MONEY MAKING MARKETING

Finding The People Who Need What You're Selling And Making Sure They Buy It

Dr. Jeffrey Lant

Published by JLA Publications
Division of Jeffrey Lant Associates, Inc.
50 Follen Street, Suite 507
Cambridge, Massachusetts 02138
Tel: (617) 547-6372

Special Preface For The Second Edition

Dear Friend,

As I bring you this new Second Edition, the national economy is, at best, faltering. Any number of states are in outright recession; others teeter on the edge of economic downturn. What does this have to do with you if you're running a business?

Just this. It means you've got to think smarter about marketing. You've got to know more about what makes marketing work...and what to avoid. You've got to understand where you should put your limited resources...and where you should never spend them.

That's why I recommend this book to you. Thousands of businesses both in the United States and abroad are now using its detailed methods to make more profitable marketing decisions...to put more money in their pockets and get rid of wasteful marketing. Now you can do the same! I guarantee it.

How can I be so sure? Because for over a decade now I've been helping literally millions of businesses make more money...through my consulting, books, lectures, articles, on radio, on audio cassettes, on video...and most recently through my new card-deck, "Jeffrey Lant's Sales & Marketing SuccessDek." All this time I've asked *everyone* getting my message and using it successfully to contact me with success results. I hear from these people — my friends — every day with reports of how much better off they are using the kinds of information you've got right at your fingertips. And in due course I want to hear from you, too, with equally good news.

The mere fact that the economy may be rotten where you are is not important. Business cycles have always been a part of life. What's important is what you do to maximize your profit and cut your expenses both when times are good...and when they're not. To this end, I'm ready, willing and able to help you...if you do everything you can to help yourself, including immersing yourself in these profit-making methods and using them rigorously. When you do, you'll be better off. When you are, don't exult silently. Tell me. I love hearing about your success!

Jeffrey

Cambridge, MA

January, 1991

MONEY MAKING MARKETING

Finding The People Who Need What You're Selling And Making Sure They Buy It

Dedication

To the memory of Paul Bloom, who radiated the secret of successful marketing: true concern for other people.

ISBN 0-940374-19-6
Revised Second Edition 1991

Acknowledgements. As always, many specialists have been generous with their time, knowledge, and materials. As always, this book is better because of it. Some of the following are noted in the text. Others are not. Whether specifically cited in the text or not, all have helped make this a more useful book for you.

I am beholden to copywriter *par excellence* Robert Bly; census data specialist Angel Broadnax; mail guru Dr. Luther Brock, "The Letter Doctor"; listening specialist Dr. Frank Cancelliere; advertising expert Bruce David; marketing and sales specialist Jeffrey Davidson; consulting and sales guru Fred Dent; persnickety copy editor (and bloated diction deflater) Professor Robert Dobson; marketer and information impressario Jeff Geibel; Bonnie Gorbaty, goals-setting strategist; designer and printer overseer John Hamwey; sales expert Ronne Jacobs; marketing specialist Professor Geoff Lantos; computer wizard Jackie Mazloff; direct response card deck guru Bill Norcutt; intrepid and inventive book marketer Dan Poynter; profit-making mail maven Galen Stilson; co-op advertising expert Karen Taylor; art marketing magician Sue Viders; and the protean book marketer Russ Von Hoelscher, an inspiration to me! And to Bill Reece, who helped me with the Revised Second Edition. I am in their debt, one and all.

TABLE OF CONTENTS

Introduction

Why I Wrote This Book, What's In It, How To Use It

We are citizens of a thrilling period when enterprise after enterprise and business after business are being created. New products and services are being developed at an amazing rate.

Sadly, large numbers of them fail, simultaneously destroying the dreams and aspirations of millions of people, many of whom have only the vaguest idea of why they are not lounging on Easy Street, as they were sure they would be.

One of the chief reasons for this debilitating, disheartening process is a general lack of marketing skills and a failure to employ the marketing procedures which ensure success.

I have written this book, my eighth, to solve this problem. With it, you'll know precisely what you must do to solve the two continuing marketing problems of your business: how to sell to your prospects and how to sell to them again.

If you can solve these two problems, your business will be the success you want it to be, and, as a result, you will derive from your business the lifestyle you wish to have. That's the benefit of mastering marketing. That's the benefit of mastering this book.

Background To MONEY MAKING MARKETING

Like all the books I write, this one is densely packed with relentlessly thorough how-to-do-it information. This kind of information has, over the years, become my trademark, and I am proud of it.

For over a decade now, I've been fighting an unremitting war against "how to" books that don't tell you how to, books that presume, books that assume, books that leave out the precise details you must have to make a technique work for you. These details are just what you'll find here: I guarantee it.

Perhaps you already know this about me. Perhaps you're one of the millions of people who now read my Sure-Fire Business Success Column. It's a feature which runs in publications nationwide and regularly provides *precise* information on how to solve a wide variety of business problems.

Or you may be one of the tens of thousands of readers who are already profitably using one or more of the other books in my seven-volume "Get Ahead" Series, among the most thorough how-to books ever written.

The "Get Ahead" Series now includes:

- **THE CONSULTANT'S KIT: ESTABLISHING AND OPERATING YOUR SUCCESSFUL CONSULTING BUSINESS.** It's the one book the United States Small Business Administration specifically recommends to new and aspiring consultants in any field.

- **THE UNABASHED SELF-PROMOTER'S GUIDE: WHAT EVERY MAN, WOMAN, CHILD AND ORGANIZATION IN AMERICA NEEDS TO KNOW ABOUT GETTING AHEAD BY EXPLOITING THE MEDIA.** If you want to promote anything through the free media, here's just what you need to know and do.

- **MONEY TALKS: THE COMPLETE GUIDE TO CREATING A PROFITABLE WORKSHOP OR SEMINAR IN ANY FIELD.** Here's the information you need to establish yourself, part- or full-time, in the multi-billion dollar world of talk.

- **TRICKS OF THE TRADE: THE COMPLETE GUIDE TO SUCCEEDING IN THE ADVICE BUSINESS.** It's the most detailed book ever written on how to profit from problem-solving information.

- **CASH COPY: HOW TO OFFER YOUR PRODUCTS AND SERVICES SO YOUR PROSPECTS BUY THEM...NOW!** You're going to be writing lots of copy for ads, brochures, flyers, cover letters, proposals, *etc.*, *etc.*, *etc.* This book tells you how to do it right!

- **HOW TO MAKE A WHOLE LOT MORE THAN $1,000,000 WRITING, COMMISSIONING, PUBLISHING AND SELLING "HOW-TO" INFORMATION.** This is the resource you use to make really big money from books, booklets, audio cassettes and special reports.

Furthermore, if you're running a nonprofit organization, there's my well-known book **DEVELOPMENT TODAY: A FUND RAISING GUIDE FOR NONPROFIT ORGANIZATIONS.** Use it to raise the money you need from corporations, foundations, and individuals.

And now there's the Revised Second Edition of **MONEY MAKING MARKETING.**

I have written this book with one overriding purpose in mind: to tell you precisely what you need to do, in precisely the way you need to do it, to sell any product or service.

Unlike other marketing books, no words are minced and nothing is theoretical. As a consummate marketer myself, I tell you *exactly* what you need to do to succeed. There's not a nostrum in this book; only unrelentingly precise step-by-step information. You may not like having all this information: it suggests that the road to success is not an easy one and that you must continually accomplish a host of tasks to travel it fruitfully. My mother says people don't want to know all they have to do to get ahead. They just want to know and do a little bit and hope that that will be enough. If it isn't, they want a scapegoat readily available to explain their failure to succeed. She's got a point. All Americans like to talk about success. Most don't want to do what is necessary to succeed. And all those who fail want to make sure they are never held responsible for what happened to them.

If this is the way you think, you'll be disappointed with this book, because it places the burden for achieving marketing success just where it ought to be: on you. It says that this success can be yours if you think smart and consistently use the dozens of techniques spelled out in this book. It also says that if you don't use them, your resulting failure will be nobody's fault but your own.

However, if you are willing to accept the responsibility for your success and acknowledge how much you must regularly do to achieve it, I can be of the utmost assistance to you. After all, few other how-to writers go to the lengths I do to ensure that you have the exact information you need to succeed and are willing to work along with you to reach your objectives.

In **MONEY MAKING MARKETING,** here's how I can help:

The book is composed of 11 chapters, one appendix and a samples section.

Chapter 1 presents the reasons why you may not now be effectively marketing and what to do about them. It then gives you the precise mental and technical prerequisites you must master to succeed in marketing. No other marketing book I've ever seen contains this vital information.

In Chapter 2, you'll learn how to do your marketing research in the least expensive and time-consuming way while still gathering the information you need about your market. I know you're busy and hate research, so I've made realistic recommendations on how to get the data you need for the least expense and time commitment.

Chapter 3 provides the information you need to create a manageable marketing plan. Here you'll learn about the Rule of Seven and how to arrange your marketing activities so that they reinforce each other and ensure that your prospects know who you are and how you can help them.

After mastering Chapter 4, you'll know exactly what you need to know about how to create effective, persuasive, economical marketing documents. Many of them you have never seen before. Billions of dollars are wasted annually on marketing documents which talk about you rather than your prospects. This section is a remarkable departure from what you may previously have read about documents, and, if you master it, you'll cut the costs of every marketing document you'll ever produce and increase their persuasiveness.

In Chapter 5, you'll learn what you must know about how to effectively utilize the mail to market your product or service. Mail marketing is expensive and, for most people, ineffective. Now make sure that every time you use the mail to promote your product or service, you will make a profit, not just help fill your prospects' waste baskets.

Chapter 6 provides step-by-step guidelines on how to use the free media, radio, television, newspapers, magazines and newsletters, to market your offering. I am nationally known as the "unabashed promoter". Now find out why, in a characteristically pungent and detailed look at how to get any media source anywhere to carry your message to your prospects for free.

In Chapter 7 you'll get the low-down on how to profitably use classified and small space ads as marketing vehicles. An ocean of advertising dollars is wasted each day. If you've been advertising, you already know many of your ads are a complete waste of money. Now learn how to stop this destructive practice and make the advertising you do profitable.

Phone Profit is the topic of Chapter 8. Using it you'll never be in doubt again how to use the telephone most effectively to prospect for clients and close sales. Most people are horrifyingly inept on the telephone. This will never happen to you, though, when you've mastered the steps of phone profit.

Step-by-step sales techniques are offered in Chapter 9, Solution Selling. In this fast-moving chapter, you'll get the information you need to increase the percentage of sales you close and develop long-standing relationships with more buyers. If you can't sell and can't close, your business will never prosper. I am a sales fanatic. I am always selling and always tinkering with my techniques to see what works, why, and how to do things better. Here's the best of what I've learned in a lifetime of selling.

Chapter 10 is rich with a variety of marketing techniques, everything from how to find premiums on which to print your logo and message to the essentials of co-op advertising and direct-response card decks. This chapter is studded with techniques to improve your marketing and, like the rest of the book, the names, addresses, and telephone numbers of specialists in a wide variety of marketing areas. It's worth making special mention of these resources, since I have combed the nation to find experts with additional information of value to you in selected fields.

Finally, in Chapter 11 I tell you what you need to know to use any talk program, be it workshop, seminar or lecture, to your advantage as a marketing opportunity. Most people giving talk programs fail to make the best use of them, fail, indeed, to make any use of them at all. As you begin to understand and use the techniques in this chapter, every talk program you give will become the consummate marketing success.

Going on, the Appendix deals with how to find a marketing consultant and what such a consultant wants to know about you. Complete guidelines tell you how to present yourself and your problem to a would-be consultant and how to ensure that the one you retain is the right one for you.

Thereafter, you'll find a Samples Section with illustrations of pertinent forms discussed in the book, and a copy of my Sure-Fire Business Success Catalog. Remember: if you didn't order your book directly from me, you are not on my mailing list. If you want to continue to receive this catalog, you'll have to write to let me know. The Sure-Fire Business Success Catalog is a unique resource which you can only get through me. I know why no one else has it: it's very demanding to put together. Since you'll probably never have the time to spend locating and evaluating as many business get-ahead materials as I do, take advantage of my effort. Request and use the Sure-Fire Business Success Catalog.

A Little About Your Author

If you've read any of my previous books or articles, you already know I am a fanatic about two things: marketing and providing precise, step-by-step information to my readers. In **MONEY MAKING MARKETING,** this fanaticism is clearly apparent. Either I have perfected each technique in this book myself or, in selected instances, have called upon designated specialists to share their expertise. As they can tell you, where I thought the information they provided was insufficiently detailed, I sent it back and asked them to try again! I know what you need to succeed, and I've made sure you've got it, although it has occasionally been at the cost of badgering the experts!

The advice I offer you is the advice I follow myself. I work daily, as you must work, to identify prospects and develop the means of meaningfully connecting with them so that they know I understand their problems and that my products and services can solve them. I work, too, to reconnect with past buyers and clients, to see what's bothering them now and how I can improve their lives through what I'm offering. All that I've learned as a result of daily practice in marketing is now laid out for your benefit. You get information on what works and why, what you must do, how you must do it, and even when you must do it to sell your products and services.

Nothing in this book is theoretical. Each technique has been tested and retested to make sure it works. But if you find this isn't helpful enough, here's my pledge:

If you don't understand how something works, don't see how it applies to your situation, or think, imagine!, that something has been left out, call me at (617) 547-6372. When you call, I'll answer the telephone and am ordinarily ready to deal with you right then. So be prepared!

If the information you need is available in this book, I'll send you back for further study. Don't expect me to be warm and charming, either, if the information you need is right under your nose!

If it's available in another one of my books, I'll tell you where and how to find it. If it's something I've left out or inadequately explained, I'll provide you with as much information as I have on the subject. And if yours is a long, complicated matter needing my sustained consideration, I'll give you my best estimate of what it will take for me to solve the problem and produce the result you want. Fair enough? How many other authors do you know who unhesitatingly give you the opportunity to refine what they say in this way? In case you don't know the answer, I'll tell you: precious few.

Understand that I am not just writing a book, I am entering into a relationship with you to solve your marketing problems. Over the course of many years working in this way with lots of readers, I have made many new friends. I hope you will be one of them. I hope that I will be of assistance to you, and I hope that, in return, you'll share your techniques with me. I have lots to learn, too!

One Final Word

Try hard not to fight the style of this book. Learn the techniques. Use them and understand why I am recommending them. Some people would rather that I present things more in line with the prevailing American sentimentality and soft thinking. But I'll share something with you: my objective in this book is to help three people. I want to help myself, of course. I'm a writer and your buying this book keeps me living the autonomous lifestyle I must have. I also want to help you. I feel a tremendous responsibility to my readers, all of whom I regard as clients, to be as complete and honest as I can be. Finally, I feel a strong sense of responsibility to *your* prospects and clients.

If you have a product or service that makes people's lives better, then it is your responsibility to do whatever is necessary to get it into their hands, as quickly as possible and so make this a better world. Towards this end, I am impatient about people who talk a good game about wanting to market, but never find the time and will never do the things which must be done to bring their offering to their prospects' attention. I am at the service of those who want to build a better world. They know I am there to help them. It is only those Flatworms, who talk about action but do nothing to implement it, who find my style taxing. Keep this in mind as you work your way through what is admittedly a demanding book, a book which may very well affront your current operating techniques.

With this warning in mind, we are now ready to approach the captivating subject of marketing. When you are finished with this book, when you are master of its techniques, you will be ready to embark on one of the most thrilling adventures of your life, an adventure flush with possibilities, needing every ounce of your energy and creativity, calling for diverse tactics and techniques, and resulting in the most satisfying feeling of all: the welcome knowledge that you are helping yourself by helping others.

This is what marketing can do for you. And I am delighted you have decided to learn its secrets and master its possibilities with my help. You will not be disappointed.

J.L.
Cambridge, Massachusetts
January, 1991

CHAPTER 1

MMMM

Very Candid Thoughts About Why Your Current Marketing May Not Be Working, The Excuses You Make For Not Marketing, And The Mental And Technical Prerequisites You Need To Make Your Marketing Successful

I deal with people regularly whose marketing is not working. They are not getting connected to new prospects and transforming them into buyers. They are not getting their current clients and customers to buy from them again. In short, they have not yet mastered the two essential points which are the basis for every successful business.

Here are the leading reasons why most people's marketing is not working. Look at them closely. Do any of them apply to you?

- **You don't know to whom you're marketing.**

The successful marketer can tell you precisely who he's marketing to. He can tell you exact demographic information about who this person is, where he is, his age, sex, educational and income levels, and other pertinent information. Marketing success starts with an exact answer to the question "Who?" Without fail, I have found in my marketing workshops across the nation that participants have only the most general idea of who has the problem their product or service can solve. The extent to which you are vague about who you are marketing to is the extent to which you are handicapping your marketing.

- **You don't know why your customers buy.**

Knowing who you are marketing to is the beginning of marketing success. Knowing why your customers buy is equally essential. They involve both what I call Ultimate Benefits and Benefits. Ultimate Benefits include the prospect's desire for:

- health
- friends
- salvation
- security
- prestige
- sexual fulfillment
- money
- freedom
- time
- belonging

And many other similar reasons all of which can be regarded as Ultimate Benefits.

Benefits include such things as:

- less expensive
- faster
- cleaner
- more organized
- less space
- brighter color
- nearer
- sweeter
- tastier, *etc.*

A good way to think of Benefits is that they are always comparative. Whereas Ultimate Benefits are things to which you can devote your life, Benefits — and the products and services which provide them — are comparative and always changing. It is very unlikely you would ever drop your interest in being healthy (however unhealthful your habits), but you could easily be induced to change your commitment to a product or service that was no longer as comparatively attractive as one offering you a better benefit.

Your job is to find out what your prospects want to achieve in terms of Ultimate Benefits and show them how your product or service with its clearly-defined benefits enables them to achieve the Ultimate Benefit they want.

• **You're not client-centered.**

Too many people selling products and services focus on themselves, on what they are selling, and not on the prospect and why he is buying. The first rule of successful marketing is to "know thy client". Know who he is. Know what his problem is. Know what he wants to accomplish. Know why he wants to accomplish this. Know when he wants to accomplish this. And then show him how he can get precisely what he wants with what you're selling.

I know you don't think of yourself as selfish, and if anyone called you selfish you'd indignantly reject the idea. Yet your marketing may very well be distinguished by its selfishness, by the fact that you know far more about yourself and what you are doing than you do about your prospects, their current situation, and the objective they want to reach. Until this equation is reversed, and you understand your client as well as, if not better than, you know yourself, you'll be handicapping your marketing.

• **You have no marketing plan.**

To my utter and continuing consternation, most of the business people I talk to, all professing a desire to succeed, have no plan. Let me tell you something: if you don't have a marketing plan, you'll never reach any truly substantial objectives. This plan must consist of the following parts:

- a clear, precise dollar objective for each year for each of your products or services. Once you know how many dollars you want to raise, then you can objectively evaluate all the different means available to you to do so.

- an exact indication of which marketing alternatives you'll use, in what ways, and how often.

- techniques for converting your prospects to buyers and those for upgrading your buyers so that they'll buy more of your problem-solving products and services.

Unless your plan addresses each of these three areas in specific detail you cannot expect your marketing to be successful.

• **You are not persistent.**

Most people expect too much from a single marketing endeavor. This is a mistake. A single direct mailing. A single classified ad. A single article. Any single marketing technique will not ordinarily produce dramatic results. And you should neither expect it to nor be disappointed when it doesn't. Instead, the essence of building a successful business through marketing is to work for a solid, certain return on each thing you do, always remembering that this return may take some time and many further steps. You must know precisely who you are marketing to and connect with them again and again and again and again, until such time as they awake to the fact that you exist and that you can help them solve their problems.

Marketing is not a sport for the fainthearted or the impatient. You must work at it daily. You cannot allow yourself the luxury of getting discouraged — if you are certain you understand the problems of your buyers and are addressing them directly. But you must work to refine who you are trying to connect with. Once you have made this decision you must approach them using many ways to ensure that they know what you can do for them. And once they know, you must persist so that they never have the opportunity to forget. Never.

• **You expect the prospect to do too much work.**

Successful marketers realize that we are the epitome of the service business. We make it easy, seductively easy, for people to buy what we are selling. The marketer is by definition always alert to how he can make it easier for his prospect to buy.

Sadly, not even people who are self-professed experts in marketing are always aware that this is their job. While I was writing this book I was asked by one of the country's largest marketing publications to submit an article based on my book **MONEY TALKS**. I did so and, as usual, closed the article with information on how readers could get the book, including its postpaid price and my name, address, and telephone number.

The editor, a self-professed marketing expert, vetoed including this marketing information, saying it was not appropriate for a news article. I strongly demurred, pointing out that serving his readers was his job and that this information did just that. He did not accept my point, and there was nothing I could do about it but tell him, in the strongest possible terms, that he understood nothing about the function of marketing, which is to serve people, not to make their lives unnecessarily difficult. It was a point which he, supposedly at the apogee of the profession, didn't understand. Is it any wonder, therefore, that thousands of other presumed marketing experts don't get it either?

I'm going to say this now and I'll repeat it through this book. Your job is to make it as easy as possible for the prospect to follow up whatever kind of marketing activity you use and to buy your product or service at whatever time of the day or night he wishes. You cannot wait until you are ready to sell your product or service to do so. You must be prepared to do so when the prospect is ready to buy. It is his wishes and desire for action which are paramount, not yours. When yours become paramount, your business suffers.

• **You don't go for the jugular.**

The best marketing is simple. It is simple and direct. It clearly indicates what the prospect's problem is. Knows what the prospect wishes to attain. And lets him know in no uncertain terms that what you are offering is precisely what the prospect needs. I call this going for the jugular, and it is something which most overly-genteel marketing experts seem unable to do.

From my direct experience, I know the real problem with most marketing, including most of your marketing, is that it is entirely wasted. That it doesn't connect with the right person. That it doesn't persuade him you understand his problem. That it doesn't convince him your product or service meets his intense need. And certainly doesn't convince him he must take action now — or be worse off than he is today. If your marketing fails on any of these counts, there is no point in doing it. Indeed, you are doing nothing more than throwing your dollars out the window and scattering them into the wind. Whether you meant to do this or not, this is precisely the result which most of your marketing delivers.

Listen up! As a result of this book you will learn what is really bothering your prospects. You'll know where they hurt. In your marketing you'll remind them of this pain in the most dramatic way possible, while simultaneously reminding them they need not be so pained — if only they use your product or service. People don't buy merely because what you are offering is a good idea. They buy because they must buy. And it is our job as marketers to show our prospects, in dramatic detail, why it is strikingly in their interest to take action now to get what we are selling.

• **You are boring people.**

Over the course of any given year, I read hundreds of marketing documents. Most are of lamentable quality. But think! Behind each document stands one person, and often a complete team of people, who have spent their time and dipped into their dreams and their money to bring forth what can only be described as a completely useless document. One of the chief problems with these documents is that they are deadly dull.

Don't take my word for it. Read the ads, the brochures, the direct mail pieces that come to your attention over the next day or two. How many of them actually are intrinsically interesting? Let me tell you something. If you cannot interest your prospect, cannot catch him up in the dramatic possibilities of what you are offering, cannot offer him a vision of a better world, then your marketing has failed. This means that by definition marketing documents must be among the most captivating documents written.

The essence of these documents must be action. People buy to change. Your documents must show, in thrilling language gilded with enthusiasm, that you can move your prospects from a place that no longer satisfies them, that in fact may be fraught with outright pain and discomfort, to another, better situation. A situation which is available to them if and only if they take immediate action to acquire and use what you are offering. Do your documents do this? Or do they pile boring fact on prosaic fact on mundane fact until the end result is the very essence of boredom?

- **You fail to connect with your prospects and customers sufficiently often.**

Marketing is an again-and-again process. So long as you have correctly identified the prospect who has the problem your product or service can solve, it is your responsibility to stay in constant touch until he buys what you're selling. People have short memories. People are slothful. People don't take action even in their own best interests. People, in short, need to be constantly reminded what you can do for them.

It is not enough intermittently to remind people you exist and can help them solve their problems. You must create a regular program for initially snagging the prospect and then for continuing your association both with prospects and buyers. You must make such contact at least every 90 days and must continue it either until the prospect buys or until you are firmly convinced that he is a Flatworm, interested only in mouthing the clichés of change and progress and not in doing what is necessary to make things better. Once you have determined that that prospect is a Flatworm, then it is perfectly acceptable to spurn him. But not until.

Marketing means correctly identifying your prospect and then, using a variety of techniques, connecting with him over and over again — but at least seven times in 18 months — until the truth dawns: you and what you are selling are essential to his life. Unless you are willing to handle your marketing in this unrelenting fashion, don't even start, because to begin without a commitment to following through is to ensure that your limited resources will be wasted.

- **You let past buyers and customers get away.**

This point is a natural extension from the one above. When I ask the small businesses, nonprofit organizations and independent professionals to whom I consult what they are doing to attract again people who once used their services but have now drifted away, the answer is usually "Nothing!" To my utter horror, most organizations spend far more time attempting to gather new prospects and clients than they do attempting to make current buyers happy and reattract those who (we must presume) were at one time happy with them. This is a mistake.

Marketing breaks down into these finite, defined tasks:

- upgrading existing buyers so that they buy more of your problem-solving products and services;
- reattracting past buyers who were at one time happy with your problem-solving products and services and again inducing them to use what you are selling and so reenter their lives, and;
- connecting with new prospects and converting them from prospects to buyers.

This is the order in which you should be handling your marketing endeavors. The only time this doesn't apply is when you are launching an entirely new enterprise that does not already have customers. Then, of course, by definition, you must spend your time solely attracting new prospects. But once you have transformed these prospects into buyers, you must spend the bulk of your time amortizing the investment you made in getting them in the first place, by doing what is necessary so that they'll buy again and buy more than they originally did.

- **You don't seek to upgrade your buyers.**

The buyer who has just bought from you offers you the best opportunity to sell again, assuming that you have not solved all his problems with what you have just sold him and that he has the money to pursue another solution. If these two conditions are met, then it is your responsibility to upgrade this buyer, to get him to buy something else and solve another of his problems.

No business (I hope!) would disagree that it is necessary to keep on good terms with recent buyers of their products and services. However, in practice, most businesses have no organized way of doing this. That is because they don't think like marketers.

Instead, they suppose their job is done when they have sold the customer the product or service that meets the need he brought to your attention. This is not the way marketers think. Why? Because we don't sell. We solve. Our job is to find out, to really find out, what the customer is trying to achieve and to sell him everything he needs to reach this result.

Here's what I mean. As you know, I have a quarterly catalog chock full of dozens of business success materials. My buyers often call to order one or more of them. But before I close the sale I seek to upgrade them by discovering what they are really trying to accomplish. If I can discover what they are trying to do, it is almost always possible to upgrade the order and so make a more fruitful contact for both me and the buyer.

By the same token, if a person orders from me by letter (as many do), particularly when they order the books that I have written and which are grouped naturally into series, I immediately attempt to upgrade the order, as you'll see. I am not merely interested in selling what the prospect or customer first wishes to buy. Not by a long shot.

Instead, I am interested in finding out (either by asking directly or by deduction) what single problem or related set of problems the prospect wishes to solve and then I offer him the appropriate solution. This is entirely different, I need hardly tell you, from the way most people conduct their business.

Let me stress that your job doesn't begin to be done when you have sold the prospect what he originally expressed interest in. Any half-trained clerk can do that. Instead you should be striving to ascertain what problem the prospect wishes to solve and then proposing the appropriate solution to it, which, of course, may well involve selling much more than the prospect originally intended to buy. However, if you concentrate on what the prospect wishes to achieve, he will not be resistant to you as you upgrade his order. Quite the reverse. He will be grateful for your attention to his interests.

- **You are not ready to sell when your prospects are ready to buy.**

Most businesses sell at prescribed times, like 9 to 5. This is a mistake. You must be prepared to deal with your prospects and buyers and to sell to them when they are ready for action. Not when you are ready to serve them. These days there is no excuse for not setting up a twenty-four hour prospect-and-customer service center, no matter how small your business. As you'll see later, even a simple answering machine, properly used, allows you to do this.

Every business talks about service, but the polished marketer is a service fanatic. He realizes that any imposition of buying conditions on his buyers is fatuous. Having found out who has the problem his product or service can solve and having done what is necessary to imbue and develop trust in that prospect and lower his anxiety that he will be sold something he doesn't need, it is then the marketer's responsibility to make it as easy as possible for that prospect to buy. This means that if the prospect wants to buy at 2 a.m., you must be ready for him. I'll tell you something. The chances are you're nowhere near ready for this now. But let me tell you something else. After you finish this book, you will be.

- **You think like an order-taker, not a marketer.**

You will hear me talk about order-takers many times in this book. We all know the type. When you call a company to order something, the order-taker (if we're lucky) does nothing more than take the order. He is not interested in the problem we are solving. He doesn't ask us for information. He doesn't make any attempt to find out what we'd like to do. He volunteers no helpful information. At best, he merely writes down the order and works to fulfill it.

This unimaginative system only works well, however, if you know precisely what you want, know precisely what the seller has to offer, and can go unerringly to that one thing you need without needing further information. It is like the difference between a full-service stock broker and a discount brokerage house. Both can work. But the discount brokerage is solely for those who know what they're doing.

Unfortunately, most people don't, and therefore order-takers are usually severely unhelpful. To the degree they manifest these unhelpful characteristics, they retard the prosperity of your business.

The essence of this book is to get you to think like a marketer, not an order-taker. It is contained in these words, "Don't sell. Solve." The order-taker merely sells. Nothing more. The marketer's job is much more important; he solves. He attempts to understand what the prospect's problem is and what he wants to accomplish. And then makes appropriate suggestions which will solve the prospect's problem. By indicating he knows how to solve the prospect's problem, he ensures the prospect will buy. The order-taker does nothing more than write down what you think you want and takes your money, usually sullenly. Let me tell you something: most people are order-takers. But I don't want this catastrophic fate to befall you. Heed the instructions of this book, and you must rise to the eminence of the marketer and prosper accordingly as the order-taker (on his minimum wage) cannot.

• **You don't use "'What Next?' Thinking".**

A successful marketer always knows where a contact with a prospect or buyer is going next and knows in precise detail exactly what he wants to happen, when he wants it to happen and has arranged how it must happen. Recently I did an experiment with one of my marketing groups. I asked each of participants to bring his basic marketing brochure to the class.

Once there I asked that each one tell me who the brochure was written for and what the writer expected the prospect to do upon receiving it. Many answers were given. "To read it," some said. "To call me," others offered. "To schedule an appointment" a third group suggested. "To ask for more information."

"But", I pressed, "precisely what do you want your prospect to do and when do you want him to do it?" "To read it and call me," a man said. "Anytime?", I quizzed. "Yes, anytime." I then asked whether he was set up to take the prospect's call in the evening. "No, only 9 to 5." "Then you don't mean 'anytime', do you? You mean your time." And so it went.

The expert marketer knows precisely who should get his materials. He understands that person's problems as well as, often better than, the prospect does himself. And he has offered the prospect complete instructions on what to do and how to do it to solve his problem. Your marketing must involve exact answers to a series of "What next?" questions.

The prospect receives your marketing material. What precise thing (or things) do you want him to do?

The prospect needs further information about what you are selling. How do you want him to get it? Have you provided him the essential information he needs to make getting it easy?

The prospect wants to buy one of your products. How can he do this? When can he do this?

And so on through the dozens of questions which must be precisely answered as you identify prospects and move them through stages until they become customers who buy from you regularly. At each stage there is either one or a series of "What next?" questions, which you must successfully answer and in detail if you want this relationship to prosper.

• **You think provincially.**

This is a terrible problem. I get, as you may imagine, heaps of mail. Over the course of the last several months I've been doing an informal survey using the letters I receive. About *one quarter* of them do not provide an area code with the telephone number. There could scarcely be a plainer indication that these people are provincial thinkers, that they have made the determination to serve people and make money within a rigidly-defined area and to exclude all others who have the problem they can solve. May I say that this is the height of folly for most people who sell products and services?

Remember what I said and will say again: "Don't sell. Solve." If you are interested in solving problems and not just selling products and services, you will look to whoever in the country, indeed the world, has this problem, and you will consider how best you can prosper by making the appropriate problem-solving product or service available to them.

The sad fact is, most people (even purported marketers) think provincially. But why? Why? I help solve the management and fund-raising problems of nonprofit organizations and the organizational development problems of small businesses.

True, there are many such organizations in the Greater Boston area. But more true, there are thousands of times as many beyond this geographical locale who can benefit from the knowledge, skills, and techniques which I have developed. Why deprive them of what I can do to help? Why deprive myself of the income that results from successfully building a business that can accommodate all their needs with appropriate problem-solving products and services? The way in which this can be done I call the Mobile Mini-Conglomerate, a 10-part wealth-producing machine, which I fully described in **TRICKS OF THE TRADE: THE COMPLETE GUIDE TO SUCCEEDING IN THE ADVICE BUSINESS.**

But whether you use all parts of the Mobile-Mini Conglomerate or not, whether you sell only a single product or service, ask yourself whether you are not foolishly limiting your territory to your immediate area when there are thousands, perhaps millions, of people who could benefit from the very things you are now solely selling locally. I think you'll find, as I have, that the answer is yes, and as you gear up to meet the need and solve these problems your life will be changed forever and, working properly, your prosperity assured.

- **You are disappointed when people don't buy from you immediately, and you get dispirited and give up.**

Gloomy people are continually trooping through my life, most despairing because they are not selling as many of their products or services as they would like. Usually I have little patience with them, because I find them unrealistic about their chances for success and unwilling to do what is necessary to succeed.

If you are going to succeed in business, you must make yourself into not merely a competent but an enthusiastic and realistic marketer. Each part of this equation is necessary. To be enthusiastic about any marketing gambit without being realistic about the results you can expect from it, is to risk grave, even crippling, disappointment. By the same token to be simply realistic without being enthusiastic raises the possibility you will fail to impart to your prospects a sense of excitement about what you are offering, and you will therefore fail to inspire them about the possibilities of what you are selling. Either course is disastrous.

When you have a product or service to sell, you must realize that you have embarked on a lifetime of marketing. It cannot be episodic, intermittent, or handled as an afterthought. It must indeed be the core of your business, for in the long run marketing is one of the twin axes on which successful businesses are built. The other is the integrity of what you are selling and its ability to do what you say it can do.

Almost without exception the gloomy people coming to ask for my advice are undermarketing. They are doing too little, to the wrong people, in the wrong way, without a plan and without the relentless determination and brilliant inspiration that distinguishes the most successful marketers. Their failure is therefore entirely predictable.

Try to remember as you approach your marketing that people are assailed each week by thousands of different sales possibilities. We have therefore learned, out of a need to secure our autonomy, to screen out even those messages which offer what is good for us. As marketers we must realize that this screen exists and that each year it becomes more difficult to get through it, whatever the level of need of our prospects. Yet our task remains clear; we must get through that screen, that often-obstinate layer of defense, for unless we do, two people suffer — ourselves and our prospect.

Thus, I say this to you and you must adopt it as your marketing credo. If you have correctly identified a person who needs your product or service. If what you are selling compares favorably to other available offerings. If, therefore, the prospect will be better off using what you are offering. Then you must continue to do what is necessary, using as many of the existing means of marketing as you can, to bring your understanding of the prospect's problem to his attention and to let him know that you can solve it. So long as you are in business, this is what you must do and so long as these conditions apply, it is jejune to give way to despair because your prospects neither act as quickly nor as intelligently as you would like to take advantage of what you are offering them.

These are the leading reasons your marketing is not working as well as it should. Let me tell you something: these are all reasons that can be dealt with. If you are willing to do what is necessary (that big if!), you can transform the pallid facsimile of marketing you now use into an activity which is at once exciting, cost-effective, soul-satisfying (as solving people's problems ought to be), and even fun. It is up to you. Sadly, however, people give me excuse after excuse about why they cannot achieve this result.

Excuses Which Block Successful Marketing

Being human, we are continually in search of a scapegoat to spare us the aggravating thought that we ourselves are responsible for our fate. But let me tell you something: if your marketing is failing, it is more likely failing because of you than because of the inadequacies of your prospects and buyers. This being the case, you must jettison the following excuses. If you find yourself saying them, you'll have proof-positive that you are part of the problem, not part of the solution.

- **"I don't have any time for marketing."**

If you do not market, you cannot exist. Marketing is an essential precondition for business success. You know this. But what you may not know is how to make the best use of your time, how to transform every contact with every prospect and every buyer into a satisfying marketing experience for both of you. That is the purpose of this book.

The real problem is not that you don't have the time but that you may not use the time you do have as productively as you could. This is a problem that I continually contemplate, hoping in the process to find additional ways of making each prospect contact I have more productive. This kind of sustained attention to marketing works.

You will find that if you work regularly at your marketing, work regularly at constructively connecting with your prospects and customers, your business must prosper. Moreover, if you focus resolutely on how better to serve your prospects and customers, you will find that each contact becomes a reverberating contact. Such a contact not only succeeds in satisfying this individual but through this individual reaches others, thereby helping promote your firm and spread constructive information about what you can do.

- **"Frankly, I don't need to do any marketing. My customers find me."**

One of the distressing things I have discovered over the last several years is the arrogance of many people who market products and services. Why is this?

I think there are at least two answers. On the one hand, many marketers feel superior to their clientele. After all, most people coming to them do know less than they do about both the problem solved by the product and service and its solution. Thus, the marketer is perpetually in a position of superiority. After awhile, as Lord Acton knew only too well, this situation proves corrosive and leaves the marketer thinking he is not merely knowledgeable but superior. Arrogance is the direct result.

The second answer is that after a time a business which functions reasonably well does get a group of people who return for its products and services and who tell their friends. Thus, the need for the kind of aggressive marketing which distinguished the business in its early days is no longer as necessary. Being human, these business people become slothful.

Such sloth, however, has its price. The business reaches stasis. It grows no more and is ruled by routine. Routine is dull. And as this dullness permeates the customer base, they may well lose interest. As they do, the business shrinks and dies.

Thus, business people saying "I don't need to do any marketing" end up either moving towards arrogance or towards dull routine. Either way a terrible thing happens — people who need what they are offering do not get it and the businesses themselves fail to reach their fullest potential. Is this what you want?

Perhaps it is. If so, fine. Each of us in business must make a decision about how energetically we wish to pursue what we are doing. But I tell you this: I am in business to solve problems. And I have made the decision to do whatever is necessary to place me and my problem-solving products and services in contact with people who need the results they deliver. I will go anywhere at anytime in any way to connect with these people. This spirit irradiates all my business dealings. And if you are serious not only about doing well for yourself but doing good for others with what you are offering, it will irradiate yours as well.

- **"I'm afraid people will decline my offering."**

Every successful marketer knows that far more people will decline his offer than accept it. And that this will always be the case, even where he is making his offer to the precise group of people who have the problem his product or service can solve. Indeed, the more successful the marketer, the greater the numbers of people who will regularly decline to consider and use what he is offering. What is important to consider, however, is that truly great success is only achieved concurrently with even greater failure. What matters is whether you can profit, directly or indirectly, in the midst of such considerable failure. If you can, the failure is inconsequential and must be considered nothing more than a related condition of success.

I spend large amounts of my time developing precise profiles of my various markets and creating marketing devices which ensure that I reach them often and with impact. Most of the people I reach, whatever the level of their need, will not respond. I accept this as a condition of business. But I do not look upon this in any way as a rejection of either me or what I am offering. Rather I see it as a continuing failure of perception on the part of the person with the problem to understand that I hold the key to the solution he needs and as mandating the need for me to try him yet again in perhaps yet another way with perhaps yet another line of persuasion.

You must always consider the reasons for the rejection of what you are selling. But you must never give way before them. Instead, consider this rejection as a form of curious communication between you and your prospects. What does their silence indicate? Can it mean that:

- you are attempting to communicate with the wrong person?
- you have failed to understand what they want and why they want it?
- you have not compelled their interest in any one of number of ways, including the offer itself, the words you have used to describe it, your very ink and paper?
- the prospect was overwhelmed with other matters, other offers, at the time yours arrived and so never really saw it at all?

Or any one of a number of other reasons.

It is always your job to attempt to answer these questions. It is never acceptable to take umbrage at the situation or become dejected about it. Whether your offer is accepted or not, something is being communicated to you, often less clearly than we would like, no doubt, but still subject to our consideration and reflection. For what we discover can and must modify what we do with the next marketing gambit which we will employ to connect with these same people, whether they buy or whether they have not yet done so.

- **"I don't have enough money to do my marketing properly."**

I hear this quite a lot, and it irritates me because it is so obviously beside the point. Marketing is anything which connects you, with your problem-solving product or service, to prospects and customers, whose problem you can solve. Some of these things are costly. Many are not. This book gives you information about each.

I am, as you'll come to learn, a Scotsman by descent. I loathe spending money. I am parsimonious in the extreme. But I also have rampant ambition. I desire to connect with every conceivable person who has the problem my products and services can solve. Is there a tension here, then, between my frugal personal and business habits and my galloping personal and business desires? Not at all. The solution, dear reader, is in finding the creative means of reaching your objective while simultaneously minimizing your expense. That is the chief purpose of this book and must be a continuing objective of your business.

I delight, as I wish you to delight, in finding ever less expensive ways of reaching ever greater numbers of prospective buyers. You must take, as one of the clear objectives of your business, pruning pennies from your marketing budget while simultaneously raising the number of people you wish to reach. This is the challenge of your business, the purpose of this book, and the mark of a canny marketer.

From now on, from this very minute, I ask you to scrutinize each of your marketing endeavors using these questions; "Must I really spend this much money to reach this objective? Am I reaching the greatest number of prospects in the most constructive way with this expenditure? Or can I reach more for less by doing something else?"

If you internalize these questions and act accordingly, you must work to cut your marketing expenses, and you'll find yourself in touch with ever greater numbers of people. The thrill of, on the one hand, slicing expenditure, and, on the other, increasing the reach and the profit, is one of the most satisfying aspects of being in business. It is open to you, too, if only you will determine to become one of the great marketers.

- **"I have no help."**

Another curious excuse.

It would be nice if each of us had a squad of eager marketing experts at our beck and call. Nice. But not always useful.

I can tell — and often do — many satisfying horror stories about the large amounts of money firms have spent on marketing consultants, public relations agencies, advertising firms and all the other minions of marketing without gaining in return a fraction of their initial investment. I delight in these tales. They at once attest to the sloth of humans who are always looking for others to do their work for them and the naiveté of the ingenue as he contemplates the purported expert. Sadly, this unsatisfactory experience is all too common.

But this need not happen to you, if you use thoughtful consideration and due caution. This begins with the realization that no one — no one! — will ever be as interested in building your business as you are. No one will ever know the features and benefits of your business as you do. No one will ever have your understanding of your prospects. And if you don't have this interest, this knowledge, and this understanding now, you will — or you will wither away. You can retain a firm to assist you, but you cannot always retain the interest, knowledge, and understanding you need to make that relationship productive.

Your immediate lack of help is no bar to your success. As you know, I work largely by myself. I handle all my marketing, my very considerable marketing, myself and treat it like the exciting adult game that it is. By handling your marketing yourself, by making your own mistakes and forcing yourself to learn who your buyers really are, what they really want to achieve, and why they really buy what you're selling you will become the specialist you need to be.

Thus, when you are ready to retain outside help you will be in a position fairly to evaluate what you are getting, as most businesses, even the richest and most powerful, are not. It goes without saying that the mere fact that such outside helpers are adept at selling you (who want help) on the need to use their services is no guarantee that they are as good at selling your prospects on the need to buy your offerings.

Having help when you are small, particularly if you become dependent upon it or fail to understand the essential elements about both your market and about how to connect with it, can be detrimental to your long-term interests and ought to be assiduously avoided. Instead, recognize that mastering the essentials of successful marketing to smaller numbers of prospects ensures your success as you begin to approach larger, even staggering, numbers. Only the numbers involved, not the essential preconditions of success, are different. You must understand this. Therefore working alone at the beginning can be the best possible thing, so long as you are willing to learn from all that you do, continually experiment, and become a relentless marketer.

- **"I don't know how to market."**

After you finish this book, master its precepts and implement its techniques you need never say this again. And if you do, you are a Flatworm.

So now we have explored the basic reasons for marketing failure and the run of unpersuasive excuses people hopefully offer to extenuate such ignobility. Having considered them, it is time to move beyond them, gathering insight into the necessary mental and technical preconditions to be a successful marketer.

Mental & Technical Prerequisites To Be A Successful Marketer

It is one of my fervently-held beliefs, substantiated daily, that people in business fail more often because they have not mastered the basics of marketing than because of the generally more exotic reasons they often advance. That is why you must give proper consideration to the mental and technical prerequisites which are necessary to be a successful marketer. In this connection, nothing is more essential for achieving marketing success than using it to reach a goal to which you are completely and enthusiastically committed.

On Goal-Setting

Marketing is not an end in itself. It is a means to an end. That end is your goal. Failure to posit a goal means, by definition, that your marketing is operating in a vacuum and thus can never be as focused and directed as it ought to be. To the extent you have failed to state and dedicate yourself to a reasonable goal which marketing can assist in achieving, that marketing becomes relatively pointless and undirected.

To a considerable extent, the failure of many people to achieve the business success they say they desire is found in their failure to be goal-oriented, to have a meaningful goal and to live and work to make that goal a reality. In this situation, how can marketing, which is nothing more than a means of helping you reach that goal, possibly succeed?

Quo Vadis?

A goal, by definition, is a general statement of a situation you desire for yourself. It suggests what you want to achieve, when you want to achieve it, and the extent to which you wish to achieve it. "I want to be financially self-sufficient by age 45 with an annual income from investments of $50,000." Note the aspects of this goal statement.

It advances a condition ("financially self-sufficient"), a precise time ("by age 45") and an extent ("an annual income from investments of $50,000.") Without this kind of a goals statement, you have no target to reach. Therefore it doesn't matter where you go, since you have indicated to yourself that any destination will do just as well as any other. Sadly, this is the way most people nowadays approach their personal and their business lives.

You must realize in setting your goal that you are running against the current of most people you know. In subtle ways they let you know that they are meanderers, content to drift wherever life takes them. "Have a nice day, " they say. "I take what comes," they tell you. "I live one day at a time," others offer. Think! There are thousands of equally destructive shibboleths emanating effortlessly from the cadre of Flatworms which surrounds us.

You are different.

Therefore you must have a goal. Or goals. For make no mistake about it, you can have goals for every aspect of your life. The methodology I am advancing here is necessarily devoted to business goals, but the techniques are applicable to all aspects of your life.

But I tell you this, and strongly so: if you fail to set and commit yourself to precise goals, you are allying yourself with the least productive, least useful, least valuable kinds of people in our society. Whatever tawdry attractions they may display, they are in fact despicable. And like the race of the blind urging the one-eyed man to destroy his sight to join them in companionable darkness, they will do everything to reduce you to their level. Misery, after all, loves company. What stands between you and these sad creatures is your goal and your resolute commitment to achieving it.

Brainstorm Your Goal

If you have never previously written a goals statement (for having it in your head is not good enough), you may wonder at what to do. Indeed, you may wonder at what you really want to achieve.

Often people react to events. Essentially they are negative movers. Something must happen to them before they know what they want. Again, you are different. A goals statement and a commitment to realizing your goal enables you to be proactive and positive, to take direction of your life and move at will wherever you wish to go.

Begin this process by writing down all the goals you wish to achieve as a result of your business. They may include (but are certainly not limited to) goals for the following:

- money
- possessions
- utilization of your skills and talents
- influence
- recognition by your peers
- people with whom you wish to work and be associated.

While brainstorming, don't be judgmental. Write everything down. If you've always wanted a chauffeur-driven limousine, this is the moment to write it down as a possible goal. You will find that it takes awhile before you list all your goals for each of these subjects. Many you have repressed, feeling that they were "unrealistic" or because of peer pressure. This is not the moment to consider either.

In time you will have an impressive list of possibilities. Now is the moment to evaluate them and to see whether you really want them or whether you are being influenced by others who have determined that you should have them. Remember: if you do not commit yourself to the goal and internalize it and feel energized by it, you will not reach it. Or if, by chance, you do, it will leave you prey to the "Is that all there is?" feeling.

The Values Exercise

In considering what should be done to evaluate the goal and either accept or reject it, I turned to goals specialist Bonnie Gorbaty, my friend. She advises that once you have advanced a desire (that chauffeur-driven limousine) and your reasons for wanting it, you must check both against your values system to make sure this is something you really want.

Desire

chauffeur-driven limousine

Reason for desire

I want everybody to see how successful I am. I want to drive around town with the telephone in the back of the car. This will help me save time. I can also do paperwork on the way to my appointments. Further, it will give me the right sort of social cachet when I go out.

Once you have written your desire and the reasons for it, you've got to compare what you've written with your values, the underlying rules by which you live your life. The values exercise only works if you are rigorously honest with yourself. You'll find this very difficult at first. We are so accustomed to having other people look over our shoulders monitoring what we do and influencing us with their opinions that even when we're alone, it's hard to be honest. Yet if these are the reasons why you want your limousine, you'd better say so.

Now assess what you've written.

"The truth is I like to drive myself. I find it difficult to write in a car, always have. I've never liked people who were ostentatious about their wealth and such an effect is not consonant with the general image I'm striving to portray in my business and personal lives."

If this were your honest response to your purported desire, it would make a lot of sense just to jettison it from the list of possibilities. You should continue to do this with all your desires until you have found that set (usually compact) that does square with your values system and which you can therefore work enthusiastically to reach.

N.B. I didn't select this example at random. Last year I earnestly considered getting the limousine I thought I had always wanted. First, however, I put myself through this goals-setting process. After completing it, I discovered that I didn't want it at all and that the limousine wouldn't fit my current lifestyle. I dismissed it without a pang. That's what happens to false goals. You'll walk away from them without a second thought and move on to those which really are important to you.

Note: Bonnie Gorbaty recommends that you should consider your values in the following way:

- Values that shaped your past work experience. Over the past three years why have you done what you've done? What values have shaped your decisions? Are these values still important to you? If not, what has changed?

- Values that make your current work worth doing. Why are you doing what you're going?

- Values you want to achieve in your work in the future, particularly the next three years. Are the values you want to achieve in the near future the same as you have right now?

- Values you want to change. Certain underlying beliefs you have had in the past may no longer be useful in reaching your goals. What are they? What do you want instead?

Prioritizing Your Choices

You can't do everything. And you certainly cannot do everything well. Recently in counseling a fellow in goals-setting, I had him do the exercises above and return them to me. He had selected enough goals for several lifetimes! As a result he was threatening the realization of any truly substantial goal. After he worked with me, he selected the goals which were really important to him. So must you.

As humans we are decidedly limited in what we can do. Many Americans, facing the groaning sideboard of life, refuse to admit this. As a result they become the consummate nibblers, ultimately emerging as experts only in the nibbling process itself. I call this "smörgasbording", and you have to work hard to avoid this inglorious fate.

You must now confront your desires list. As you do so review it with the following five questions of goal-setting expert Paul Meyer.

- "Have I considered this desire in the light of where I stand now and where I want to go? Does it fit into the direction I wish to go?"

- "Have I developed a detailed, written plan and a deadline for its achievement?"

- "Do I have a burning desire to achieve this goal?"

- "Do I have supreme confidence in myself and my ability to reach this goal?"

- "Do I have the iron-willed determination to follow through to reach this goal regardless of what other people say, think, or do?"

Unless you can answer each of these questions positively, what you have selected is not truly important to you and cannot be considered an achievable goal. Thus, get rid of it and move on to those you can embrace enthusiastically.

Your Written Plan Of Action

Is there anyone in America who doesn't know the importance of keeping a written goals statement? Yet how few people do it.

This plan must consist of the following parts:

- The Goals Statement. As described above this statement of 20 to 50 words consists of the condition you wish to achieve, the time in which you want to achieve it, and the extent to which you wish to achieve it.

- The Benefits Statement. Here, you write down the benefits that will derive by reaching your goal. If there are no benefits to be gained, there is no purpose to reaching your goal. Think hard! Why do you want to achieve this goal? Write down each and every reason.

- Obstacles to achieving the goal and how you will deal with them. Each goal you set will have obstacles to achieving it. So much is obvious. But what specific thing will you do to overcome these obstacles? Say you hate making marketing telephone calls, that the telephone paralyzes you with fear. The obvious answer (as described elsewhere in this book) is to identify the particular form of call reluctance to which you are subject and to implement recommended techniques to overcome your problem.

- The Action Plan. The Action Plan consists of the logical action steps from start to finish required to reach your goal with due dates for achieving each step. This plan is based on rigorous "What Next?" thinking, working backward from the goal and concluding with the very first step that must be taken and when you will take it. Built into this plan must be an evaluation segment which allows you to check your progress, see what is working (and why) and what is not working (and what you intend to do about it.)

When your goal is to achieve business success, your action plan and your marketing plan will overlap considerably. After all, marketing gambits are your primary means of achieving business success.

Visualizing Your Goal

In the ebb and flow of daily life, it's easy to lose sight of our goals. "When you're knee high in alligators," the joke runs, "it's easy to forget your objective was to drain the swamp." So it is. That's why you need to use visualization.

Surround yourself with visual tokens of what you want to achieve. If you want to deposit $1000 each month in your investment program, photocopy 10 one hundred dollar bills and post them prominently. It will be a constant reminder to you to achieve what you set out to achieve. This reminder will both help you structure daily reality and prod your subconscious, which has got to help you with its work, too. "Out of sight, out of mind" runs the adage. Remember it. Place your goals around you and keep them prominently in your mind.

Learn to involve all senses in realizing your goal. See yourself opening the envelopes with the checks which total the $1000 per month you need. Feel yourself walking to the bank with these checks. Believe yourself filling out the deposit slip. You get the idea. You must experience having the goal long before you have in fact achieved it. Indeed, the achievement must seem to be nothing more than an inevitable extension of the reality you have been living long before it becomes a fact.

Expect To Achieve Your Goal

Without a doubt one of the gravest problems I confront in my workshops and with my clients is their failure to believe they can reach the goals they have set. In so doubting, they sabotage their ability to reach them. Many say this: "If I don't commit myself to any goals, I'll never be disappointed. Whatever I achieve will be to the good, and I won't worry about what I don't achieve. On the other hand, Jeffrey, you could well be disappointed if you fail to reach your goals. My way is the safe way."

This is the quintessence of mediocre thinking and ensures that you will never achieve anything substantial.

I guarantee this for you. That you will be further ahead with a written goals achievement program supported by your values system, even if you don't achieve it completely, than you will be if you let matters take a drifting course. Moreover, you will have the satisfaction of knowing that you have done the best you can and need not wonder, as these others must wonder, what you could have achieved if you had set your mind to it. They can never know. But you will. And you can justly feel proud.

To assist in sustaining this expectation of success, use the following techniques:

- Affirmation Cards. Carry your goals with you everywhere. Review them. Before going into a meeting which can help you realize your goal, ask yourself whether you have done everything you could do to make this meeting successful and bring yourself another step closer to your goal. After the meeting, do the same thing. Did you do everything you could to help achieve your goal by helping the prospect achieve his goal?

- Before And After Work Reviews. The process of achieving your goals must be part of the very fiber of your being. This means reviewing your goals before and after work: before, to remind yourself where you are going so that you work accordingly; after, to review whether you made progress and to see how you could do better tomorrow. After a time, the process of achieving your goals will become increasingly automatic — which is just what you want.

- Daily Action Plan. You should be making progress to your goals each day. This means doing — each day! — the five most important things that will help you reach your goals. Start with them. Each of us is necessarily limited in what we can accomplish each day. So therefore do the things you must do first. Then follow with the items of secondary importance. Most of us are fresher and more optimistic in the morning. That, then, is the period you should use to tackle the toughest jobs, for these are the jobs which, when achieved, will give you a feeling of accomplishment which will irradiate the entire day and move us closer to our goals. Early achievement in a day is therefore worth much more than later achievement.

This entire goals setting process is summarized in a compelling quotation of Paul Meyer which you should memorize and post prominently. "Whatever you vividly imagine, ardently desire, sincerely believe, and enthusiastically act upon must inevitably come to pass." I believe this and I live this. And so should you.

Resource

Goals-setting and goals-living are important. If you don't have a goal, you're marketing effort will never be as successful as it could be since you will never really be committed to it. Why should you? What's the point of doing something if you don't really know why you're doing it? That's why you must set a goal.

In doing so, you'll want to be aware of the expert goals-setting services provided by my friend Bonnie Gorbaty. She provides workshops on the subject and strategic planning for small groups. Reach her at Inner Resources Unlimited, P.O. Box 28, Newton, MA 02161 (617) 964-2730.

You'll also find two tapes by goals-setting expert Paul Meyer helpful. They are "Power Of Goal Setting" and "Self-Motivation For Winners." Bonnie Gorbaty makes them available.

Technical Prerequisites For Marketing Success

Setting goals is a necessary but not a sufficient precondition for success. You must possess the technical skills to reach your goal. In marketing these consist of the following 5 skill clusters:

- research
- listening
- writing
- speaking
- organization.

Research

Successful marketing means positioning yourself in the current market, adapting to changing conditions in this market, and benefitting from the rise of new markets before others are even aware they exist. Each of these objectives can only be successfully achieved through research.

What I have found in practice is that many business people are peculiarly ignorant about their markets. They are thus entirely at the mercy of events. Only research — knowing every last thing you can know about your existing markets and about developing markets — will ensure that you'll be in a position to command change and not be whiplashed by it. This means knowing where information about your markets can be found and knowing how to get to it quickly. This will be explored at length in Chapter 2.

Listening

A good marketer is a superb listener. People who know me know I'm extremely adept at getting people to talk about themselves, not only their dreams, hopes and aspirations, but also their anxieties and fears. Both are important for the marketer. Out of an understanding of both the dreams and anxieties comes the marketer's targeted proposal to his prospect. If he has understood what that prospect has said and if he offers the appropriate solution, there is a very good chance the prospect will take it. Why not?

How few people actually listen to anyone else. How few people actually take the time to frame an appropriate, meaningful response. The prospect, sensing that you are working hard to give him what he wants, will want to do business with you. Listening is one of the things that makes this possible. Yet because listening is something we've done since birth we're ordinarily entirely heedless of it. Of course, you'll say, I listen.

Allow me to doubt that. You may hear. But you may not perceive. And listening is the art of clear perception. Because so few people do it well, I turned to my friend Dr. Frank Cancelliere, a listening expert, for advice on how you can become a more effective listener and thus a far more effective marketer.

How We Block Listening

Effective listening is blocked when:

- We hear only what we want or expect to hear.

- We ignore information that conflicts with what we think we already "know."

- We evaluate and pre-judge sources before understanding the entire message.

- We don't all perceive things the same way.

- We forget that words are only symbols, the meaning of which is in the user, not the word itself.

- We let our emotions distort the input.

- We become distracted by "noise", which can be external or internal.

Failing to master these situations will adversely affect your ability to market to your prospect successfully.

What can we do?

Moving To Understanding

The listening process is a process of understanding, as is the entire process of marketing, properly understood. Accordingly to the late Dr. Carl Rogers, the noted humanistic psychologist, evaluation is the major barrier to interpersonal communication. Rogers says that real communication occurs when this evaluative tendency is avoided, when we listen with understanding to what the other person is trying to tell us. This means seeing the expressed idea and attitude from the other person's point of view, sensing how this feels to him, achieving his frame of reference in regard to the thing he is talking about.

Unfortunately, to get to this point, where we can really perceive what is being said to us, we have to learn how to work through the noise which assails us. This noise, says Frank Cancelliere, is both internal and external. The external noise we are all familiar with. It is everything from a jet breaking the sound barrier to office distractions. But the internal noise may be worse. This noise comes from the "tape recorder" continually running in our minds. The tape is composed of messages (both articulated and non-verbal) from our egos, our psyches, and our own experiences. Stress is such an internal noise and, of course, it precludes effective perception of others.

What can we do about all this?

Becoming A Better Listener

- An effective listener constantly strives to enter the speaker's world of feelings and ideas to experience them from his point of view. Knowing what he is feeling, thinking and understanding enables you to respond appropriately and to move towards the mutual understanding that will bring the sale. Effective listening means truly caring about the speaker and conveying a sense of respect. Better listening begins with empathy.

- A good listener makes a conscious, perceptible effort to give the speaker his full attention, establishing a situation which makes him feel comfortable, both physically and psychologically. He keeps interruptions and distractions to a minimum.

- The practiced listener establishes eye contact with the speaker while observing everything that is going on. This means paying attention to inflections, body language, tone of voice, and the speaker's choice of words, as well as to physical position.

Does all this seem obvious to you? I think many of us have heard this before. I doubt whether most of us make a conscious effort to ensure that we really hear our prospects and customers. But if we don't we have failed as a listener and hence as a marketer.

The Principal Listening Responses

There are really four responses we can use when listening to a speaker. They include:

- The Understanding Response. This captures the essential feelings expressed by the speaker, indicating a desire to have an empathetic relationship with the speaker. According to the knowledgeable Cancelliere this is the most difficult response to learn. It requires the listener to respect the speaker and reflect back his feelings.

- The Probing Response. Here, you seek additional information, directing the discussion along a certain line. More information may in fact be needed, but seeking it in this way risks diverting the speaker from his direction. The trick in marketing is to establish an empathetic connection with your prospect and then let him, with your interest, concern and sincerity firmly established, provide you with the information you need to serve him.

- The Recommendation Response. This offers a suggestion and indicates that your intent is to teach. You're implying what the speaker should think or do, either subtly or overtly. Making a recommendation to your listener can only occur after the empathetic link has been established, and you have let the prospect tell you all you need to make the suitable recommendation.

- The Judging/Evaluating Response. Here you express a mild form of criticism, indicating that you've formed an opinion about what the speaker has said. The speaker may, in fact, have said something wrong, but this response can create guilt feelings that block further trust-building communication. Of course this is disastrous in marketing.

The Maestro's Recommendations

As you've probably already gathered, Frank Cancelliere's advice is to use the Understanding Response whenever possible in marketing to your prospects and in all other listening situations. It serves the speaker's need to be heard, understood and accepted. The other three responses he calls Directive Listening. They focus more on your needs than the speaker's. If the speaker senses this, the development of the mutually beneficial marketing relationship may be thwarted.

To achieve this kind of beneficial listening, here's what Frank suggests you do:

- Listen without interruptions.

- Don't jump to conclusions.

- Don't prematurely evaluate what you are hearing. Certainly don't evaluate until after you've achieved understanding.

- Be patient with the speaker.

- Always look the speaker in the eye. Talk to the speaker, not to a corner.

- Ask questions to clarify the speaker's meaning.

- Don't rush the speaker.

- Don't finish the speaker's sentences.

- Refrain from giving advice to the speaker unless you're asked.

- Control your need to assert yourself. Allow yourself to be filled with what the speaker is saying. Out of what he tells you will come your appropriate response.

- Let your body lean into the speaker and indicate that you are fully attending to what he has to say and doing so with enthusiasm.

Pursuing understanding in this way will enhance the likelihood of getting it. And as you achieve understanding you can make the appropriate response which will enhance the likelihood you and the speaker will do business together.

Resource

Dr. Frank Cancelliere speaks, conducts workshops and consults in the fields of management, sales and communications. You'll find him both knowledgeable and client-centered. He is Chairman, Department of Management, Long Island University, C.W. Post Campus, Brookville, NY 11548 (516) 299-2361.

Writing

To succeed in marketing means to be a successful writer. By this I do not mean having the skill to write The Great American Novel. Not at all. It means being able to write active, client-centered prose, studded with meaningful buyer benefits. As I intend to discuss this again in the chapter on how to create effective documents, I shall not tackle the subject in detail here. Suffice it to say, however, that much of the marketing writing I see is cumbersome, flaccid, verbose, meandering and downright dull. Don't let this happen to you.

The job of your marketing writing is to capture the prospect's imagination, to catch him up in the potential of what you are offering and, through the language of movement, to compel his attention and engender his excitement and his trust.

Resource

To write marketing copy such as I've just described, use my book CASH COPY. I can also enthusiastically recommend two books by my esteemed colleague Bob Bly, *The Copywriter's Handbook* and *Create The Perfect Sales Piece.* If you find you just can't write this kind of copy yourself, call me and I'll be happy to help.

Speaking

As a marketer, you will be speaking continually. Your success as a speaker consists of knowing what to say and knowing how to say it. Knowing what to say and how to say it vary depending on the situation you're in when you are the speaker. Generally speaking there are three situations you will face:

- when you are speaking to your prospect directly, one-on-one. Here there will be considerable conversation with both parties talking.

- when you are speaking to a small group. Here there is a chance for you to make your points and for most, if not all, of the group members to have their say, too.

- when you are speaking to a larger assembly. Here people come to hear you. You will make the primary presentation. The remarks of others will ordinarily be limited to questions or short comments.

Each of these is a characteristic marketing situation and hence to give yourself the broadest possible flexibility in marketing your products and services, you must become adept at them all.

Speaking One-On-One

Following Frank Cancelliere's advice will help you make this situation a success. To be a perceptive listener puts you well on the way to success here. But listening is not sufficient for success. Here, then, are some tricks of the trade for making your one-on-one marketing situations a success:

- Focus on the person you are speaking to. Everything about you should clearly suggest you are interested. Give him your full attention.

- Be positive. Tell the person you want to help him solve his problems. Be sincere.

- Lead with questions about his situation. Don't talk until you have gathered the information you need. As the person presents you with this information, ask follow-up questions which enable you to clarify the facts.

- Once you have the information you need and the speaker has told you what he has to say, then make a clear presentation and offer precise follow-up steps. If you need to assess what you've heard before you can submit a proposal, say so. Tell your speaker precisely what you are going to do and precisely when he'll hear from you again. If you can summarize the information on the spot and make your recommendation, do so. The important thing is to indicate that you have heard what the other person has said and are ready to offer the appropriate solution.

In a situation where you are speaking to one other person, the essence of success rests on three things: exuding sincerity and interest in his problem and enthusiasm and confidence that you can help solve it. Asking questions which provide you with the information you need to follow up appropriately. And presenting either your considered proposal forthrightly and/or letting your prospect know precisely how and when you intend to follow up this meeting.

Success In A Group

There are two group-speaking possibilities. Either you are hosting the meeting at which you'll make your presentation, or you are speaking to a meeting someone else has called. Clearly, you have more control in the first situation.

- **Where You Are The Host**

When you have called the meeting and are speaking to it, do the following:

- Send an agenda in advance to all those attending. Indicate not only what the topics at the meeting will be but the questions which must be resolved. The more specific you can be about the outcomes for the meeting, the more likely it will be a success.

- Start the meeting promptly. It is never a good idea to penalize those who arrived in a timely fashion because others did not. If one of the no-shows is a key person, move to those parts of the agenda where his involvement is not so important, and continue.

- Begin your presentation by telling those attending what needs to be accomplished, when it needs to be accomplished, and how you propose that it be accomplished. If you are making recommendations about a matter, make them briefly and set forth succinctly the chief reasons for them. Both recommendations and reasons should be presented in the most upbeat and enthusiastic way possible.

N.B. It is a good idea to summarize the key points of your remarks, your recommendations and reasons for them and distribute them to members of the group. Do this when you are finished talking, not before. That way, if a negative speaker follows you, many group members will be distracted by what you've passed out and will not be according him the full attention you should have received.

As you make your recommendations, look at the people in the group. If people in the group have helped you formulate these recommendations, look at them and thank them for what they have done. Your objective as a speaker in a group is not only to present information but also to help build a group consensus which will stimulate action. That is why you must involve as many members of the group in your presentation as you can.

- If you expect negative comments and criticism, address them point by point in your remarks with your best responses. Many groups divide naturally into three parts. Those who agree with you. Those who disagree with you. And those who have no opinion one way or another. Your task as a speaker is to make it easy for your adherents to support you. To neutralize the opposition of those who don't. And to give good, solid reasons for supporting you to those who have no feelings on the matter one way or the other. Each of these is important.

- After you've finished your presentation, summarize your key points. Remind people what needs to be accomplished and how your recommendations will help accomplish it. End on the upbeat with a benefit statement. Tell them in clear, precise detail exactly what your recommendations will deliver. The more specific you can be about this, the better. It is a good idea to distribute this benefits list to the participants as an indication that you have done your homework and know precisely where your recommendations lead. Count on it: no one else will have this kind of persuasive supporting information.

- Now ask for questions. If you are smart, you may well want to plant a question or two from a supporter about what you have suggested. This enables you to underscore key aspects of what you are proposing. If a question is hostile and you do not have the information, don't bluff. Say when and how you'll respond to it. In such a situation it is important to indicate you remain in control, even when you don't have the information you need.

The most dangerous questioners are those who are able to undermine your presentation using your own information, facts, assumptions and ideas. Make sure you have thought about what you're saying and handing out. A negative questioner who attacks you personally (while irritating) is usually a blessing in disguise. Most people respond negatively to a personal attack even where the questioner's underlying ideas are positive and worth hearing. Your job in this situation is to remain calm, confident and, above all, courteous. Let the questioner huff and puff. Stay cool.

- At the end of the meeting, make sure you are the one to summarize what happened, what will be done and how it will be done. That way you can put the best face on what occurred. Make sure that your version is the official one by working with the notetaker (you are having one, aren't you?) so that what you say is properly recorded. In a week this will be the accepted version of what happened so it bears your consideration.

- **When You Are Not The Host**

Matters change, of course, where you are not the host. In this situation, you are relatively less in control. This being the case, you must work with the host to ensure the most advantageous result for you both. That is the key to this kind of meeting. What you want to achieve is no different, but you must work with and through the host to make sure you get it.

- Ask the host what he wants the meeting to accomplish. Also find out who supports these objectives and who opposes them. Write down the reasons people give for each point of view. You can use them in your presentation.

- Have the host communicate the objectives for the meeting to all expected to participate. These must be sent in advance. Be careful that these are your objectives. You'll be better off if you draft these materials yourself. Either way, review them before they are sent. If you don't, you may well find materials being sent which undermine your position.

- Write your introduction for the host. You wish to be introduced as the consummate problem-solver for whatever problem is being discussed. An intelligent introduction will properly position you before members of the group. You will be seen not as an outsider but as an expert come to assist them in solving their problem through your product or service. This is precisely what you want.

- Have the host introduce you to people as they arrive. Get their cards and arrange them in front of you in the way they are sitting so you can address them by name in your presentation. Or get their names in advance from the host.

- After the host introduces you, make your presentation. This time include the host in your presentation. "Tom and I have been discussing the best ways for your agency to get the money it needs for its meals-on-wheels program." What you say must be perceived as a joint effort. Don't hesitate to end crucial sections with, "Isn't that right, Tom?" to further commit the host and indicate the partnership to the group. Indicate this partnership even in the documents you distribute. Here's a possible heading, "Recommendations stemming from a meeting between Jeffrey Lant and Executive Director Smith." You are the less threatening and the more part of the team as you bring in your host.

- If there are hostile questions, you need not answer them all. You can have your say and ask your host, your partner, to answer, too. The more you have involved your host in your presentation, the less hostile the questions will be.

- At the end, summarize just as you did before. This time, you can summarize the results yourself and have them distributed by the host to participants to ensure that your point of view is well represented.

Speaking To An Assembly

This important matter is discussed in detail in Chapter 11.

Organization

To be organized in business (or, for that matter, in personal) affairs means to be focused on the objective to be achieved, disciplined about achieving it, knowledgeable about the means to achieve it, and in command of the time needed to achieve it. Each is an absolute precondition of organizational success. If you are not so organized you cannot be a successful marketer.

- **Being Focused On The Objective**

Organized marketers are focused marketers. They know precisely whom they are trying to reach. Precisely why they are trying to reach them. What these people will respond to and what they will not. And what they want these people to do once the connection has been made. Once the marketer is working on this task, he must resolutely see it through. Other tasks must be regarded as any other interruption, namely, as something which undermines his ability to connect with his prospects and move them to become customers. Collectively, I group all these interruptions under the "Dog Ate My Homework" Syndrome. We are all subject to it.

Instead of being focused on the marketing task at hand, crucial to the success of our business, we instead allow ourselves to give way before the tyranny of the insignificant. "I can't do what I ought to do, because...

- I have a cold."
- My mother-in-law is visiting."
- My boyfriend argued with me last night."
- My car got stuck in a snowdrift."

And all the other picayune matters which seem, at the time, to be sufficient reasons for putting aside the task which we purportedly wish successfully to conclude. But let me tell you something. Not one of these excuses, however cogent at the time, will help you connect with your buyers and so bring your marketing to a successful conclusion.

Focus is the first component of successful marketing. The minute you allow yourself to be diverted from the task at hand you are becoming disorganized.

- **Being Disciplined About Achieving It**

This point is intimately related to the one above. To be disciplined means to go about the task at hand in good times and bad, when you feel like it and when you don't. Trifling people do things only when they care to. Disciplined people do things when they do not. Trifling people believe in the Myth of Inspiration. They can give as a perfectly self-convincing excuse "I don't feel like it", before pushing the crucial project away, believing they await the siren call of inspiration. Disciplined people never do. Instead they say, "Slow and steady wins the race."

The reason many of my readers and students hate marketing is because it must be done day-in, day-out. One marketing gambit, however successful, is never sufficient. Marketing must be done again and again and again to the same people before they take the action that will benefit them. And when you are finished, it must be done again, to convince the laggards and to keep in touch with those who have at last acted.

How can you remain disciplined, indeed enthusiastically disciplined, in the face of what so disheartens those with a less realistic view of life and what it demands for success?

- To stay disciplined, you must focus on two objectives simultaneously: the completion of the task at hand and the role of the completed task in delivering the Benefit and the Ultimate Benefit both to you and to the person using your product and service. Thus, as I sit down to overcome my natural inertia and to write one of my problem-solving process marketing articles, I focus on the following benefits to be derived by all the parties involved in the process of using this as a marketing device:

  - The article helps my prospect reach one of his objectives through the information I provide. As a helpful person, this makes me feel good and is, of course, useful to the prospect, who thereby moves closer to achieving his objectives.

  - It brings me favorably before the attention of many people whose problems I can solve with my products or services. It increases the prospect's trust that I can solve his problems and increases the possibility he will put himself in touch with me, now or in the near future.

  - It is cheap. I get my message to the attention of thousands of people at limited cost. I can therefore redirect my money into other projects, both business and personal, while increasing the profitability of this activity.

  - It generates inquiries from people who, by skillful follow-up, I can transform over time into buyers.

  - It produces buyers who respond directly to the offers attached to the article. These buyers not only make me a richer man today but, through my upgrade process, ensure that I shall be still richer tomorrow, all the while solving the problems of prospects in need.

All these benefits come from the completion of this single marketing task. Set against so much to be won, is it not a little thing to overcome my natural sloth and aversion to work? And so I do. And so will you.

- **Being Knowledgeable About Achieving It**

Every organized person is an intelligent person. He knows what must be done and knows how to do it. You cannot be organized in marketing without knowing the means, in precise detail, which connect you to your prospects and which enable you to keep your current buyers and upgrade them. Fortunately, that's where this book comes in. With it, you have achieved another step in the admirable process of becoming organized and benefitting accordingly.

- **Being In Command Of The Time Needed To Achieve It**

Marketing takes time. Often lots of time. But with successful marketing the payoffs can be spectacular. Essentially the time you need is eaten away in three ways:

- through other bona fide tasks of running your home and business;
- because of the picayune interruptions under the "Dog At My Homework" Syndrome; and
- because of procrastination.

To be successful at marketing, the engine which fuels your business, means to be successful at handling the three general problems which cut into the time you have available to handle it properly. We all have enough time if we handle our affairs in such a way as to make it available for what really needs to be done and which will in the long run be most productive for us and our business. Thus, to get time we must:

- Prune away the inessential. From long dealings with thousands of business people and those aspiring to success in business, I know that too many spend too much of their time on trivia.

Evaluate your activities by these simple questions:

- Is what you are about to do essential in connecting you with your prospects or buyers or in some other direct way building your business?

- Do you need to do it yourself?

- Or is your time best utilized doing something else?

Unless the activity you have undertaken is directly relevant to improving your business, principally through connecting you to your buyers, either don't do it or have someone else do it.

In the great days of Britain's Indian Raj, Lord Curzon, the Viceroy, commanded a subcontinent. He had only to snap his fingers to summon squads of palace servants. Yet this obsessive man used to write in his own fair hand the place cards for the viceregal dinner parties. Therefore I use what I call the Curzon Test on my business activities to determine whether what I am about to do is important, necessary, and will in fact build my business and connect me with my prospects and customers. If I have any doubts, I abandon it. So should you. In this way, you will find yourself with additional time which you can invest in these important activities.

- Don't mislead yourself into thinking you are concentrating on the important when you are, in fact, doing nothing more than faltering because of the trivial. No excuse is an acceptable excuse as to why you have not satisfactorily handled your marketing, if you are really interested in assisting your prospects and building your own business and prosperity. You can train your mind accordingly, as I did years ago.

While I was writing my first book I came down with bronchitis, a terrible problem. In the beginning I gave way before the disease. Then, still in its grip, I rallied my determination and took action. Each day, still feeble, I arose and went to my desk where, through a slick of sweat, I wrote my 750 words. Often I finished in the middle of a sentence, returning to my sick bed exhausted but triumphant. There, in the midst of this disease, I came to know that one could truly shuck off the trivial impedimenta which daily assail us and by focusing on the truly significant transcend our human limitations and reach the goal enthusiastically adopted. Remember this!

This means learning to overcome procrastination, too, for while you are in its grip you cannot successfully market. If procrastination assails you, both you and your prospects go without the benefits which come with your marketing. To overcome it, try this:

- Focus on the benefits to be gained by the task you are putting off. The problem may be that you don't really see any benefits. If this is true, perhaps the task isn't worth doing. But if you do want the benefits, use them to motivate your mind to start the task.

- Outline the task from start to finish in logical order. Outlining is an action activity. By doing it you will be both breaking down the project into smaller, more manageable bits and, through the sheer fact of outlining, moving towards its completion.

- Now start to solve the problem by beginning to work on any part of the task. You need not start at the beginning. Start where you can start. Finish what you can finish. Then move to complete what remains.

- Reward yourself for what you are doing. But make it a meaningful reward. Reward yourself for finishing parts of the project. Reserve a significant reward for yourself when you are entirely finished. You deserve it. But the real reward is in the mind; you now know that procrastination need never undermine your activities. Having conquered it this time, you can conquer it whenever it threatens you.

Resources

If procrastination afflicts you, use *Procrastination: Why You Do It, What To Do About It* by Burka and Yuen. They offer sensible suggestions and candid good humor, not least about their own bouts with this universal and debilitating problem.

To become a more organized person in general, use *Organize Yourself!* by Ronni Eisenberg with Kate Kelly.

Energy And Determination: The Last Essential Prerequisites For Marketing Success

This has been a long chapter, I know. Yet these prerequisites are important. Important yet neglected by virtually every marketing book. Their authors assume that you know all this. But having worked with so many businesses over the last years, I know differently.

Business people who do not have the necessary prerequisites for marketing success ensure their own problems. It is the responsibility of people who say they are interested in helping others market better to know this and to do something about it. Now, at least, I have — or at least almost. For there remain two more essential prerequisites: energy and determination. Without them your marketing effort will falter.

Energy, in relation to marketing, comes, it seems to me, from two sources: the brain and the body. I shall not dwell here on the need for good physical health, except to tell you that the demands of marketing are considerable and demand that you be fit. I remember a few summers ago teaching a class of M.B.A. candidates at a local college. Most were fat, some grossly obese. As they waddled into class, I could not help but think that to them marketing must always remain a mystery beyond their understanding. How could they understand and implement the quintessential action-discipline when they had trouble walking into a classroom?

Arguably more important, however, is the energy that emanates from your mind, the energy that informs your entire approach to marketing. This energy rests on twin supports: the knowledge that you are doing good for others, others who need what you are selling, and the knowledge that in the process you are doing well for yourself. So long as you believe in the necessity and importance of your offer, there need never be any weakening dichotomy between these objectives. Hence your energy will be unified and more intense. Everything you do will be directed to a point worth your work. This integrity of purpose is the ultimate source of your energy. And it is to this integrity of purpose you must return when depleted, as you inevitably will be.

It is this integrity of purpose which also acts as the generative source for the determination you must also have to succeed. For make no mistake about it, in marketing even those who need what you are offering will decline what you are selling, either directly or indirectly, again and again.

If you are willing to take no for an answer, if you are willing to have them go without the product or service which will enhance their lives, then indeed marketing is not for you. If you are not so willing and are determined to do what it necessary to help your prospects, and, in the process, yourself, then you have the single most important prerequisite for success: iron-willed determination to do what it takes to help the people who need you. Such being the case, we are now ready to move into the specific techniques which will enable you to find the people who need what you're selling and make sure they buy it.

CHAPTER 2

MMMM

How To Handle Your Market Research: Getting The Insurance You Need To Make Sure You're Heading In The Right Direction

Is there any American who doesn't dream at one point or another about launching a successful independent business? I doubt it. Yet for too many of those who do begin such a business the experience is an almost unrelieved disaster. No wonder. They jump from the condition of exhilarated inspiration to actual selling without doing anything in between.

This is a terrible mistake.

Business is not a variation on Russian roulette. Certainly successful business isn't. It is an exercise in continual assessment. Assessing the state of your industry. Assessing what your competitors are doing and why they're doing it. Assessing your distribution channels if you have a product. And your promotion channels, whatever you're selling. It's finding out from your prospects and customers what they like and what they don't like, why they are buying from your competitors, and what it will take to get them to buy from you.

Thus, going into business means transforming yourself into Sherlock Holmes. For make no mistake about it, the admirably deductive Holmes is the inspiration for this chapter and all the marketing research you must do forever after. Throughout this chapter I shall be advising you to think like Holmes. And I'll tell you right now, if you haven't spent any time with this insightful man, study a volume of his stories today to correct this shocking lapse in your education. For you see, Sherlock Holmes is the patron saint of market research, as you will see from a tale of my introduction to the subject.

An Anecdote

My first real glimpse of market research came when I was 18 years old, a college freshman. Just before spring break one of my enterprising friends, a sophomore named John Edwards, told me he was going to Ohio to visit cities where he was considering establishing his summer business. John, all of 19 (but far more experienced than I), owned a dozen bicycle-powered ice cream wagons. He was attempting to figure out where he would deploy them that summer. He inveigled me into going with him into the fleshpots of Ohio to help him gather the intelligence that would enable him to make his decision.

He started from the essential point, for he had clearcut objectives he wanted his marketing to help him reach. He needed a city sufficiently far away from home so there would be no parental interference (essential for an autonomous-minded teenager) and one which would produce sufficient revenue to pay for his summer living expenses, the cost of his labor and supplies, and the profit he needed for his next year's college expenses. The trip was designed to produce the information he needed to make a decision about where to establish his enterprise.

No fool he, he needed a willing dogsbody and researcher to assist him. And who better than his friend who had all the necessary prerequisites: love of library work, a need for no more than living expenses, and the kind of deference to a superior which only a freshman could feel to a worldly sophomore. And so my first market research trip was launched.

John Edwards, the quintessential entrepreneur, made that trip pay off. We went to Columbus. To Toledo. To Akron. And to who knows where else checking on the things John needed to know: mean temperature (the hotter the city the better the ice cream sales), the number of hills (remember his wagons were pulled by bicycles), the percentage of population with air conditioning (the more that had it, the less likely they were to need ice cream), neighborhoods where there were the most children (his prime customers), ease of getting supplies, prevailing summer wages for teen-age help, and the many other things he wanted to know and which, once gathered, were carefully entered in his elaborate log books.

Helping gather this information was how I spent spring vacation my freshman year while others sported on the Florida coast. But there was a lesson in thoroughness here I have never forgotten, though the experience took place over 20 years ago. The fact that John's summer business was as successful as he wanted should come as a surprise to no one. *He* had always known it would be. And he had a right to that warm feeling of certainty, based as it was on hard numbers and information and from his deductions from them which would have done credit to Sherlock Holmes himself.

I am therefore dedicating this chapter to John Edwards, still my friend, for the lesson he taught: that one is never too young to learn the importance of thorough market research and its role in the establishment of a successful business.

What You'll Learn In This Chapter

This chapter is divided into the following 6 parts. If you satisfactorily solve these six problems, all but one of which *must* be solved *before* you start your business, you'll vastly increase the chances that what you do will be successful. The six problems are:

- discovering the state of your industry;
- sleuthing out your competition to find out what they are doing and why;
- gathering information and insight into your product distribution channels;
- finding out what you need to know about the available means for promoting your product and service;
- surveying potential prospects to find out if they have bought from others; if so, why; and what it would take to get them to buy from you;
- surveying existing clients to determine why they are buying from you, to make sure they continue to do so.

Background To Successful Market Research

I am aware that most people reading this book will not like market research, will find it boring, and may even regard it as a waste of time. Some suffer from the curious delusion that it hobbles their creativity and inspiration. Others couldn't be dragged by wild horses into the libraries and research facilities where at least some of it must be done. Still others like to go by their intuition and "trust their gut," a common problem of entrepreneurs. Nonetheless, I say this as strongly as possible: jumping over the market research stage is the height of folly.

- Market research is insurance. It transforms business from a gamble into a calculated risk, a very different thing.
- Market research enables you to position yourself athwart the great trends in your industry and those which affect your prospects and society as a whole long before lesser minds have even discerned them. You are thus ready to act long before others, both in entering a field and in getting out.
- Market research gives you the confidence you need to proceed with determination. You'll know where you are going, why you are going there, and how to get there — all essential in achieving business success. No one who fails to undertake this kind of basic research is ever entitled to this feeling. That ill-prepared person can only have faith and hope. You'll have knowledge.

The Essential Precondition Of Marketing Research

I live in an area where the number of highly-trained professional people is extremely high. Yet large numbers of them are living far below their earning capabilities because they have failed to master even the most basic elements of market research and to take appropriate action based on what they've discovered. Indeed, some take pride in this state of benighted ignorance, feeling that it confirms their standing as a right-thinking humanist. What rot!

These people, whom I see daily, have made the classic mistake of marketing. Instead of assessing the capacity of a market to sustain them, they have instead selected a field of endeavor (usually for purely personal reasons) and then looked for their market. Smart marketers, by comparison, assess a market and then create a product or develop a service based on the need they have ascertained. How very different this is!

Thus, the essential prerequisite before beginning your market research is to make a tentative selection of the product or service you are considering developing and promoting. You cannot know until such basic research is finished whether there is any need to be satisfied, any market to be found, any distribution channels open to you and hence any point in moving ahead with what you are intending.

Until the following market research steps are finished, anything you decide must be tentative. Or else you risk the terrible consequences of going ahead unprepared, as so many people I come in contact with have. Their sad consequences often include diminished earning power, flickering self-esteem, anxiety, irritation and that undermining sense of a life wasted and incomplete. If by following a set of sensible marketing steps you can avoid this result, don't you think such time and money as you must spend to accomplish it worth the cost?

Understanding Your Industry

Nothing you do in your business will take place in a vacuum. Each of us exists in a complicated series of interrelated worlds. You cannot establish a successful business without understanding how you'll relate to what is happening around you. The first place to start is with what is happening in your industry, which like all industries is made up of several essential parts. These include customers, competing product and service suppliers, distribution channels, and promotion vehicles which reach customers. Thus, you must seek to know something about each.

Not surprisingly, some of these things are easier to get information about than others. All, however, are essential. This being the case, let's ease you into the marketing research business as we go forward, animated by the spirit of Sherlock Holmes, in search of the information you need to ensure the success of your enterprise. First task: developing a bird's-eye view of your industry.

The Industry Profile

The business of business is assessing change and adapting its products and services to new conditions. This assessment begins with the state of the industry in which you operate. Each assessment is based on a blending of what has happened in the recent past (no longer than the last three years), what is happening now, and what the best available information sources project to happen over the next three to five years.

Thus, some questions can be answered with near certainty. They include:

- What was the condition of your industry in the last complete reporting period?
- Why was it in that condition?
- How long was it in that condition?
- What is the current condition of your industry?
- Why is it in this condition?

Other questions produce more speculative answers. They include:

- How long will the industry's current condition last?
- What are the reasons for thinking so?
- What happens next?
- Why is this likely to happen?

Market research is always a balancing of the known past, useful only insofar as it suggests what may happen in the future, with the unknown future, which is unsettling to the extent we have no way of anticipating it and preparing for it. Market research, however, does give you a way of anticipating and preparing and hence reducing your risk and anxiety.

Here's how to gather information on the state of your industry over the recent past, currently, and as a projection into the future:

- Identify all the professional associations that are involved in your industry. There are more than you think. You'll find many of them in the Gale *Encyclopedia of Associations*. Published in three volumes, here you'll find basic information on close to 20,000 professional associations, including information on their publications. You will have to join some of these. Before you do, check with the largest local general and business library to see which publications they already carry. If you're not sure what libraries are available in your area, check the *American Library Directory*. You want to join the relevant associations not covered by any reasonably-accessible library.

- Make contact with both the government documents and business librarians of these libraries. Ask for an orientation tour. Don't be passive on this orientation. Bring in a list of questions you're going to need to have answered. Thus, after the librarian has given you a broad overview of the collections and storing system, you'll get expert help on locating what you need to know. For instance, given my interest in homebased businesses, I would take a list of questions like these:

  - How many homebased businesses are there in Massachusetts?
  - Are they separately tracked by any state agency or are they lumped together with small businesses? By a federal agency? If so, which ones? Where are their documents kept? If this library doesn't have these documents, where could I look for them?
  - How many such businesses are there nationally? How can I find government publications about them?

You get the idea. By asking the kinds of questions you are likely to have to keep on asking (so long as you are interested in this market), you'll get a private training session on how to use the materials they have and you need. You'll also identify holes in their collections and later be in a position to recommend suitable additions.

- Note the hours of the libraries you need and the names of the librarians you'll be dealing with; find out from them when their least busy times are. That's when you'll want to call. You'll get better, more thorough attention then. I find I am continually using the services of librarians, and I follow these rules to good effect.

- Pay particular attention to the relevant offices at all levels of government involved in gathering information about your market. Much of what you want will probably be done by the U.S. Department of Commerce, but not all. Your task is to identify all the departments of governments which are involved in gathering and publishing information about your market.

Find out which specific offices are involved in this process. When you do, write and ask to be put on their mailing lists. At the very least, you'll probably receive notification when new publications are available. From time to time, you can bring these to the attention of the librarian at the facilities where you customarily gather information and let them spend their money getting the information you need.

N.B. If you write regular articles on your market, as I do, stay in touch with the public relations officers of the government agencies producing the material. Ask for review copies of the documents they produce. By citing the department (and making sure they see your article), you're ensuring that you'll be sent materials whenever you need them.

- Open an Expert File. As you read the publications produced by the professional associations and the various government departments, the names of experts will pop up. After a time, you'll notice the same names. These are the recognized sources in your industry. Make contact with these specialists.

To do so, use what I call a Sophisticated Fan Letter. Here are its elements:

- Lead off with a knowledgeable compliment. Tell the specialist you liked his recent article (or appreciated the wisdom of his quotation) and tell him where you saw it. Tell him why you liked the article. The specialist likes compliments, of course, but he'll be grateful to know what particularly interested you.

- Follow up with information about your work. Let him know you will be happy to be a source for him. Never just ask for something for nothing. Be willing to enter into a mutually productive relationship. Specialists always need to know what practitioners are doing. Let him know you're willing to tell him.

- Then ask for the information you need. But don't ask for information that the specialist will have to work for weeks to find. Ask for citations for books, articles, and other information sources. Ask, too, if he has published on the subjects in which you are interested. Or whether he knows other experts who have and can provide you with their names and addresses.

I write these kinds of letters regularly, and the chances that they'll be answered are very, very good. I learned this when I was a child and used to write to present and former U.S. government officials as well as current heads of state. A surprising number took the time to send back very personal responses. Take heed from a little boy's successes.

N.B. Stay in touch with these experts. Put them on your mailing list and when you have information that might be valuable to them, let them know. If they're interested, they'll contact you. If they use it, make sure you are fully identified with name, address and telephone number. This then becomes yet another way of unabashed promotion. Using these techniques, I have ended up in dozens of articles and many books, including several best sellers such as *What Color Is Your Parachute?*

- Identify publishers of newsletters and other specialty publications in your field. Some of these will be published by the associations you find in *The Encyclopedia of Associations,* but not all. Indeed, you'll find only, about one-third of the associations in the country in these books. Many of the others will have information you need but are more difficult to find.

For newsletters and specialized publications try the following:

- *Oxbridge Directory of Newsletters.* It's published by Oxbridge Communications, 150 Fifth Ave., New York, NY 10011.

- *Standard Periodical Directory.* Also published by Oxbridge Communications.

- Check, too, with Howard Penn Hudson's Newsletter Clearinghouse, 44 W. Market Street, P. O. Box 311, Rhinebeck, NY 12572 (914) 876-2081. Also publishes *The Newsletter On Newsletters.*

From these three sources, you should get at least one lead (and will often get dozens) to follow up. Here's where Sherlock Holmes comes in again. You must follow these leads back to their original sources, back to where the information originated. Thus, as you approach an information source, you must:

- Note the facts. What is being said about your industry?
- Where did these facts come from?
- Are you in contact with the place whence the facts originated? If not, how can you either gain deeper insight into the story being reported and/or make sure you are notified about future information on this topic?
- Take into account the source's bias.

Apropos of this last point, you will need to be in your business for a time before you can adequately assess an information source's bias. Many sources are biased in one direction or another. All information is based on one set of propositions or another. To be able to properly evaluate the information you see, you need to understand the bias of its author. Unfortunately this only comes with time. If you are in doubt, however, never hesitate to contact the originating source for the information, wherever he is.

- Pick up the telephone and call the reporter who wrote the story you have just read on your industry. Don't be coy. Identify yourself. Say that you are a practitioner in that industry and would like to follow up any of the particular points of interest. *N.B.* As will be described later, don't miss this opportunity, too, to say that you'd be glad to be kept in mind as an expert source for later articles. Confirm this in a letter.
- Write to the author of the article (the Sophisticated Fan Letter) requesting what you need to know.
- Call the Congressman's office after you've just read what he has to say about the state of your industry. Ask for any written documents and fact sources used in coming to this determination.

In short, don't merely be a passive receptacle for information. Understand that information is a commodity and the more you have about your industry the better off you'll be. Recognize that much helpful information, despite what you may think when you see the avalanche that makes it into print, is not available through printed sources. Much is only available from the horse's mouth. So get to know the horse.

The Industry Profile

Using these techniques (and others which are discussed elsewhere in this chapter), you'll gather (and continue gathering, for the process never stops) an enormous amount of information. Now you need to put it into a form that's easy to use. Develop an Industry Profile Sheet including the following questions and your best answers:

- Past State of the Industry

- What was the condition of the industry in the last complete reporting period?

Here you will log the information you have gathered based on the last complete report done of your industry. Include the name of the reporting body and its address and telephone number. If you know the name or names of the people who did the report, log this information. These are specialists of importance.

Find out, too, when the next report will be done. If the report is being done by a government or regulatory body, it is usually done at regular intervals. The originating body can usually tell you when their next major (or interim) report will be available. Get yourself on the mailing list for this report if possible. Whether you get on this list or not, note the name, address and telephone number of the person responsible both for writing and publishing this report and shipping it.

Note the names of all the experts who appear in this report. Follow them up as I have advised. If you are going to be a leader in your field, and certainly if you are going to have the information you need to succeed, you're going to have to be in touch with these specialists.

- Why was your industry in that condition?

List the specific reasons why the industry was in the condition discussed in the information you've gathered. Be specific. Thinking like Sherlock Holmes, ask yourself whether you have followed the information thread back to its source. If prices in my industry have been going up in part because of a general rise in paper prices, then the sleuthing instinct suggests keeping abreast of such prices. One way of doing this is to continue to monitor the subject through the professional associations of my industry and their publications. Another way is to make contact with the professional association of the paper manufacturers themselves who will obviously be closely monitoring the situation. Have you done this with each of the significant variables in your equation? Have you identified the appropriate sources for the information you need?

Now use these same techniques to answer the questions: how long was the industry in that condition?; what is the current condition of the industry?; and why is it in this condition?

Do the same for the projection information you've gathered; how long will the industry's current condition last?; what are the reasons for thinking so?; what happens next?; and why is this likely to happen?

By answering these questions you'll have an excellent profile of the immediate past and present of your industry and a reasonable glimpse of what the future may bring. Moreover, all your information will be accompanied by an indication of where it came from, who is responsible for it, when an update can be expected, and how you can get it. You are therefore in a position to keep yourself current forever after.

Handling This Market Research Expeditiously

I can just hear you groaning about doing all this work. I know you see the value of it. But perhaps you're wondering whether all this is *really* necessary. It is if you wish to correctly position yourself as circumstances change. Either you can be in a position to benefit from the change which will come. Or you'll be in a position where you'll be its servant.

The truth is, the first time you do market research is particularly time-consuming. You don't have your information sources. You don't know where to look. And you may have a limited understanding of the climate in your industry. All that changes over time. As in so many things, the good foundation you give yourself will pay off later. But you have to spend the time necessary to give yourself that essential foundation. It's up to you.

Let me tell you about one character you know who used this kind of market research to his decided benefit: Rhett Butler of *Gone With The Wind.* At the beginning of the Civil War when lesser men were investing in Confederate bonds, he did some market research on cotton and on England's need for a product which would shortly be in short supply because of the Union blockade. He bought up bales of the stuff at a discount, shipped it to England and waited until it brought a dollar a pound, at least 10 times what he paid for it and the basis of his subsequent fortune. Market research. You can't beat it.

Resources

The key to market research is knowing where to look, how to find information and how to interpret what you've found. These resources will help.

- To find information more easily, use Todd Alden's *Finding Facts Fast: How To Find Out What You Want And Need To Know.* Short but sweet.

- For information on on-line computer databases, see the *Datapro Directory of On-Line Services.* It is available in two volumes. It includes tutorials for both the novice and the more experienced searcher and also publicly accessible databases of every kind. Available from Datapro, 600 Delran Parkway, Delran, NJ 08075. 800-328-2776.

- Use information provided by the Bureau of the Census, which does many more things than count us every decade. You'll find an excellent introduction to the work of this bureau, the data it gathers, and how to use them in *Census '80: Continuing The Factfinder Tradition.* This 490-page text is available for $8.50 from the Superintendent of Documents, U.S. Government Printing Office, Washington, D.C. 20402. Stock #003-024-02262-1.

Sleuthing Out Your Competition To Find Out What They Are Doing And Why

Competitor intelligence builds on what you've already learned about gathering research on your industry. Like it or not (and you'd better learn to like it), competitors, like taxes, will always be with you. Fighting them had better not be your first response. Learning from them, benefitting from them, and always outsmarting them is far more useful and, ultimately, far more satisfying. Remember your Sherlock Holmes.

Some Background Remarks On Competitor Intelligence

We live in an age of spy novels, often flamboyant espionage revelations, and rampant fascination with illegal intelligence. This, however, is not what I am talking about. I am talking about what you need to know in order to use publicly-available information sources and so learn what you need to know about your competitors and what they're doing. You are then in a position to deduce the reasons for why they are doing this and whether they know something you need to know, too.

As competitor intelligence expert Leonard Fuld, the author of a superb book on the subject, notes, fully 95% of the material even major corporations need about their competitors is commonly available. This doesn't mean that it's always easily available, but it does mean that through the use of research techniques you can find out what you need to know.

Finding out about your competitors, as Richard Nixon might have learned to his profit, is more a function of using information you can gather from readily-available sources and common-sense techniques than retaining desperadoes for midnight safecracking. Here's how you do it. *N.B.* As you consider these techniques, consider how you can use them in gaining insight into your industry, too.

Getting Started

Essentially, gathering information successfully on your competitors is a function of knowing what you are looking for and where to look. Let's begin with the first of these: knowing what you are looking for. Here you need to master the following points:

- Be clear about the question(s) you are trying to answer. Know precisely what you are looking for.
- Learn how your industry works. If you don't know how your industry works, you'll be frustrated finding out what you need to know about it.
- Know where to look for information.
- Organize your literature search through each available source.
- Review the material you retrieve, making sure you gather not only the information itself but the source of the information and making appropriate deductions from the information.
- Develop a list of specialists to talk to and others with information you need. Get the facts you need about reaching them and decide how you will do so.
- Interview these specialists and log their information.
- Analyze what you have learned.
- Make your decisions accordingly.

An Example Of Competitor Intelligence At Work

Lest this series of steps seem too abstract to you, let me give you an example which should convince you it is not.

Last year, one of my competitors launched a major series of national workshops. These workshops, offered in most states, almost identically duplicated some of my own popular workshops. Unlike my workshops, however, these were being entirely marketed through ads in major newspapers, both those with a national circulation and major urban dailies. That meant they received far more visibility than my programs do, for mine are ordinarily marketed by colleges and professional associations which don't use these kinds of high-visibility marketing vehicles.

As properly-concerned (and previously-briefed) friends sent me illustrations of the ads running in their communities, I invoked the spirit of Holmes, patron saint of marketing. I wanted to know how successful these programs were, both financially and from the standpoint of satisfied customers. I also needed to discover if there was a way I could benefit from what was happening without having to enter into ruinously costly direct competition with them. This was the puzzle.

Well, What Would You Do?

I set about solving this problem in this fashion:

- Through my own contact bank in the industry, I discovered that I had a friend who was teaching some of these programs and was involved in their administration. I swapped some of my expert wisdom for some of his. Lesson: don't just ask for information, swap information. People are much more likely to be helpful to you if you are helpful to them.

Second lesson: don't ask the question you need to know right away. Instead, ask a series of questions which build to what you need to know. If I said, for instance, "How much money have these programs grossed?", I might very well be rebuffed. My source might very well refuse to answer such an intrusive query. By asking questions like, "How did your Mobile program go? Did you get more people in the morning or the afternoon?", you will get the prospect (for he's that) talking about himself and hence can lead him around to telling you more than you would get otherwise.

- I sent a friend to count the house at a program. By arriving 15 minutes before the end of Program 1 and staying an additional 90 minutes until the start of Program 2, he was able to get a very clear indication of the number of people attending both programs without spending much time. During the lunch break, when the speaker isn't busy, he asked a series of innocent questions like, "Is this about the size house you usually get?" or "I bet you do a lot better in big cities, don't you?". Again, the end result is more information that you'd get by insistent direct questioning.

- I called up the advertising departments of the newspapers being used to promote the programs and inquired about the cost of the ads. I multiplied this by the number of cities in which the programs were taking place. This gave me a good indication of the marketing costs. Having these costs I could then compare them against what I already knew about the number of participants.

Your Deduction, Dr. Watson?

Having done so, it was clear to me that the sponsors were in deep trouble. They had spent too much on marketing and were pulling in too few registrants to make a profit. Now here's where competitor intelligence begins to pay off substantially.

Profiting From Competitor Intelligence Through Creative Problem-Solving In Your Own Best Interests

- The Insurance Step. You must be prepared to consider how your interests can best be served whether the competitor's scheme flourishes or flops. I reasoned that if the competitor were not attracting sufficient numbers of people to his programs, he needed a way to draw more revenue from each participant. I therefore proposed a straight cash-for-books deal so that he could sell my products at his seminars to his benefit, thus increasing the value of each registrant-purchaser.

N.B. In proposing this deal, I did not say anything about my having deduced his poor cash position. Instead, I concentrated on showing how much better off he'd be if he could increase the amount of money each participant spent. Never tell a competitor what you know. Instead use what you know to get what you want from the competitor. Keep in mind that had the competitor's programs been flourishing, I should have used the same argument. His reasons for accepting my offer, however, would have been very different.

- The Next Deal. As the competitor's programs faltered, I considered how I could benefit from the situation. Clearly, I was benefitting already because of the competitor's faulty market analysis and the fact he had tripped and hurt himself. So much was quite satisfying. But was there not another way to benefit? Yes! Through the names the competitor had collected. The people who had inquired about the programs and those who had actually attended. How could I get my hands on them?

I reckoned that the competitor was now committed to carrying through at least some part of his workshop program but now knew the cost of attracting participants through expensive paid ads. He might therefore want additional names of prospects both to sell his programs to and his other (back of the room) products. Voilà!

Why not a straight one-for-one swap of his new names for mine? That way I could get access to his very-expensive-to-acquire names without my spending anything more than the cost of the paper to print the names on and my time. (Of course, mailing my information to them would necessarily be extra.) So a swap was arranged. Again, nothing was said about the underlying reasons for this transaction. Yet these were why this beneficial transaction took place.

- The Planning Deduction. By carefully monitoring my competitor's mad (and ultimately riotously self-destructive) tarantella, I was able to make certain deductions about the state of the industry, the size of the market we were competing for, its interest in these kinds of workshop programs, and the lack of wisdom of marketing them through costly newspaper ads. It reinforced the sense of the workshop promotion methods I have advocated in **MONEY TALKS**. Take heed.

He Who Engages In Market Research Laughs Best

My erstwhile competitor is now in bankruptcy, several hundreds of thousands of dollars in debt, my sources tell me. The mailing I did to his names, however, was profitable to me and, because I asked those who wanted to remain on my mailing list to let me know, gave me continuing access to a market I wouldn't have had otherwise.

Last Words On Competitor Intelligence

If you know about your competitors, you can:

- get a glimpse into your market. Researching your competitors is another facet of researching your industry.

  - properly position yourself. You'll make changes in what you're selling and the way you're selling, in part based on what you know of your competitors.

  - make deals with competitors, because you'll understand what they need and why they need it. Deals which might otherwise be difficult or impossible become likely because you know the competitor's circumstances and can act accordingly.

  - obstruct deals you might otherwise have made and let the chips fall where they may. Knowing what your competitor needs and why he needs it may just persuade you to withhold it.

Resources

If you really want to learn about what your competitors are up to, you need *Competitor Intelligence: How To Get It, How To Use It.* Leonard Fuld understands how to get the information you need and gives you thousands of tips on how to do it.

If you're opening a retail establishment, use Wayne A. Lemmon's *The Owner's And Manager's Market Analysis Workbook For Small To Moderate Retail And Service Establishments.* Follow his guidelines for defining your market and estimating its support for what you're selling *vis-à-vis* your competitors.

Gathering Information And Insight Into Your Product Distribution Channels

As a marketing fanatic in good standing, I am continually reviewing materials on marketing, including those dealing with market research. One of the most surprising things about these generally lackluster books is the complete lack of any discussion of product distribution channels. Yet it seems obvious to me that (if you have a product) your market research can never be complete unless you know precisely what product distribution channels are available to you and the ease of gaining access to them.

Incredibly, even those conscientious people dedicatedly following the guidelines of the existing marketing literature will still have no information about how to distribute the products they create. This is suicidal. Hence, this section which advises you on what to do to see whether anyone would be interested in distributing your product once you have it, and how easy it will be to gain access and work with your distributors. Here are the steps:

- See if you need a prototype. Too many product manufacturers produce their product only to discover that distributors are not interested in handling it. The way to avoid this is to produce a prototype which, when accompanied by your marketing literature, enables you to make a reasonable presentation. (I admit this may not always be possible. How can you make a prototype of a book, for instance?)

In circumstances where a prototype just won't work, produce the smallest possible number of the item you can. Yes, your per-item costs will be higher. No, you may not make a great profit on a small run. But you can amortize these higher costs later when your product succeeds — if it succeeds. And if it doesn't — as most products don't — you'll be grateful you kept your exposure low.

N.B. At this point, you should also give consideration to having this prototype (and all that goes with it) reviewed by an expert in the field. This is where your specialist file comes in handy. Write this specialist a letter saying you'd like to have your product reviewed for both completeness and marketability. Ask the specialist whether he does this kind of work and if so on what basis. If he doesn't, ask for a referral. You may also want to approach the relevant professional association. What you are looking for is the answer to two key questions:

- How does my product compare with prevailing industry standards?
- What are its chances of being successfully marketed?

- Draw up a list of all the ways your product can be distributed *by others.* That is the purpose of this section. The marketing channels you control yourself are discussed elsewhere in this book. Here you are simply attempting to list all the ways other people can distribute your product and the ease of getting access to them and persuading them to carry your product. This is very much in keeping with my general philosophy about using other people's money to promote and market what you've developed. If other people won't do this, there's probably a very good reason why you shouldn't either. That's why you start with these steps when you've got a product to promote.

The distribution channels you must review may include (but are certainly not limited to):

- catalog houses
- vendors with retail outlets
- wholesalers who sell by mail
- wholesalers who sell through sales representatives
- publications and associations selling direct to their readers and members
- providers of workshops who sell to program participants.

You need a complete list of every conceivable distribution mechanism appropriate for your product to which you can get access only by persuading another person of the value of what you are selling.

Understanding Product Vendors

All product vendors, whichever marketing vehicles they use, want to sell profitable products. At any given time their list of products is composed of the following product categories: products which are selling up to their expectations, products which are plodding along producing a regular profit (but not setting the world on fire), products which are either losing money or just making a trickle of profit, and products which are just being tested for their market potential and are not yet in any of these categories. Here's how the vendor considers each category:

- The Sizzlers. Vendors love products which are best sellers. Why not? But they also worry about them, wondering if their momentum has peaked, and it's time to bail out. The only way to displace a sizzler is to persuade the vendor that this market is about to be exhausted and that this season's hot item is about to be a has-been. Vendors, still seeing the steady stream of money coming is, will usually doubt your reasoning. Hope, after all, so often is stronger than good sense. Just ask the vendors who sold Cabbage Patch dolls the year *after* they were the big sellers.

- The Cash Cows. Cash cows produce income for the vendor year-in, year-out. The only way to displace this kind of item is to demonstrate that yours is now a new, improved version which will continue to offer the vendor the same level of profitability. The implication is that if he doesn't adopt it (and his competitors do), his cash cow will become moribund. Here you must convince the vendor that the new product is demonstrably superior to the one he is currently carrying.

- The Marginals. These are products which vendors carry to round out their product line. They would very much like to exchange them for more profitable items, but they need to be convinced that the product is at fault and that the lack of sales is not due to a limited market. Vendors may be reluctant to drop a marginal item after having brought it to their market only once, reasoning that the market has not yet become sufficiently familiar with it to enable them to determine if the product is at fault or the market simply knows too little about it.

- Test Items. These are products which have only recently been added to the vendor's line and may or may not be doing well. The vendor doesn't yet know whether he's nursing a sleeper or whether he's ill-advisedly accepted something marginal. To dislodge a test item, the vendor has to be willing to admit that he made a mistake, has to be willing to write off the money he's invested to promote it, and to bet that your product really will do better. Understandably, vendors may be unwilling to do this, unless they are absolutely sure a market for this test item doesn't exist.

As you can see, while a vendor is certainly looking for new items (and often despairs at the poor quality of much that is offered to him), it is not an easy thing to get him to adopt a product for marketing. No wonder. He is taking a calculated risk with each product he adopts and wants to make sure that he has a reasonable chance of recovering both his investment and making a profit. You must therefore find out what he needs to make a decision and calculate your chances of being able both to provide it and to persuade him to take what you've developed. You should do as much of this as possible before you put any significant funds into producing the product.

Creating The Vendor List

Before you approach anyone, do your homework to find out whom you are approaching. Part of being a successful product developer means knowing who can sell your products and developing a good personal and business relationship with them. The time you take now to work with them will be repaid later when you go forward with your product. Here's what you need to do now:

- List every conceivable kind of marketing outlet through which your product will be sold by others.

- Search for directories and other information sources listing the names of each particular vendor within each category.

- Select a representative sample (say 10 vendors) within each category to personally contact. How do you select them? You'll find in marketing products that in most industries and in most categories certain companies are the best known and command a significant percentage of the market. If these companies smile upon your product, then it is indeed likely to flourish. They are the most difficult to get access to in most cases. They are, however, crucial to the success of your offering, and you must do what it takes to discover how they work. These should be part of the group you approach for market research information.

- If your directories do not have the name of the appropriate individual reviewing new product suggestions, call to find out the name you need, his title, address, and telephone number. Log this information. Remember: if you do go ahead with your product, it will be in very helpful indeed.

- Now write your Vendor Research Letter. This two-page letter is designed to find out how each vendor works in reviewing new product ideas. You need to know:

  - precisely what the vendor needs from you to make his decision;
  - how long the lead time is from your submission of an idea to the vendor's report;
  - the discount the vendor requires;
  - whether you or the vendor pays freight costs;
  - what product supplies the vendor requires you to maintain;
  - what marketing materials the vendor needs from you;
  - how long after your product is accepted before the vendor begins marketing it;
  - how many product ideas are submitted annually to the vendor;

- how many are adopted;
- what the vendor feels may be competing with your product;
- what volume of sales the vendor requires to continue selling the product;
- what specific aspects of a product like yours make it attractive to the target market, and what features the vendor thinks your product must have to succeed; and
- what it takes to open a vendor account, including credit references, the completion of special forms, *etc.* Find out how long it takes once the forms have been completed to establish the account.

These questions should appear on page 2 of your letter. This page should be self-contained and should conclude with your address and a self-addressed stamped envelope and this question: "If I have any further questions, may I call you? When is the best time to reach you? Please include your direct dial telephone number."

The first page of your letter should:

- indicate your interest in having a product adopted by this particular vendor;
- let the vendor know you want to get all the information necessary to make the most complete submission. Remind him this will benefit both of you.
- ask the vendor to complete the questionnaire on the following page and return it to you in the enclosed envelope;
- thank the vendor for the time he spends on this matter.

If you have a product sample available, tell the vendor you do and have a box on the second page he can check if he's interested in seeing it. Send this sample at once, even if you will not be producing your product right away. This is a useful qualified prospect lead. If you don't have a product sample, send whatever information will help the vendor understand what you've got in mind, why it's important and what market your product is intended for. You are not making a submission right now, but you do want the vendor to know as much as possible about what you're doing so that his answers will be more complete and so you can build a relationship.

After The Letters Are Sent

Sadly, only about one in ten of these letters, helpful though they are for both vendor and product developer, will actually be answered. Sometimes this is due to sloth, sometimes to the avalanche of mail the vendors have to deal with. Either way, it means you must follow up. Wait three weeks. Then send a second letter and a second questionnaire. In the second cover letter:

- tell the vendor how important this information is to you and that it will enable you to serve him better by giving him precisely what he wants.
- indicate that if you don't hear from him in 10 days (two business weeks), you'll be calling him.

Then follow up with a call and take the information down by your own hand.

Of course this process is time-consuming, and it does cost money. The alternative, however, is to trust your (perhaps faulty) instincts and rampant enthusiasm and go ahead without knowing whether anyone wants to sell your product or not or without having any understanding of the difficulty of gaining access to these vendors, who in turn have access to your market. To me, that is an entirely unacceptable, far too risky, alternative. By doing the research, however, you get the following benefits:

- You'll find out whether your vendors are really interested in your product. And you'll come to have some qualified prospects who look like prime candidates for selling your product.

- You'll be able to assess the chances of having your product accepted by those vendors to whom you didn't write. If your product has been favorably reviewed by a number of the vendors you've contacted, chances are other vendors, with whom you haven't yet been in contact, will be equally impressed. By the same token, if few or even no vendors are interested, it's unlikely others will be.

- You'll get information about what features of your product attract the vendors and what improvements they think you might need to make.

- You'll begin to build a good relationship with them. Remember: people often buy products because they know and like the developer. Not least, the vendors will certainly know you are conscientious and interested in helping them. This is no bad thing.

Now Assess

You may find this work tedious. It certainly can be. But it is absolutely necessary. Remember: business should not be a roller coaster ride you take blindfolded. It should instead be a process of gradually moving into perhaps previously unvisited terrain with which you are already familiar because of your research.

Take the information you've gathered and honestly assess it.

- How easy was it to get access to the vendors you'll have to work with once your product is generally available?

- Do you know precisely what you need to do to get your product adopted by these vendors?

- Have you made a conservative assessment of the chances that your product will in fact be adopted? Or are you still riding high on the fuel of your enthusiasm?

- Are you willing to do what it takes to modify your product so that it becomes more appealing to the vendors along the lines they suggested?

- Are you willing to keep approaching particularly the so-far uncooperative vendors in the many ways open to you to persuade them they ought to be doing business with you? In short, are you willing to take no for an answer and give in to the discouragement that necessarily accompanies this draining process — or have you learned rejection is part of achieving success and how to deal with it?

These questions must be satisfactorily answered before this part of your market research process can be considered completed. If they are not, you are taking a fearful, probably unwarranted, risk.

Finding Out What You Need To Know About The Available Means For Promoting Your Product Or Service

In marketing, you can get to your prospects through ways you control yourself and through ways controlled by others. You must use both if you expect your product or service to be successfully (read "profitably") marketed. This means assembling, as part of your ongoing marketing research and certainly before you have finally created either your product or service, a list of available non-vendor related marketing vehicles controlled by others. These include (but are not limited to):

- Every kind of free publicity source open to you, including appropriate radio and television shows in your marketing area, columnists and other writers who feature products and services like yours, newsletters and other specialized publications reaching your target market which will both feature your problem-solving process articles and run feature articles about you.

- Advertising sources that you could pay full price for (but don't want to), including remnant advertising and per-inquiry direct-response cards.

Foolish marketers spend their own money to reach their markets. This is all very well if money is no object for you, but anathema to those of us who have other ways to spend our cash. Thus, as part of your marketing research, begin to make contact with those sources which will enable you to reach your prospects through the expenditure of the least possible amount of money. I know you can spend your money to reach them. But do you really need to?

Contacting These Prospect-Connecting Resources

Unless your field is highly specialized and highly localized, you will find dozens of possibilities for marketing your product or service through non-vendor related marketing vehicles. Here's what you must do:

- List every conceivable kind of non-vendor related marketing vehicle of both free publicity and reduced-rate paid advertising available to you.

- Under each category begin listing each specific source available to you. Thus, if you are selling a consulting service for raising money for nonprofit organizations in the Greater Boston area (guess to whom this applies!) and wish to use radio to promote your problem-solving capabilities (as you would), you need to list every conceivable public service program in the area.

You have two ways of getting this information. You could call each radio station directly and ask for the name of the proper program for what you want to talk about, the public service director, his address and telephone number. Or you could locate, by using a book like **THE UNABASHED SELF-PROMOTER'S GUIDE** and its detailed list of resources, the local directory of such programs. The larger the city the more likely there is such a directory. The smaller the town, the more likely you'll have to make the calls and gather the information yourself.

- Once you've gathered this information, develop a two-page letter (plus attachments) to send to the marketing source you want to deal with. This letter should:

  - indicate you are gathering marketing research information for future use. You are not asking for the cut-rate advertising space now or asking to be featured by any media source today. You are gathering information which will enable you to assess the likelihood of these events occurring later.

  - ask this marketing source to kindly complete the enclosed questionnaire. Indicate to him that it is in your mutual interest for him to take the time, that it will enable you to work most effectively with him in the future.

  - include a self-addressed stamped envelope so you can get the information back.

  - thank the source for helping you.

The Packet You Should Send To Free Publicity Sources

What you are trying to discover from a free publicity source is whether they would be interested in featuring you and if so in what way. Before they can answer these questions, they need to know who you are and what you are offering them. Thus, provide them with information about:

- the problem you are in business to solve. If they are not convinced about the seriousness of the problem and the fact that it concerns the audience they serve, you will not get publicity from this source.

- how this problem can be solved, including information about your proposed product or service.

- your credentials to solve this problem.

N.B. You'll find detailed information on how to develop these documents in Chapter 6 on unabashed promotion. What you are trying to discover at this point is which of the thousands of available media resources are appropriate for you to spend your time approaching to get this kind of publicity. If your market research is thorough, you won't be wasting your time later by approaching the wrong source.

Your Publicity Source Questionnaire

Begin your questionnaire to free publicity sources with the following pungent preamble: "You have very limited time. Most people contacting you concerning the publication of articles/appearances on your media show, haven't done their homework. I want to! I want to give you exactly what you want in the exact form you want it, so that we can work together to bring the best problem-solving information to your readers/listeners. Please let me! Please read the enclosed information sheet about the problem I am in business to solve and let me know how I can work with your station/publication." You can also headline the page with these words in capital letters, italics or bold printing, "This is not a request for space or air time but for information which will enable us to work profitably together!!!"

The questions:

- Given what you now know about my problem-solving skills, please tell me which program/department of your radio/television station or publication would be most likely to be interested in what I'm offering. Please include the editor/program director's name, address and direct dial telephone number. When is the best time to call this person?

- Would you be interested in my keeping you up-to-date on developments in this field and possibly using me as a Recognized Source when issues on this topic arise? If so, I shall send materials to you regularly. You may reach me twenty-four hours a day at (your telephone number).

- Would you be interested in my submitting an article on trends in this field? If so, please specify the editor to whom I should submit the story and the length you would like. Topics I would currently suggest for stories include (list your ideas). Please check off the ones in which you are interested. *N.B.* Be as specific as possible with the article topics you suggest and make them as timely and useful as possible.

- (For publications) Would you be amenable to an article for advertising-space swap? If so, please specify your conditions.

- (For electronic media) If your guests ever cancel at short notice, would you be interested in keeping my name on file to call to cover for you? I would be happy to make myself available to you when the need arises.

The Response

Despite the fact that people in the media constantly bemoan the low quality of the article and program submissions they receive, you can count on few of them responding to this questionnaire. That means you'll have to send a second letter (about two weeks after the first). Ultimately, you'll have to follow up by telephone about ten days after the second letter is sent.

There are two reasons for this lack of response. In the first place, media people are not well-organized; in the second, they get plenty of proper submissions to select from. Their need for you at this point is probably less than your need for them. You'll have to compensate for this by working harder to get through and show what you can do for them. (Keep in mind that later, after they know how good you are, their dependence and reliance on you will increase — and so will your leverage!) Of course all this takes time. But, again, it is better to know in advance how many real sources of publicity are open to you and to plan accordingly rather than proceed blindly.

The Difference With Paid-Advertising Sources

Let me remind you what I'm talking about here. When you want to buy an ad and wish to pay full price for it, you control the undertaking. You can decide the size of the ad, the content of the ad, when the ad will be run, where the ad will be run, and how often the ad will be run. You will pay accordingly for the right of having your way.

When you want to get cut-rate advertising, however, the seller largely controls the process. This means you need to find out whether he is willing to deal with you and under what circumstances. Because letters about discounted advertising prices involve the possibility of cash changing hands (even if it is not the full amount the seller wishes), there is a very good chance they will be answered and that you won't have to follow up with a telephone call. Very good, but not perfect.

In this case, your cover letter should:

- indicate you are thinking of buying advertising in the publication or card deck under consideration;

- clearly state you want to know about possibilities other than full-rate advertising;

- invite the seller to complete the enclosed questionnaire and return it to you. In this case, you need not include a self-addressed stamped envelope.

Here are the questions you should include:

- Who is the person we should be dealing with for remnant space and per-inquiry advertising? Please include his name, title, address, and direct dial number.

- Do you sell remnant ads? If so, in what sizes and for what prices? How near your advertising closing date are such ads available? At this point, do you require camera-ready copy?

- Will you inform the advertiser in advance of what remnant space you have available and give him a selection of options?

- What are your payment terms for remnant space ads?

- Do you accept per-inquiry advertising? If so, on what basis?

- Do you accept credit card payments?

The Point Of Knowing This Information

The whole point of market research is to minimize your risk of failure and enhance the likelihood of success. It should suggest an overall marketing strategy and which specific tactical possibilities you should use to reach your prospects, not just once but over and over again. What you are trying to discover is both how hard it will be to get free publicity and to get cut-rate advertising in the publications which enable you to connect with your prospects.

With this information in hand, you can determine where you should spend your limited time and money, how much time and money it will take to connect with your prospects using these alternatives, and how long you must wait for a return. Given what I shall say later about the return you can expect from these vehicles, the real question you are asking is, "Can I hold out this long before I get that return?"

Surveying Potential Prospects To Find Out If They Have Bought From Others; If So, Why; And What It Would Take To Get Them To Buy From You

We are all familiar with market surveys. Usually they enter our life at dinner time when some hapless (short-term) employee calls us and, in a pitiably beseeching voice, asks if he could have just a "few minutes" of our time to ask just a few questions about our preferences concerning the obscure product under discussion. We are human. We have held low-life jobs ourselves. We understand the value of market research. We agree.

After thirty minutes of the most pertinacious questioning ("Are you sure you can't be more precise about how many of these you have bought in the last decade?"), we are regretful of our kindness and of our lost dinner. After 50 such questions, we hang up in a fury, damning market research and all its minions.

We remember that all too often such research is nothing more than a clumsy, stupid business involving the unknowing talking to the uncaring about the unattracting.

Need I say that this conclusion, however reasonable it appears at the time, is most unfortunate? Market research surveys are something all of us need to use. But here, as elsewhere, there are better ways to proceed than the one outlined above.

Succeeding With Market Surveys

Market surveys work if you:

- know why you are developing them. What questions are you trying to have answered?
- keep them short and easy to answer;
- get them to the right people, the people who constitute your market;
- give your prospects some incentive for responding;
- use what you've learned to improve your product and your marketing; and
- keep assessing your market to stay abreast of developments and changing trends.

Let's look at each of these points in further detail.

Know Why You Have Developed Your Market Survey

You take a survey to find out crucial information about your market. You want to know why your prospect buys, from whom your prospect buys, how much your prospect buys, and what it would take to get your prospect to buy from someone else, namely you. Admit it. If you knew all this about your prospects, your marketing would be much easier, wouldn't it?

Keep Your Market Survey Short And Easy To Answer

The problem with too many surveys is that they attempt to do too much. By being too ambitious, however, they risk achieving less. No wonder! Most people don't like to take the time to complete the questions. Thus, resolve to produce more market surveys of fewer questions. Ten questions is a perfectly good number for a survey. If possible, the questions and their answers should be arranged to fit on a single 8 1/2" by 11" flyer.

Begin with a preamble telling the respondent you need information which you will use to produce a better product or service for him. Say that it is for this reason and for this reason only, you'd appreciate his taking the time which will, in the near future, produce something better for him. If this is the truth (and it had better be!), remind the respondent. Market surveys properly understood are a crucial part of client-centered marketing. Now decide which of the three major kinds of questionnaires you will use; those with open-ended questions, close-ended questions, or a mixture of both.

Open-ended questions allow the respondent to give you whatever answer he wants to the question. "Why do you buy bran muffins from the local convenience store?"

Close-ended questions direct the respondent to one or more of a number of possibilities. "Please check any of the following answers which best describe why you buy bran muffins from the local convenience store? ❑ Price ❑ Location ❑ Flavor ❑ Freshness."

There are pros and cons to each type.

Open-ended questions are more difficult to answer. The respondent has to think about them. Always in a hurry, usually not giving the question the time it needs to be properly answered, the respondent may give you misleading or incomplete information. On the other hand, he may well give you information which suggests something you had never thought about.

Close-ended questions may be considered too structured. You'll very likely get answers, but you may find that items at the beginning and end of your list get more response, simply because of where they're placed. Thus, they may not accurately reflect the prospects' thinking. In any case, only continuing surveys which replicate results can convince you that you have, indeed, gotten a true impression of your prospects and why they act the way they do.

Personally, I prefer a questionnaire which is composed of both open-ended and close-ended questions, about five of each. This allows those who need guidance and structure to have it and also allows for longer, more spontaneous answers. Open-ended questions are sometimes most helpful when you are talking to people on the telephone or face-to-face, because they easily allow for follow-up. The catch is, these questions must be asked by someone who is adept at follow-up techniques.

Good Questions To Include

If you're uncertain of what to ask, use the following as guidelines:

- the reasons your prospects are buying the product or service
- which of your competitors they are buying from
- how much of a given item they are buying
- how they came to learn about this item
- what they like about this item
- what they dislike
- whether they are recommending it to their friends
- how loyal they are to your competitor
- whether they would consider changing to a new vendor
- if so, on what basis.

N.B. When your survey is close-ended, give people no more than six choices per category. Always conclude with the final possibility "Other. Please be specific."

A Few Words About Questionnaire Lay-Out

- Double-space your questionnaire.

- Allow for generous margins and lots of white space on the page. Too many words frighten the respondent.

- Always allow space for the respondent to write other personal comments which may not be covered by your questions.

- Make sure your name, address and telephone number appear on every page of your survey and instructions about how the respondent should return it to you.

Give Them To The Right People, The People Who Constitute Your Market

Market survey questionnaires are valuable only to the extent that you ask questions to which you need the answers and get the answers from people you want to serve. Thus, you must get them into the hands of the right people. There are essentially three ways of doing this:

- by mail
- by telephone
- in person.

What are the pros and cons of each?

By Mail

We have all received questionnaires by mail, and most of us do what most other people do: throw them away. This is what most people will do with your questionnaire, too. There are ways, however, you can increase the likelihood that people will respond to it:

- write a strong cover letter pointing out why it is in the respondent's interest to complete the questionnaire;
- include a stamped self-addressed envelope;
- tell the respondent that if he completes the questionnaire, you'll share the results with him;
- let the respondent know he'll be receiving a premium when he returns his questionnaire to you (see below).

Despite these inducements, don't expect a great response from a mailed questionnaire. Even though the respondent really will receive a benefit from working with you on the development of a superior product or service, this benefit is too far removed from his present cares to provide sufficient motivation for doing the questionnaire now. And if it is not done now, it is unlikely to be completed at all. Although I must say that in one famous case, I did receive a completed questionnaire back in the mail more than 18 months after I'd sent it out!

By Telephone

Telephone surveys have a greater chance of getting a better response than mail surveys. But they can also succeed in rousing the ire of your prospect if they are not properly conducted. My suggestions for an improved response and more civil reception to you and your callers include:

- sending a letter in advance advising that the prospect will be called and then following up with the call;
- making sure the respondent can talk at the time you call. Ordinarily, the caller assumes that this is a convenient time for you without bothering to ask. Personally, I detest this presumption.
- stating at the outset of the conversation how long the survey will take and rigorously adhering to this limit;
- asking the respondent whether he'd like to have information on how the survey turns out. *N.B.* What this means in practice is your sending information about the new improved product or service you've developed based on respondents' answers. This is a very clever way to open up your next contact with this prospect, demonstrating as it so clearly does your client-centered behavior.
- informing the respondent about any premium you may be offering for assisting you and ensuring that this is sent to him promptly after the interview.

Note: further suggestions for improved telephone contact with your prospects, perfectly applicable here, are found in Chapter 8, Phone Profit.

My experience with telephone surveys is that they can be a most effective device for getting information from your prospects *and* (a very important point) for getting them interested in the development of a new product or service that will be of assistance to them. To conduct a survey and then not offer to tell people what the results are (and so both send them information on what you have developed and confirm your commitment to the client) is unbelievably stupid. The key, however, is making sure you are calling at a time when it is convenient for the prospect to talk and not abusing the privilege of gaining access to him. Abide by these rules, and you'll get the information and the marketing hook you need to return to him in future.

Where The Names Come From, How Many You Should Contact

Market surveys can be effective despite a limited sample population if (but only if) the people surveyed are in fact representative of your general market. Thus, you must take particular pains to make sure the names you get are representative. This is where your previous research into your market comes in handy, for your prospects can include:

- members of pertinent associations in your field
- subscribers to publications
- individuals who have bought products and services similar to yours and whose names are available through people like list brokers. Be aware that the cost of renting names with telephone numbers is expensive, another reason for keeping the survey population to moderate size until you know you must add more names to get a conclusive result.

My advice is to approach these prospects in stages. Start with a mailing of 1000 pieces. See what the response is like. If you are getting a coherent response, this may be sufficient for your research purposes. If, however, the results are not conclusive, consider sending another 1000 pieces.

When doing a telephone survey, think smaller. With telephone numbers at hand, a caller can make between 6 and 10 calls an hour. If you have said you'd follow up the letter with a telephone call, it will take a week for one person to attempt to contact 500 people. Not all, of course, will be available at the time the initial call is made, which will lengthen the survey period.

Thus, the key to this kind of market research is to think in stages, going on to another stage as you feel the need and (where the telephone is involved), to think small. In all cases, however, making sure you are getting to the people who could actually use your product or service is crucial. When you've made contact with a person who cannot use what you're selling, graciously ring off.

In-Person

In-person surveys are far more likely to yield the information you want, but are also far most costly in terms of your time and expense. Thus, the best way of handling such surveys is to do them where substantial numbers of your prospects are already gathered. A trade show, for instance, is the perfect place for such a survey.

In such cases, if your circumstances allow, you should sit with the respondent, ask the questions, and fill in the questionnaire yourself. Under these conditions, you may well select a mix of close- and open-ended questions, the latter allowing you to follow up for further information. This kind of information-rich interview is not always possible to arrange, even at a place where large numbers of prospects have gathered. Do the best you can! The key is not to let a gathering of large numbers of your prospects take place without attempting to ascertain from them the information you must have to refine your marketing.

Give Your Prospects Some Incentive For Responding

Any time you launch a marketing survey, you are deciding to intrude into someone's life. Of course I well understand that your motives are the very highest. You can only serve the prospect by understanding him and catering to his wishes. Still, even the prospect who understands this, is giving you something of real value now — his time — for something that may not be of value to him until much later, your improved product or service.

Under the circumstances, therefore, you should immediately reward the prospect with something useful and of value to him now. This is a gracious act. It also has the benefit of firmly establishing you as client-centered, a fact which it is always in your interest to publicize.

What you give deserves much attention. It must be something:

- the respondent can use;
- he'll keep on hand;
- which has your name, address and telephone number on it and an indication of the service you provide;
- which doesn't cost you much money.

The unimaginative satisfy these conditions by giving the respondents something like a pen or a keychain. You can do the same. It's scarcely criminal. But I think you can do better.

I send one of my "Get Ahead" articles packed with useful information for the respondent. It meets all the conditions above, clearly shows I want the respondent to be better off (always through his connection with me) and offers another benefit as well; it concludes with a Resource Box indicating a product or service the respondent can get and use. Thus there's the prospect of an immediate sale for me. You don't get that with a keychain.

Use What You've Learned To Improve Your Product And Your Marketing

Too many market surveys are taken and then simply gather dust. Don't let this happen to you. Depending on the questions you've asked, your survey will help you to:

- focus on the right prospects;
- understand their problems and position yourself as the person who can solve them with your product or service
- appear (and actually be) more client-centered than your competitors;
- offer the benefits your prospects want, not the ones you want;
- refine the product or service you offer;
- be more confident and hence more resolute in your marketing. You won't need to be tentative and cautious, as so many unprepared marketers are. You'll know where you are going, why you are going there, and what to expect when you get there. This is a tremendous advantage and gives you a sense of sureness which impresses people.

Keep Assessing Your Market To Stay Abreast of Developments And Changing Trends

Only those fatuous creatures who believe in a static universe forego the benefits of continuing market research. This chapter has focused on the research you must do *before* you start selling to your prospects. Yet it cannot end without giving you a firm indication that this research must *continue* after you begin selling to them.

There is, however, one significant difference between this pre- and post-operating research. After you're in business, you can be a target for others. Now you can lose customers to those who are more clearly perceived as client-centered. Now you can lose the chance to serve prospects, who can also end up with your competitors. It's to ensure that this doesn't happen that you must keep surveying your market after you've begun operations.

At this point, you'll have two additional kinds of surveys to use:

- surveys in which you ask your current and past buyers to assess the product or service you deliver. (One-dimensional surveys)

- surveys which ask your current and past buyers to compare the product or service you deliver with what they have experienced from your competitors. (Comparative surveys)

Use a one-dimensional survey to find out if your customers feel your product or service is satisfactory (and why) and how they feel about the way you treat them. Such surveys can include such questions as:

- Why did you buy our product or service?
- What problems did you expect it to solve?
- Has it met your expectations?
- Have you gotten the service you needed to make the best use of what you bought?
- What improvements can you suggest to what we are selling?
- What suggestions can you make to help us improve our service?
- Please summarize your feelings about the product or service you're using.
  N.B. These summary quotes are very important and can be used in your own marketing. However, if you intend to use the user's name, you must get his permission to do so.

Use a comparative survey to find out how you stand *vis-à-vis* your competitors. Use questions like:

- Why did you select our product or service to use?
- Did you compare it to other products or services? If so, please tell us which ones?
- What didn't you like about the other products or services you reviewed?
- If there was one reason which was most significant in persuading you to get our product or service over the other ones you reviewed, please list it.
- If you wavered in considering whether to use our product or service, could you say why?
- How do you feel about our product or service now? Would you invest in it again? Please summarize your feelings about it.

Distributing Surveys To Your Buyers

The one thing you never want to be in marketing is surprised. Surprises in this business are usually unpleasant. That's why you should be surveying your market regularly. Once you have customers and buyers, this is easier to do than beforehand. Simple surveys of the kind I've been recommending to you can be distributed to your buyers in the following inexpensive ways:

- as package-stuffers when you ship your products;
- at the end of talk-programs for which you've received payment (thereby making it a service);
- at regular intervals in your relationships with service clients.

N.B. If you're selling a product like a book, you can ask all your readers to write to give you their reactions. Not least, this supplies you with a hefty file of glowing testimonials, for most people will only write if they are really angry about your offering or completely enthralled by it. *Do* write me!

The Benefits of Keeping In Touch With Your Market

When you keep in touch with your market you can:

- both create and update your products and services so that they have a higher likelihood of succeeding. People who don't survey their markets are in fact attempting to impose their ideas on a market rather than taking inspiration and direction from their market. This is the height of hubris and as all those familiar with their Greek drama know, such pride goeth before a fall.

- reposition yourself in response to new trends. Even where a product or service stays the same, it may have to be repositioned in response to changing market trends. A product marketed one year primarily because of its competitive price can the next year, in response to different circumstances, be marketed because of its safety value. The reasons why people buy the same thing change as circumstances change.

Why don't people recognize this? Day after day in this age of low inflation I continue to get direct mail advertisements talking about the benefits of the product as an inflation-fighter. This shows me that the sender is desperately ill-informed and in immediate need of the repositioning market research would have enabled him to make. Learn, reader, learn.

- Review and improve your service. It's not enough to have a high caliber product or service. It must be aptly delivered to your market. You must be sure you have the right product or service, are promoting it in the right fashion to the right audience, and must be sure this audience is happy with how you are handling them. Again, market research enables you to do just that. The problem is integrating this research into your business life.

Towards Integrating Market Research In Your Business Life

Few people truly interested in building a successful business would dispute the benefits of market research. They are plain. The real problem, however, is integrating this research and its findings into the jumbled reality of your life. For we all know that the rough and tumble of every day life is scarcely amenable to the clean organizing and discipline of both practical research and implementation based on that research. This is where creating a practical, realistic plan comes in. Luckily for you, the constituents of this plan are in the next chapter.

Resource

Many books have been written about market research. Most fail to realize the distinct limitations in resources, particularly time, money, and personnel, we small business people labor under. I've found one pair of writers, however, which does offer helpful suggestions. Use George Breen's and A.B. Blankenship's *Do-It-Yourself-Marketing Research*. It has a special small business emphasis.

CHAPTER 3

Developing A Marketing Plan You Can Successfully Live With And Work From

Let's face it. We all know the benefits of having a written marketing plan. Yet I'm sure not one in a hundred businesses actually has one. Every sort of reason, all self-convincing, is given for not having such a plan. But without it you cannot move resolutely towards your goal. You risk wasting the money you spend on your marketing, since you will not necessarily be hitting the same target population over and over again, and thereby reinforcing the effectiveness of your earlier marketing and ensuring the success of your later marketing.

The object of a marketing plan is clear. It enables you to:

- target the right population;
- consider all the means of reaching it;
- ascertain which are the best means given your circumstances;
- hit the same prospects again and again, thereby reinforcing all you do and making it more successful;
- know what happens next and where you should be spending your time and resources;
- evaluate what is working and what is not and to plan accordingly.

The Problem With Plans

All marketing books advise you to have a written plan. This book is not different in that regard. But the other books advise you to prepare highly elaborate plans. Now I know you. You are not going to take the time to prepare such a plan, even if it is in your own best interest. You don't really like planning, and you find a hundred other (almost legitimate) reasons to postpone it.

As a result too many of your marketing efforts are scattershot and so lose their impact and diminish the value of your investment. Thus my task, as the consummate realist, has been to recognize both your need for a plan and your aversion to creating one. I had to come up with a solution to this very real problem. This chapter is the result. I advise you to follow its guidelines closely, since what you have here is the crux of the plan you must have.

Using A GNOME To Craft Your Marketing Plan

Long ago I discovered you could make any enterprise succeed by remembering five letters and using them to arrange the matter at hand. These letters are GNOME. Use them to craft your marketing plan, and I guarantee you'll have vastly improved results. Here's what the letters stand for:

G = Goal
N = Need
O = Objective
M = Method
E = Evaluation

Goal

As I've said before, marketing is not something you do in a vacuum. Marketing is always the handmaiden, never the mistress. It must always work for a purpose beyond itself. That purpose is your Goal. The Goal is best understood as the "where" concept. Where are you going?

The Goal states in general terms what you are working for. No one can tell you what that is but yourself. But some possibilities include financial freedom, freedom to control your own time, building a business that gives you status in your community, a means of supporting yourself and your family, and the ability to help others through the product or service you are selling. All of these — and many other possibilities — constitute perfectly reasonable goals. But you must have a goal before you institute your marketing. Otherwise you won't know why you're marketing and for what you're marketing.

Need

The Need, by comparison, is best understood as the "why" concept. Why do you need to accomplish this goal? This question demands a good long look at yourself as you are, not as others see you or want you to be. Your needs will largely determine what you will do and how you will do it. For a goal to be truly something you want to and indeed must work for, it has to be based on your needs. Powerful needs include:

- safety and security;
- recognition and love;
- power and dominance.

N.B. While these needs are quite distinct, you can, of course, be working to realize several of them through a single goal.

Objective

The Objective is the "when" and "how much" question. When do you want to or must you realize your goal and satisfy your need? And how much must you have to satisfy your need? These are not abstract questions. Say your goal is financial freedom by age 45. Perfectly reasonable. Say you must have it to satisfy your need for safety and security. Again perfectly reasonable.

This need for safety and security is ongoing. It must regularly be satisfied. Thus, setting an objective answers the questions "When do I need to satisfy my need for safety and security?" and "How much must I have to satisfy my need for safety and security?"

There are short- and long-range answers to these questions. In business, you satisfy this need by paying your bills regularly and by generating a sufficient surplus over and above these expenses to invest and so satisfy your need for safety and security. This means you must have a monthly objective and a series of longer range objectives, ultimately expressed in a life plan. Each objective can be satisfied through an aspect of your marketing methodology.

Your objective at any given time is best expressed as two numbers, one being the number of products or services you must sell and the second being the time by which you must sell them to realize your objective and so satisfy your need, thereby moving towards your goal.

But you cannot reach your objective without a precise budget. These budgets should be both short- (one month) and long-term (one year). Each must be composed of your necessary expenses and those items (such as pensions, health insurance, disability insurance, other benefits, and savings) which help you meet your needs. How much marketing you must do is directly determined by these needs. And these needs, in turn, are determined by your personality and ultimate goals. Marketing is not just something you do. Properly understood, it is a crucial means of enabling you to fulfill yourself. Thus, how intelligently and energetically you pursue your marketing is a direct indication of what you think of yourself and the products and services you are offering.

Method

The method is the "how" question. What means will you use to realize your objective. Here it is time to introduce you to the critical concept of the Rule of Seven, a concept you will be reading about throughout this book and which you must incorporate into your marketing thinking and implementation.

As I review businesses around the country, I am regularly struck by the fact that most are not succeeding to the extent they could. Many in fact are outright failing. In many instances this is unnecessary, a condition brought about by the lack of knowledge of their owners and a failure to understand and use the Rule of Seven.

Marketing fails for many reasons. One of the chief of these, however, is a failure to hit the same group of carefully considered prospects, prospects who have the problem your product or service can solve, not just once but again and again and again. That's where the Rule of Seven comes in. You must resolve not to start *any* marketing enterprise to *any* group unless the following conditions apply:

- it has the problem your product or service solves;
- you have worked to understand this problem and to clearly identify the benefits this group gets by using your product or service;
- you are committed to connecting with this body of targeted prospects a minimum of seven times within an 18-month period.

The reason for the Rule of Seven, which will be discussed in detail shortly, is clear. Most people do not respond to an offer the first time they see it. This is because of natural sloth, a lack of trust in your offer (because of a lack of familiarity with it), a feeling that if it is important it is certain to be repeated, and the desire to pursue other options (with only limited resources). Therefore, unless you are prepared to persist, you are preparing to fail. If you will not so persist, you are best advised to desist altogether and not waste your resources. Do you clearly understand this?

Evaluation

Some marketing works. Other marketing does not. Each thing you do must be evaluated to see if the result can be improved or needs to be scrapped. This is where evaluation comes in, the "what happened, why and what now" questions. Without evaluation, you will not know what is really worth doing next (and so increase your profit) and what you should avoid doing (and so reduce your expense).

Drafting Your Plan

Note the wording here. No plan is ever written in cement, especially the first one you do. The problem with the first plan you draft is that it is the *first* plan. By definition it can hardly be perfect and is very likely to be built on a certain number of hopeful assumptions rather than hard fact. So be it. If you plan conservatively, you'll live through this plan and be able in subsequent plans to remove the optimistic assumptions and incorporate findings based on your experience. But we all have to start somewhere. Don't let your lack of experience be the reason for not proceeding. If this holds you up, you'll never get started, with devastating consequences later when increasingly precise planning is crucial.

N.B. You cannot fully draft your plan until you finish this book. This is particularly true as regards the method section of your marketing plan. **MONEY MAKING MARKETING** is a compendium of methods. You must find the ones which are most appropriate given the market you want to reach, the resources you have available and your determination to make your marketing work. Therefore, understand that you will only be able fully to utilize this chapter after studying all of this book.

Base your marketing plan on the GNOME system. Begin with a preamble consisting of your goal or goals. Follow with your most candid current understanding of your need. Be aware that this may well change as you come to understand yourself better — and acknowledge what truly makes you function. This will not come at once.

Follow with a precise statement of the objectives you wish to realize for each product and service within a precise period of time. To begin, state your objectives for a three-month, six-month and twelve-month period. The objectives, as stated above, must take into account the money you need to operate your business and achieve your goals. If either point is not included, your objectives are not complete.

Now start working on the heart of your plan, the methods you'll utilize to reach your objectives. The methods section must be composed of the following parts:

- a listing of all the marketing methods available to you to reach a precisely targeted group of your prospects. Each possible method must be considered in turn as you determine which of these methods will be the ones on which you concentrate at present to reach your prospects.

This list should include all the ways of reaching people who don't know you or who know you but haven't yet bought and ways to reach those who already know you and have already bought. Possibilities for reaching the former group of people include such options as:

Direct Mail

- renting lists
- swapping lists
- contacting people who have responded to your classified ads
- contacting people who have responded to your space ads
- contacting people who have responded to your post card deck ads

Paid Advertising

- ads from which you expect to make direct sales

Free Publicity

- including programs and articles by and about you on radio, television, newspapers, newsletters, magazines, and books

Telemarketing

- calling people who don't know you

Trade Shows

- exhibiting

Workshops And Seminars

- giving a wide variety of talk programs

Catalogs

- getting your products into other people's catalogs and having your literature used by other people as package stuffers

Retail Outlets

- getting your products into appropriate retail stores.

Many of these methods can be adapted, as this book demonstrates, into effective ways of getting to people who already know you and have bought from you. In addition, you can reach this group through:

Add-Ons

- getting your current buyers to buy from you again soon

Newsletters And Other Informational Communications

- showing your buyers you can solve their problems and incorporating information about your sales offerings.

The first rule of crafting a constructive marketing plan is to know each possible way to reach your market and then to give consideration to which of them you will use given the constraints under which each of us works. You cannot, of course, know which of them you will use unless and until you use the research methodology set forth in the previous chapter. There is no point in trying to get radio time, for instance, if your research into your market has suggested that no radio program director is interested in putting you on his show.

Like it or not, each of us who markets products and services must adapt to the constraints of our market. It is important to remember that our market consists both of those who actually purchase what we are selling and those who are the agents placing us in contact with those buyers (whether they do so for a fee, as a retail store, or without one, such as a media publicity outlet).

Thus, in drafting your plan, begin with a complete listing of all the available marketing vehicles which connect you to your buyers. Evaluate these, keeping in mind your constraints and the following principles. All things being equal, select the marketing alternative that:

- enables you to reidentify and reapproach the same prospects again rather than having to approach new prospects from scratch;

- has natural follow-up potential. You must learn to think not in terms of isolated marketing endeavors, but in terms of sequences. Whatever you do must be capable of being followed up, of reaching the same audience again. As you consider any individual marketing activity, consider at the same moment how you will follow it up and whether such follow-up is indeed available to you given your resources and the constraints of your market;

- enables you to get complete information about your product or service into the hands of your prospects. No marketing activity can be considered complete unless and until your prospect has *everything* he needs to buy what you're selling. This includes complete details on the offer (including the benefits it supplies the buyer and its price), your name, address, and telephone number and, where applicable, credit card buying information;

- costs less over a comparable activity that costs more. If you can reach your buyers with the benefit and price information they need to take action but which costs you little (such as publicity) instead of much (as in paid advertising), use the less expensive alternative and increase your profit accordingly. All marketing (even purportedly "free" publicity) costs money and other resources. You should always make an attempt, however, to see whether you can reach your market for the least possible amount before making the (perhaps avoidable) decision to spend your money, which may well be your profit margin;

- piggybacks on other people's money (such as getting in their catalog) rather than spends your own money (such as creating your own catalog). Particularly where you have only a single product to sell and are not yet familiar with the means of marketing it, learn your business and reach your prospects on other people's money, not your own. Having done so, then expand;

- allows you to get and use a marketing option for which others must pay cash (like advertising space) by rendering something the publisher wants (like merchandise or a problem-solving article). Again, think of the money you were going to spend as your profit. It may very well be. Husband it accordingly.

Structuring Your Plan On The Rule Of Seven

Keeping these principles in mind, begin to draft plans which enable you to contact your prospects *at least* seven times in 18 months. Given the number of marketing alternatives that exist and which are discussed in this book, there are literally thousands of seven-step possibilities which enable you to connect with your prospects and connect with them again and again and again in an 18-month period. What follows are four possible plans from the incredible number of alternatives available to you. Your task is to understand why these particular plans are sensible ones and then to construct your own, taking inspiration from what I've given you, but not necessarily connecting you with your market in the same ways.

Plan 1: Selling A Service

Keep in mind that as you construct your marketing plans, you must always write down the precise group being approached, the type of approach you'll be using, the date you'll be using it, and what you want the prospect to do when he finds out about your product or service. Also ask yourself if you are certain the group you are approaching has the problem your product or service can solve, how you know, whether you have clearly indicated this in any materials you will provide them, and whether you are certain this marketing vehicle is open to you. Having done so, you are ready to proceed.

- Once you have identified the coherent body of prospects you want to approach, begin by writing Direct Mail Letter 1. Include with this sales letter and response coupon a client-survey questionnaire which will enable your prospects to tell you which problems they want to solve and hence which of your services they are interested in. You'll be approaching this entire body of prospects again, so either make duplicate sets of labels or enter a separate data base in your computer. Send this letter in April.

- Before sending this letter, contact the editor of the newsletter serving this population. Arrange for one of your problem-solving process articles to be printed at the same time you are contacting your prospects by mail. This article must deal with a problem connected with the subject of your service. This article should be printed in the April/May issue.

- Telephone those prospects who returned your client-survey questionnaire and schedule meetings with them. These are qualified prospects. If time allows, use telemarketing techniques to schedule meetings with others, who have not so far expressed their interest in having you help them solve their problem. Make calls within a two-week period in April/May.

- Now send Direct Mail Letter 2. If you have signed up a client since the time you originally wrote, say so. If this client has achieved any success in reaching his objective, say so. Your goal is to give prospects a feeling of your momentum and an indication that others are already *en route* to solving their problems. Use envy to create interest. Again enclose a client-survey questionnaire to elicit interest from prospects. Send this packet in June. *N.B.* It is perfectly acceptable to enclose a copy of the article that has just run in their newsletter. This underscores the fact you are someone with problem-solving skills and something to offer.

- Make additional telephone calls to schedule meetings with prospects. These calls are ongoing.

- Provide a problem-solving workshop on the topic of your service at the prospects' annual fall meeting. Begin to reach your prospects through an article by or about you in advance of the meeting. This is particularly important if the organization is not planning a special meeting announcement. If they are, so much the better. If the annual meeting is in November, you'll want your article to appear in October.

- Have information about the prospects' problems and your problem-solving services distributed to all people attending the meeting. You should arrange to have your materials placed in the conference registration packets. If you cannot arrange this, at the very least make sure all participants in your sessions get these materials. November.

- Pass out a client-survey questionnaire at your program. Collect the completed questionnaire at the end of the program. Follow up accordingly with letters and telephone calls. November.

- Make sure your remarks are reported by the organization in their newsletter. The preferred issue is the one immediately after their meeting. December.

- Send Direct Mail Letter 3 to all those who were not in attendance at the meeting. Let them know if others are using your methods satisfactorily. Let them know you are still available to help them. Advise them you'll be calling to schedule a meeting to discuss their needs and your services. Enclose testimonials from satisfied clients, people who attended your workshop program, a précis of your remarks to the annual meeting and other supportive data. January.

Further Words About Plan 1

Please note, this plan connects you to your prospects more than 7 times and will, if further developed (as it must be), do so far more than the requisite 7 times in an eighteen-month period. Fine. Seven is, after all, a minimum. You are encouraged to add as many more ways of reaching your market as make economic sense. The point is that even here, by the time you have finished approaching your market this many times in this period, you are a known entity, the standard against which others will be compared. This, of course, is just the way you want it.

Before going on to the next plan, reread the one above keeping in mind my inviolate marketing principles. The object is for you to understand why this set of steps makes sense and to see how you can both replicate them and creatively deviate from them to sell your own services.

Plan 2: A Product Sold Through Wholesalers

- Identify a satisfied wholesaler who has profited from your product. Develop a strongly-worded letter from this satisfied wholesaler to his peers (if he is not directly competing with them) urging them to sell your product, too. This will be the cover letter for a packet including information about your product (features, benefits, and price) and response card. January.

- Coordinate the mailing of this letter with an announcement in publications read by wholesalers about the availability of this product. Even where a product is not new, continue to update publications with information about sales. Trade magazines are interested in how well products do. Make sure you keep them abreast of sales of your product and its availability to wholesalers. January/February.

- Follow this letter with a telephone call. If wholesalers are not presently able to add new products, find out when they will be. Tell them you'll keep them abreast of developments with your product. If there is paperwork to be completed or samples to be sent so that the wholesaler has complete information, take care of it. January/February.

- Approach a trade publication written for wholesalers. Write an article on a subject of interest to them which enables you to include information about your own product in a Resource Box. March.

- Continue to get testimonials from satisfied wholesalers. Send these along with periodic reports to other wholesalers about the success of your product. Begin in May and follow-up regularly.

- Attend trade show where wholesalers will be present. Pass out materials including information of use to wholesalers and facts about the benefits to be derived from carrying your product. October.

- Follow up all those with whom you make contact at the trade show. October.

- Send an end-of-the-year report to all wholesalers with whom you have been in contact during the year. Point out how well wholesalers who carried your product have done by selling it. Include a client-survey questionnaire to ascertain the possible interest of those who are not yet carrying it. December

Plan 3: A Catalog

- Announce in trade publications you are seeking appropriate merchandise for your catalog. Have the publication run your name and address so that readers can send you a sample and ask for a copy of your catalog. Add these names to your mailing list. June.

- Announce publication of your catalog in print media sources read by those interested in your merchandise. Again indicate that a copy of your catalog is available by contacting you. Make sure your telephone number and address are run with this announcement. September.

- Mail your catalog to prospects, both those who have bought from you before and those who have not yet done so, including names you may have rented. Ask those who have not requested your catalog (the rented names) to contact you if they want to remain on your list. This augments your list. September, *etc.*

- Develop an upgrade letter. Include it in all outgoing packages. Ask people who have just bought to buy something else, something which nicely supplements their first purchase. Thus, if a person buys from my catalog a book on how to publish books, I suggest they also buy my book **THE UNABASHED SELF-PROMOTER'S GUIDE.** It makes sense and is appropriate for an upgrade letter. September, *etc.*

- Write a problem-solving process article for the publication whose readers would be interested in merchandise in your catalog. Include a Resource Box at the end of the article, asking readers to write or call you for your catalog, or swap the article for an ad with similar copy. October.

- Swap your mailing list for that of the publication which has carried either your announcements about the catalog or your article. People reading that publication have a higher likelihood of knowing who you are. October.

- Offer to enclose package stuffers with information about the publication whose readers are interested in your merchandise in all your outgoing packages and mail. In return, ask for free advertising space in their publication or a reciprocal package stuffer arrangement. Make sure any stuffers you use clearly state that the person receiving it is not on your mailing list and that if they want to be, they must contact you. Again, you pick up extra names this way. Begin in September, and carry on thereafter.

- Mail your next catalog to your mailing list. January.

Plan 4: Books

Because so many of my readers are authors or would-be authors, I'm enclosing this special (partial, if suggestive) marketing plan for books. As with all other products or services being marketed, the problem with books is that they are generally marketed with a scattershot approach. This, of course, is a huge mistake. Moreover, all too often complete buying information is not included with the mention of the book, which makes that mention generally useless. Thus, if you want your book to sell, consider the following:

- If you are marketing your book through stores, make sure the books are actually in the stores before launching any general marketing effort. To do this you must target the retailers first and interest them in the product. If you fail to do this, you are handicapping your marketing effort unless you can satisfactorily arrange for mail order sales. When selling to bookstores, as to any other market, focus on the benefits they derive from carrying the product, not the product itself.

- Once you have been assured books are in stores, then target a market you wish to motivate, a market that has the problem your book solves. Approach electronic media sources which connect you with this market. Schedule appearances on these media vehicles.

- Before going on any of these shows, establish a twenty-four hour order center which will both give out a marketing message about your book and take orders. Also develop a single 8 1/2" x 11" page with problem-solving information based on your book. Include ordering information. Make this available to all listeners of every program you give. Make sure the media host gives out the number of the order center and how to get the free problem-solving information. Promise that you'll send this information out promptly to your listeners/prospects.

- Simultaneously approach appropriate print media sources which connect you with your prospects. Again, ensure that each article is run with complete follow-up information. If you ask your prospect to do more than pick up the telephone or drop a card in the mail to you, you are probably asking for too much.

- Don't talk about your product on the order center message tape. Talk about the problem you can solve. Thus, if your book is about marketing, say, "If you want to sell more widgets, leave your name, address and telephone number on this tape and Jeffrey Lant will send you 10 suggestions on how to do just that." Need I say that the tenth suggestion is order details for your book?

- Follow up each person promptly. Keep a list of who called. Check them off as they order. If they don't order in two weeks, send a follow-up letter with order information. If you cannot fulfill your book orders directly, provide complete details about which book stores carry your books or otherwise how to get them. Remember: don't concentrate on the book. Concentrate on the problem the book solves. If you are connecting with the right people, the people who have the problem, then they'll want to get the thing that helps them solve it, in this case your book.

- If possible, stagger your appearances on local media. More and more handle interviews by telephone wherever you are. See if you can schedule these.

N.B. If you concentrate on selling your book, you will date yourself. If you concentrate on solving a problem, you can come back again and again so long as the problem exists. Each time, you can disseminate information about your book. Only at such time as the problem itself is no longer thought to be important by media sources or the book itself is irrevocably dated are you precluded from using this approach.

How Many Of These Step-By-Step Marketing Plans Should You Have?

The real question is not whether you can build marketing plans on the Rule of Seven. As you see, once you begin to get into this, you should have no trouble developing many more than the minimum of seven required contacts with your market. No, the real question is determining how many such plans there can be and how many you can operate at once given your limited resources. Let's deal with the first question.

Successful marketing is based on working with clear target markets and convincing them that your product or service is for them. Too many people never get the hang of this. But you must.

One of my books is entitled **TRICKS OF THE TRADE.** It is designed for people who sell problem-solving information. I could market the book generally for anyone with such information, or I could work to convince each particular group with problem-solving information that this book was especially written for them. I take the latter route.

This means working up a marketing plan for *each* of the hundreds of American markets composed of people who sell problem-solving information for a living. These markets range from agricultural consultants to zoologists. *Each* of these markets needs a marketing plan composed of at least seven steps. And if you are to gain dominance within that market, you must go beyond the minimum of seven (and keep doing so). For the moment you stop, your dominance fades.

At any given time, I am operating at different stages dozens of these plans. Some are just beginning. In these markets, neither the product nor I may be known at all. In other markets, I have not yet completed the minimum of seven steps. In still other markets, I am way beyond the minimum of seven steps. In these markets, of course, I have achieved the dominance we all desire for our products and services.

Just how many of these market-specific plans you develop and implement depends on two things: the resources at your command and the goal towards which you are working. If your goal and resources are limited, you can perhaps get by with only one or two such step-by-step plans. You will, of course, help many fewer people with your product or service and you will reap a severely limited return, but if this is acceptable to you, who can cavil at such an inglorious utilization of these methods?

If, on the other hand, you wish to fly higher, then you will seek to launch and maintain as many of these plans as your mental, physical, time and financial resources at any one time permit. It really depends on where you are trying to go and how fast you want to get there. The key is husbanding your resources, learning to supervise as many of these plans as possible and making sure that, once launched, they continue to bring you into sustained and substantial contact with your market. This means you must:

- not begin a sequence of marketing steps towards a certain market unless you are resolved to connect with it at least seven times in 18 months

- always understand that the burden of follow-up is on you. In the marketing game it's always your move. To be sure, you will often have to wait for others to make up their minds, but you must realize that what you do is more important than what others do. Thus, if someone has not followed up appropriately, you must realize it is your obligation, always your obligation, to do so. This never changes no matter how rich and important you get. If you want your marketing plan to work, if you want to reach the people who have the problem your product or service solves, it is always your responsibility to move the matter to the next step.

- constantly evaluate your standing *vis-à-vis* any particular market. Have you been in touch with this market lately? If not, why not? Do you know how and when you'll next be in touch with this market? If not, why not?

Use this methodology, and I guarantee you'll see substantial results. Most businesses don't. Instead they start a marketing effort but fail to complete it, with predictably unhappy results. Don't let this happen to you!

Evaluating Your Results And Modifying Your Plan

Successful marketing means continuous evaluation and tinkering. You must not only know what you are going to do and how you are going to do it, but what happened once you did it and (as near as possible) why this method produced the results it did. Thus, you need to keep in mind the evaluation questions:

If your marketing effort paid off:

- Have you asked yourself why?
- Can it be repeated? Or is this success based on a unique situation?
- If it can be repeated, have you begun the process of repeating it?
- Can you extend the successful technique to other, similar markets? If so, which ones?

Thus, when a marketing technique has been successful, you must ask and answer two essential questions: can it be replicated with the existing group of prospects? And can this technique be used with other, similar markets? It is never enough to rest on your success and not use it. Each marketing success must be analyzed and reviewed to determine whether you can repeat it with the same group and duplicate it with similar groups.

If your marketing effort has not paid off:

- First, ask the elementary questions.

    - Have you approached a group with the problems your product or service can solve?
    - Was your ability to solve their problems clearly stated?
    - Did you make it easy for this group to respond to your offer?
    - Was your offer competitive with other offers this group may be receiving?

If you have answered all these questions affirmatively, then you are ready for the next set of assessment questions. Whereas the first set deals with whether you are approaching the right market in the right way, the second set deals with whether you should continue or not.

- Second, ask the continuation questions.

    - If your marketing effort failed to make an initial profit, did it nonetheless yield additional prospects for your product and service? If these were converted from prospects to buyers, would this effort be profitable? In other words, is there the prospect of future revenue from either the existing buyers (because you have other products or services that solve their problems) or from the as yet unsold prospects? If so, your marketing effort may well be profitable and should be continued.

- Can you reapproach the same group of prospects to reinforce the fact that you can solve their problems? Or did you approach a group which cannot be recontacted in this way? If you made sales from your initial marketing activity (although it is not yet profitable) and if you can reapproach the same group and reinforce your problem-solving message, then you must continue.

- Did your marketing effort fail to be profitable because you are allowing too much time to elapse between contacts with your prospects? If this is the case, it is your responsibility to increase the frequency of these contacts to reinforce your message more often.

- Did your marketing effort fail to be profitable because the prospects had never heard of you before? Had no reason to trust you? And were assailed with many other related problem-solving offers? If so, if your product or service compares favorably to what else is offered to them, you must continue to bring it to their attention.

- Did your marketing effort fail because it was too expensive? Can you therefore think of a way of reaching these prospects for less cost, thereby enhancing the likelihood of a profit?

What is clear is that if the first group of questions above applies, that you are not hitting the right people with the right offer, you should not return to that group again. On the other hand, if the second group of questions applies, you should.

My personal rule of thumb is once I have made the determination that the market I am approaching has the problem my product or service can solve and that what I am offering compares favorably with other offers available to them, I do *whatever* is necessary to ensure that my offer is brought before them again and again and again (always keeping in mind that this must be a minimum of 7 times in 18 months). I thereby ensure that these prospects *must* know that my product or service can help them solve their problem.

If, however, by that time they have still failed to buy, I can safely assume they are Flatworms, the creatures who like to talk about making progress but who resist taking the necessary action to ensure that this progress occurs. And if I have come to the decision that they are Flatworms, I consider them no longer and go on to more fruitful possibilities. As you must do, too. But by all means always let these Flatworms know what they are missing by not taking action. This may wake a few more up.

Writing And Keeping Your Marketing Plan

Keep your marketing plan in a three-ring binder. Allow sections for your goals, needs and objectives.

In the methods section, make sure that each plan has at least 7 steps in an 18- month period. Allow space for the method to be employed, the name(s) of any people you have to deal with in implementing this method, when you want to use this method, and your estimate of what you expect this method to produce. Leave space for a complete log of all contacts.

If you maintain this contact log, you'll be able to tell at a glance if this particular plan is being held up because you've failed to follow up or because someone else has. In either case, *you* need to take appropriate action to get things moving again. Remember: each marketing action you take must never be considered alone and in isolation. It must always be considered in relation to the other steps in the plan and to the action that comes next. For instance, you must ask yourself whether there is any point in getting on a radio show if the host will not allow you to give your name, address and telephone number so that those interested in your problem-solving product or service can contact you. Thus, your plan is built on answers to the "What next?" question.

The evaluation section should list the results of each marketing activity in which you engage, including the number of people contacted, the number of dollars generated, the cost (in terms of money and other resources) to get these dollars, the likelihood of being able to repeat this activity and the desirability of doing so. In this section, you are answering the question "Should this be repeated?" and providing your reasons for continuing or stopping.

Get into the habit of filling out these log forms as you work on these activities. Thus, you'll have a complete record of not only what you decided to do but what happened when you did it. This is invaluable as you continue the necessary planning that builds a successful business.

Last Words On Marketing Plans

Keep your plan short, simply written and action-oriented. Good marketing plans are based on a series of questions to which you have precise answers.

- Am I focusing on the right market?
- Does this market have the problem my product or service can solve?
- Is my offer competitively priced?
- Have I thought through at least 7 ways to connect with my market in the next 18 months?
- Do I know if these ways are available to me? Is there any reason why I cannot use one or more of them?
- Have I considered if there is a more advantageous way to achieve the same result with my prospects than the one I am contemplating?
- Have I thought through how to follow up each step and so again bring my product or service to the attention of my prospects?
- So long as I am sure that my product or service is a good one and that it is needed by the people I am contacting, am I willing to make the commitment to do what it takes to bring it to their attention?
- Have I evaluated and incorporated information from previous marketing efforts, both more successful and less successful, into my planning and implementation to improve future efforts?
- Have I arranged my marketing activities so that if I succeed in realizing them I shall reach my overall goal?

If you successfully answer these questions in your ongoing marketing planning, you will be well along on the road to success.

Now it's time to take yet another step towards that goal by learning how to create the persuasive marketing documents which will convincingly represent you and your products and services to the people who have the problems they solve.

CHAPTER 4

MMM

Essentials Of Creating Effective, Inexpensive, Persuasive Marketing Documents

I am well aware there are many reasons for having documents, but this chapter concentrates on just two: to get the attention of a buyer prospect and to provide him with sufficient information so that he either directly buys what you are selling — or takes the next necessary action which ultimately results in his buying what you are selling. These are, to my way of thinking, the only reasons that matter.

Those of us running small businesses, independent professional practices and nonprofit organizations ordinarily don't have vast sums of money at our disposal. We have to be chary about every expenditure, for we do not have the means available to recoup an unfortunate expenditure the way the big guys do. This means that we cannot afford to put sizable amounts of money (and I personally regard even the most minute expenditure as 'sizable') into documents which "raise our public image," "get the word out," or any other of those asinine things which I continually hear people say to and around me.

No, for me the reason for business documents is plain; either they provide the prospect with sufficient information, incentive and directions to buy your product or service directly and **now**, or they provide him with precisely what he needs to know so he takes the next necessary action in the marketing chain, an action which will lead in due course to your making the sale of your product or service and so solving his problem, too.

Here, therefore, is what you must achieve with **every** document you produce, without exception. You must:

- attract your targeted buyer prospect, indicating to him that you know what his problem is and that you can solve it with your product or service;

- provide him with sufficient information so that his natural mistrust and hesitation to take action are overcome. You must provide a complete indication that you know what his problem is and show either conclusively (if you expect to make the sale from this document) or preliminarily (if you expect the prospect to take an action which will lead in due course to the sale being made) that your product or service can solve it;

- anticipate his comments, criticisms, and objections and provide him with the answers, information, data and material he needs to overcome them;

- precisely indicate how the prospect can easily take action either to purchase your product or service now or move towards doing so;

- speak directly to the prospect, connect with him, begin to build the relationship which must be an essential outcome of your contact with him.

Each document you write to be read by others should have these characteristics. For remember: *whatever* you turn out to be read by a client or client prospect is a marketing document, whatever other purpose you may ascribe to it. What is important to remember is that marketing documents have far more in common than you may suppose, given their differences in format. That's why it's especially important to learn these steps. Once you realize what the real purpose is of each document you create, you will necessarily produce stronger, more client-centered documents — and hence make the sales you must make to stay in business.

Hideous Mistakes That Are Made In Marketing Documents (Even By The Big Guys): A Quick Check List

• Talking About Yourself First

While writing this book, I had occasion to read and review many marketing books and other sales materials. On the cover of what was in general a quite good book about creating successful documents, there was a series of documents that made a mockery out of almost everything the writer was presenting to his clients/readers.

The cover was made up of a series of very standard brochures (designed and written by the author?). Those that sold services each had on its cover a photograph of the seller, a line about the service he or she provided, his address and telephone number and a cute graphic. I wanted to scream with rage when I saw these examples of what the author surely feels are successful marketing documents (in this case brochures, mostly for independent consultants). Nothing could be further from the truth.

A typical one said, "George Duncan. Writer/Consultant. Direct Mail and Direct Response Marketing." It then provided Duncan's address and telephone number.

I want to tell you something: Mr. Duncan got taken. A worse example of pedestrian stupidity would be hard to discover!

Ask yourself this question. Even if you are interested in "direct response marketing" (a terrible use of jargon by the way), are you really interested in seeing, first and foremost, a photograph of George Duncan? Are you really interested, secondly, in the fact that Mr. Duncan is a "writer/consultant"? Are you really interested, thirdly, in the fact that he provides "Direct Mail and Direct Response Marketing"? I don't think so. In fact, I know you are not!

If you were a client prospect for Mr. Duncan (an important distinction), what you'd probably be interested in is selling more of your widgets by mail, reaching more of the right people, and doing it for less money. These would be your primary interests. Only later might you be interested in knowing about George Duncan. This is the point.

Too many marketing documents, like this terrible one prominently positioned on the cover of a well-known book on writing sales materials, are written for the ego-gratification of the people paying for them. Let's face it: it's nifty to see your mug staring grandly out from a stack of thousands of marketing documents ready to charm your would-be customers. There isn't a person in the world (I don't care what he says to the contrary) who doesn't get a thrill from this kind of self-glorification. It's our way of letting the world know how swell we are — and who can resist that?

You.

You can and must.

Mr. Duncan, sadly, didn't, and I have good reason for thinking his brochures ended up as most marketing pieces end up — as expensive exercises in self-glorification which persuade neither new prospects to become clients nor existing clients to seek out and use your services and products again. Take my word for it. This is a very serious problem.

As I hope I have by now made crystal clear, the only purpose of any marketing document is either to make a direct sale to a prospect or to get the prospect to take the next necessary step which will in due course lead to the sale. Ask yourself, is Mr. Duncan's picture calculated to achieve either of these results? I sincerely doubt it.

Hence, while the designer of his brochure certainly benefitted and the printer and the people who produced the ink and the paper and the shippers who delivered these beauties to Mr. Duncan — while all these people, I say, succeeded with the brochure (they made *their* sales, after all) the guy who really should have benefitted, the pitiable Duncan, did not. Still, he may take what pleasure he can from the fact that he is a sort of unlikely philanthropist, giving his bounty to so many who have such good reason to be grateful for his otherwise unproductive purchase!

• Providing No Clear Indication That You Understand What The Prospect Is Attempting To Achieve

Difficult as it is to admit, prospects and clients don't want to help you make a dandy living. They want to help themselves achieve that dandy living — and achieve all the other substantial benefits they so ardently desire. Never forget this. Thus, the way to get the attention of the prospect is to indicate, with the very first line, that you not only understand both the problem the client has and (directly or indirectly) what he is trying to achieve, but that, in due course, you can help him get it.

In this sense, then, the hapless Mr. Duncan would have been better off with any one of the following openers:

- "Every time you send a sales letter, it costs you money you may not get back. Are you confident you are getting the best results for every letter you send?"
- "George Duncan knows 10 ways to make your investment in direct mail pay off. Turn the page to find out what they are and begin making your investment in direct mail more profitable for you..."
- " 99 out of 100 people receiving *your* sales letters throw them away. Is this a result you can live with? Turn the page to find out how to improve your results... "

Get the idea?

The original brochure, the terrible marketing document, focused on George Duncan and, as such, no doubt made him happy to look at it. But at what cost? Good marketing documents begin by showing the prospect that you, the seller, understand the prospect's problem(s). And Duncan's client prospects have a whole host of problems:

- Most of the money they spend on direct mail is wasted money. The sales materials either make the wrong offer or go to the wrong people, or, having been received by the right people, are so poorly conceived and designed that they fail to get a response. Yes, there is tremendous waste in the mail order business. The direct response advertiser knows that the overwhelming percentage of the money he spends to approach his market will be money virtually thrown away. As a result he sweats through a lot of lonely nights wondering if, on the 1 to 2% he'll get back on a cold mailing, there will be sufficient money to run his very-expensive enterprise. Does Mr. Duncan's opening deal with this deeply-disturbing problem? No. It simply shows Mr. Duncan's winsome visage sporting a closely-cropped beard. Does the mail marketer care about that with his life and fortune continually on the line? You tell me!
- Even the tiniest improved return, 1/2 of 1%, will raise profits substantially, the more so as more pieces of mail are sent. Does this brochure indicate that Mr. Duncan can help achieve a better result? No, it does not.

I don't mean to belabor this point, or continue to point out the foolishness of Mr. Duncan's marketing investment (or the depth of ignorance either of his designer or copywriter). That, by now, should be obvious. But I do want to spare you the same ignominious result. This means snagging the attention of the prospect or client *immediately*. Nothing is calculated to do that better than a strong indication that you understand his problem ("Every time you send a sales letter it costs you money you may never see again!") with the explicit or implicit suggestion that you can do something to help. Isn't this irresistible?

• Providing Meaningless Information About Who You Are

I call this the Resumé Syndrome, and it's pervasive in our culture, destroying in its path millions of marketing documents.

Most resumés are based on facts about where people have *been*. But marketing documents succeed by giving the prospect a strong, believable indication of what problems you have solved. Of what you have *done*. And of the part your product/service played in delivering this benefit.

Particularly when you are selling a service using problem-solving information and techniques, your prospects want to know that you have solved this problem before (which is why people selling this kind of service are usually older; it takes awhile to accumulate the kind of track record you need to convince client-prospects you are the right person for them).

Everything you do must be put in terms of problem confronted, problem solved, and the difference that this solution made in the life of the client. You must answer the question "What results did I get?" and the question "What difference did it make?" Then, and only then, can you begin to diminish your client-prospect's natural anxiety about dealing with you. If you don't provide this information, his anxiety, which may so frustrate you, will only be the perfectly natural result of your failure to market properly.

• Providing An Insufficient Indication Of What You Do To Solve The Prospect's Problem

Note the wording here. I am not advising you to give away the store by telling your clients and prospects how your service is done or how your product is constructed so that they can either provide the service for themselves or create their own product. Quite the contrary. But I do want you to provide information about *what* you do. I am a fund-raising consultant, as you may know. I help organizations raise capital, project and operating funds from corporations, foundations, and individuals. Here's what an indication of what I do might look like in my marketing documents:

"Jeffrey works directly with you to:

- *review* your past fund-raising efforts. Which have worked and why? Jeffrey provides you with the kind of information you need so that you'll know and so that unsuccessful efforts can either be improved (or dropped altogether) and successful activities continued. Your time is valuable. Your resources are limited. Jeffrey knows that. That's why this thorough review is so helpful.

- *train* members of your Board of Directors, staff, and volunteers. Most people have never had any training in effective fund-raising techniques. Furthermore, most people find fund-raising distasteful and intrusive. Jeffrey is sensitive to these feelings and has developed specialized training techniques to help people overcome their anxieties and become active, productive fund-raising volunteers.

- *develop* persuasive fund-raising documents. There is a knack to writing effective fund-raising documents. Jeffrey has it! Working with him, you'll learn just what should go into a document and what should be left out. Moreover, the documents that are created will last for at least a year and will need minimal updating after that, a terrific time-savings.

- *target* just the right corporations and foundations to approach for funds. With over 24,000 active foundations and many millions of corporations to chose from, it can be difficult to know where to spend your limited time and resources for best results. You want to get the money that your organization needs, but you don't want to waste your time. That's where Jeffrey comes in. He'll help guide you to the most likely sources of funding and provide clear step-by-step advice about whom to approach, how to approach them, how to handle the solicitation meeting and the on-site visit and all the other often-difficult details which are an intrinsic part of successful fund-raising."

Get the idea? You need a paragraph for each service you provide and, importantly, for each objection or obstacle raised by the prospect. Each paragraph should start with an action verb, for what your product/service is really doing is actively *moving* your client from one place to a better place. You must give your prospect a sense of this movement and convince him that you can move him to where he wants to go.

What you are doing here is providing information about what you'll do (but not how you'll do it); you are addressing objections raised by the prospect, and, by providing the information the prospect needs to make a decision, you are lowering the prospect's resistance to buying from you.

What is important to point out is that I have never said *how* I do these things. Just *what* I do. The precise "how to" step-by-step details are left for the relationship I have with the client, in this case a nonprofit organization seeking money. Thus, I have given the potential prospect information he needs to make a decision and in the process calmed his fears about do-nothing consultants who draw large fees and do little in return, while not threatening my own trade secrets, the crux of what makes my service worth having.

But you're probably asking yourself, "Don't prospects want to know precisely what you'll do, precisely how you'll go about solving their problems?" The answer is that I am **never** asked by my clients how I will do this work. Think of the last time you selected a dentist. Did you ask him precisely how he would be filling your teeth or constructing your bridge? Certainly not.

Prospects have a need to know that I know what I am doing and that I can successfully institute these measures and techniques with them. But once this need has been met, they do not ask detailed questions (as you might have thought they would) about how the system operates in practice. In fact, if they are happy with the results you bring them, they'll probably never ask you any detailed questions, unless they entertain a personal or professional interest in what you are doing.

Be honest. How many marketing documents have you ever seen which provide the prospect with this kind of detailed, helpful, anxiety-relieving information? I'll tell you: damned few. Now what about yours?

- **Providing No Indication Of What You Want The Prospect To Do And How You Want The Prospect To Do It**

Every document you produce to succeed in marketing must provide a clear indication of what you want your prospect to do to follow up and how you want him to do it. At no time must the prospect be left with a feeling of "Now what?". (Can you believe, for instance, that there are still considerable numbers of people who, while including their telephone numbers on their stationery, do not include the area codes? And those who, while adding their street addresses, do not include their zip codes? Not surprisingly, I regard these people as either slipshod or demented, and who can blame me?) It's your job to make sure this never happens. Thus, include complete step-by-step details of what you want the prospect to do and how you want him to do it.

As I have said many times, this should include your ability to deal with the prospect twenty-four hours a day. By that I do not mean that you personally, in the flesh, must be available twenty-four hours daily. But you must provide some means, some system, so that if your prospect is ready to act at 3 a.m. on a Sunday morning, your system can oblige him. I have a twenty-four hour order line, always primed with a marketing message (call me and find out!). Everyone offering a product or service, whatever its nature, should have nothing less. I'll have more to say about this later.

Focus on Specific Problems Of Your Prospects

Too many people create marketing documents which are too general, attempting to be all things to all people. This is a mistake. If you are attempting to reach widely varying audiences, then create different marketing documents for each. General Motors doesn't attempt to sell everything it produces from a single brochure and neither should you. Many participants in my marketing workshops feel distinctly unhappy when they hear this advice. They are afraid that by being specific they will someday, somewhere, somehow lose a dollar from a specific individual who will read this specific brochure, not find himself in it, and go elsewhere.

Let me say again and again that marketing is specific. And that in the age of computers and telecommunications it is becoming more specific yet. The "big secret" is that ours is an age of factionalism and that with modern technology each faction can be served precisely what it wants, in the precise way it wants it. Why else would Burger King run as its slogan "Have it your way?" Ladies and gentlemen, if it can be done with the lowly hamburger, then it must be done with whatever *you* are selling.

Each single marketing document produced by you (whatever form it takes) must be directed to a highly-targeted audience. Must demonstrate that you understand what this particular audience wishes to buy and why it wishes to buy it. Must indicate that *you* understand exactly what Ultimate Benefit your targeted buyer prospect wishes to have. And then must work to persuade this audience to take action immediately — either to acquire the item being presented to it — or to take the next logical action towards securing it.

The entire process breathes a necessary specificity which all too many marketing documents simply don't have. It is better to have two quite precise documents which work (even though they admittedly take more time and money to produce) than to have a single marketing document which, by attempting to convince disparate groups, fails, thereby wasting your time and money. Don't you agree?

Document Modules

Successful documents are composed of building blocks, each block of which has a specific purpose and which works first to lower the prospect's resistance and increase his trust in you and second to move him towards either immediate purchase or along the buying chain which will, in due course, result in his acquiring your product or using your service. Here are the modules you need:

Headline Module

Let's face it. Most people don't read well or thoroughly. They don't understand what they read and don't ordinarily take the time to figure it out, even when it's in their best interest. That's why your headline is so important.

The headline really has four functions:

- It snags the attention of your prospect.
- It defines the audience you are trying to reach. Right from the start, the headline must be so written that the response of the person reading it is "Here's something for me!"
- It delivers a complete message. The best message is "You, client prospect, have a problem. I have your solution."
- It draws the reader into the copy which follows, copy which will indicate in detail how much you understand the prospect's problem and how you can solve it.

Headline Writing Tips

There are basically eight different kinds of headlines you can use.

- *Direct headlines* lay your sales message right on the line, "Two shirts for the price of one until November 1." You'd have to be an idiot to misunderstand this plainly-stated message. (*N.B.* Idiots exist in exuberant profusion.)
- *Indirect headlines* make their points in a more roundabout way. "If you've got ring around the collar, it's time for a new shirt." As you have probably already guessed, I'm not big on this kind of indirect approach. It asks the reader/client prospect to go through another step. You risk losing him. You can do this, of course, but why not simply state your message clearly, right from the start?
- *News headlines* provide information about a new product, an improvement in your existing product or service or a new application for something you've been selling, "New Postal Mail Batching Regulation Could Lower Cost Of Your Next Direct Mailing." Such a headline may seem pretty boring to you, but let me tell you something: as a person who runs an expensive mail order business, I'd read a headline like this (and the copy that inevitably follows) in a minute. It promises a benefit to a highly-targeted prospect and as such is irresistible.

• The *How-To Headline* offers the prospect the promise of a solution to one of his very important problems, a problem he is willing to spend money to solve. "How To Raise The Money You Need For Your Nonprofit Organization From Corporations, Foundations and Individuals, Even When You Hate To Fund-Raise!"

A how-to headline tells the targeted buyer-prospect very directly that there is a solution to his problem and that by reading on he'll get it. Again, another irresistible headline. My advice is if you ever get stuck writing a headline, write a how-to headline first. If you can't, it's a dead certainty you don't understand the problem your buyers have or how your product or service can solve it.

• The *Question Headline* asks a query important to the prospect with the suggestion that the copy that follows will provide an answer — and thus, in due course, lead to the purchase of your product or service. "If you became disabled today, do you really have the resources to support your family?"(Such a headline could be used to sell disability insurance.) Such questions engage the attention of the prospect. Once he's engaged you provide an advantageous means of solving his problem.

• *Command Headlines.* These are headlines which briskly tell the prospect to do something, to take action. "Send in this coupon today for your free copy of the Sure-Fire Business Success Catalog: 135 ways to make your small business more profitable!" Many marketers are meek marketers. They are afraid to antagonize their buyer-prospects by coming on too strong. Many other marketers are arrogant marketers; they feel that what they are selling is so sublime that their buyers ought to kowtow to them in gratitude for its even existing. They are therefore certainly not going to lower themselves to providing their buyers with directions on what to do.

Need I say that both these types, so commonly found, are both sadly mistaken? I am going to say over and over again that people are slow to take action on their own behalf. They give themselves lots of "good" reasons why they cannot do even that thing which is so obviously in their best interest.

You will come to find out just how long it takes people using your particular product or service to take the action they ought to take much more quickly. Each business has a Lethargy Quotient, and you'll come to learn what yours is. Your command headlines will come out of a knowledge of how slowly your prospects act and how badly they need what you are selling. The more slowly they act and the more badly they need your product or service, the more likely you are to use the command mode to get their attention and push them towards beneficial action.

• *The Reason-Why Headline.* Once you have listed all the benefits of *using* (not buying) your product or service, you can write a "reason why" headline. It simply summarizes how many reasons there are for the prospect to use your product or service. "17 Reasons Why Your Nonprofit Organization Should Be Using **DEVELOPMENT TODAY: A FUND RAISING GUIDE FOR NONPROFIT ORGANIZATIONS** To Raise The Money You Need." I'm one of those people who feel that many (perhaps most) buying decisions are made for other than rational reasons. But I also believe that once a person has decided to buy, he wants the reasons which, in the first place, did not cause him to buy. But whether a person buys rationally or not, this headline indicates that he'll have a complete list of all the necessary reasons for taking action. These reasons are useful for the rational and essential for those who act otherwise.

• The *Testimonial Headline* offers the endorsement of an individual who is happy with your product or service, thereby offering proof that it actually works. "Judi Boyko of the Natick Visiting Nurses says, 'Dr. Jeffrey Lant and his book **DEVELOPMENT TODAY: A FUND RAISING GUIDE FOR NONPROFIT ORGANIZATIONS** helped us raise more than $80,000 from corporations, foundations, and individuals for our desperately ill elderly clients.' " As you'll see in a minute (for I intend to discuss the questions of testimonials again shortly), the person who provides you with a testimonial need not be a celebrity. Indeed, I feel that celebrity endorsements can often backfire. Not all Americans are stupid. They know that Mr. Known-By-All is getting big bucks by endorsing a product which he probably doesn't know whether to wear, eat or drive, thereby engendering the very reasonable cynicism of the buyer.

The testimonials we little guys use have to be different. They must be from someone like the prospective buyer. They must say to the prospect, "Here's somebody just like you, with problems just like yours, who used this product/service successfully. See, you don't have to worry. So why don't you get the lead out and get it yourself?" If our testimonials do this, they are successful testimonials and, as such, are much more useful (and a whole lot less expensive) than those offered by sports stars featured in underwear ads.

A Few Words About Headline Writing

Let me tell you something about headlines. There are days when you can write them and days when they just won't come for love or money. Depend on it and prepare accordingly.

Don't just write one headline. Write at least *three* headlines for each of these headline categories. Write three Testimonial headlines. Write three Reason-Why headlines. And then begin to test them. People really are funny. It's often difficult, if not impossible, to suggest in advance which headline will really grab the attention of your buyers. So don't try.

Write lots of examples and keep using them on people. As I have already said, a single marketing document cannot suffice except, perhaps, for the tiniest company. If you are offering more than a single service or a single product, more than likely you'll have to have more than a single document. This means trying out lots of headlines on your prospects.

One thing is certain; if you write your headlines properly, they will do the following:

- alert the prospect that you know what his pressing problem is and know how to solve it (through your product or service);
- snag his interest (since you are dealing with his problem) and persuade him to read on into the copy that will help close the sale — and so move him towards a solution;
- lower his anxiety. People want help, often desperately. But they are afraid that the person who pretends to have the solution they often urgently require is not the knowledgeable authority they actually need. Your prospect's justifiable anxiety will be lowered, however, if you have spoken to him in language he understands about a problem he knows he has, and if your copy follows through and delivers more persuasive evidence of your understanding of his problem and information about how your techniques solve it. This, then, is precisely what you must do.

Tricks of the Trade for Writing Persuasive Headlines

- Don't try to be cute. As I watch commercials on television, listen to them on the radio and read them in all sorts of publications, I realize the staggering waste in the advertising field. This may not matter for the big guys, but it certainly matters when you don't have heaps of capital to draw on. For us on the micro end of business, each dollar has to count. That's why it's better for you to be straightforward and direct.

Use a direct headline or a how-to headline or a reason-why headline. Let the prospect know right from the start that you know what his problem is and that you have what it takes to solve it. This kind of marketing strategy cannot fail — so long as you are dealing with people who really have this problem and really want to solve it.

As I must reiterate throughout this book, those people who either don't have the problem or who don't want to do what it takes to solve it were never really your prospects in the first place and if they don't like your headline or don't respond to it, it's no loss whatsoever. So long as those with the problem and with the commitment to solve the problem are attracted by your headline (and by the body copy which follows) and take the necessary action to solve their problem, then you can fairly reckon your headline to be a success.

What this all means, of course, is that you should be very wary of puns, double entendres, strange words and jargon. Oh, yes, beware of jargon! *Anything* that stands between you and the prospect with the problem you can solve should be avoided. Keeping this in mind, from now on listen to every commercial, read every advertisement, especially examine every headline with these questions in mind:

- Has this advertiser attracted my attention in a way connected to the product or service he is selling? Or has he simply used any device to engage (my no doubt) momentary interest? Back in the dark ages of advertising (but still seen today) ads would be headlined "SEX". Of course, people looked (sex sells, right?) only to discover that the ad was about toaster repairs. If you were expecting sex and got, instead, a lead to a properly-functioning toaster, you might reasonably be irked — and might take it out on the advertiser. Instead, the way the advertiser attracts your attention should be directly connected to the ultimate benefit he is selling. "No more burnt toast" is, in this connection, an infinitely better headline than "SEX".

- Has this advertiser clearly indicated whom he is trying to attract? People like very firm guidelines. They rightly want an answer to the question, "Is this thing for me?" If there is the slightest hesitation, they are right to go on to something else where this confusion doesn't exist. Keep asking yourself: is it absolutely, beyond-the-slightest-shadow-of-a-doubt clear that the advertiser is talking to me? If you cannot be absolutely sure, then the ad has failed. Be sure that your marketing materials are not similar fiascos.

- Has this advertiser delivered a complete message in his headline? (Remember: 'No More Burnt Toast.' It may not win the Nobel Prize for Literature, but it is a complete, clear, targeted message).

- Has the advertiser promised you a benefit ("No more burnt toast") that induces you to listen to the remainder of the ad or read on into his copy? Take particular notice of this point when you are, or could be, a prospect for what the advertiser is selling. I pay much closer attention to the marketing message when I might be a customer and I always ask myself "Has this message worked and, if not, why not?" You do the same.

The Problem Module

You are probably already getting bored with my saying that people buy products and services because they have a problem they want to solve. Still, I'm going to say it again — and again and again. And I'll tell you why. While I was writing this chapter a fellow from Houston called to tell me he was having problems selling his stress-management workshops. He couldn't figure out why, but within three minutes of listening to him I knew that he was selling workshops and not health. Despite the fact that he had a copy of **MONEY TALKS**, my workshop and seminar book on hand (in which this problem is discussed in relation to talk programs), he didn't understand what I was talking about! No wonder he was having problems!!! People don't buy stress management workshops. They buy health! And they want health because they are having one or more problems in their lives which make them uncomfortable. That's where the Problem Module comes in.

From now on, you should be keeping a list of every problem your clients and client prospects have. The more problems they have, the more solutions you can reasonably offer them — to their delight.

First, list their problems, one by one. When you start this exercise, don't worry about putting them in any order. But do worry that you get *every single problem* of your prospects and buyers, no matter how insignificant you really think it is. The fact that you think it insignificant is insignificant! What matters is how your prospects and clients feel about it. Here is a very partial list (for in real life the list can go on much further) of the problems my clients and prospects face on the matter of raising money from corporations and foundations:

They:

- feel uncomfortable asking people for money. They are afraid they will be rejected and humilitated.

- don't know which corporations and foundations to approach. There are so many! They are therefore afraid the necessary research will eat up a lot of time and not necessarily bring any return at all. Moreover, they are afraid that if they approach the wrong corporation or foundation, someone may tell them off for wasting their time and being incompetent. At the very least, they may never know what happened, for the funding source may not get back to them.

- if they are executive directors, they are afraid the board will not assist them. That the board will have unreasonable expectations about the fund-raising and will place the total onus (especially for failure) on the director, thus possibly leading to a "fall guy" situation for the executive.

You get the idea.

Where do these fears and anxieties, these problems, come from? How do you know these are the real fears and anxieties of your prospects? They come from your ongoing contact with your prospects, clients, and customers — by listening to them (and writing down what they say), by reading their professional publications and attending their meetings, in short by empathizing with them. Be honest. Do you really do this kind of homework with your clients and prospects, or do you, like most people, "wing it" and hope for the best? You can lie to me, you old fox, but by your marketing results, ye shall be known.

The object of marketing is to ascertain precisely what problems your would-be buyers have and to indicate that you know what they are and can solve them. Successful marketing need not be flashy (indeed should not be flashy) but it should be solid, intelligent, and relentlessly focused on the prospect's problems and your very-believable solutions.

Benefit Module

As I've said over and over again (I certainly hope you're not tired of hearing it either) people buy benefits, not products, not services. So you had better have a Benefit Module packed with the kinds of meaningful benefits your prospect really wants to have.

You have to let the prospect know that, yes, there is a solution to their problem and that, yes, you, with your product or service can provide it. Let's go back to my fund-raising consultation service example above. First, I listed the problems that people have, their anxieties, the things that upset and unsettle them. It is the fact that they are unsettled (first) and only (second) their aspiration for something better, which induces the prospect to take substantive action. Here are the benefits the prospect wishes to achieve:

Benefits

- You can have the money you need for capital acquisitions and improvements, for acquiring a new building or improving the one you've got. For running the programs you now have or adding new programs to serve new client groups. For taking care of those nagging operating expenses like rent, heat, electricity. For building an endowment fund, so that in future years your program will have a cushion of security against whatever takes place.

- You will learn how to invest your time wisely, how to approach the right corporations, foundations and individuals in the right way with the right documents with a reasonable expectation that you will get the money you need. No more wasted time for you. No more uncertainty. And you can therefore go about the often-distasteful business of fund-raising with a new, more confident outlook, an outlook which will improve your success!

- You will have fund-raising letters which will produce the money you need. Direct mail is expensive and can often be disastrous for an agency. Now you'll have the reasonable assurance that your letters will reach the right people with the right message and persuade them to give money to your organization.

See what I mean?

There should be a benefit for each anxiety the prospect has and for every aspect of your product or service.

How do you know these are benefits? Ask your clients and prospects what benefits they desire. Again, listen to what they talk about. Read their publications. Attend their conferences. In short, be empathetic in an active, involved, committed fashion. Don't be so interested in your own need to make the sale, in your own need for money, about how you'll make the presentation to the prospect. Focus instead on the prospect; hear the prospect, draw information (both hard factual information and soft "feeling" information) from the prospect. Then and only then are you ready to use this information, to fashion and construct an approach which will induce the prospect to take the action which is entirely is his best interest.

Ultimate Benefit Module

The Ultimate Benefit, as you'll recall, is the *real*, the final, the truly most important benefit the individual buying your product or service will get by buying and using it. Let's take the example above. The first benefit is listed as having the money the executive director needs for capital, project and operating expenses. This is a benefit, no doubt about it. But it is not the Ultimate Benefit. Let's say I am addressing this marketing document to executive directors of health agencies, a large chunk, by the way, of my market. While they would agree that having more money is a benefit, it is because of the Ultimate Benefit(s) that they would act. These Ultimate Benefits include:

- keeping their clients healthy. When they buy a fund-raising service that has every possibility of delivering the financial results they want, what they are really buying is health. And not just health in the abstract, either, but health for elderly, infirm citizens who cannot leave their homes, health for teen-age mothers, health for low-income people. In other words, Ultimate Benefits for very precise groups of people.

You, as a marketer, have got to make the buyer see, feel, taste, and visualize this Ultimate Benefit. In this instance, therefore, I am not selling a service, I am not selling simply money (although this is part of the attraction to be sure), I am selling health, an absence of pain, a dignified end of life to people who need this service.

In selling this benefit, you are also selling a series of other benefits, including:

- Inner-gratification to the executive director. In a world where lots and lots of people have lost their way or have become mindlessly, terminally selfish, imagine how deeply satisfying it must be to an executive director who can, day after day, really help people be better off. This inner-gratification, this end to the destructive question "Is that all there is?", is one of the Ultimate Benefits I sell. What else?

- A Better World. Yes, when the elderly infirm get treated with dignity as well as having their needs met, one can say without fear of contradiction that one is providing a better world and can, as a result, look the world squarely in the eye and fear no man's nagging scrutiny. Can you imagine being able to sell such an Ultimate Benefit? Well, I do.

As I have said before, each feature (which I'm getting to) has a benefit and each benefit (or cluster of benefits) should have an Ultimate Benefit. It is your job to make the prospect vividly aware of:

- the prospect's problems;

- the benefits that are available to the prospect, if the prospect takes action;

- the Ultimate Benefits the prospect really is buying, for often prospects rely on you to put into words what exists only as something vague in their minds;

- how you will work to gain these results and these benefits; and

- what features your product or service offers and why they are important for the prospect in reaching his objectives.

The Features Module

Once people are snagged by these points, they want and need to know *exactly* what they are buying, the features of your product or service, those traits, attributes and characteristics of which it is composed. Again, let's return to my fund-raising consultation example. The Features Module is composed of information about precisely what the prospect is buying.

To show you what I mean, let's take my Co-Operative Service Contract, one of the two options I have available to help solve the prospect's problems and deliver the actual benefit and then the Ultimate Benefit they desire. Here are some of the features of this contract:

- One-hour weekly meetings for a year. Each meeting concludes with a list of approximately ten tasks which you complete by the next weekly meeting. Tasks include gathering guidelines from corporations, foundations and individuals; submitting proposals to corporations and foundations; and arranging and having interviews with corporate and foundation grants officers.

- Two two-hour progress report meetings with your Board of Directors during the course of the year. These meetings allow your Directors to ask questions of Jeffrey and enable him to advise the Board about which aspects of the fund-raising effort are succeeding — and why — and which aspects are not doing so well and what can be done to improve matters. These are very candid, very frank sessions which lead to adjustments being made in the way the fund-raising activity is being carried out.

- Drafting, editing and finalizing persuasive fund-raising documents. Successful fund-raising is based on paper, lots and lots of paper. During Jeffrey's consultancy, he will work with you to develop persuasive fund-raising proposals for submission to corporations and foundations, deft cover letters for these proposals, sequences of fund-raising letters, volunteer training materials, telephone solicitation scripts, and many other documents which will become the permanent property of your organization and which, with minimal updating, you can use for years.

I'm sure you get the idea.

Remember: the features of your product or service need not be drily rendered. Again, include and stress not just the facts about your features (you'll draft a fund-raising proposal) but the benefit of the system you use ("with minimal updating and editing, you can use this document for years.") In even the simplest of marketing documents, you can reinforce the impact of each section by adding not just facts but reminding the prospect of the benefits attached to each fact.

Success Module

As I'm sure you're aware, people these days are very skeptical about the claims made by people selling anything. At some level, they know that marketing is handled by marketing specialists who are adept at getting people to take action, but who probably really don't know a lot about the product or service in question. Whether the product or service is good, such people are paid to get us to take action.

We are therefore correct to have those cautionary words "Caveat Emptor" tattooed on our bodies for easy reference; having them on the hand you use to grab your wallet probably makes the most sense. This kind of skepticism these days is entirely natural — and need not work against us. Indeed, you should start with the assumption that your prospects will be skeptical about you, your product and service and that they are right to be so skeptical. Properly handled, however, this skepticism need not deter them from buying what you are selling. The Success Module helps you achieve this result.

The Success Module is composed of information about people, organizations, and businesses who have used your product or service and used it successfully. It says, in effect, "Here are people just like you who had the same kinds of problems that you have. They used our product or service, and as a result they have solved their problem or are well along towards doing so."

There are several important factors to keep in mind about the Success Module:

- To get information about how your product or service functioned, ask people to tell you. Particularly with products, where you are not on hand working with the buyer, you will not always know what people liked about your product and what benefits they produced for the buyer. So, ask them to share this information with you and give them something for doing so.

- What you give them should have, of course, some relation to the product/service you are selling. For instance, if you wanted to find out how your new vitamins made people feel, you might ask them to contact you and give them in return a free article/pamphlet listing all the body's daily vitamin and mineral needs and the best ways to have them fulfilled.

- The success must be put in a context. It is not enough to have a success. You must tell people what difference the success made. Here are the kinds of successes to keep in mind:

  - If you and your competitors produced the same success, your success is the more meaningful if your product/service costs less.

  - If your product or service costs more, did you deliver more than what is being standardly offered by your competitor?

  - If your success was not impressive on raw numbers, but your competitors during the same period produced no success at all, you need to point this out. Otherwise prospects could easily get the wrong idea.

All this is called Creating the Success Context — the success which is meaningful when set into its particular context and compared with what others were doing during the same period.

A subsidiary part of the Success Module is the Testimonial File. It stands to reason that buyer-prospects like to identify with others like them who have used your product/service. Make it easy for them. Most testimonials fail in this regard. The most stupid (and I mean stupid!) use this kind of testimonial, " 'I loved this product!' Mrs. S.J., Des Moines."

An endorsement like this strikes me as futile and actually undercuts the standing of the seller. "If," one properly asks, "Mrs. S.J. loved the product so much, why didn't she allow her name to be used?" One is immediately lead to the conclusion (so detrimental to the marketer) that there is *no* Mrs. S.J. at all. What do you think this conclusion does to the marketer's credibility?

Instead, do not just use real names but also use identifying characteristics which help the prospect identify with person offering the testimonial and say, in effect, "This person is like me. Therefore his endorsement is a valuable one." Hence, " 'I love this product!' Dr. Jeffrey Lant, 43-year old home-based business owner." The key words here are "home-based business owner", always assuming that the endorsement is for something that category of buyers would find helpful. That's the key; the endorsement is meaningful if the person reading it can say, "Hey, this guy had the same problem I have, and he used the product/service to solve it. He benefitted. I want that benefit. Ergo, I want that product/service, too!"

But how, pray, do you get this information from people, these endorsements, testimonials and the context facts which make them valuable? You ask for them!

From now on, never send out a product or perform a service without asking the buyer/client to rate you, to tell you what he liked (and, for that matter what he doesn't like, so you can get continually better and offer better problem-solving products and services), and to tell you why he liked it.

Tell them you may be using some of these comments in your marketing and advertising efforts and ask the individual if he minds your using his name? Ask him at the same time for pertinent information which would be of helpful in constructing a meaningful testimonial/endorsement, the kind of endorsement which other prospects will identify with. Such information may include:

- the person's name, age, sex, place of residence, type of business, kind of product(s) used, and years used.

In other words, the kind of context information you need is directly related to the kinds of people you are trying to reach and whom you want to buy your product or service. If it kills me, I shall continue to conduct my unrelenting war against the "Mrs. S.J., Des Moines" type of endorsement, so ridiculously futile, and I urge you, by adopting more sensible standards, to join my crusade!

People Module

Many documents, particularly brochures featuring someone offering a service, provide biographical information. Most of this information is completely useless and doesn't help sell your products and services. The reason for this is plain: most information consists of futile biographical details, information on where the marketer went to school, what degrees he has and how many children. What possible benefit can the prospect get from any of this selfish information?

As before, the prospect needs to know not where you have been (The Resumé Syndrome discussed above) but what problems you have solved. And what successes you have had solving them.

Just see what I mean.

Standard Resumé Fare: "Dr. Jeffrey Lant holds four college degrees. He holds the B.A. *summa cum laude* in history and political science from the University of California, Santa Barbara (1969); M.A.(1970) and Ph.D. (1975) degrees in history from Harvard, and a Certificate of Advanced Graduate Studies in Higher Education Administration (1976) from Northeastern University, Boston."

Successful People Module: "Dr. Jeffrey Lant, who received his Ph.D. from Harvard, has worked with several hundred nonprofit organizations over the past 10 years as administrator, trainer in successful fund-raising techniques and management consultant and assisted organizations to raise the money they need from corporations, foundations, and individuals. With those organizations he has served as management consultant, *each* has had significant success, success which can be confirmed by the executive directors of each organization."

You get the idea.

The first box, the standard resumé fare, is impressive, no doubt about it. But it says, "Jeffrey Lant is an impressive fellow." Which is a good thing to know but rather hard to know what to do with. On the other hand the Successful People Module says, "Jeffrey Lant has been successful solving the problems of people just like you. What he has done in the past, which can be confirmed by those who have used his services, augurs well for your investment and what you can expect to receive in the future." The second box, therefore, lowers the reasonable anxieties of your buyers and provides the kind of information they need to know about you, so that they feel confident and comfortable making the decision that they must make to move matters along.

Next time you pick up a brochure — or any other marketing document — browse through it quickly. Are you being given information about the person offering the product or service which leads you to say, "This is an impressive person" (but I don't know if he can solve my problem)? Or can you honestly say, "This is an impressive person who can solve my problem based on what he has done in the past"? You tell me!

Follow-Up Module

You already know I am a fanatic about follow-up. Most marketing documents are passive. They say, in effect, "Here we are. Now you figure out how to get in touch with us. We're above helping you."

The truth is most marketing documents are arrogant documents. They do not contain the kind of information the prospect needs to make his following up easy. Instead, they act as if the prospect should be glad, actually glad, that anyone is there to see to his needs when he calls. Need I say that this line of reasoning, of which I see examples every day, is nonsensical?

Before you can include any follow-up information in your marketing documents, you need to come up with answers to the following questions:

- Have I provided complete follow-up information to my prospects, including the name of my company, street address (don't simply rely on a post office box!), telephone number with area code and the name of the person with whom the prospect will first come into contact?
- If I am not in the office, have I set up a system where the prospect can leave his message? Is the message greeting him clear? Does it thank him for making the call, provide him with a sales message, and provide complete details about the information you will need to expeditiously process his query/call?

- Have I provided a twenty-four hour system so that when the prospect is ready to act, I am ready to assist him?

You cannot write a satisfactory marketing document until you have satisfactory answers to these questions.

A Few More Words On These Points

- Think through all the logical possibilities about how people can contact you and make sure you have provided them the information they need to do so. Therefore, simply giving people a post office box has always seemed nonsensical to me. Not only does a post office box unsettle prospects (who often have very good reason to doubt the good intentions of the person using it), but it makes it impossible for people to walk in and acquire your product/service. Do you really want to remove this option from your buyers?

- People following up marketing documents of any kind feel better if they know whom to contact and what will happen when they call. Face it. It's difficult for people to pick up the telephone and call for information (much less walk into a new place with which they have not done business before.) They know that in most instances the first person they talk to will not know what they are calling about, will not have the information they need, and will not know how to handle their call or visit. They know this because these unsettling and aggravating circumstances happen to them daily. Is it therefore any wonder that people return again and again to the people and situations they know, even if these are not quite perfect? They are at least known!

When you send out a marketing document, indicate whenever possible to the people receiving it exactly whom they should call and precisely how their call will be handled. Then make sure that you follow through on this commitment.

- We can't always be in our offices. I know. But even when you are not present, you can expeditiously handle your contacts with your prospects and move them towards completion. This starts with your answering machine message. Most people's messages are atrocious. They are written for the convenience of the seller, not the convenience of the prospect.

I have, for instance, a friend who is a marketing consultant. But his answering message is no more useful than anybody else's, despite the fact he should know better. His message simply says, "This is Tom Brown. I'm not available to take your call right now. But please your name and number after the beep, and I'll get back to you." Do you see anything wrong with this message? I certainly do!

Telephone messages should be marketing messages. They should provide information about what you do and the problems you solve. They should reinforce your expertise in the minds of your clients, and they should provide your prospects with yet another indication of what you do and the problems you solve.

In this regard how about this message for my friend's answering service, "This is Tom Brown, marketing consultant. I'm out helping people sell more of their products and services right now. And I'd like to help you do the same, so after the beep leave your name, number and an indication of how I can serve you. I'll get back and help you sell more of your products and services just as soon as I can."

See the difference? The first is passive. It leaves all the work to the person placing the call, the person who needs your guidance. It is unhelpful, even arrogant. The second message is brisk, precise, client-centered, helpful. If you were a customer, which would impress you more?

Remember: it is not enough, never enough!, to provide your message once. You must use every opportunity to reinforce it in the minds of those who are already using your products and services (you want them to keep you in mind so that when the opportunity arises they'll pass your name along to someone else who needs you via word-of-mouth marketing) and those who are not.

Providing your marketing message once will never be sufficient. You must use every opportunity you can to indicate particularly to your prospects that you can solve their problem — and that if you are not available right now to help them, it's because you are working to help someone else. You are, aren't you?

- You must provide a twenty-four hour response system. This point naturally follows the one above. Most people work the standard 8-hour day. But it's a terrible mistake to shut off your ability to solve other people's problems, or at least to indicate to them how the problem-solving process can be started, merely because you are off having a good time somewhere. Therefore, provide a twenty-four hour marketing service so people can leave you the information you need. You must be prepared to solve your prospects' problems, when they are ready to have them solved. Think through just how you will do this before you even consider writing a document of any kind.

Further Words On Document Modules

- Keep a file for each module. Whatever you write in your documents will quickly become outmoded. Prepare accordingly. Keep a file for each of these modules. Add information as it becomes available. When you write new documents and update existing ones, you'll have readily available all the information you need for them.

- Always test what you've got against other marketing documents, particularly ones created by your competitors. If they score a telling point in their marketing documents, make sure you can do as much in yours.

- Ask your clients and customers to comment on your modules before you use them. We are all dependent on our customers, and there's absolutely no reason to find out what they really like after we've put out our documents. Work to find out beforehand.

- Don't hesitate to throw away your golden words. Situations and circumstances change. And you — and your documents — must change, too. If a marketing document is not working, throw it away — even if you have 3,000 of them in your garage. Learn what you can from the unhappy experience of producing a document that doesn't work, doesn't entice prospects, doesn't help make the sales both of you need. Then throw them away — without a second thought. After all, we've all written a bad document. The trick is how to profit from even this unfortunate situation.

Turning Your Modules Into Document Copy

Once you've addressed each specific section of your marketing documents and gathered the material you need, it's time to begin putting what you've got into the right form, the form, that is, that will attract the most buyers and persuade them to take the action you both need: to buy your product or service. This task is called copywriting, and it can be very frustrating.

There's nothing mysterious about copywriting. It is best understood as the art of writing up the information you have gathered about the client prospect's problems, anxieties, objectives, benefits, and Ultimate Benefits in such a way that the prospect understands precisely how your offer will benefit him and precisely how to act now so that he gets the benefit he desires as quickly as possible.

Tips For Writing Persuasive, Punchy, Interesting Copy

Whole books have been written on the subject of writing persuasive copy, and if you check out my Sure-Fire Business Success Catalog at the back of this book you'll find recommendations to some of the best of them, including CASH COPY: How To Offer Your Products And Services So Your Prospects Buy Them Now! But writing the kind of copy you need won't be all that difficult, if you keep in mind some sensible suggestions:

- Don't use jargon. Jargon is a word or series of words which are used by people within one profession or trade but not generally understood by outsiders. Even when you are talking to people within a trade or profession, use the simplest, most easily-understood language first. It is not always a sign of intelligence to use complicated language and in terms of marketing documents is usually a mistake.

- Write in "you" language. Don't discuss your products, services, and benefits generally. Speak directly to your buyer. In this connection, it often helps to visualize a particular person and address your remarks to him.

- Use conversational language, the kind of language I am using in this book. I call this kind of language "conversational accessible", because it is easy for the reader to understand what you are saying and to feel it is being written especially for him — as it should be!

- Settle on your image and make sure all the words you use are consistent. There are basically two images: warm and cool. The warm image (which I call "The Accessible Expert") can be used when you have a reasonable assurance that your client prospects understand their problem and will take action reasonably quickly to solve it. The cool image (which I call the "In-Common Technocrat") is used when your client prospects are likely to move slowly towards taking action and need another, insistent push to take the action they need. The image you decide to use depends not so much on you as it does on which clients you are trying to attract, on their needs and on how quickly they are likely to take action. This point is very commonly misunderstood.

Most people look at themselves and decide how to shape their image. It is more sensible, however, to look at the people you are trying to attract and try to discern what they need you to be. Then present yourself accordingly.

- Break your copy into short sections. Long paragraphs tire your reader and make him less likely to read your copy, indeed may even irritate him to the point where, even though he needs what you are selling, he may simply decide it's not worth all this effort.

- Use short sentences for the same reason as above.

- Alter the length of your sentences. Variety is not only the spice of life. It is the essence of interesting writing. If your copy is not interesting, your prospects are not likely to wade through it.

- Put the most important points first. I've already stressed the importance of your headlines. After the headline, make sure you've added your most telling selling points. People want to know right away what's in it for them. Make it easy on yourself. Tell them.

- Be concise. Americans almost always overwrite. This is a problem you probably have and one which you must get over. Get to the point as soon as you can. Be specific about the problem the prospect has and how you can solve it. If people really want to solve their problem (and are as such real client prospects), they want to know immediately how you think you can help them. No lengthy preambles are necessary.

- Make sure you include women as well as men in your copy.

- Don't hesitate to end with prepositions. We all talk this way. There is, therefore, nothing wrong with using them in your marketing documents.

- Use sentence fragments. Again, we use them all the time when we talk. If they help increase the conversational quality of your writing, it is probably a good idea to use them.

- Begin sentences with conjunctions like "And", "But", and "Or." Long sentences are difficult to wade through. When your sentence gets too long, rather than linking it with a conjunction, simply start the next sentence with one. It's perfectly acceptable and is inherently more interesting than a long, ponderous sentence.

- Use bullets, numbers, indentations, and other breakers. Look how this section — and indeed this entire book — is arranged. It is packed with punctuating devices, methods which set off important bits of information and which simultaneously make it easier for you, the reader, to follow what is being said.

Don't hesitate to use:

- <u>underlining</u>
- CAPITAL LETTERS
- **boldface type**
- *italics*
- colored type (at what it would cost to demonstrate this, you'll have to imagine the color of your choice!)
- ➩➩ arrows and notes in the margin ➩➩
- reverse type
- boxed copy.

Your task is to indicate the importance of any body of copy to your would-be customer, and then make it easy for him to read it — and take action to follow it up.

Knowing In Advance Whether Your Copy Will Work

Too many people write copy and have no idea whether it will actually work with their client-prospects. You should know in advance whether it will work. Check what you've written against the following points:

- Does the copy logically follow from your headline? If you want your prospects to have confidence that you'll follow through and give them what they expect, what you say you'll provide, start right away in your copy. Give the information your headline leads them to expect.

- Is the copy interesting? Or it is deadly dull? Face it. Most copy is deadly. It doesn't grip the prospect's attention. Yet let me tell you something. The problem the prospect wants to solve is of gripping interest to him. Sometimes, indeed, it is of actual life and death interest, and as such is compelling to him.

If your copy is dull and lifeless, the prospect is right to deduce that you don't understand his situation, don't fathom his interest and his need for a solution, and won't do what you can as expeditiously as you can to solve his problem. Under the circumstances, is it surprising he decides not to do business with you?

- Is your copy specific? Use real numbers and concrete examples. Specificity is one of the keystones of convincing marketing copy. Whenever possible, provide concrete numbers and examples to lower the anxiety of your prospects and convince them that you can solve their problem. What do you think is better: "Jeffrey Lant has a lot of experience raising money for nonprofit organizations," or "Jeffrey Lant has spent the last 8 years working with 77 health and human service nonprofit organizations for which he has raised over $10 million." You tell me!

- Is your copy easy to read? This point follows directly from the one above. If what you have written is not easy to read, it cannot be interesting. I live in a neighborhood where everyone is trying to persuade everyone else how bright he is, how interesting, how substantial, how important. As a result, most people hereabouts come across as stilted, pompous and self-centered. Don't let this happen to you! Before you let a single marketing sentence loose in the world, go through it with a blue pencil and start cutting words out of it. The more words you cut, the better your copy is going to be, because it will be inherently more interesting and easier to read.

- Is your copy believable? Too many marketers make claims which are just too exaggerated to be believable. Don't be one of them! Of course, there are people in the world who are looking for get-rich-quick schemes, or their equivalent in every field. They'll be disappointed that you haven't promised to deliver the moon for a nickel. But they are not your audience — not now or ever. Focus on the reasonable prospect. The prospect who knows it takes time, commitment, and treasure to achieve the result he desires. This person will act when you've convinced him that what he wishes to achieve can be achieved in a reasonable fashion. Frankly, this is just the kind of customer/client we all want — and that we should work hard to get and retain.

- Is your copy persuasive? Ask yourself if you'd buy a used car from the person presenting himself in your copy? Have you really demonstrated that you understand the prospect's problems, the prospect's anxieties about solving this problem, the benefits the prospect wishes to achieve (including the Ultimate Benefit for which he really is striving)?

Have you conclusively demonstrated that you know how to solve his problem and that you have either a product or a series of service-related techniques which will enable the prospect to achieve his objectives? Have you shown the prospect that you have had meaningful successes in the past with similar problems and, therefore, that this prospect can have a reasonable certainty of achieving similar success with your product or service? If you can answer these questions satisfactorily, then and only then can you say you have written persuasive copy.

- Is your copy concise? It could probably be shorter— and if it can be shorter, it should be shorter.

- Is your copy meaningful? Does it have any real relevance to the prospect? In other words, does it really address the real-life problems, anxieties and aspirations of your prospect? Is every line directed not at making you look good, grand, important and significant but instead aimed at the prospect's self- interest? Ask yourself, "What does this line, this word, this phrase, have to do with my prospect? Does it convince him I understand his problem and can solve it with my product or service?" If you are unsure cut it out, because if you don't know why that bit of information has been included, I can guarantee you your prospect won't know either.

- Does your copy flow smoothly? Face it. You are writing an interesting feature document in which there are two protagonists: you and your prospect. The prospect's attention has to be snagged immediately, and he must want to read on, lured by the prospect that you have what you really should have, namely a solution to his problem in the form of your product or service.

Are there annoying breaks in your copy? Are the words too long? Are the passages without a break? Is there just too much prose on a page, making it look like a daunting task to get through it? If so, your copy doesn't flow — and your prospect will not finish it. May not, indeed, start it, thus depriving you both of the connection you must have.

- Does your copy call for action? The entire point of any marketing document you write will be lost unless the prospect takes action upon finishing it. When the prospect finishes your document, he must feel excited, must understand that you understand his problem and have worked hard to come up with a solution that he can implement with either your product or service.

Think of it! When a prospect realizes this, he must be thrilled. Thrilled that at last he has connected with someone who, in this impersonal world, actually cares enough about him to have created this solution. And in the midst of being so thrilled, the prospect must be prepared to accept your call to action. What, after all, is the point of getting your prospect excited if you are not prepared to move the prospect to the next step in the sales sequence: to picking up the phone, filling out and sending in a coupon, writing a check and mailing it to you? What indeed!

Love Letters And Goat Breeders

In time you'll develop a feeling for whether you've written brisk, action-oriented, persuasive copy. Until you do, review your copy in the light of the preceding guidelines and these two key points:

- Write all your copy as if you were writing a love letter. Love letters are, of course, the ultimate marketing documents. Imagine the immensity and importance of the task of trying to persuade someone to spend his life with you! This is the kind of enthusiasm, excitement and passion which should emanate from all your other marketing documents, too. Your objective is to sweep your prospect off his feet and make him love you. Don't aim for anything less. When you've finished a marketing document, apply the Love Letter Test to it. Have you done what you could to engender the utmost enthusiasm, even love, in your prospect? If not, your copy needs to be improved.

- Or try this. To test whether you have written meaningful or futile marketing copy, try a simple test I've developed. Add the words "goat breeder" to the end of any marketing sentence, paragraph or document. If you are not marketing to goat breeders (for some of you may be!) and the section still makes sense, you have failed to write precisely-targeted marketing copy. Instead what you have written could apply to anyone and so does not definitely apply to the people you are trying to motivate. Your copy needs to be rewritten before it will entice your prospects. Try it. The Goat Breeder Test is an infallible guide to detecting meaningless marketing copy, which may sound good but is meant for nobody in particular. Winning marketing copy is precisely directed copy.

The Document Formats You Need And When To Use Them

Once you've got your modules and have reworked them along the lines of the points listed above, you are ready to go to work on the actual documents themselves, those bits of paper you'll get into the hands of your prospects which urge them to take action. But what format should you use?

Usually a small business, nonprofit organization or independent professional has two marketing documents: a brochure and a card. These may or may not be enough depending on whom you are trying to reach and what they need to know about your product or service. Therefore, in deciding which document formats to use, you ought to consider the following:

- Brochure
- Business Card
- Précis
- Success Case(s)
- Features/Benefit List
- Competitor Comparison Listing
- Company Capabilities Statement
- Question-Answer Brochure

Building, Molding, And Shaping Your Persuasive Marketing Documents

The best marketing documents, the documents which will get your prospects to take action and buy your product and service to solve their problem, are not written off the top of your head. They are carefully crafted in response to what you know about the problems and anxieties of your buyers and what they need to know about you to take expeditious action.

Building Your Persuasive Brochure

There is nothing "standard" about the brochure I am about to describe for you, except, perhaps, its size. Your brochure should:

- Attract with a cover headline. Put a headline on your brochure which indicates that you understand the prospect's problem and can provide a solution. Make it crisp, to the point, and not about you;

- Start with a problem list. Inside, list the kinds of problems (in priority order going from most important to least important) your prospects have — problems, of course, that you can solve with your product or service. Remember: people are buying you for your ability to provide them with a solution;

- Indicate that you (your company, nonprofit organization, product or service) can provide the solution to these problems;

- List the problem-solving products or services you have available. Describe them in terms of the benefits customers get when they use them, not the features that each is composed of;

- Provide information about others who have used these products and services successfully, who have solved problems similar to those the prospect has;

- Provide information (if you are selling a service) on the people who will solve the prospect's problems — on the successes they have previously had with similar problems;

- Provide complete directions about how the prospect can follow up, to whom he'll speak and when he can call. The name of the game here is "complete".

- Indicate that additional information is available in case the prospect wants or needs to know more. This information may include a features/benefit list, a précis, success cases, and capabilities statement. Always let the prospect know that you have thought through his possible objections and have other information available in case he needs it before he can make up his mind.

The Question-Answer Brochure

The question-answer brochure, as its name suggests, is made up of question-answer modules, questions that your prospects might have about your product or service and your precise answers to them. This brochure is arranged logically and should contain answers to the following kinds of questions:

- Do you have the following problems? (List them.)

- Do you want to achieve the following results? (List them.)

- If you do, then our product/service can probably help.

- What is (name of product/service)?

- How does it solve your problems?

- What are the benefits of this product/service?

- Has anyone else worked with this product/service successfully? What happened to him?

- Have satisfied customers provided testimonials about the product/service?

- Who are the people you'll work with in getting the successful results you want? What have they done in the past that leads you, the prospect, to feel confident they can help you get the results you want?

- What are the exact features of the product/service?

- Can I (the prospect) try your product/service in a limited way before committing myself totally? What happens if I want a money-back guarantee, a refund or decide to end the contract?

- Can I have a demonstration or schedule a meeting to learn more? Whom do I contact?

- What happens then?

- What do you need to know about me (the prospect), my problem and the objective I want to achieve before we go any farther? (If you need to get information from your prospect in order to make a successful presentation, this is a good time to request it. Don't wing it. If you need information, ask for it.)

- Do you (the seller) have different options available to help me solve this problem? (If you have different ways available of solving the prospect's problems, this is the time to lay them out — to let the prospect know you have several ways available to solve his problems, presumably involving differing commitments on his part up to and including price.)

- "This all sounds good but I (the prospect) am still unsure. I need to solve my problem but want to make sure I'm not wasting my time and money. What should I do?" Indicate that you understand this caution and are quite capable of providing further information about how your product/service can solve the prospect's problems, necessary referrals to satisfied clients, testimonials and additional information in (name the other documents you have available with further information and how the prospect can get them). Indicate that you want to make sure the prospect is happy because you are not looking for a one-time-only-sale but an ongoing relationship and want to begin on the right foot.

- "What do I do now?" If you are ready to order, here's how to do so. (Now provide complete order information with details about how to call in orders, the credit cards you take, when the prospect may call — I hope it's 24 hours a day! — and everything else the prospect needs to be able to take action **NOW**, even though **NOW** may be 3 a.m.

If, however, the prospect is not ready to order now, then make sure you have provided the name of a person whom he may call or write for further information. This should be a specific person whose telephone number and address are provided. If the prospect has read this far in your sales document, he is very much a qualified prospect and if the sale is lost at this point, it's your fault — not the prospect's!

- Conclude this document with a flourish. Tell the prospect you want to work with him in solving his problems and achieving the beneficial result he wants to achieve. Reiterate one or more of the leading benefits that can be gained by working with you. It is always a good idea to remind the prospect about precisely what he is buying from you — which is not, please remember, a product or service but some much more exalted benefit of far more attractiveness to the prospect than the money it costs him to get it.

A Few More Words About The Question-Answer Document

Many people ask me if there is not too much information in the Question-Answer Brochure, if people will really wade through so much detail. My answer is an unequivocal yes. People who have the problem that you can solve, people, that is, who are qualified prospects and not merely browsers, want to know as much as possible about how you can help them. Is this surprising?

Think of how few people you meet really take an interest in your problems and objectives and can offer you something substantial to solve them. Think how glad you are to connect with these people. If one of them comes along, you want to know as much as possible, don't you, about how he works and what he might do for you? If you agree with this, why should your prospects be any different?

Print this document on gray, beige or ivory laid paper to give it a serious, professional look and feel. You should use black ink and a solid (non-eccentric) type face.

Précis

As you are only too well aware, most documents people receive get thrown away as soon as they receive them. This is a problem all people in marketing live with — and have to learn to solve. That's where the Précis comes in. The Précis' *raison d'etre* is to provide your prospects with information of such importance that they'll want to keep it on hand, thereby ensuring the longevity of your marketing documents. But how, pray, does this miracle take place?

The Précis is composed of 10 bullets which provide your prospects with useful information about the problem they want to solve — and which you are in business to help them solve. It is a fast-moving, information-dense document usually composed of bullets of about 50 to 75 words each, telling your prospects what they need to accomplish but not how to accomplish it. For the "how" they need to buy your product or service. Nonetheless, the "what" information is sufficiently valuable for them to want to keep it on hand.

Let's build a précis around my fund-raising books and services for nonprofit organizations to give you an example of what I have in mind.

Opening Your Précis

The précis, like all marketing documents, begins by focusing on the problem(s) the prospect wishes to solve and on the benefits (including the Ultimate Benefits) he wishes to achieve. Importantly, it also contains information about what can go wrong if the prospect doesn't follow good, solid advise in attempting to solve his problem (*i.e.*, if he doesn't buy your product/service).

Thus, here's the opening section to a paragraph directed to executive directors of nonprofit organizations. It is most important that you know precisely to whom you are directing this précis (whose problems, that is, you want to solve) and speak to them particularly.

"Of course you want to raise money for your nonprofit organization. You may want to rehabilitate your building — or acquire a new one. You certainly have existing programs which call for funds — and I'm sure you have ideas about how you could improve your services, if only you had the money to do that. Then there are those nagging, ongoing operating expenses like salaries, rent, heat, electricity and all the others that have to be paid, month-in, month-out. Finally, wouldn't it be nice to begin to acquire an endowment fund or to augment the one you've already got?"

"Successful fund-raising can do all this for you and more. Yet, as I'm sure you know, fund-raising can often be a difficult, aggravating, frustrating business — with no guarantee that you will raise the money you need, the money that will enable you to provide your important services to the people who need them. That's why I've developed this handy check-list for successful fund-raising. You may not be doing any fund-raising just now, but keep this check list on hand for when you begin.

- Plan Ahead. Everyone is in favor of planning. In theory. But successful fund-raising is based on it. If you plan to begin your annual fund-raising in September, you need to begin planning in January.

- Involve Your Board of Directors. No organizational fund-raising can be successful until it has the full and enthusiastic support of your Board of Directors. This means involving them in the planning process to ensure that once you have determined what capital, project, operating and endowment objectives you want to reach, the Board will approve and support them.

- Develop Persuasive Documents. Bad documents hurt whether you are approaching corporations, foundations, or individuals. Make sure your documents are punchy, persuasive, and persistent.

- Target Corporations and Foundations. Unsophisticated organizations send their proposals out to anyone whose address they can get. This is unwise and expensive and will not produce the funds you need. Spend time picking the right corporations and foundations which you know, in advance and through your homework, that are interested in the work you do — and may want to support it.

- Follow Up Every Proposal You Send Out. As you may not be surprised to learn, people are not waiting expectantly for your letters, hoping to give you money. Fund-raising is a business of persistence and persuasion. Follow-up every letter or proposal you send to a prospective donor, individual or institutional. If you don't have the time to follow-up, don't bother to contact them in the first place.

- Keep Thorough Records Of Every Contact You Make With Every Potential Funding Source. Most nonprofit organizations severely neglect their corporate memory. Imagine how helpful it would have been for you had your predecessor kept records of all the corporations, foundations, and individuals he had approached. Your life would have been a lot easier. Now that it's your turn, keep extensive records of all your interactions with prospective funding sources. It will make your current fund-raising job easier and will be a godsend for your successor.

- Follow-Up Every Proposal That's Turned Down By A Funding Source. That's right. Successful fund-raising involves persistence. Most people ask for a contribution prematurely in the cultivation/solicitation process and abruptly stop dealing with donor prospects if they are declined. Wise fund-raisers persist. This often means having to turn a "No" into a "Yes!". To do so successfully means asking a donor (particularly foundations, corporations and major individual donor prospects) who has just declined to contribute, why they made this decision. What they tell you in response will provide you with what you need to know to continue — and develop — your relationship.

- Develop A Coordinating Committee. Successful fund-raising means raising money from lots of different groups in a coordinated fashion. Local small businesses, professionals, civic organizations, staff, past Board members, organizational clients — and others — all need to be solicited to provide resources so your services can continue. The work of overseeing the many committees which must necessarily become involved in this process is done by a central Coordinating Committee. Make sure you have one.

- Send Out Fund-Raising Letters. Many agencies send out an annual fund-raising appeal, but for most organizations a single letter — all too often sent during the December holidays — is inadequate. Instead, develop a strategy which brings your need for funds to provide needed services to interested individuals not just once but several times during the year.

- Differentiate Between Those Who Have Previously Supported You And Those Who Have Not Yet Done So. People who know about your organization and are already supporting you should be approached in a different way from those who may not yet know what you do and have not yet supported you. Make sure, therefore, you produce different letters to each group and follow-up in different ways. Remember: those who are supporting you now are your most valuable contacts."

Notice that there are, so far, nine different bullets. Nine points which are useful to the organization. Please note that these bullets contain information which tells what the organization needs to do to make its fund-raising efforts successful, but does not tell them how to accomplish it. That's where your product or service comes in and that's why the tenth bullet of any paragraph is always the "Buy Me!" bullet. Thus:

"• Work With A Good Development Consultant. A good consultant will help you with the strategy and tactics of successful fund-raising. Will help with the planning process, work with your Board of Directors, develop persuasive fund-raising documents, identify corporations, foundations and individuals who ought to receive them; make sure you go to the right places seeking the right amounts, develop a sensible community fund-raising effort and create the right kinds of letters and other documents you need to make it successful. All this, in fact, and more is precisely what Dr. Jeffrey Lant can do for you.

You may already know about Jeffrey. He has worked successfully with a wide variety of nonprofit organizations to raise the money they need for capital, project, operating and endowment objectives. Each of his clients has been significantly better off after working with him than they were beforehand. The executive directors he has worked with will be happy to provide enthusiastic recommendations for what he has helped them accomplish.

His methods are contained in his well-known book DEVELOPMENT TODAY: A FUND RAISING GUIDE FOR NONPROFIT ORGANIZATIONS, a step-by-step plan for successful fund-raising. It is $28.95 postpaid from Jeffrey at 50 Follen St., Suite 507, Cambridge, MA 02138 or by calling (617) 547-6372 with your MasterCard or Visa.

If your current fund-raising efforts are lagging behind your goals or if you want to plan for a successful fund-raising effort for your organization, call Jeffrey to receive further information about how his service works and how he will work with you to raise the money you need. Fund-raising need not be the frustrating, time-consuming, uncertain activity it so often is. If this is how you feel, take action now. Call Jeffrey at (617) 547-6372 and let him help you begin getting the money you need to provide the services so that those who benefit from your work will keep on doing so."

Notes On The Précis

The tenth bullet should always contain information on:

- what you want the prospect to do;
- when you want the prospect to do it;
- how you want the prospect to follow up;

- how the prospect can acquire your product (complete order information, please!);

- what further information you have available if the prospect does not make a decision to purchase based on this single document.

In this bullet, too, you must work to diminish any anxieties or reasonable doubts the prospect may have about your ability to solve his problem. Hence, there must always be information about how you have already successfully solved similar problems for others similarly situated. It is perfectly permissible to use testimonials and recommendations to prove that you can, indeed, solve the prospect's problem — anything that lowers his anxieties about you and makes it perfectly obvious to him that you are the right person with the right skills and the certified track record who can help him solve his problem.

Variations On The Précis Format

A good précis should fit on a single side of a single 8 1/2" by 11" sheet of paper. If you write as much as I do, of course, that may mean you'll have to have your précis typeset! Either way, it leaves the backside of the paper free for further use. I suggest using third-party recommendations, including testimonial quotes from satisfied users/customers, articles about you, your products and services (if you don't have any now you will after you've finished Chapter 6 on unabashed promotion) and excerpts from articles by you, articles which underscore the importance of the points you've made in the précis or which provide additional useful information to your prospect.

Now you have a very impressive-looking marketing document indeed, and one which your prospects will not only want to keep on hand — but need to, thereby ensuring a much longer life for this document (and hence the chance it may actually be used!) than most marketing documents have. They generally last no more than the time it takes to open an envelope, for the prospect to glance at them and throw them away. Since you do this yourself, you know that takes under a minute!

Final Words On The Précis

- Print your précis on colored paper. As with your brochure and question-answer brochure, select a color that will underscore the importance of the information you are providing people: gray, beige, or ivory laid.

- Print about 1000 of these to start. The cost of a précis is very, very low. A two-sided 8 1/2" by 11" precis costs about $60 per thousand in my expensive neighborhood and probably less in yours.

The Success Case

Whether you are selling a product or service, prospects want to know who else has used it successfully. The first rule of successful marketing, therefore, is to make sure your product/service is *used* by someone — and used successfully. This can be a problem when you are just starting out, when you have a new product or service. But I'll be telling you in chapters that lie ahead just how you can get your products/services reviewed, and thus build the necessary constituents of the Success Case.

The Success Case says, very simply:

- Someone just like you had a problem just like you do.

- This person wondered, just as you are wondering, whether his problem could be solved and whether our product/service could solve it.

- This person wonders no more, because the product/service did work for him.

- Moreover, we intend to tell you not only that it worked but also about the context in which it worked — that is, what benefit it provided *vis-à-vis* the benefits others were achieving (or not achieving) at the same time. The last bit I call the Context Statement, and it is crucial to the success of your Success Case.

Here's what a typical Success Case might look like if I wanted to sell both services and products to one of my designated nonprofit client prospect constituencies, visiting nurses agencies.

Your Colleague, the Natick Visiting Nurses, Is Raising Money They Need For Capital, Project, Operating, And Endowment Objectives From Corporations, Foundations, And Individuals. So Can You!

Does having the money you need to carry out much-needed building repairs, for paying for the free care you provide citizens in your town, for covering operating expenses, and for building an endowment sound good to you? I bet it does. It was equally important to your colleague the Natick Visiting Nurses, especially Executive Director Judi Boyko, and members of their Board of Directors.

Like you and your Board, however, they wondered whether the time, effort and expense they put into fund-raising would get them the money they needed to do what they wanted. Like you, they are not particularly keen on fund-raising, seeing it like most people as an often frustrating and certainly aggravating activity. So they thought about getting help.

They wondered, however, whether a consultant *really* would help them — or would simply be another expense they didn't want and couldn't afford. Well, let me tell you something. Now they know the right consultant can make a world of difference!

The Natick VNA retained Dr. Jeffrey Lant as fund-raising counsel 8 months ago to assist them in raising money for making improvements on their headquarters, to pay for the free care which was a great drain on their revenues, and to augment their endowment fund, as well as provide other money they needed. The 12-month fund-raising objective was $80,000.

Since retaining Dr. Lant, $65,000 has already been raised from corporations, foundations, and individuals and it is now expected the original objective will be realized. But *already* the sum raised is over 8 times what the Natick VNA had raised in a typical fund-raising effort. Think of it! Eight times! And at a cost of only about 10 cents on the dollar, which includes consulting fees. In short, the experience has already been very profitable for the Natick VNA.

With the money that has already been raised, the Natick VNA intends to reshingle the roof of its headquarters and make certain long-needed improvements in its attic space (transforming it into a modern work area). It has already provided specialized training to its personnel, and has provided additional free care to area residents. In addition, a significant sum has been put into the Natick VNA endowment, a fund which will continue to generate money in perpetuity for the free care program. Isn't this a result which you, too, would like to have?

The credit for this result goes to many people, including the Natick VNA Board; Judi Boyko, Executive Director; and to the fund-raising consultant, Dr. Jeffrey Lant, whose precise step-by-step techniques have been followed in approaching corporations, foundations, and individuals.

You may already know about these techniques. They are found in explicit detail in Dr. Lant's classic book on how to organize successful fund-raising, **DEVELOPMENT TODAY: A FUND RAISING GUIDE FOR NONPROFIT ORGANIZATIONS.** You'll find this book helpful if you decide to organize your own fund-raising effort or to work with Dr. Lant. You can order a copy (it's $28.95, postpaid) through Jeffrey Lant Associates, Inc., 50 Follen St., Suite 507, Cambridge, MA 02138 or by calling (617) 547-6372 with your MasterCard or Visa.

For further information about Dr. Lant's work with the Natick VNA, you may contact Judi Boyko, Executive Director, at (617) 653-3081 or Dr. Lant at (617) 547-6372. You may also wish to call Dr. Lant to see about how he can work with you to raise the money you need for your capital, project, operating, and endowment needs. Call now for information on how you can get a no cost, no obligation meeting which will start you on the road to successfully raising the money you need. Call today. Fund-raising is often a long, difficult, and frustrating process. Starting early will help ensure both the result you want and your continuing ability to provide your services to the people who need them.

More About Success Cases

- Success Cases are built on the presumption that most people are cautious, that they'll take action on their own behalf only when they are reasonably sure they are not gambling their money and other resources but intelligently risking them. The facts in the success case tell them that you understand their problem and can — with your product or service — help solve it, precisely because you have already done so with someone else, someone who is named and who is available to provide additional information to the prospect should the prospect need it.

- What happens, however, if you cannot provide this kind of precise additional information? You do the best you can! Everyone who uses your product or service is not going to want to be identified as a successful user. The best reason for not wanting to be so identified is because your product or service deals with a delicate human situation/problem which the user does not want generally known.

But this is where your creativity comes in! Say you sell a product that stops bed-wetting. I can scarcely imagine a satisfied client (be that parent or child) who's going to want to provide you with the kind of information you need for a Success Case. So instead, get the endorsement of some physicians or child psychologists, who'll say precisely what you need to have said — and will provide you with the kind of authoritative endorsement you need. If you have this kind of endorsement, the actual cases you use in your Success Case can — and should — be anonymous. But, as you see, you still use them because now the anonymity doesn't matter and, indeed, establishes you as a person of sense and sensibility.

- Success Cases provide as much specific information about what your buyer/user/client has achieved as possible, without telling the prospect anything about how you achieved these things. It should be enough — and usually is — for the prospect to know that you have achieved these striking results. He isn't ordinarily interested in how they came about. Knowing that your product or service brings about such satisfying results is quite enough for him to want to go ahead to do what is necessary to get them, too. Do not feel obligated to provide the prospect with the "how" information. If he really wants to know that, he will; when he buys your product or service and begins using it himself.

- You can create a Success Case the minute there is success to report. Those of you selling services may feel constrained to wait until your relationship with the client is over before using that client and his situation to attract new clients. Don't be silly! The minute you have an attractive success on hand, a success others would like to duplicate, go ahead and use it. Of course, be aware that whether you use the success while you are still working on creating it or whether you wait until your relationship with the client is over, you still must secure the client's permission to cite it in your marketing documents.

A Few Words On Securing Client Endorsements

So long as you are in business, you are in the business of securing endorsements from satisfied clients and users of your product for use in your own marketing efforts to attract new users/clients.

- When sending out your products, make sure you enclose a brief form or letter asking people in the warmest possible terms to tell you what they think of your product. Because people often have difficulty responding to an open-ended question, provide them with choices. "Did you find this book ❑ Helpful ❑ Very Helpful ❑ Not helpful at all?" Always conclude, however, with an open-ended question which allows them to provide a quotation which you can use later: "Please tell me in your own words what you think about this product and what it has done for you." Give them some incentive for responding to you. If I were selling my book **THE CONSULTANT'S KIT**, for example, I'd tell people that if they wrote back to let me know what they thought of it, I'd send them a article on the 10 leading mistakes consultants make — and how to avoid them. To people interested in establishing a consulting business (the people, in short, who buy **THE CONSULTANT'S KIT**) this would be a sufficiently meaningful premium to ensure response.

Only *after* they had responded and (assuming what they said would help attract and interest future clients) would I respond to them and ask for permission to use their remarks in my advertising. And the letter I'd send to them requesting this permission would be warm, personable and directly from me. In other words, an Esteemed Colleague letter, letting them know how important they are to me and to my business. Such letters, of course, are irresistible — as they are intended to be.

- If you are selling a service, request such a testimonial from your clients at a moment when they are happy, at a moment when you have helped secure some success for them. This need not — often should not — be at the conclusion of a relationship with a client. Do it when the success is new and the client is happy about it. Don't wait.

Tom Hopkins, whose sales training programs are now legendary, suggests that this endorsement be put on audio tape, so that you can play it for future prospects. If you use this technique, make sure you:

- Provide the person giving the endorsement with the points you'd like covered in it. These points should include the period of time you worked with the client, the kinds of services you provided, the way in which you provided them, the results which were achieved, the importance of the results to the client, and information about what was happening at the same time in the industry. In other words, if you managed to achieve success at a time others were struggling, future clients need to be made aware of this fact. Do not rely on the imagination and creativity of the client to come up with the kinds of topics which will do you the most good in future sales interviews. Prompt the client yourself.

- Identify the client by name and position. Remember: you want future prospects to say, "That person is like me. That person works for the same kind of organization, has the same kind of title, and the same kinds of problems." If your prospect recognizes this similarity between the person providing the endorsement on the audio cassette and himself, you are way ahead in the game of getting your next client. This information can either be given by you at the beginning of the cassette or provided by the client. (Remember: you'll ask him to give it and what you need will be included on a list right in front of his nose during the taping.)

N.B. Make sure you follow the same techniques when you are requesting a written letter of endorsement/testimonial. To rely on the imagination and creativity of those who do not have the vested interest you do in securing future clients is not very smart.

Variations On The Success Case

Face it. You probably deal only with a limited number of products and services. While you need a separate Success Case for each, you can gather a number of endorsements for any single product or service in a single case. Be creative about how you let people know about these endorsements.

If you have a retail outlet, put people's comments in the window under a headline, "Here's what our satisfied customers say about 'Grandma's Cookies'... You'll love 'em, too! Come in and see!!!" As is well known, people love the look and sound of their names. So ask people for their opinions — and then display their comments prominently, if possible with their names. Show the customer that you value him and his opinion — even to the extent of publicly posting it. That customer will not only come back. He'll also tell his friends. After all, you've got to be running a great place since you recognize his worth!

The same principle, of course, applies when selling a service. Give people in insurance testimonials and endorsements from people in insurance. Give people in the media testimonials from others in the media. People they might know — but whom they can empathize with, even if they don't know them.

I call this document The Success Cluster. It gives the prospect the feeling that lots of other people just like him are happy with what you are doing. This reduces his anxiety and makes him keen to join this joyous, productive bandwagon.

The Features/Benefit Chart

This document is easy to explain. Part of the information you gathered for your modules dealt with the features of your product/service, what it is, how it works, and what it does and the benefits of each feature. As I said then, each feature must have a benefit — or what's the purpose of the feature in the first place?

The Features/Benefit Chart should be a complete listing of every feature of your product/service and the corresponding benefit. Think how helpful this chart would be — and how sad it is that you have probably never seen one in your life! Here's what one might look like:

The Features and Benefits Of Using **THE UNABASHED SELF-PROMOTER'S GUIDE: WHAT EVERY MAN, WOMAN, CHILD AND ORGANIZATION IN AMERICA NEEDS TO KNOW ABOUT GETTING AHEAD BY EXPLOITING THE MEDIA**

FEATURE	**BENEFIT**
366 pages long	"Complete" is the word here. You get everything you need to know to promote your product or service through the free media — radio, television, newspapers, magazines and newsletters. You don't need anything else. Precisely what you need is included. All is readily available at your fingertips.
Large 8 1/2" by 11" pages	Not only is the print easy to read but the book is chock full of a samples section of documents which will help get your message out to the media. These samples — which include a log of media outlets contacted, letters, and forms — can be photocopied and used by you — as is. You don't have to change the format. A tremendous time-savings.
Precise step-by-step directions tell you how to approach radio and television programs to get your product/service featured.	To market your products/services, you either have to use paid advertising or free media — your own money, or someone else's. Which do you prefer? **THE UNABASHED SELF-PROMOTER'S GUIDE** tells you precisely how to target the right radio and television outlets, what materials to send (and includes samples of them you can use). It tells you how to follow-up everything you send; what to do when the media people don't respond, and what to do when you do get on the air to make maximum use of your appearance to sell more of your products and services.
Step-by-step guidelines on how to get articles about yourself, your products and services inprint media — magazines, newspapers, and newsletters.	If you say good things about yourself, your product and service (as you do with advertising), people say, "Well, of course he's going to say good things. It's his product/service." But if other people say good things about your product or service, it's a public endorsement. Don't you think people are more likely to believe this? **THE UNABASHED SELF-PROMOTER'S GUIDE** tells you precisely what you need to know, and includes all the document forms you need, including letters to send to the media and guidelines for following up your correspondence to get results, to get articles about you, your product/service, articles which constitute valuable third-party endorsements you can use over and over again.

Tips To Producing A Persuasive Features/Benefit Chart

- Lead off with your strongest features and your correspondingly strongest benefits. People want to know right away what you've got and whether the benefit is a significant one for them.

- Ten features and benefits are ordinarily adequate. Remember: those prospects who act rationally should by then have a pretty clear indication that this product/service is for them. Those who act emotionally have more than enough information about why this purchase (which they'll make for other reasons) can be defended logically. You've given them all the ammunition they'll need to use on themselves after they've already decided to buy!

- Keep your Features/Benefit Chart to one side of an 8 1/2" by 11" paper. Use the other side for endorsements, testimonials and third-party media validation, including media comments about your product/service and articles (and article excerpts) by and about you.

- Use a bright attractive paper. Canary yellow is a good one. You have something to be proud about with your product/service. This Features/Benefits Chart clearly establishes that — so use a bright, cheerful paper color and bold typography with clear, direct headlines.

N.B. An extra added benefit of the Features/Benefit Chart is that any anxiety you have about your product/service should be laid to rest, including any hesitation you may have about presenting it to people. Here, in one easy-to-read, easy-to-present document is all the information people really need about what you are selling — and why it is clearly in their own best interest to buy and use it. If your prospects agree that the benefits are, indeed, real, then you will have no trouble selling the product/service. They'll convince themselves they need to use it.

The Competitor Comparison Chart

All of us have competitors. That much is clear. But not all of us need to use a Competitor Comparison Chart. The only time you need to use such a chart is when you are in a situation with a recognizable competitor offering a product or service most people would use first because of its superior name recognition and well-established marketing position.

A Competitor Comparison Chart is never used by an industry leader. Why should they dignify their competitors by giving them any attention whatsoever, even by drawing attention to the weaknesses of the competitors? It is only used by those who are attempting to take on an industry leader and want to point out in the bluntest possible way how far superior their own product is to the one being offered by the leader.

A Competitor Comparison Chart is a relative of the Features/Benefit Chart. It lists the features of your product/service and the benefits and then points out whether the competition has these features or not (it had better be not!). Go back to my illustration above. Say that my **UNABASHED SELF-PROMOTER'S GUIDE** was competing against a book entitled *The Complete Guide to Publicity*. Here's what the Competitor Comparison Chart would look like:

Feature of THE UNABASHED SELF-PROMOTER'S GUIDE

Step-by-step information giving you precise guidelines on how to target the right radio and television shows for your product/service. Tells you exactly what information they'll need to know about you, your product/service, and how to present it. Provides complete document samples you can use. Tells you how to approach radio and television personnel; what to do when they don't return your calls, and how to handle the interview once you have made the appointment, so you get the maximum benefit. Contains over 100 practical suggestions, with complete step-by-step details on how to use them to your profit.

Benefit of THE UNABASHED SELF-PROMOTER'S GUIDE

Your objective is to get free air time to promote your products and services and to know precisely what to do so that you make the best possible use of your time. This is exactly the benefit you'll get when you use THE **UNABASHED SELF-PROMOTER'S GUIDE.** Complete is the word here. You won't miss an opportunity. Won't be embarrassed by not knowing what to do and will sell more of your product —without committing your scarce advertising dollars.

Comparison With Competitor Product

"The Complete Guide to Publicity" is only 60% as long as **THE UNABASHED SELF-PROMOTER'S GUIDE.** While the subject of how to get your product/service on to radio and television shows is mentioned, you are not given the precise step-by-step guidelines you need. It is easy to make a mistake when approaching broadcast personnel, and thereby lose your chance of getting precious airtime. We provide you with the exact step-by-step information you need. *The Complete Guide To Publicity* doesn't. Do you want to take a chance? Or do you want to have what you need when you need it? You tell me!

You get the idea.

A Few Words About The Competitor Comparison Chart

- If you are the industry leader and wish to put together such a chart, you needn't mention your competitors by name. Just point out what you've got and what your competitors do not have. Refer to your competitors generically.

- If you do name competitors and point out the inadequacies of their products/services, make absolutely sure you know what you are talking about. If you make a mistake and the prospect finds out, your overall credibility is necessarily lowered. If you make a mistake and the competitor finds out, at the very least he'll ask you to cease and desist from distributing that erroneous information. After that, in our litigious society, it's anyone's guess what could happen. Be absolutely sure you are correct in what you say!

- Comparison charts can be enormously helpful to prospects and enormously powerful and persuasive marketing tools. So long as the prospect trusts you, he is going to trust the information you gathered. This trust will be helped if you tell the prospect precisely what the benefits are of doing business with your competitors. There is, therefore, no need to run down your competitors. This is a foolish sales technique.

Unless the competitor actually offers no benefits whatsoever (yes, this does happen), you are actually better off pointing out what the competitor can do. Then when you point out what the competitor cannot do, the prospect is the more likely to believe you. You have, after all, been fair. My work convinces me that prospects want to deal with people from whom they can get a straight answer. Indeed, getting that straight answer may be so valuable and important to them that they might even be willing to sacrifice a benefit they could have by buying from someone else for the benefit of continuing to have the advantage of your candor.

- When discussing your competitors, be straightforward about what they can offer. Don't laud. Just present. Make your best case as to what you offer by comparison and why you don't have a given feature that your competitor may be offering. Then be equally direct about the features the competitor is missing, why these are important, and what you are offering the prospect.

Yes, this is the wisest way to build credibility with the prospect, for the real purpose of the Competitor Comparison Chart is to build rapport with the prospect, to show him that you can meet his needs, which the competition cannot. In a situation where your competitors and you each offer the same benefits, if you follow these techniques you are bound to be successful, for you'll have the considerable advantage of the prospect's trust.

The Obstacles/Objections Sheet

Face it. Some of your prospects are going to have objections to buying from you and will have to overcome obstacles to doing so. This is where the Obstacles/Objections Sheet comes in.

By now, you should be well aware of the exact objections that your prospects have to doing business with you. Indeed, one of the secrets to successful marketing is to know the precise objections your customers will offer and to be prepared to deal with them, to make sure you are never surprised.

Thus, begin by keeping an obstacles and objections file. Write down every obstacle and every objection your prospects have about your product/service. This may hurt! We all want to be liked. We all think that our product/service is sublime, don't we? We certainly don't want to think about the objections that people have to it. But unless you know these objections and are thoroughly prepared to deal with them, you are courting failure.

Here are some of the objections to **THE CONSULTANT'S KIT:**

- "It's expensive. $30 is a lot of money to pay for a paperback book."
- "How do I know this book is going to help me? I'm worried I'm going to spend my money and get nothing back of any real value."
- "I'm worried that I don't have what it takes to succeed. Sure it's easy for you, a Harvard Ph.D., but what about me? I don't want to spend my money foolishly."

These are characteristic objections I hear. That's the point. You are in the business of listening for people's objections and then giving people what they need to overcome them. You don't persuade people to overcome their objections. You provide them with the material and information they need, and they'll persuade themselves.

Your Responses

- $30 *is* a lot of money — particularly if you were just buying a paperback book. But you are buying complete step-by-step guidelines to making money from your problem-solving information. You are not merely buying a book. You are instead investing in yourself to create a profit-making business that will give you the satisfaction of profiting from what you know and can do and give you freedom of control over your own time and destiny.

Regard **THE CONSULTANT'S KIT** as an investment, not an expense. If you follow the carefully laid out steps, you'll be able to take what you know and can do and turn it into a profitable part- or full-time business. Remember: you are buying techniques that work, including over 70 pages of specific forms, documents, and formats. All you need to add is your problem-solving knowledge and you're in business!

- Wondering whether this product — or any product — can help you makes good sense. We know this book can work. Already over 26,000 people nationwide in hundreds of consulting fields are profiting from this book. It's the *only* book on consulting specifically recommended by the U.S. Small Business Administration to new and aspiring consultants in any field. It's the only book on consulting recommended by *What Color Is Your Parachute?*, the best selling career-guide ever published, and it's recommended, too, by the *Harvard Guide To Careers*. Moreover, I stand by this product.

If for any reason you don't want it or don't think it will help you, and you want to return it, you have 30 days to do so. When you buy **THE CONSULTANT'S KIT,** you get a complete 30-day money-back guarantee. I know this book — and it's thorough step-by-step practice-building techniques — can help those who are really interested in becoming a successful consultant. If you're one of them, you have absolutely nothing to lose.

- Many people wonder if consulting is right for them and if they can build a successful practice. That's only natural. That's why I include a series of self-assessment exercises in **THE CONSULTANT'S KIT** so you can see if you have what it takes to become a successful consultant in your field. But let me tell you something: the primary requisite is having problem-solving information at your disposal — and knowing how to use it to solve other people's problems. If you've got the problem-solving information your clients need, you have the critical prerequisite to becoming a successful consultant. With this information — and by following the precise step-by-step techniques in **THE CONSULTANT'S KIT**— you can build a lucrative practice. If, however, after you review these exercises you decide you don't have what it takes, or simply don't want to try, return **THE CONSULTANT'S KIT** to me for a complete refund.

See what I mean?

Tips About The Obstacles/Objections Sheet

- Anticipate that price will always be one of the objections. Hit it head on. You must not let your prospects feel they are "buying" a product or service but that they are investing to secure the ultimate benefit(s) they want. What people are really buying from me is job-satisfaction, the satisfaction that comes with helping others, money, and freedom of control over their own time. If $30 will help them achieve these four key life objectives, then it is money exceptionally well invested and anyone with half a brain knows that.

- List the objections in priority order, the one you hear most often first. Again, if your prospect's objection has been satisfactorily answered, there is no reason why he shouldn't take immediate action — always supposing that he has the money he needs to be able to do so. For make no mistake about it; a person who doesn't have the money necessary to buy your product or service was never a prospect in the first place.

- Draw it up in columns. Put the obstacle/objection on the left side of a single 8 1/2" x 11" sheet and your considered response to it on the right. Don't hesitate to underline key points, circle them, put them in CAPITAL LETTERS, or use arrows to direct the prospect's attention to them. It is important that the prospect get the message, and graphics can help you get it across.

- Don't hesitate to use the back side of this form. Fill it up with testimonials, third-party (media) validation, excerpts from articles about your product/service. Tell your prospect, too, that you have other information available which he may find of service, and then list the names of the available documentation.

Company Capabilities Statement

People buying from you want to make sure you can do the job for them, want to make sure you have readily available resources — including personnel, machines, and expertise — to solve their problems. That's where the Capabilities Statement comes in. It provides prospects with detailed information about the kinds of problems you solve and the resources you have available to solve them.

To write a compelling Capabilities Statement you need, first of all, to take an inventory of everything you have available to help solve your prospects' problems. Such an inventory may include, but is not limited to, precise information about:

- Your personnel. Whom do you have available on staff and precisely what problem-solving skills and technical information do they have at their command? As I have said before, when you talk about people, you must be very careful not to fall victim to the Resumé Syndrome, must not merely provide information about where they have been, but the skills they have and the problems they have solved and can solve.

N.B. If you work with independent contractors, you need to ensure that these people are available. Before presenting information to prospects about your capabilities when these capabilities depend to any significant degree on the services of independent contractors, it is very wise to check to make sure these contractors are available to you during this period.

- Your machines. What machines do you have available, and what problems can they solve?

- Your location. Perhaps the location of your business is a key point in your favor. I know it is for me! Being located in the heart of a major urban center just steps away from major transportation and across the street from Harvard University has always been one of my selling points. Make sure you, too, derive the maximum benefit from this capability.

- Your financial resources. For some jobs, your ability to raise the capital you need is a consideration. If it is, and if you can raise it expeditiously, say so.

I'm sure you get the picture.

Tips on the Capabilities Statement

- You can bolster this statement considerably by using endorsements and testimonials along with it. Clearly what prospects want to know is, "Do you have the resources available to solve my problem?" What will help diminish their anxieties, however, is if you clearly indicate that, indeed, you do have these resources and that others in the past have found your use of them satisfactory. The Capabilities Statement, then, should make good use of the endorsements of satisfied customers. In effect you are saying "We have what you want. We had what they wanted. They liked what we did. You'll like what we do for you." A very nice sequence, indeed, and one which should prove convincing to your prospect.

- Keep this statement up-to-date. Pay particular attention to your personnel resources. When an employee completes a new course, for instance, he now has new skills which can help prospects solve their problems. Taking a course *per se* is not important. Having the skills to help clients is, however. Every time someone in your organization acquires a new skill, make sure your Capabilities Statement is updated. Remember: there is no reason for having an employee unless that person is able to solve problems — both for you and for your clients and customers. It is amazing to me both how few employers seem to realize this and how scandalously fewer employees.

Note: It is a superb idea for you to have a Problem-Solving People File. Each individual — including, again, yourself — associated with your organization should be required yearly to list his successes for the year; what he has accomplished and what difference accomplishing this objective meant. He should list the skills he has — and has acquired during the year — and the problems he can now solve. This holds true for whether one is a secretary or chairperson of the board. No one should be considered too grand or exalted for completing this critical task.

Remember: your customers and clients — and, of course, your prospects — are buying solutions, not products, not services. You certainly need to know that your personnel —including, of course, yourself — can deliver these solutions, and this information needs to be readily available to help persuade your prospects to take action. If your prospects clearly understand that you and your personnel can solve their problems, then they will surely want to do business with you. I wish that more employees realized this, for all too often they see their jobs in terms of following routine, not solving prospect and customer problems. Thus, each year, each employee — including you! — should be required to list the skills he has, the problems he can solve, and the people who ought to be interested in having these problems solved. This problem-solving skill file is what really impresses clients and lets them know you can do their job.

The Lowly Business Card

Everything in this chapter has focused on creating marketing documents which demonstrate to the prospect that you know what his problem is and can solve it. That is the essence of marketing. Your business card should also be designed to meet these two objectives.

Your business card should, therefore, not merely include your name, address, telephone number and company name. It should include a check list of the problems you are in business to solve. This check list should appear on the back of your card. It should ask the prospect to check off which subjects are of interest to him and to get back to you for further information. In short, the card should be used as any other prospecting document.

Remember: your job as a marketer is to get into as many of the prospect's brain cells as possible — and stay there. Taking up parts of the prospect's brain with your name, address, and telephone number is not very helpful if the prospect doesn't know what problem(s) you solve. Given that his problem is more interesting to him than your name, if you only include on your card the information about yourself, you are leading with your weaker suit.

For the back of your card, list at least 6 leading problems you solve. Prioritize them in order of which problem most people ask you to solve. Sure, plumbers solve lots of problems, but if most people call on you to put in new bathroom pipes, lead off with that problem-solution. As in all marketing documents, make these problem-solution bullets interesting:

"Here are some of the leading problems we solve. Check off the one(s) in which you are interested and return this card to Dr. Jeffrey Lant or call him. He'll supply you with further information about how we can help solve your problems and help you realize your objectives.

- ❑ We help people launch a profitable part-time/full-time consulting business in any field.
- ❑ We get people off to a fast start in creating profit-making talk programs.
- ❑ We have just what you need to know about raising capital, project, operating, and endowment funds for your nonprofit organizations from corporations, foundations, and individuals."

See what I mean?

Use your card as a prospecting device.

Ask people to check off the subject(s) in which they are interested and either write or call to get further information. If you maintain a mailing list, make sure you ask them to send the necessary information so they can get on it.

Your object is to make your cards interactive, to get the prospects involved in your business by letting them know you have solutions to the problems they want to solve. Even the lowly business card can accomplish this. But do you think most cards do? I'll tell you something: they don't! Most cards say, in effect, "I think I'm swell. And if you want to find out anything about what I do, you have to do all the work yourself." Don't you think that's just plain stupid? Business cards are marketing documents, although they are tiny ones to be sure. They should be designed and used accordingly.

Some people will say, "But what if they do send you back the card? Then they won't have the information about you on hand." Nonsense. You'll be right back in touch with them with information which is far more meaningful, more comprehensive than that contained on the card, and because they have indicated the subjects in which they are interested you can target these precise areas, which is exactly what you ought to be doing.

Tips About Your Business Card

- Don't just provide information about yourself. Ask the prospect to get involved, to tell you what his problems are and, by extension, to let you know what he wants to achieve. Then get right back in touch and show him how you can help him realize his objectives.

- Always put a note on the bottom of your card such as, "Turn this card over and tell us how we may be of service to you... " Don't assume the prospect will be bright enough to turn the card over. Besides, think of how few people actually use this technique. There is precious little reason — just now — why the prospect should turn your card over. But when people start implementing the suggestions in this book, all that will change!

- Always follow up the inquiries that this procedure generates. If you are slow to do so, the prospect can rightly deduce that you are not client-centered. Hence he is quite right to take his business elsewhere.

Some Words On Lay-out, Design, Color, And Paper

Again, here we are at a subject that others have dealt with in entire books. Shortly, I shall be providing you with recommendations to a few of the best of these. However, there are a few simple design and printing rules you should always keep in mind to produce the most compelling marketing documents you can for the money you have available.

- Build your documents around a dramatic client-centered headline. Make this headline bold and compelling from a graphic standpoint.
- Don't drown the page in copy. It wearies the eye. Allow for sufficient white space. This space should be so arranged that it accentuates the importance of the copy around it.
- Break up your copy visually, again to emphasize your important points.
- Graphics should emphasize significant points in the copy. All too often I find myself asking of the graphics I am reviewing, "What are they doing there?" Make sure you know.
- Any graphics that you use (including the layout itself) should direct your prospect's eye to significant parts of the copy you've written.
- If you use a photograph of yourself, make sure you are leaning into your prospect, leaning through the frame that surrounds the photograph. Your prospect must feel you are reaching out to touch him, as indeed you are.
- Everything should be so arranged on the page that the prospect's eye moves naturally to the "Call for Action" section of the document, the section which tells the prospect what to do next: pick up the telephone and send in his check.
- Never copy from a copy. It looks tawdry.
- Do consider printing on a bright colored paper. Beware, however, of anything gaudy.
- Establish a long-term relationship with a designer whose judgment you trust. You need someone who understands what you are trying to do and will work with you to achieve it.

Once you have achieved the desired effect in your marketing documents, both with the copy you've created and the look, you're ready to begin using them to connect with your prospects. The next chapter shows you one way of doing this.

Resources

As long as you are in the marketing business, you'll have to give consideration to the such details as designing, typesetting, and printing your documents. Thus, it's to your advantage to learn as much about these subjects as you can. The following books will help.

- *Getting It Printed: How to Work with Printers and Graphics Arts Services to Assure Quality, Stay on Schedule, and Control Costs.* This book by Mark Beach, Steve Shepro, and Ken Russon has information you need.
- So will Judy E. Pickens' exhaustive volume *The Copy-To-Press Handbook: Preparing Words And Art For Print.*
- Also check out Al Beechick's handy little booklet *Resource Manual for Typesetting with Your Computer.* It will help you save money with your typesetting. Available from Arrow Connection, P.O. Box 899, Pollock Pines, CA 95726. (916) 644-2341.

CHAPTER 5

MMM

Money Making Mail Marketing

At some point you are going to have to use the mails to market your products and services. Beware! For most people, this is a costly snare that produces neither clients nor customers. Indeed, all too often, resorting to the mails to sell your products and services is a complete waste of money. That's why you should read this chapter closely and follow its recommendations religiously.

I have combed the direct-response literature and have been chagrined, to say no more, at the stupid notions that abound. Making money through the mails is not easy. Neither is getting people to respond to your offers. Nor even getting them to send you an expression of their interest is easy. No wonder!

While estimates vary as to how many advertising messages people are subjected to weekly (different sources generally report between 2,500 and 7,500), we all know it's more than we can handle. We are suffering from:

- information overload
- too many options
- the continuing erosion of seller-credibility due to rampant product- and service-hype, and
- confusion about which product and service really does meet our needs.

This is the bad news.

The good news is that these problems can be overcome. And that you must overcome them if you expect to use the mails successfully.

I want to tell you this from the very beginning. I am a mail fanatic. I love getting mail. I love sending mail. I love the way the mail works. And I have ever since I was a child. Now I rely on mail to (in part) bring my problem-solving products and services to the attention of likely buyers and bring their responses to my offers, those delightful bits of paper that are redeemable in the currency of the land. Of all the many subjects that are part of my business, few get the kind of sustained attention from me that profitably using the mail does. Therefore, please pay particular heed to what I am about to tell you.

Why Most Mail Marketing Fails.

Face it. If you're like most people, most of the mail you receive you toss out with only the most cursory of glances. You do so for a variety of reasons:

- You are the wrong person to receive the particular offer. Letters coming to my address for "Mrs. Jeffrey Lant" go right into the trash. I'm not married and never have been.
- The timing is wrong. The offer is coming to the right person but you have no particular interest in it at the time you receive it. Why do I need to know about a vacation in the sun-drenched Caribbean in the midst of a steamy Cambridge July?
- The timing of the seller is right (and the offer is acceptable) but my own personal timing is off. I'd like go to the Caribbean in March but I'm broke.
- The seller's timing is acceptable. My personal timing is acceptable. It's the kind of thing I'm interested in (in the abstract) but the benefits don't seem very substantial or alluring.
- The seller's timing is acceptable. My personal timing is acceptable. It's the kind of thing I am interested in but I can't figure out what they want me to do to follow up. This makes me feel the seller is disorganized.

- The seller's timing is acceptable. My personal timing is acceptable. It's the kind of thing I'm interested in but there are lots of little errors in the seller's copy. I see a misspelled word. There are grammatical errors. The captions don't seem to go with the photographs. This, too, makes me feel uncomfortable.

You get the idea.

But as you see, most of these problems are not prospect problems. They are seller problems. The seller — you! — has:

- selected the wrong audience for his offer;

- offered his offer at the wrong time;

- not made the benefits of taking action now sufficiently plain;

- not made it easy to follow up the offering;

- has made errors in the copy of the marketing documents the prospect is reviewing.

Fortunately all these problems can be dealt with. This still leaves what I regard as the biggest problem of all. It, too, is solvable but most people never succeed in solving it.

When you approach your prospects through the mail, your attempts to connect with them — to get them to buy your problem-solving products and services — all fall under the Rule of Seven. This means that you must be prepared to make an investment in your prospects until such time as they recognize your inevitability, buy what you are selling and so begin to solve their problems.

Let me say this as strongly as I can: unless you are prepared to target a defined group of prospects and hit them over and over again (using other means I'll discuss other than the mail), then don't even consider beginning to use the mail to approach your prospects. You must hit your prospects, either using the mail wholly or in part, at least 7 times within an 18-month period before those prospects wake up to the fact that you can solve their problems.

Now do an experiment. Take this week's mail. Take those pieces which are business-related and have problem-solving product and service offerings. Mark those that have come from companies for the first time and those that have come from companies more than once. Now track this group of letters. Every time a piece comes in from the company, number it. At the end of six months, ask yourself the following questions:

- If I am the right person to be receiving the company's offer in the first place, am I more likely to buy something now than I was when I first learned about them?

- Have I heard about these companies and their offerings in other ways besides the mail? In other words, have they reinforced the impression they created by mail through the use of other means of getting at me?

- Am I likely to buy the offering of a company which has only sent me one piece of mail and that I have heard about in no other way

- Why not? Is it because I don't know enough about the company or its offerings? Do I wonder about the track record of the company? Do I have too many questions which remain to be answered?

Let me help you with this section.

You are far, far more likely to trust a company and its problem-solving products and services that make an investment in you over a period of time, that realizes that while you may be the absolutely right person for this offer you may not want to take action or may not be able to take action now, than you are to trust a company you've never heard of and which only approaches you once. This stands to reason, doesn't it?

Why, then, are most of the offers I receive in the mail, day after day, single-shot offers which are never, and I mean never, followed up by the people making them? I cannot stress sufficiently that these people —and you, if you do this — are wasting their money. They might as well throw it out the window and spare themselves a lot of frustration and aggravation.

For most people, offering most problem-solving products and services, single-shot offers don't work. I shall return to this point later. For now, suffice it to say that if you are only going to hit your prospects once, you had better be offering a sufficiently high-priced product or service so that with a 1% response to your offer you can pay your expenses and make your profit. There are two other alternatives: you can sell something your customer will need to reorder from you (and thus in due course make your profit), or you can give your customer a range of options (such as in a catalog) that increases the likelihood that you will offer him something he wants to get right now. Otherwise, don't even consider mailing anything at all.

Preconditions For Mail Success

You are already correctly getting the idea that there are preconditions which help ensure success in using the mail. These conditions ensure that the people receiving your mail-marketing piece promptly follow up what you have sent them either with money or a request for further information. These preconditions include:

- Exclusivity. If you are the only person able to make this offer and if your prospects clearly understand the benefits of taking immediate action to secure the very real benefits to be derived from using your product or service, then mail may well work for you. If the prospect wishes to solve his problem and has nowhere else to turn, he can be convinced to turn to you.

- Trust. If the prospect has a problem and already knows about you and has reason to believe you can solve his problem, he will be likely to respond to your mail offer. Remember: one of the reasons you don't respond to the mail offers you receive is that you know nothing about the people making the offer. You know they use the mails. But you have no idea if they can solve your problems. Rather than make a mistake, you do nothing even though you need a solution to the problem. If you knew through personal knowledge that the person sending you this offer could in fact solve your problem, you'd be more likely to take action, wouldn't you?

N.B. There are many ways to build up this feeling of trust in your prospects. You can do so by repeatedly sending them problem-solving information and offers via the mail. You can also connect with them through articles about you and your problem-solving products and services in the publications they read (see Chapter 6). You can increase their trust when they attend your problem-solving workshops and seminars (see Chapter 11).

In short, using the various possibilities of the Rule of Seven, you can ensure that these prospects know who you are and realize that you can solve their problem. That they don't know precisely *how* you can solve their problem, is irrelevant. That they feel you can solve it, is very relevant indeed.

- Persistence. If you can identify a defined group of qualified prospects and hit them again and again and again with offers which are clearly seen to solve a problem which is meaningful to them, you are more likely to succeed. In other words, you must work hard to ensure that the people getting your offer really have the problem you can solve and that you can convince them that you can solve it. You must be able to connect with this exact group again and again. Having, in short, ensured that they do indeed have the problem you can solve, you are also investing in them.

This means you do not expect them to take action immediately but, because you have carefully selected them, you do expect them to take action sometime. This is a key difference. I no longer expect my prospects to take immediate action on their own behalf, even though they have the problem and I have the solution they need. But, because I have exercised care and consideration in deciding who gets these offers, I do expect them to take this important action at some point unknown to me and, as yet, unknown to the buyer.

And if they don't take this action within a reasonable period (about which we'll discuss later)? What then?

Then, like the Red Queen in *Alice In Wonderland*, I say, "Off with their heads" and drop them from my mailing list, life and consciousness — without a backward glance or second thought. Just as you must do. If after the investment you have made in them, they have still not taken action, they must be regarded as Flatworms and treated as such. This means assiduously avoiding them. I mean this. And you'll come to mean it, too —or you'll never successfully learn how to use the mails to your benefit.

The real question becomes how long you make an investment in your prospects. The answer to this cosmic conundrum will be revealed to you shortly.

Key Constituents Of Profitable Mail-Marketing

Basically, you will make money using the mail if:

- You have an absolutely clear understanding of the problems your prospects have and how your problem-solving product or service will solve them and what benefits, as a result, your clients will gain by using what you are selling them.

- You have a highly-targeted list of these prospects, a list you can use over and over to hit them. In other words, you are not expecting a single letter or a single offer to sell your prospects but are intending to approach them over, and over again, until even the slowest-witted among them understands you can solve his problem — and takes the necessary action.

- You have written copy that is heavy both on the benefits to be derived from using your product or service and on the need to take action NOW to secure these benefits.

Make no mistake about it. If you solve these three problems, you will be well on your way to profitably using the U.S. mail.

Selecting The Right Lists

From the moment you start in business, you should begin working on developing your mailing list. There are very few businesses that are not better off using mail to promote their problem-solving products and services. Very few. Such businesses usually rely solely on a walk-in clientele and have no desire to expand beyond this limitation. I hope this isn't you.

The easiest way to determine whom to contact by mail is to begin by listing all the problems that you solve (and the corresponding benefits you offer). Then write down both the people who have these problems and how you can reach them. Here's an example of what I mean.

Problem	**People who have this problem**	**Benefit I offer**	**Mailing list I can use to reach them to bring my understanding of their problem and my solution to their problem to their attention**
Massachusetts visiting nurses agencies are hard hit by Medicare cutbacks. As a result they are being asked to provide more and more free care to needy local residents but are not being reimbursed for the service. They are, therefore, having increasingly severe cash problems.	Executive directors and Boards of Directors of Massachusetts based visiting nurses agencies.	By using my step-by step fund-raising techniques these organizations have an enhanced likelihood of raising the capital, project, operating and endowment funds they need from corporations, foundations and individuals. As a result, they could have the funds they need to provide this free care and not have to reduce their endowment funds or take on operating deficits.	Membership directory of the Visiting Nurse Association of Massachusetts, Inc.

You may say "But surely, Massachusetts isn't the only state with this problem." That's true. If I want to target organizations in, say, Connecticut, I would use the same kind of chart, but the last frame would have different information in it. If I wanted to target a national audience, I'd use the same chart, but, again, the last frame would have different information in it.

What is important to point out is that we live in an age of increasing ability to target the precise people we want to get to. These people expect those of us selling problem-solving services and products to be very, very clear about why we are coming to them and the precise benefits they can expect when using what we are selling. If you are not prepared to target your offering, you are prepared to fail with it.

Selecting The Right People To Target, Getting The Names You Need

There are various ways to get names to build your mailing list. And of course you need a mailing list because you are going to be approaching these prospects — always supposing they really are prospects for your problem-solving products and services — over and over again. Here are ways you should consider using:

- Get membership lists from societies you belong to. Can you solve any of the problems of these members? Then this membership list becomes a suitable mailing list.

- Write articles about problems you can solve. Always make sure your complete name, address and telephone number follow the article. Ask people to write to you or call to get additional information on how you can solve their problem. There will be much more on this in Chapter 6. For now remember any marketing mailing you do is not about selling products and services. It is about solving problems.

Thus, it is perfectly acceptable to write, "For more information on how your visiting nurses agency can raise the money it needs to provide free care, contact Dr. Jeffrey Lant at 50 Follen St., Suite 507, Cambridge, MA 02138 or call him at 617-547-6372." The people responding to this blurb are qualified prospects and should both find a place on your mailing list and be followed up in other appropriate ways, too.

- Swap lists. Once you've got about 500 names of prospects, it's time to seek out others who want to get access to your names and who have a list you want to use. I think, for instance, of a fellow I know who writes books on accounting for nonprofit organizations. My nonprofit list is perfect for his problem-solving offer. Similarly people who have used or inquired about my fund-raising services would be a good list for him. A situation tailor-made for a swap.

- Swap your problem-solving products and services for lists. I have a friend who lets me use a membership list of her society (which is updated every year), a group which is composed of people who need my services. In return, I help her with her marketing letters. You could do something similar.

- Use electronic media programs. This works just like print media except that you should set up your order center (I'll tell you how in Chapter 6) so that people call you right while you're on the air. These people are prospects for the problem-solving product or service you were discussing on the air, right?

- Distribute your prospect-questionnaires wherever you go. Whoever responds to them is clearly a qualified prospect and should be added to your mailing list. Use some creativity and imagination about where you distribute these questionnaires. I put them into magazines on airplanes, on top of the cigarette machine at conventions. I stuff them into my outgoing mail. I distribute them at mass meetings where there is no chance of my getting the complete list of those attending. The cost of the survey documents is slight compared to the value of the prospect name and prospect interest I get in return. *N.B.* I have never known anyone as aggressive about distributing these surveys as I am. You'll have to work long and creatively to rival my record!

- Get people to use stuffers for your products/services in their mailings. All the people who inquire about your product/service or who buy it belong to you and become part of your prospect name bank (a/k/a mailing list).

- Swap articles for ads in publications. Again the responses belong to your name bank.

- Get yourself listed in professional directories. Look for books of resources and get yourself listed. I am, for instance, the only person in *What Color Is Your Parachute?*, that two-million copy best-seller, whom the author recommends as a resource on the subject of consulting. He also provides my address so that his readers can contact me for further information. I'm there, of course, not because author Richard Bolles sought me out (that would have been nice), but because I sought him out. Nonetheless all the names I get as a result become part of my name bank.

- Rent Names.

I have left the costly alternative until last. Most people, of course, think of it first. The fact is, you can build up a nice and growing file of prospects to whom to send your mail offerings without great cost. And this is precisely what you should be doing. When you are small and without significant resources at your disposal, you have to be clever about cutting corners, about getting the prospect names you need without spending lots of cash. It is better to swap some articles with a publication and get their mailing list than it is to rent the names for one-time use.

Why?

Because when your articles appear, you'll be exposing your prospects to you (increasing your name recognition and their sense of trust that you can solve their problems with your products and services) and to your products and services (thanks to the Resource Box which will follow your article). You thereby increase the possibility that when you use that mailing list for your offers, you'll get the response you need to make it profitable. It's supremely frustrating to me that more people don't understand this technique and don't use it. Why not? It's easier to call a list-broker and place an order for a list for a one-time only mailing. This is, however, for most people a prescription for financial disaster.

Resources

When you do get to the point where you need to rent names, be advised that you are about to undertake a very costly business. To maximize your chance of doing it right, see *Mailing List Strategies: A Guide To Direct Mail Success* by Rose Harper. Also check out a superb book by expert Nat Bodian, a long time direct mail pro and former nominee to The Publishing Hall of Fame, entitled *NTC's Dictionary of Direct Mail and Mailing List Terminology and Techniques*, published fall 1990 by NTC Business Books. The *NTC Dictionary* is a revised, retitled update of the widely acclaimed *Encyclopedia Of Mailing List Terminology and Techniques*, which had been out of print for two years. Get Bodian's for $49.95 from NTC Business Books, 4255 West Touhy Ave., Lincolnwood, IL 60646-1975. 1-800-323-4900.

Writing Persuasive Marketing Letters

As you surely should by now be aware, I feel strongly that most marketing letters fail because they concentrate on the virtues of the senders rather than the problems of the receivers, your prospective clients. People are selfish. We live in a selfish universe. People are self-centered and are most interested in reading about themselves, in helping themselves, in learning that you can help them. Face it. This is the way *you* are. And this is the way your prospects are. So don't fight it. Use it — to the benefit of both the prospect and yourself.

Building Blocks Of Your Persuasive Marketing Letters

Persuasive marketing letters are crafted. They should contain the following essential building blocks. You should already have the material for these successful building blocks in the information files I previously suggested you maintain. If you do, writing the letters you need should not be that difficult. Here are the blocks you need:

- The Anxiety Block. People buy products and services because they have a problem to solve, an anxiety to resolve. They buy less for the hope of getting something new and more with the expectation of preserving something they already have and are afraid of losing. Fear of loss is a more powerful motivator than the likelihood of gain. So use it to your advantage. Open your letters with lists of aggravating, infuriating, debilitating, painful problems the prospect has right now.

- The Solution Block. No matter what kind of anxiety Americans have, we are not constituted to live with it. *We have to have a solution.* Even if that solution is only hope. You must follow the anxiety with your forthright statement that the prospect's problem does have a solution.

- The Problem-Solving Technique Block. Here you indicate that there are precise techniques available to solve the prospect's problem. You indicate that they are available, you can provide information about them ("We have a developed a 15-point action plan which helps get you donations from corporations and foundations") but under no circumstances do you tell the prospect precisely how these techniques work. That information is proprietary. They get it only when they buy your product or service. Here you are, instead, telling them that you have the techniques.

- The "Don't Take My Word These Techniques Work" Block. Your buyer is going to be skeptical about your ability to solve his problem. And the buyer has very good reason to be so skeptical. Each of us has swallowed the claims of some seller, only to be sadly disappointed afterwards. This has happened to you! And this has happened, too, to your prospects. They want to believe that you really do understand their problem and that you can really help solve it. But they are afraid, based on their experience, that they are going to be ripped off. They are afraid your product or service won't work, and that they'll have another expensive disappointment on their hands. That's why you need the "Don't Take My Word For It" Block. It's composed of testimonials, endorsements, third-party recommendations and other soothing words from real people just like them and from respected above-board reviewers and media sources.

- The "Here's What To Do Now" Block. This block provides your prospects with their marching orders, with information about what you want them to do now and how you want them to do it. Be clear. Be precise.

- The "What Happens If You Don't Take Action" Block. This block provides information on what happens to the prospect if he doesn't do what you are suggesting he ought to do in his own best interest. What will he lose by not taking action? It is your job to describe not only the benefits the prospect expects if he takes action but to let him know what will happen if he doesn't. Don't expect the prospect to play the part of the Ghost of Christmas Future. That's your role!

The letter you'll create using these building blocks I call The Success Letter, and it is a crucial marketing tool.

Here's a sample Success Letter for your consideration. This one I might send to the executive director of a Massachusetts visiting nurses agency.

Dear (Named Prospect):

If you're like other visiting nurses executives, you're worried about your ability to provide free and reduced-cost care to those who need it. This is a very real worry. Your Medicare reimbursements have dropped substantially — but the need for the reduced and free care keeps on rising.

Fortunately this terrible problem has a solution which you can begin to implement today.

This same problem faced Mary Smith at the Community Health and Visiting Nurse organization: how to provide care to the people who need it at a time when such care was becoming increasing expensive and yet federal reimbursement for it was decreasing. Now Mary, her Board of Directors, and the agency are well on their way to solving this problem.

Six months ago they retained me to provide assistance in raising the money they need from corporations, foundations, and individuals. Since that time, we have raised $65,000. This is the product of hard work on the part of many people concerned with solving the problem.

Not all this money is going to the free-care fund. Some of it is for improvements to the agency's physical plant. Other funds are being directed to a special project helping local frail elderly. Still more is being invested in the organization's endowment fund so that the agency can continue to provide this much-needed service in the years ahead.

Many people were involved in this already successful (though as yet incomplete) result. Mary, her Board and staff have all pulled together — with the result you see above.

And I'm proud to say I've had my role in this imposing effort!

As development counsel to the Community Health and Visiting Nurse organization, I:

- reviewed the previous fund-raising efforts of the organization;
- helped establish the fund-raising objectives and the dollar amounts we'd seek;
- persuaded the Board about what they had to do in the fund-raising effort;
- drafted persuasive marketing documents to be presented to corporations, foundations, and individuals;
- targeted the corporations and foundations to approach for investing in the work of the agency;
- worked with Mary to make sure there was proper follow-up, including telephone calls and visits, and
- wrote the letters and marketing materials used in soliciting funds from local citizens.

Step-by-step, I've been there to assist in this successful fund-raising effort. The result is already impressive. Contributions are over 300% higher than last year. And we are by no means finished!

Isn't this a result which you, too, would like to have?

You can. You can have it either by following the precise step-by-step fund-raising suggestions of my well-known book **DEVELOPMENT TODAY: A FUND RAISING GUIDE FOR NONPROFIT ORGANIZATIONS** (information about which is enclosed). Or we can work together directly just as I am working with Mary Smith, her Board and staff at Community Health and Visiting Nurse.

If you select the second alternative, working together to raise the funds you need, let me invite you to schedule a no-cost, no-obligation meeting here in Cambridge. During this meeting we can begin to discuss your fund-raising needs and how I may be of service to you. Because fund-raising is a long, often-frustrating process, I urge you to set up this meeting as soon as possible. You can do so by calling me at (617) 547-6372.

Of course, I would like to point out that I cannot guarantee you that your result will be as profitable as that of Community Health and Visiting Nurse. No one can. Just how profitable the experience is depends on a number of factors, including your ability to find the time to work with me, the willingness of both your Board to assist in the fund-raising process, and your staff to do what is necessary so that the project succeeds. You know this.

But what I can tell you is that no organization which has ever worked with me has ever failed to make substantially more than the cost of the fees they invested. And they were therefore the more able to provide the service they are in business to provide. There is every likelihood that, at the very least, this too would happen to you. And I'm happy to provide you with the kinds of satisfied-client recommendations that will make you feel comfortable this is the case. To start with, Mary Smith assures me she will be willing to speak to you about what I have done for her organization. You may call her at (617) 223-6789 to ask what I've done and how I've done it.

So why not call today for your appointment. You have nothing to lose. But the sad fact is that if you don't call, and make no effort otherwise to raise the funds you need, there will be a price to pay — but it will be paid by those who need the services you provide. Since I'm sure this is not acceptable to you, I am looking forward to hearing from you soon and to working with you so that you'll have the money you need to continue to provide the care they must have.

Looking forward to hearing from you very soon and to working with you,

Sincerely,

Jeffrey Lant, Ph.D.
President

Some Comments On The Success Letter

- You needn't wait until the end of a successful engagement to write the Success Letter. As soon as you have recorded a success which others would like to duplicate, that is the moment to write and send your Success Letter.

- It is perfectly acceptable to mention not only one success but several. Using the letter above as an example, it would be quite all right to mention other successes with other health agencies. Why not? The more extensive your track record, the less anxiety the prospect ought to have about working with you. *N.B.* If you have lots and lots of successes to report, you can include a separate sheet, listing information about how to contact the people you worked with or who used your product. Use discretion. Some indication of your track record, however, needs to be in the cover letter. It may be that your prospects will never get beyond it and, you want to make the best possible case for yourself as soon as you can.

- If you cannot guarantee the result of using your product or service, it is a good idea to say so in this letter. We live in a very litigious society. You need protection against suit. As the author of self-help books, trainer and management consultant, I cannot guarantee results. The reason? Because I don't control the person I am working with. The result is dependent on what they do, on how they use my information, on how successfully they follow my directions. So, I protect myself by advising them that I cannot guarantee that they'll have as much success as the person I am referring them to.

But don't be stupid about this. Point out why! Ordinarily, buyers of your product and users of your service will have to use it properly to get the best results. I believe in firmly letting them know that success is a two-way street, that I'll do my part if they do theirs and that together we'll get the success they say they want. This is perfectly reasonable. It is also sensible for you. It is a form of protection and gives you a moral advantage to boot, for you'll feel better if you've been honest about what both parties to the compact involving your product or service have to do to make your working together a success.

- Refer your prospect directly to satisfied customers, people who are willing to speak up for you. Of course you have to clear it with these customers in advance. But it's infinitely better if you can actually use real people to support you.

As I've already said, sometimes this just isn't possible. Sometimes you deal with sensitive or restricted information. Sometimes a client will not wish a competitor to know that you have assisted him. This subject therefore demands sensitivity. If you cannot cite the precise names and follow-up information of satisfied customers, then say why — and give as much generic information as you can about them so that the prospect reading your materials will say, "I understand why he cannot provide me with the precise information but I'm still clear that this product/service helps people like me."

More About The Success Letter

- Success letters are built on a very simple but compelling structure. You, the prospect, have a problem. I have a problem-solving product or service. You are worried that what I am offering won't do the trick, that you'll be taken advantage of again. So I am going to do what I can to persuade you that I am honest, honorable and that what I am providing you actually will work — if you do your part in this endeavor. You're still worried, of course (I know you've been taken advantage of many times in your life). But don't take my word for it.

Contact the people whose names and follow-up information I give you here. They are like you. They've had the problem you have. And they can persuade you better than I can that you will get a solution — and not be ripped off. Understand this structure and why it has been created — and you'll be well on your way to writing persuasive marketing materials every time.

Don't think you can only send one Success Letter to your targeted prospects. You haven't forgotten the Rule of Seven already, have you? You must consider sending a series of Success Letters. Here's a suggestion:

- Send the first Success Letter when you have a demonstrated success to report to prospects who'll be interested in this success (because they have the same problem) and want to replicate it for themselves.

- Send Success Letter II to the same group when you have more success to report. Perhaps Buyer I has had additional success (you'll see to it that he does, won't you?). Perhaps you now have the success results of Buyer II to report.

- Send Success Letter III when you want to tell the same group of prospects about your continuing success with either existing or past buyers (who continue to use your products and services) or new buyers who you haven't told them about so far.

In short, persist.

Too many marketing people (and you become one, of course, the minute you attempt to sell anyone anything) attempt to be clever in what they send out. I don't. My marketing materials always focus on the problem the prospect has and on persuading him that I have the ability to solve it. That's it.

Personally, I don't believe in fancy graphics, fancy papers, fancy inks, fancy letterheads. I do believe, however, in focusing relentlessly on the buyer and his problem, on doing everything I possibly can to persuade him that I have the solution to his problem through my problem-solving products and services.

Of course you can use the fancy papers, inks, and typographies to persuade the prospect that you are the right person to solve his problem. But they are not as important as your continuing ability to focus on the important problem the prospect wishes to solve and demonstrating in conclusive detail that you, with your product or service are the right person to solve it. Never forget this!

- By the same token, too many marketing people give up on a target market too quickly. Do you take action the first time you hear about something beneficial for you, something which will help you solve a pressing problem or service? Answer that! Of course you don't!!! And neither will your prospects. That's why your success letters need to be sent out in sequences, need to target the right prospects and need to hit them again and again and again.

How often do you have to do this? The right people with the right problem you can solve need to hear about you at least 7 times in 18 months before you can reasonably expect them to take the action which is in their own best interest. If this demoralizes you, you are demoralized about the human condition more than marketing. A good marketer is a consistent, persistent, dedicated, unrelenting marketer. Which is just what I intend you should become — to your own benefit and that of the people who need what you are selling.

What To Send With The Success Letter

A good Success Letter is supported by a number of other marketing documents which underscore the need of the prospect to take action now and your ability to solve the prospect's pressing problem.

Remember, for the price of a stamp, you can include five 8 1/2" x 11" pages or, as printers say, 10 pages of material back-to-back. This works out to your being able to send your prospects something like 4000 to 5000 words of material (assuming your material is typeset). In short, you can send your prospects material the length of a rather long article, all dealing with their favorite subject — themselves and their problems. Isn't this an article you would read if someone were good enough to write it for you?

Here are some ideas for making up the packet of materials you'll send to your prospects:

- A Précis. The problem with marketing documents, as you well know, is that people throw them away. Thus, solve this problem by giving your prospects information of value, always making sure that this information includes complete details about you and your ability to solve their problems. This information has a higher likelihood of being retained by the prospect than the usual marketing materials they receive.

- Third-party media validation. Has there been a story about you and your ability to solve the problems of your prospects? (If not, you'll soon learn, in Chapter 6, how to generate such a story.) Has information been published about your problem-solving products or services? Share it with those who need to know and be reassured that you can solve their problems.

- Recommendations, evaluations, good soothing words by those who are known to your prospects or who are like the prospects.

- Information about people and organizations who have successfully used your problem-solving products and services.

- Information on the pressing nature of the anxiety facing the prospect, giving facts about how widespread the problem is. This information, of course, is designed to move this problem up in the list of what the prospect will focus on now. Sure, the prospect may regard the problem as one needing a solution, but perhaps he doesn't rate it very high. Improve your rating by including information (it may be taken from any standard media source or from Congressional records and the testimony of experts) on the degree and extent of the problem the prospect has — thereby urging him to get moving to solve it.

- Your prospect-survey questionnaire. If the prospect completes this questionnaire and returns it to you, he is giving you permission to sell to him and making your next step infinitely easier. Never send out a mailing unless you have included the prospect-survey questionnaire and given the prospect the opportunity to tell you what problems he wishes to solve and in what order he wishes to solve them. (See Samples, page 261.)

- Your company's brochure. Yes, there is a place for the thousands of brochures you've printed. Here it is. By all means, feel free to include it in your mailing — but as a back-up piece. The brochure should contain good solid back-up information about you, your products and services. You should follow with it, not lead with it. This is a mistake almost every marketing mailing I see makes. Don't you make it, too!

- Information about related products and services. Whenever possible, include information about other products and services you offer. By all means, include an order blank with information about them. Such an order blank may be in the form of a mini-catalog.

Remember: people having a certain problem, people wishing to achieve a certain result, may also have other, related problems. So, put yourself in the position of offering to solve them. For instance, if I am contacting nonprofit executive directors about my ability to solve their need for extra funds, I am certainly going to include an order blank not only for my fund-raising book **DEVELOPMENT TODAY** but for Deborah Ashton's book **THE COMPLETE GUIDE TO PLANNED GIVING: EVERYTHING YOU NEED TO KNOW TO COMPETE FOR GIFTS**, because those who are interested in raising money principally from corporations and foundations also ought to explore the possibilities of raising money from planned gifts. This makes sense.

Always think in terms of how you can solve the related problems of your buyers — and work to offer them products and services which solve these problems. This is a cluster mentality, and it leads in due course to the creation of your first catalog, a marketing document which is best understood as a cluster of solutions around a common theme offered to a targeted group of prospects.

Tricks Of The Trade For Creating Profitable Catalogs

There is scarcely a business that wouldn't be better off with a catalog. Whether you are primarily a service business or a product business is irrelevant, since the real business you are in is solving the problems of a targeted group of buyers. Sometimes their problems can be solved with a service. Sometimes they can be solved with a product. Why shouldn't you benefit by selling them both?

That's where your catalog comes in. To be successful, a catalog must have a theme, must identify a targeted group of prospects and must focus on a related group of problems. Properly understood, catalogs don't offer products and services. Instead they offer solutions — solutions to a targeted collection of problems around a common theme.

Want to see a good example of such a catalog? Turn to my Sure-Fire Business Success Catalog at the conclusion of this book. Notice how simple it is graphically: no colors, no pretty pictures, no textures. Nothing, in short, but solutions to problems, the kinds of problems that particularly small business people are likely to have. That you, in short, are likely to have.

This catalog works because it relentlessly focuses on the prospects' problems and on a series of related solutions, solutions that, when adopted, lead to Sure-Fire Business Success.

Here are the things you need to keep in mind as you develop your own catalog:

- Start by writing down the problems your targeted prospects have. Don't start with products and services. Start with problems. If your catalog is to succeed, it will do so because you more than any other individual in touch with the prospects understand what their problems are, what their aspirations are, and what Ultimate Benefits the prospects wish to achieve. Read this paragraph again. It's crucial for making money with a catalog.

- Now find the products that help solve these problems. For your catalog to be profitable, these products cannot be readily available to the prospects. If they can walk into any local retail outlet and find the product, it's not likely that this is a product you'll want to carry. Still, this condition shouldn't prove too onerous. Take books, for instance.

Each year some 45,000 titles are published. Only about one out of ten of these ever makes it into most bookstores. Perhaps another 10% are promoted in catalogs of various kinds. But that leaves a very significant selection of books that have no natural and readily available marketing outlet. That's where you come in! The published items in my catalog are not easy to find. They solve problems but they have their own problem — too few people know they exist. *Voilà!* The perfect set of circumstances for a profitable catalog — so long as you can get the catalog into the hands of people who have the problems being solved in it.

- Approach the manufacturers and find out what product review and discount terms they are offering. Let me tell you something: the first time you contact the manufacturer you won't be offered the best possible terms. Depend on it. Ask for a complete list of terms and conditions. You'll get better terms if you:

  - sell more products

  - store the manufacturers' products

  - forego the right to return unsold merchandise.

Start slow. Start small.

Start by having what are called drop-ship agreements, agreements whereby you do not commit to selling a certain number of products and do not store the products yourself. Enthusiasm is often a killer in business, particularly when it precedes experience. My hunch is that your catalog will be too vague and diffuse when you begin it, will not deal sharply with the problems your prospects have and will not be sufficiently focused either on the prospect or his problems.

The longer you are in business, the more sophisticated you'll become about this targeting process. It is the essence of a successful business. But it only comes with experience. So start small. Make your mistakes when you're small. And learn from both your errors and your successes.

- Your first catalog should be no more than a single back-to-back 8 1/2" x 11" sheet. Although it's short, it should have:

  - a hard-hitting headline which speaks directly to your targeted prospects. They need to know the minute they see it that that sheet is for them.

  - warm, intimate, conversational copy. This is a critically important point. Stop here and read a couple of pages of my catalog. A real person is speaking to you. The language is warm, accessible, conversational, intimate. There's nothing dull or impersonal about it. It is a problem-solver speaking to a person who has a problem and wants to solve it. This is just the kind of copy you have to write, too.

  - section-headings which point out which problems you'll be solving in this part of the catalog

  - easy-to-follow instructions about how to get the items you are offering. You'll also improve the profitability of your catalog if you make it possible for your buyers to use their credit cards like MasterCard or Visa and have a twenty-four hour answer line where they can place their order when they want to, not just when you want to take it.

Please note: these items may include services. The crazy notion exists in some quarters that only problem-solving products can be offered through a catalog. Nothing could be further from the truth. Problem-solving services that pertain to the common theme can also be offered. Just as with the products, you must work out the business arrangement you'll have with the service provider before you put him in the catalog. Remember: you can take a percentage of the sale or can swap for services. It's up to you.

More Notes On Successful Problem-Solving Catalogs

- As your profitability warrants, expand your offerings to more problem-solving products and services. As people begin to understand that you can solve their problems, they'll want to buy other products and services from you. Why not? Finding a supplier you can trust is one of the most difficult problems all buyers face. When they've found they've solved it in relation to the solutions you are offering, they'll be back regularly.

- Institute regular mailings. As I hope I've already made clear, one of the reasons why many marketing efforts fail is because the people undertaking them don't approach their prospects often enough. The prospects forget about you and what you can do for them. That's only natural. But it's the responsibility of the marketer to make sure they don't. Regular mailings about pertinent problem-solving products and services to the prospect ensure that you'll be remembered. The extent to which you are both perceived as the prospect's problem-solver and remembered as the problem-solver also ensures that the money you have previously spent on the prospect has been well invested and not thrown away.

Just what does regular mailings mean? I have found quarterly mailings to be productive. It's also as much as I can handle. L.L.Bean, one of the country's major mailers, mails 10 times yearly. They have learned that the prospect is not always ready to buy when they are ready to sell. But they are confident that when the prospect is ready, they'll be there because of the frequency of their approach.

More Sage Advice About Your Problem-Solving Catalog

- Your catalog is more than a collection of products and services. It is a series of solutions. As such it is of interest to publications that also offer solutions to the same group of targeted buyers. The publication of your catalog should therefore be promoted in the same way a new problem-solving book or product is promoted, because the catalog, in its own right, is a solution device and as such is deserving of publicity.

Why don't more catalog producers understand this? I think it's because they see their catalog merely as a list of products (and less often services). I don't. I regard my catalog in the same way I regard my books: as a means of solving the precise problems of a targeted group of buyers. More than likely there are publications that also serve the interests of these buyers. Publicizing information about my catalog thus becomes yet another service that the producers of these publications provide to those people, their readers.

Based on this principle, it is no surprise that my Sure-Fire Business Success Catalog receives constant publicity (it *is* published quarterly, after all). But what does surprise me is how very, very few catalog providers even think about doing the same thing. Don't be one who misses this opportunity!

- Offer to provide your catalog to workshop leaders, teachers, professors, or professional associations for distribution at their meetings as a service to those attending. Of course this benefits you. But far more importantly it benefits the workshop leader (who is thereby perceived as client-centered) and the association (which scores extra points for doing something more for its membership). Ask yourself who could benefit from distributing your catalog and then let them know it's available. I announce the publication of my catalog in many publications and in this announcement I make it plain that those who wish to distribute it as a service to their clients need only call to let me know how many copies they need.

It goes without saying that in these instances, I won't know who the catalog is given to. Thus, there must always be a line in the catalog telling the recipient that if *he* has not requested the catalog from me directly and if he wishes to keep on receiving this problem-solving, good-for-him information, he'll need to write or call me at once to ensure that he continues to get it. In this fashion, you are further perceived as client-centered — and, of course, you continue, at the most limited expense, to build your mailing list. The same line in your catalog ensures that if you do rent lists those who receive the mailing will have the opportunity to get back to you and so become part of your permanent prospect bank.

- Make your catalog interactive. Don't just ask your prospects to read it. Don't merely ask them to order from it, either, although that's certainly not the worst thing they'll do with it! No; use the catalog as an ongoing assessment device.

Ask your prospects to check off problems they'd like to solve (problems, of course, that ultimately relate to the products and services you are selling). Ask them, where appropriate, to do something for you, something that's also in their interest. For example, I ask my readers to ask their local libraries to order one or more of my books and to send me a copy of the letter they've sent (remember: the Rule of Seven applies to library buyers, too!). In return, I'll send one of the more universal of my problem-solving process articles which contains get-ahead tips they can profit from. A fair exchange.

- Make sure you offer a Money-Back Guarantee on your products. Some people are not going to like what you sell them. That's life. So give them the option of returning it to you, without questions. Fewer than one in one hundred of my buyers actually exercises this option, but I suspect many, many more are reassured by it, justifying their purchase with the notion that if they don't like it, they can always return it.

If the buyer returns what he has bought and includes a letter of complaint about it, I respond. I ask him to tell me in detail what problem he is attempting to solve so that I can see about recommending something more appropriate for his situation. I always act as the problem-solver. Never just as the problem-and-service seller. Problem-solvers should feel free to suggest alternatives to the solution they originally offered, the solution which failed to please the buyer. A product-seller is probably stuck when the buyer returns what he's sold. A problem-solver never is. Which are you? For keep in mind that once you are regarded as the problem-solver by your targeted buyer, he'll be more than likely to buy again from you. But if you are perceived only as the seller of a product that failed to meet his needs and disappointed him, he'll probably avoid you like the plague.

More Notes On Successful Catalogs

- People read in strange ways. They will scan the beginning of your catalog to see if there's anything of interest. They will check the end. And if they like both, they may read the middle. They will read the top and bottom of pages before they read the middle. They will read the right hand page before they read the left. They will read headlines before they read text. They will read italicized, bold and underlined words before they read words in plain type. Plan accordingly.

- Send your catalog to product manufacturers and distributors that you wish to send you merchandise. If you visit me at any time now, it looks like a bookstore annex, and there's a good reason for this. Dozens of publishers and other product manufacturers are on my mailing list and regularly send me items to review. Why? First, because they have hundreds of products that have no natural distribution outlets. Second, because I assiduously keep in touch with them. And not only by sending them the current catalog either, but also:

    - requests to them to update me on their prices;

    - requests to send me their current catalogs containing their products, and

    - requests to keep me in mind as they develop new products.

The result is a steady stream of product items and plenty of possibilities for me to select from.

Final Words On Successful Problem-Solving Catalogs

In my humble opinion, too few people think creatively about catalogs. To me, a catalog presents a perfect opportunity to promote any product or service you offer and to offset the price of offering it by also presenting other, related problem-solving products and services. In other words, at the very least you should with the right kind of catalog be able to entirely cover the cost of bringing your own products and services to the attention of prospective buyers. Isn't this wonderful? For minimum extra work, you'll increase the number of people you reach and the profitability of your own items.

Too, a catalog leads naturally to a newsletter, as a newsletter does to a catalog. In fact, the catalog format I have selected already suggests a newsletter publication. And you can increase the likelihood that people will retain your catalog by inserting valuable editorial content in it, articles which provide tips on how your prospects can solve one or more of the problems they have, problems which can also be solved by the problem-solving products and services you offer.

A superb illustration of this kind of catalog is The Whole Nonprofit Catalog published regularly by The Grantsmanship Center, a large mailer to nonprofit organizations. You can get a sample copy by writing 650 South Spring St., Suite 507, P.O. Box 6210, Los Angeles, CA 90014, or by calling (213) 689-9222. Remember: in all instances, your job is to do what you can to ensure that your marketing literature will be retained. Putting useful, problem-solving "tricks of the trade" editorial information in your catalog is one way of doing this.

Building A Profitable Mailing List

From the moment you're in business, you're in the business of building and maintaining your mailing list. I cannot stress this enough. One of the most valuable possessions of your business is the specific information you have about who has bought from you, when they bought from you, how much they bought from you, and what they are interested in. At the heart of any successful business is detailed information about the buyers who support it, who are interested in the solutions offered by your problem-solving products and services.

Here are some tricks of the trade for maintaining this list in tip-top shape:

- From your first day in business treat your mailing list like a computer will treat it — even though you may be keeping it on index cards in a shoebox. This means that you have to think about the fields of information you want to maintain. These fields should include:

  - Lastname
  - Firstname
  - Title
  - Position
  - Company
  - Address1
  - Address2
  - City
  - State
  - Zip
  - Busphone (business telephone number)
  - Homephone (home telephone number)
  - Inqdate (initial inquiry date)
  - 1purdate (first purchase date)
  - 2purdate (second purchase date)
  - Amount
  - Cumamount (cumulative amount)

Then consider additional fields which indicate other connections to you (*e.g.*, "book reviewers") and areas of their interest.

Why arrange your data like this? And why run the words together in your data fields?

The reason is that you want your data arranged as closely as you can to the form in which you will someday enter it into a computer. For make no mistake about it: someday you will have enough clients and prospects and the process of contacting them will be sufficiently complicated that you will have to work with a computer, either having someone else input your data — or doing and maintaining it yourself. Either way, you have to think like a computer person. The sooner you do so, the easier it will be for you — and the sooner you can put into place those marketing procedures which will enable you to contact your prospects with utmost ease.

- You should develop a form with the information fields you need and have it offset-printed. The typesetting charge for developing these fields will be small and it should cost you about $30-$35 per thousand for the offset printing, more if your information needs back-to-back printing. These forms (simple index cards if you are not gathering many data) should then be filed, in a card-filer for cards, in a log book for 8 1/2" x 11" pages. That way all the information you need is near at hand.

From this data bank (for that's what it is), you can create your mailing list, which ordinarily uses the first eleven fields of data listed above. Remember: a data bank and a mailing list should be separate. A computer, of course, handles this chore easily, but until you have at least 500 names on your mailing list, you can probably handle it fairly easily yourself. Until that point you can maintain your mailing list on pressure-sensitive labels which can be photocopied when you need to use them. Thereafter, you need to think about using a computer.

Computers And Your Mailing List

Now that I'm computerized, I'm of the very firm belief that you'll know when you need to use a computer. You'll begin to have the sense that you are wasting a lot of time doing the same thing over and over again. When this happens to you — or about the time you are dealing with 500 prospects and clients — you need to begin working with a computer. But it doesn't need to be your own computer.

Instead, consider making a deal with a friend to use his computer. Swap computer time and assistance (for you're going to need it) for your products and services. If you can get away with inputting names and updating your data files every fortnight and don't mail more than once a quarter, it seems to me such a swap-relationship should work.

Or consider using an input/update service. My good friend Ed Simpson, Publisher of *Home Business News*, has created a service for people who aren't ready to handle their own mailing lists yet. For a modest per-name charge, he inputs your data and, for an even more modest charge, updates them. And, for another reasonable fee, he'll print out your data on pressure-sensitive labels. Until you're handling 2000 marketing pieces, pressure-sensitive (or peel-off) labels will probably suit you.

Thereafter, you'll want cheshire (or machine-glued) labels which can only be produced on a more sophisticated, wide-carriage, printer. I recommend Ed's service. It's a good one when your mailing list is small and you don't want to handle it yourself, not least because you don't want to buy the computer equipment you need to do so. You can reach him at 12221 Beaver Pike, Jackson, OH 45640, (614) 988-2331.

N.B. If you do decide to use such a service, be sure that you are getting the data fields that you must have to service your mailing list. Don't leave this to chance! Understand what you need to know about your prospects to service them and how you'll be using your data banks. It is better to create too many fields, some of which are not used, than too few and have to later re-enter or re-sort your data. Take my word for it!

Running Your Own Computer, Maintaining Your Own List

There will come a moment when your list has grown so large (over 10,000 names) that you'll want to maintain it yourself, not least because of the inconvenience of sending your data to someone else and waiting for it to be updated. Too, if you are as conscientious about your list as I am, you'll want to work with it yourself to enter the data properly and ensure that they are regularly maintained. At that point you are ready for your own computer.

This is a book about marketing, not about computers, but from this moment you need to know something about computers to handle your marketing properly. That's why I am recommending the following resources:

- John Bear's *Computer Wimp: 166 Things I Wish I Had Known Before I Bought My First Computer*. It's published by Ten Speed Press, P.O.Box 7123, Berkeley, CA 94707.

- Norma Leone's *A Mother Guide To Computers*. See #B74 in my catalog at the end of this book.

- Also be aware of the works of Alfred Glossbrenner, one of the most prolific and sensible of the computer gurus. Published by St. Martin's Press, they include *How To Buy Software: Complete Handbook Of Personal Computer Communications; How To Look It Up Online*, and *How To Get Free Software: The Master Guide To Free Programs For Every Brand Of Personal Or Home Computer*.

Let me just give you these tricks of the trade, things I have learned myself.

- Get your computer hardware from a local vendor. Unless you are a computer whiz, you are going to need service. I was given this piece of advice by a friend when I was looking, and it proved to be very sage. Get someone who allows you to call when you need to call. At the beginning, this may be often! It's only fair to tell you, you will pay more by buying from a local vendor, but in my experience, it's worth it.

- Buy your printer via mail order. It's cheaper and there's no need to pay retail prices. For a good list of mail order dealers (you'll want to shop around), join The Boston Computer Society. They maintain an excellent list of mail order and other dealer information. A year's membership is ridiculously cheap at $40, a price which enables you to join specialized user groups and entitles you to two publications. Contact the Boston Computer Society at 1 Centre Plaza, Boston, MA 02108 (617) 367-8080.

- Contact The Boston Computer Exchange and see if you can get the software you need at a special price. I did. I paid less than half the retail price for my dBASEIII+ software through this group than I would have in any store. It's well worth contacting them, although not all products are available at all times. But you can always call for free information. Or you can purchase for $10 a weekly hardcopy of their complete catalog. Furthermore, they can tell you which online data base services carry this catalog. Contact the Boston Computer Exchange at P.O. Box 1177, Boston, MA 02103 (617) 542-4414.

- Make sure the local dealer is willing to take the time you need to explain things to you and ascertain what problems you are trying to solve with your machine and why you want to get it. You can be assured that if the vendor doesn't explain things to you adequately when he is trying to sell you the equipment, he won't do so after you've already paid for it — when you really need him.

- Gėt a computer buddy. You'll spare yourself a lot of grief by asking a friend to be your guide in the early days when you are using your computer, someone who has already solved all the stupid problems you are now facing. Having such a buddy will spare you a lot of aggravation, and that's yet another reason why the specialized user groups of the Boston Computer Society are so useful.

- Rewrite the manual in words you can understand. It's a cliché, of course, in computer circles that the manuals are written by sadists. It's true. Computer manuals are among the most difficult publications I have ever read. Needlessly so, I might add, since in actual fact much of what they describe could be made much more accessible.

So write your own manual of the key processes you need to master. Don't be too proud. I always have my computer consultants write down in step-by-step detail precisely what I need to do. I never feel stupid about this. They know it. I don't. And I know that I'll forget unless they write it down, clearly. You do the same.

- Don't buy any special computer furniture right away. My hardware vendor advised against doing so, and he was right. I run my printer on a cardtable and my computer on my old typewriter table. Both work perfectly well. The only specialized equipment I advise you to get it is a glare screen for your monitor.

- Do business with a vendor who'll take your software back if you find it doesn't meet your needs. Two of the four software packages I started with proved to be wrong for what I wanted to do. The dealer took them back. Be very wary of dealing with a vendor who won't take back software that doesn't meet your needs.

If you follow these steps, you'll find that your transition from relying on someone else's computer services to providing them yourself won't be too rocky. In fact, though I was once a certified computerphobe, I was amazed at how relatively easy the transition to computerization actually was. Now I can't imagine being without it.

Mail Order And Your Computer

To end this chapter, I wanted to provide some tricks of the trade for effectively blending your computer into your mail marketing operation.

- Position your computer near the telephone. I can pick up my phone without having my eyes leave the monitor. There is a good reason for this. Whether you are simply entering a telephone caller into your prospect bank or taking more detailed information about what problem a prospect wishes to solve, you want to enter it into your computer immediately.

I find in practice that people are both amazed and pleased when I tell them they are being entered into my computer as we talk. Often they hear the soft strokes and say, "You're entering me right now, aren't you?". This also enables me to tell them precisely when they will hear from me next ("You'll be getting my next catalog in January"). They'll believe me since they know they've already been entered into the computer. I also tell them that if they don't hear from me by a certain date, there's been a problem, and they should call back. This problem, by the way, need not be one I create. The post office is notorious for not delivering mail!

- Work with a computer consultant who is expert in your data base software. Have this person adjust your software so that you can produce four-across cheshire labels. Such labels are put on with a machine by a mail-order fulfillment house which will charge you a fixed cost per thousand (I pay $20 per thousand) to do so. Don't be confused about the "cheshire" designation. Cheshire labels are produced on heavy-weight computer paper available in any good computer supply store. But the salespeople will not know it as cheshire paper, so don't confuse them by using this word. Simply ask for the heavy weight wide-carriage paper. You'll get four-across labels by having your software consultant properly configure your computer. You need four-across labels as this is what most mail-order houses need because of the equipment they are using.

- Check with your mailing house to get the proper dimensions for the four-across cheshire labels they need. Your computer must be set in just the proper way because the machines the fulfillment house has are not adjustable. If your labels are printed incorrectly, they cannot be used. The easiest way of dealing with the fulfillment house is to give them a piece of the wide-carriage computer paper you'll be printing on and have them draw the necessary margin and column lines. Sadly, fulfillment houses don't seem to be able to give you the necessary specifications for the different kinds of software, although it seems a sensible idea to me to have them do so. Instead, they give you their technical specifications which make no sense to your computer consultant. That's why I advise you to have them create a model page for you.

- Print out a copy of your list a few days before you use it. You'll find duplicates and those aggravating typos that infuriate recipients. Editing this list from hard copy is easier than doing computer searches without anything in front of you. Take my word for it. Also, unless you have entered your data using rigid editorial formats you have probably not entered them consistently, and it may be difficult for you to do searches at all.

- Perhaps I should say a further word about entering your data consistently. The post office prefers that you enter your data in capital letters without punctuation. Thus, if you were doing a label for me, it would look like this, "DR JEFFREY LANT, PRESIDENT, JEFFREY LANT ASSOCIATES INC, 50 FOLLEN ST, SUITE 507, CAMBRIDGE, MA 02138." This would be the entry style easiest for the post office to handle — and hence in your own best interest to use. Before you enter any data, make editorial decisions about whether you'll:

- enter in capital letters or not
- give everyone a title ("Mr.", "Ms.", *etc.*) or not
- enter prospects' first names or just initials (I prefer the complete name)
- enter the word "suite" or the "#" sign.
- spell out words like "road" or "street", or use an abbreviation.

Whatever you decide is probably all right, so long as you are consistent. If you are not, it'll make searching very difficult, if not impossible. If you have not been consistent, then you have no choice but to work from a hard-copy-print-out of your list.

- Try to limit the number of letters per data field to the number your mailing label can take. The reason computerized addresses are abbreviated is because labels can only take so many letters. Your fulfillment house may be helpful here.

- Make sure you use Address1 and Address2 fields. The reason is that some people use both street address and post office box address, and you'll want to include both. Also, many addresses are just too long to fit on a single line and you'll need both. Because you will be using mail merge with your data bases, make sure the software you get closes up the extra line in an address where there is no Address2.

- It seems elementary, but always make sure to have an extra printer ribbon on hand. Make sure, too, you know which stores in your area sell your kind of ribbon. Your whole operation will come to a complete stop if you run out of ribbon and you have to order it specially if no one local carries it. Yes, Virginia, even this happens!

- If you are selling products and find yourself doing more and more mailing, make sure you divide your mailing list into those who have bought from you and those who have merely inquired. The reason is that the former type of list is more valuable because it contains certified mail order buyers. Depending on the difficulty of assembling that list (Harvard-educated millionaires of Peruvian descent would be on such a list), the sooner you can rent it through a list broker and so derive extra income. Ordinarily, however, you need at least 5000 buyers.

Different list-brokers have different terms and work in different ways, but you can find out whether your list is valuable by reviewing the lists already managed by a list-brokering company and writing to them to see whether they would be interested in what you have available. For further information check with Standard Rate & Data Service, 3004 Glenview Road, Wilmette, IL 60091. (708) 256-6067.

Final Words On Money-Making Mail Marketing

This chapter has been a long one, and you'll find yourself returning to it again and again as you consider the need to approach your prospects by mail — and do so successfully.

My final word to you: don't even begin using the mails to approach your prospects unless you mean to continue to use the mails to do so. Using the mails successfully means identifying the right group of prospects, prospects who have the problem your product or service can solve, and hitting them again and again and again — until such time as they wake up to the fact that you really can help them. Impatience won't help you. Targeting your buyers and being persistent about approaching them will. And given that mail marketing is expensive marketing, you may very well want to try other means of getting access to your buyers, means which cut the amount of your initial investment and use someone else's money to help you get to your prospects. Which is precisely what unabashed promotion is all about. Read on!

CHAPTER 6

MMM

Getting Your Message To Your Buyers For Free. Using and Profiting From Unabashed Promotion

Many people now automatically think of me as the unabashed promoter, and in fact I *am* a promotional fanatic. Over the last several years I have developed a system which now gets my name, address, telephone number and information about my products and services into my targeted buyers' hands regularly — for free.

I don't buy ads. I get free publicity at least twice each day through radio, television, newspapers, magazines, or newsletters. Yes, I am a promotional fanatic. For very good reasons. Its benefits are substantial.

What are the benefits of unabashed promotion?

- Limited cost. Nothing is really free. It does take time and money to pitch your story, to identify the media outlets which could promote you, your products and services. The time and the mental energy it takes to establish the connection and see it through must be reckoned costs. But there is no direct cost for the coverage you secure with unabashed promotion.

- Third-party media validation. If you say something good about yourself (advertising), that scarcely surprises anyone. If someone else says something good about you (third-party validation), it adds credibility to you and your problem-solving products and services.

- Enhances your reputation as a problem-solver. Media make experts. You can scarcely name a celebrated person in this country who isn't a celebrity because of the media. Without media there would be precious few celebrities. By the same token, paid advertising alone has seldom created any lasting celebrities. The minute the advertising celebrity stops advertising, he's a has-been.

- Enables you to sell your product or service without appearing to do so. Remember: people are resistant to sales messages. You need to overcome their resistance before they focus on the benefits you're offering. Free publicity enables you to hook the buyer before he even realizes he is a buyer, and thus works subtly to overcome his objections to buying. It is a very good way of pulling in prospects and converting them to buyers.

- Easy to arrange. You can do much of it from your home or office. Wherever you do business, you can still run a national firm thanks to unabashed promotion. I sit at my computer keyboard and next to my telephone in Cambridge, Massachusetts. Yet thanks to the benefits of unabashed promotion, I can reach my buyers throughout this country and the other countries where I get media, all without leaving my house, simply by using the mails, the computer, and the telephone. Pretty nifty.

What You Need To Succeed As An Unabashed Promoter

Success as an unabashed promoter can be yours. But you do need certain prerequisites. These prerequisites include:

- the right mental attitude. You'll be competing for something that lots of people want, including free space in print media and free airtime on electronic media. You have got to be prepared to persevere in getting it. Why should those who have these benefits at their disposal give them to you? That's where your sales skills come in.

- good sales skills. Getting the free time and space you want is primarily a question of your ability to sell a story to the media. If you are perceived as merely seeking a promotional opportunity, you are not going to get the media's attention. They'll send you right to the advertising department. Rather, you must be perceived as offering an interesting story.

- persistence. People are going to say no to you more often than yes, particularly at the beginning when you are unknown. So what! Persist! If you can solve the problems of a designated body of people and if these are the people the media source is attempting to reach, you have an obligation to persist. Just because the media source is stupid enough to decline your invitation to appear, your invitation to help solve the problems of a designated slice of the media source's audience, doesn't mean you should be stupid enough to take no for an answer.

- expecting to get the coverage. If you have done your homework and know whom you are trying to reach, know what their problem is, and know how you can solve it, then you have every reason to expect to get the coverage. Remember: media people are not doing you a favor by putting you on. They are connecting you, the problem-solver with an apt product or service, to an audience which has the problem your product or service solves. Never forget this!

- willingness to do whatever is necessary to get the coverage. Media people are often rude, frequently lazy, generally disorganized, more than occasionally arrogant. But we must overlook these taxing flaws, for they have two special abilities: the ability to package information so that it fits the format they are working with and the ability to connect us with their audience.

Because of these skills, we, who have problem-solving products and services, must overlook their considerable shortcomings. You must resolve to do whatever is necessary to get the coverage you need. Not merely for your own selfish purposes either, but because it is in the interests of the person who has the problem you solve with your product or service to know about you. It is crucial that you always remember that the people with the problem need to connect with you as desperately as you need to connect with them. That's why unabashed promotion is best understood as a symbiosis.

Why Most People Fail To Use And Profit From Unabashed Promotion

Given the unmistakable advantages of unabashed promotion, why don't more people use it? I think for the following reasons:

- They can't talk well or cannot think on their feet and are afraid they'll be embarrassed. The truth is, however, that virtually every media show is a "puff" show. It presents people in a good light, not a bad light. Remember this.

- They are afraid the interviewer will ask them questions they can't answer. Well, this, too, may happen. But what you need to know is how to respond in such a situation. This problem, like all the problems you face, can be overcome by mastering a technique.

- They are afraid someone will criticize them, judge them, even laugh at them. Well, this may happen. What do you care, however, if you are reaching your buyer prospects and reaching them without spending any of your money? Come on, be logical!

- They're afraid they'll be perceived as self-aggrandizing. Let me tell you something: people who don't get the coverage you're getting are not going to love you. They will be jealous. But, again, what do you care? If you are connecting with your buyers and profiting from the experience, why should someone else's sour grapes cause you to lose any sleep?

- Handling all that needs to be done is a lot of work. That's true. It is a lot of work to think through whom you are trying to reach and whom the media source is trying to reach and to see if there is congruence. It's work to draft the necessary marketing documents to interest the media source in you and to play telephone tag for weeks until you finally connect. It's work to make the final sales pitch by telephone. Yes, this is a lot of work. But, frankly, the advantages far outweigh the disadvantages, not least because if you don't use free publicity to get your message across, you must use paid advertising. Remember, "paid advertising" is just another phrase meaning "your money." Keep this in mind as you consider whether to become an unabashed promoter or not.

Step-By-Step Guidelines For Successful Unabashed Promotion

You'll get your media coverage because you have clearly identified a problem and interested the media source in it. After you have sold them on the problem, they will allow you to promote your particular problem-solving product or service as the solution. Thus, the first thing you need to do to become a successful unabashed promoter is to identify the problems you are in business to solve.

You should already have a list of these problems at hand. Remember: if you cannot persuade the media source that the problem you are solving is significant, there is no reason — none whatsoever — why they should give you the time and space to discuss both this problem and your solution to it. Successful unabashed promotion is always based on your ability to identify problems and to link your problem-solving products and services closely to them.

For purposes of getting media attention I am not in the business of being a fund-raising management consultant to nonprofit organizations. No way. What I do is solve the problem of how to help them raise money so that, for example, they'll have sufficient money to feed the hungry. The fact that there are hungry people on the streets of America is a problem. My solution is to teach and work with nonprofit organizations so that they'll have the money they need to eradicate the problem and make people's lives better. Get it? In the process, I will have ample opportunities to promote the management consulting services and fund-raising books that I have available which can help the target market solve its problems. This is the magic of unabashed promotion. You need never be perceived as a seller, always as a solver.

Identifying problems should be no problem for you. To succeed in marketing, you must have a Problem (or Anxiety) File. To secure the public relations attention you wish, always lead with the problem. Always. Thus, the first document you need in successful public relations is The Problem Document, a brief (250 word) presentation about the problem you are in business to solve.

Please take note: you are not in business to make a living. You are not in business to sell products and services. You are in business to solve the problems of designated publics. Of course, I know that you want to make a living. Of course, I realize that you want to sell products and services. But if you lead with these selfish factors, you'll only increase the resistance of your prospects to you and what you are selling, despite the fact they desperately need what you are offering.

As I have previously said, you may use whatever information is available to convince the media personnel that what you are addressing is a problem. Congressional and state legislative testimony, articles by experts (including, ultimately, those by you!), statements by expert witnesses, you name it. Use whatever it takes to sell the media source on the significance of your problem.

Why is this important? Every day media personnel are faced with an abundance of information that they must evaluate. What really is more important? A scandal in Washington or the resignation of the chief executive officer of the local hospital? Every day media people must decide. Thus, you must sell them on the importance of what you are doing.

Too many people in public relations overlook this critical step, with disastrous consequences. Face it. You are vying for the extremely limited and very valuable time and space at the disposal of media personnel. To get it you have to understand something about the way they think.

To media people there are only two kinds of stories: problem stories and problem-solution stories. Read through any publication on any given day, and you'll see what I mean. The stories either deal exclusively with problems or with problems and their solutions. The kinds of stories that you will be generating as an unabashed promoter are problem-solution stories. Why? Because you are in business to solve the problems your prospects have. And you'll succeed to the extent that you offer them a solution.

Now, media people love problem stories more than they love solution stories. Problem stories are by their very nature far more exciting than solution stories, which by their very nature are calming and dull. Media people crave the adrenalin of problem stories, and they do their best to paint everything in the most lurid colors. This is a fact of life.

That's why you lead with problem information.

But media people also understand that a steady diet of horror, mayhem, revolution and convulsion is unsettling, to everyone but to them. That's why they print problem-solution stories. That's where you come in, you with your problem-solving products and services.

That's also where the second document you need comes in, too. This is the Précis, the Problem-Solving Document.

You already know about the Précis. You've already designed one. It is a ten-point problem-solving document that tells people what they need to achieve to solve the problem but doesn't tell them how to do it. To refresh your memory about what's in this document, see the sample on page 85. You'll notice it tells your buyer prospects (who are now, equally importantly, the media's audience) what they need to do to solve their problem, whatever their problem is. It doesn't tell them how to solve their problem. For that, they need what you are selling.

The Précis is a crucial document. Americans are not good at living with uncertainty, with ambiguity, with crisis. We always need a solution, even though it be nothing more imaginative than a bandaid. I designed the Précis to meet this need of your buyers for hope and for an action plan. The Précis offers both. It says, in effect, "Yes, there's a problem, and you want to solve it. Great! Because I have 10 things you can do today, right now!, to begin solving this problem." The tenth thing, as you already know, is always buying your problem-solving product or service, a step which moves them closer to the benefit they desire to achieve.

The Précis, more than your formal credentials, assures the media source that you know what you are talking about, that you can offer constructive solutions to the problem you have now persuaded him is indeed a problem. These constructive solutions are much more valuable and persuasive to him than any formal credentials you have. Formal credentials are not all that impressive to media people. Remember, they meet the great and near-great every day of their lives. They become blasé about titles, honors, degrees and credentials. Everyone is a commodity.

But the one commodity they cannot do without is information, and this is precisely what you are offering them — clear, step-by-step guidelines that will help improve the lives of the targeted population which has the problem, people the media source is also interested in connecting with. Media people understandably find this information and these step-by-step suggestions irresistible. The degree to which they do so is the degree to which you will secure the free media attention — and free access to your buyers — that you want.

The People Document

So, you have a document which deals with the problem and why it is important now. You also have a document which indicates that there are solutions to this problem, solutions which the designated public served both by yourself and the media source can begin implementing immediately.

Now you need a People Document.

Solutions are not put into place by some disembodied intelligence. They are implemented by people. This means you. Whether you are producing a product or service, you need to appear as the problem-solver, the person who understands what the problem is and how to solve it.

If you want to be successful at getting free media attention, you must be clearly seen as the person offering the buyer the solution. Why do you think people like Victor Kiam (Remington Products), Frank Perdue, and Lee Iacocca have gone public? They are not just talking about products. They are talking about solutions. Moreover, they are not talking about solutions delivered by an impersonal company, but solutions which they stand behind. In short, their solutions.

Of course, lots of people may be involved in coming up with your problem-solving products and services, but when you use media to connect with your buyers, your buyers need only know about one of them — about you, about that person who seems to them to be the most important problem-solver, the person who can help them, whether he is a selling product or service.

The media deal in personalities. Therefore if you wish to get the most attention from the media, position yourself as the problem solver, stand forth as the person who can solve the problems (through your product or service) of your designated buyer prospects.

To do this, you need the Biographical Feature Story. This document says in effect, "Here is a person who understands the specific problem or cluster of problems of a designated population. He has also devised some timely solutions which are embodied in a product or service."

To show you what this document looks like, read the following sample:

DR. JEFFREY LANT

Cambridge, Massachusetts entrepreneur Dr. Jeffrey Lant can wake up at 8:30 in the morning, shower, shave, eat breakfast — and still be early for a 9 o'clock appointment at his office.

"Yes," says Lant with his infectious smile, "I'm almost never late for work. But then I only have to walk 50 feet, and I'm at my computer keyboard plugged into the world. This is one of the very considerable advantages of running a home-based business. I've been doing this for 11 years now, and I can't imagine living any other way."

The 43-year old Harvard-educated Lant is in the forefront of one of America's fastest-growing trends, the explosive growth in people who want not only to live but to work at home. Says the casually-dressed Lant, "There are more than 18 million Americans who work either full- or part-time at home now, a very substantial and growing segment of the work force."

Why are more and more people turning to the home-based alternative? "There are lots of reasons," says Lant, who this year won Third Place in the "Home-based Businessperson of the Year" Contest sponsored by Record-A-Call Telephone Answering Machine. "It's convenient. It cuts your overhead expenses. And it reduces the false distinction in contemporary American life between work and the rest of your life." Lant, author of the nationally-syndicated Sure-Fire Business Success Column now running in over 100 publications, says "Most people artificially divide their lives between work and The Rest. I don't. I simply have a body of time which I divide as necessary into the tasks needing to be done. For me there is simply life, not tension between something called Work (which is hated) and something called The Rest (which you live for)."

Given the advantages, it's no wonder so many people are creating home-based businesses. But is it all a bed of roses? "Not at all," says Lant, who publishes quarterly The Sure-Fire Business Success Catalog packed with his very candid suggestions on how to run more effective and profitable businesses. "The deadly refrigerator is near at hand. Soap operas are a turn of the dial away. And friends call in the middle of the day wanting to talk. They reason that if you are home you couldn't possibly be working. You need discipline to deal with each of these problems."

Even more seriously, home-based entrepreneurs too often run their businesses like hobbies and not like profit-making enterprises. "Over three-quarters of the home-based businesses still make under $10,000 a year," says Lant, who himself has a six-figure income. As he points out "One of the major reasons the home-based entrepreneur doesn't do better is because she (and it still more often is a woman than a man) doesn't do much marketing, certainly no where near as much as she should. She tells me she doesn't know how. She says she doesn't have the time. She's afraid of rejection. And so the revenues stay low, low, low. It's for these people that I'm writing the books in my "Get Ahead Series."

Over the past 10 years, Jeffrey Lant has turned out a book each year. They're designed to help home-based entrepreneurs and other small business people solve some of their pressing problems. His well-known book **THE UNABASHED SELF-PROMOTER'S GUIDE** tells them how to get free publicity through the media.

"Home-based entrepreneurs have precious little capital," says Lant. **"THE UNABASHED SELF-PROMOTER'S GUIDE** tells them how to get to the people they need by working with newspapers, magazines, newsletters, radio and television and thereby cut the amount they need to spend on paid advertising." "It's relentlessly thorough," says the Cambridge management consultant, who himself is featured by the media at least twice daily.

Then came books like **MONEY TALKS**, which tells people how to take their problem-solving information and create profit-making talk programs; **THE CONSULTANT'S KIT: ESTABLISHING AND OPERATING YOUR SUCCESSFUL CONSULTING BUSINESS** (for people who'd like to establish a full- or part-time consulting practice in any field), and **MONEY MAKING MARKETING: FINDING THE PEOPLE WHO NEED WHAT YOU'RE SELLING AND MAKING SURE THEY BUY IT.** Just out in a New Revised Second Edition, it's full of specific advice on how to successfully handle the marketing of products and services for the least possible price. "I can't think of a business in America that wouldn't profit from using these techniques, which I regularly use myself," says Lant enthusiastically.

"Running a home-based or other small business isn't easy," Lant points out sternly. "Four out of five of these businesses either go bankrupt or dissolve within the first five years of operation. It's not the easiest of jobs. But it can be made much easier if people work hard on identifying the people they can serve and use all the available methods — including free media, direct mail, telemarketing, and talk programs, to name a few. These will get information out on what they do and what problems they solve." "Many of the businesses that fail could have succeeded," Lant points out, "if only they had followed common sense suggestions."

Any idea where they could get such information? "Yes," says Lant with characteristic directness and specificity. "They can write me at 50 Follen St., #507, Cambridge, MA 02138 or call me at (617) 547-6372. Either way I'll send them a copy of my Sure-Fire Business Success Catalog. It's packed with solutions to every kind of small business problem."

End

Here's what's going on in this document.

The Biographical Feature Story opens with a hook. This hook is designed to do two things: indicate that this is an interesting person, someone new, different, unusual, attractive. But also to signal to the people you are trying to reach (your prospects) who have the problem you are trying to solve that this article is for them. *N.B.* To make this exercise successful they must also be the same people that the media source you are pitching this story to (whether it is print or electronic) connects with. They must be, in short, your prospects and the media source's prospects.

Now, because this is a person story, a story about a particular problem solver, there must be considerable glimpses of this person. But these must not be random glimpses. These glimpses must cause the designated client-prospect to say when reading (or hearing) them, "This person is like me. He's confronting the same kinds of problems that I'm dealing with, and he has information I need (including a product or service) that will enable me to confront them successfully, too."

This means that your story should alternate facts about the problem with quotations from you which both amplify the problem and indicate how it can be solved. The tone in which this should be done I call Conversational Accessible. The story should be immediately accessible to the targeted prospect, in this case someone running a home-based business. There should be nothing stiff, intimidating or pompous about this article, just a look at a guy who understands the problems of home-based entrepreneurs because he is one himself and who has developed success techniques (which he is making available to you.) It's a very non-threatening, welcoming format.

Remember: you are not talking to media people in this article. You are talking *through* media people to your targeted prospects. Thus, lace the Biographical Feature Story with their fears, their anxieties ("four out of every five businesses fail within the first five years") and then suggest ways they can go about solving them, the ultimate solution being, of course, buying your product or service.

Each time your name appears in the article, which it should in every paragraph, modify it with a fact that will enhance your credibility in the eyes of your prospects (Third-Place Winner in the "Home-Based Businessperson of the Year" Contest). You must work to minimize their fears and build trust and rapport with your prospects. These modifying facts help you do just that.

Here's the thrust of this article:

- There's a person just like you who's interesting and exciting.
- This person understands your fears and anxieties.
- This person has created some solutions to them.
- One of the solutions is his product or service.
- Here's how to follow-up this article to get further information about how you can benefit using this product or service.

It's a very neat package.

And what's even neater, it can be run exactly as it is by any newspaper or magazine or easily turned into an introduction for radio or television. That's right. You are writing about yourself in the third person and creating the exact article (or introduction) you want used.

More On The Biographical Feature Story

If you work in an organization with many people, each person who's solving a problem should have his own Biographical Feature Story. Thus, in a visiting nurses agency, the person who supervises the Senior Health Monitor program gets one and so does the director of the hospice. The reason for this is clear: solutions *per se* are dull. Solutions as embodied in people are not. If you want people to take an interest in any of the solutions offered by your organization, then personalize them. It makes them much more interesting and attractive. But beyond that, the more people you get involved in your publicity, the more angles you develop, the better chance you have for media coverage.

One of the worst mistakes is to consider your organization as a single entity. It's not. Even in my business, composed of just one person, there are hundreds of media angles.

I do work, as you now know, with nonprofit health agencies. With very few changes in the Biographical Feature Story the thrust of the article could be shifted to a management consultant working at home solving the problems of these agencies. As you change the target population the article is directed to, so you change the kinds of media sources which would be interested in the article. The initial article would go nicely into a publication offering useful information to home-based entrepreneurs; the second, however, would be of interest to publications directed to health agencies.

This is a very important point. Understanding it dramatically increases the number of publications in which you can get coverage, while enabling you to use the basic shell of the article.

This may be the moment to point out one important point about unabashed promotion. Don't think in terms of a single article. Don't think of using any single article or format only once. Your job is not to be original, not to write something new every time. That's time-consuming and exhausting. No, your job is to figure out how to reach your targeted buyers, to make them feel that you (and your problem-solving products and services) exist for them, and then to use and reuse the materials you have previously created.

This necessary process becomes a lot easier if you maintain an Attributes File on yourself — and any people you work with. Include information about:

- age
- residence location
- profession
- place in which you work
- sex
- marital status
- educational institutions attended

- ethnic background
- professional societies you belong to
- hobbies
- pets.

You get the idea.

The reason for this is plain. Given that we are now well into the age of highly-targeted media, each of these facts may connect you to an appropriate media source that will be interested in you because you are like the people they want to read their publication or listen to their electronic program.

But do you want to be in such publications and on such programs? You do if they will connect you to your buyers, or, when you are starting out, to get the publicity and develop a convincing batch of clips that indicate you are a person interesting to the media.

The Last Basic Materials You Need

The final thing you need is photographs, two different kinds. You need a Standard Head Shot of yourself. It should be 5"x 7" black and white or 8"x 10" black and white. You should be leaning through the imaginary frame of the picture and through it into your buyers, as if you were about to touch them — as indeed you are.

The second shot you need is an Action Shot, you actually doing the thing you are in business to do. There may be another person or persons in this shot, although the emphasis should be clearly on you. You should look like you are enjoying what you are doing and that you are good and authoritative at doing it. You are, aren't you?

You now have the four P's in the Publicity Pod:

- The **Problem** Document
- The **Problem-Solution** Document
- The **Person** Document
- **Photographs**.

Now you are ready to start targeting the right media sources.

Targeting The Right Media Sources

No one knows the precise number of media outlets, but there are at least 200,000 of them in this country, some gigantic, others miniscule. Moreover, each of these outlets is divided into sections — different programs on television and radio and different columns, features, and pages in print media. As long as you are in business, your job is to find the ones that reach your prospects and do what you can to use them to promote a continuing, consistent picture of yourself as a problem-solver for your prospects, as someone who can help them reach their objectives by using your problem-solving products and services. You must from now on spend a portion of each day:

- identifying these crucial resources;
- understanding whom they are trying to reach;
- determining whether there is a match between those you are trying to reach and those the media source is trying to reach;
- contacting them with story angles appropriate for their format;
- following up your initial contact;
- keeping in touch with the source whether or not they use your material, so long as they continue to have the potential to reach your buyer prospects.

This process never stops.

First Step

The first part of this process is identifying the media resources who can help you reach your buyers. How do you do this?

To begin with, you have got to be aware of what media sources reach your buyers, what your buyers read, what your buyers see and listen to. So ask them. From now on ask your prospects and buyers which media they use. A trend will soon be obvious, and it will be equally obvious where you must appear to get access to them.

Second, review the likely sources. There are tens of thousands of media resources you have never heard of but which are valuable, if your prospects pay attention to them. How do you find out about them?

To begin with, read my book **THE UNABASHED SELF-PROMOTER'S GUIDE,** the most thorough and innovative book ever written on how to get through to your buyer prospects over and over again for the least possible money. I list over 175 media resources in Chapter 2. These resources collectively contain well over 150,000 media targets you would want to be in touch with, if they reach your buyers. I'm not going to replicate that list. But I shall suggest a few major resources you really cannot afford to be without:

Directory of Newspapers

IMS Directory Of Publications, Gale Research Inc., 835 Penobscot Bldg., Detroit, MI 48226-4094, 1-800-347 GALE.

Directory of Newsletters

Oxbridge Directory of Newsletters, Oxbridge Communications, 150 Fifth Ave., Room 301, New York, NY 10011 (212) 741-0231

Directory of Newspaper, Magazines, Radio and Television Outlets

Working Press Of The Nation in 5 volumes, Automated Marketing Systems, 225 West Wacker Dr., #2275, Chicago, IL 60606 (312) 346-9097. Also includes feature writer and photographer directory and internal publications directory.

General Directory of Media Sources, Including Radio, Television, Newspapers, and Magazines

Gebbie Press All In One Directory, Gebbie Press, Box 1000, New Paltz, New York 12561 (914) 255-7560.

Directory of Outlets for Publicizing Products

Bacon's Publicity Checker, Bacon's Publishing Company, 332 S. Michigan Ave., Chicago, IL 60604 (312) 922-2400

Directory of Associations and Their Publications

Encyclopedia of Associations in four volumes, Gale Research Inc., 835 Penobscot Bldg., Detroit, MI 48226-4094, 1-800-347 GALE.

These should all be available in your local library. They are expensive, and they date quickly. But if you're like me, a media fanatic, you'll want them readily at hand, even if you live a stone's throw from major libraries, as I do.

Many of these resources will be unfamiliar to you. Now. But you've got to familiarize yourself with them. Soon. This is easier to do with print media than with electronic media.

With print media, you can always write for a sample copy of the publication. Your reason? Say you are thinking of submitting an article and would like to review their format. It's true. Shortly, I'll give you some information about the kinds of articles you should consider submitting. Before you do so you should have an idea of how the publication sees itself. So ask.

With electronic media, although it may seem less easy to gauge what program formats are like in listening areas other than those near you, it is actually easier to do so. Electronic media are far more standardized than print media. The same kinds of programs exist in all markets. Thus, if you want to familiarize yourself with the kinds of programs that exist elsewhere, make yourself completely familiar with the kinds of programs that exist in your nearest major media market.

Now what?

The Familiarization Process

Okay. You've got a publication in front of you that hits your buyer prospects. Now you've got to learn how to use it, how to make it a significant part of your marketing effort. Which means how to use it with the Rule of Seven. This means doing a content analysis and figuring out what you've got that fits their format and will easily result in bringing you before their readers, your prospects.

To show you what I mean, I've just picked up one of the dozens of newsletters which cover my desk at any given time. This one is a regional newsletter for independent publishers, the kind of publisher I am. The readers of this publication are potential buyers for my products and consulting services. So I am interested in appearing before them at regular intervals to let them know that I can help them — one way or another — to solve their problems.

This particular newsletter is divided (in part) into the following sections:

- first, a president's letter complimenting people who do good things to help the association and the newsletter which it publishes;
- information on forthcoming meetings and speakers;
- short notes listing items of interest about members;
- book reviews of new titles by members;
- information on getting in their catalog which goes to booksellers;
- letters from members with current news notes on their projects;
- main article on a subject of interest to the members;
- paid ads.

Using This Information To Reach Your Prospects

Remember where I am coming from. I believe that most people marketing most things don't market enough, don't hit their buyers sufficiently often and give up before their buyers are really aware of what they are selling. Thus, the marketing that has already been done is to a significant extent wasted.

People give up, of course, for many reasons. They run out of time, energy, imagination, and money. They get bored by putting the same message out over and over again, thinking that their would-be customers are as bored with hearing it as they are with disseminating it, when, of course, the prospects are no more than vaguely aware (if that) that something is even being offered them which is in their own best interest. And so no sale is made.

That's why when you confront a publication of any kind, like the newsletter I am discussing, you must keep the Rule of Seven in mind, must make the commitment to hit those prospects over and over again until at last they understand what you are doing and understand you are doing it for them.

Let's now return to the list of possible promotional vehicles listed above, for you must analyze each publication and each electronic media source to determine how you will use each to get your message across to the prospects with whom you must connect.

Getting The Right Information To The Right People Over And Over Again

Your job now is to determine how to get into *each* section of this newsletter (and all applicable media sources) and so make the Rule of Seven work for you. Here's how you do it.

Start by knowing how many issues (in this case) of the publication there are in a year. In the case of the newsletter I am reviewing, there are 6. This doesn't mean you can only get your message in 6 times. Not at all. For you can, of course, appear more than once in any given issue.

Now, go through each feature of the newsletter and ask yourself this question, "What have I got for 'The President's Letter'?" And so on. Okay. Let's do it.

Lant Analyzes The Possibilities — And Acts

- The President's Letter. Offer to do something for the association or the newsletter. Send in a good idea. Wait. If the president doesn't notice it on his own, ask him to notice it. Yes, ask him. People forget. They mean well. But they can scarcely be expected to be as interested in your desire to position yourself positively before their readers (who they may not recall are also your prospects) as you are. So a helpful hint will not be amiss.

Why do you want this kind of publicity? Your buyers need to see you as a good person, a kind person, a helpful person, the kind of person they want to be around. People who get warm thanks for doing good things are just the kind of people they want to support.

- Information on meetings and speakers. I'll take up this question more in Chapter 11. But remember: your job is to use meeting opportunities to promote yourself as a helpful person, the kind of person who understands the problems of the readers and who can help solve them. This is what a meeting notice is for.

- Short notes of interest to the readers. What are you doing that's of interest to the readers? These notes should indicate that you understand a problem the readers are having and that you are solving it. Report on successes you have had working with clients. Publicize awards you have received indicating your understanding of a current reader problem and that you have been rewarded for devising means to solve it. Provide information on articles you have written (offprints of which are, of course, available to the readers if they contact you).

Don't just put in information about yourself. Put in information that targets your prospects and clearly indicates to them that you understand their problem and are already solving it with others. On this basis, most of the notices that are currently printed are completely wasted. They focus on the achievements of the person being publicized, but not on the needs of the people who still have the problem you could solve with your product or service.

- Book reviews of titles by members of the association publishing the newsletter. I publish books. I'm a member. I do at least one new title a year and regular new editions and reprintings of previous titles, each of which I treat as a new book. There's plenty of opportunity here.

- Information on getting in a new catalog being sent to booksellers. This is a two-for-one marketing deal. When you are a publisher, booksellers are necessarily part of the world of prospects to whom you are marketing. The Rule of Seven equally applies to getting these prospects to take action. Getting the catalog into the hands of targeted booksellers counts as one "hit" in the Rule of Seven — for that group of prospects.

But the catalog will also be read by readers of the newsletter, who are more than likely also in the catalog. So being in this catalog also functions as another "hit" at that market.

- Letters from readers with current news. Again, what current news do you have? The publication of a new book? Great reviews to report? A publishing "trick of the trade"? The news you report should help promote your products and services, not just get your name "out there" in front of people.

Now as it happens, I also look through these letters to see what others are doing that might help my marketing efforts. In this newsletter, a fellow says he is writing a book on self-publishing and is looking for material. I immediately write him with information about what I've got that will help his book. My objective? To be a part of his book (with name and complete follow-up information) and so again get to my market of independent publishers.

- Main article on subject of interest to readers. What have you got that will help shed light on a problem the readers have to which you have the solution (and which will lead naturally to promoting your products and services)?

- Paid ads. Do you really need to pay for them? Think? Couldn't you swap for the main article you'll write and forego payment for that? And if the publication doesn't pay for articles in the first place? Well, why can't you ask to get ad space notwithstanding? You see, it's all negotiable.

Submission Smarts

Don't make the mistake that most people make when they send material. Public relations "professionals" are by far the worst. They simply send materials, helter skelter. When you receive them you know instantly that you've been blitzed by a huge mailing, not by something done specially for one's own media outlet. This may be efficient for the public relations professional, but it is a lousy way to do business and rarely secures the kind of attention the client needs.

Remember what you are after:

- You want to develop a relationship with a publication. You want them to read *your* materials when they are backed up with stuff and won't read anyone else's.

- You want them to print your information regularly.

- You want them to regard you as a source for information and to feel free to call on you when they need a favor.

Simply sending out heaps of mail doesn't lead to this result. Thus, be smart:

- Accompany anything you are sending with a note, indicating in which section of the publication you want the material to appear. Include a reason if it is not immediately clear why this section applies.

- When the material appears, send a "thank you" note. You have, after all, been given something of value. But don't just make it the generic thank-you note. Talk about how the publication looks. Compliment a particular article. Make it specific for the person you are writing to.

- If the material doesn't appear, don't despair; but don't dawdle either. If you've waited for an issue or two and nothing's appeared, write a note to see why. Also send more material tailored for yet another section of the publication. Remember: you cannot afford to give up so long as this publication (or any media source) reaches the buyers you want to reach.

Let me tell you something: most people give up. I read more publications than most people, and the same tiny handful of names crops up again and again. They are the smart marketers. Most people appearing once give up at that point, rather than forge ahead. For some reason they make the crazy assumption that appearing before their buyers once is enough. It almost never is. Take heed.

Using And Reusing: So Long As People Have The Problem, Continue To Use Materials Which Help Bring Them The Solution

Before I go on to discuss lengthier articles and how to craft them, I want to discuss the use and reuse of material.

I have already hit the false notion of "creativity" in this book. For misguided reasons, people with products and services to market want to be "creative", want to be new, different, unusual. This, in practice, means coming up continually with something new. Let me ask you something: this search for creativity is all very well, but does it sell products and services?

Your job is not to be creative. It is to sell products and services. Your job is to let your targeted prospects know over and over again that you are the right person in the right place with the right information for them. To let them know that you can solve their problem. Nothing else matters. Beside this important result, the very idea of "creativity" pales into insignificance. This is why you not only use but reuse everything you do.

Resolve right now that so long as your prospects have the problem you can solve, you will use the same material over and over again until such time as you are entirely certain your prospects know what business you are in and what problem of theirs you can solve. Just because you are bored with the approach doesn't mean it isn't working. If it sells products and services, it is the right approach.

Thus, whatever scrap of news or information you send to a single place reaching your buyers, you must consider sending to other places that also reach your buyers. My rule of thumb has always been that if a single publication is going to print something, it is obviously appropriate for many others. Thus, my task —and your task — is clear: to do what is necessary to identify those other sources for which this single piece of information is appropriate and where it will also get to my buyers.

Never think in terms of a single source. Always consider how you can take a single piece of information and make it appropriate for all the publications and electronic media sources that reach your prospects. This is the creative part of promotion, not changing the message over and over but changing the place where the single message — the problem-solving message about your products and services — appears. Get it?

What You Need To Know About Articles By You

Until now, I've principally discussed how to get information about you and your problem-solving products and services published. It's one of the forms of unabashed promotion you can never do without. But you can also help your cause by getting articles by you published.

Now I am not talking about long magazine-type articles that demand heaps of research and long searching hours at your typewriter. Not at all. The object of the articles you'll be writing is different. It is not to disseminate information. It is to let your prospects know that you understand their problem, know how to solve it, and are available (through a product or service) to do so. I call this the Problem-Solving Process Article, and I use it relentlessly. It is the basis for my Sure-Fire Business Success Column which now runs in over 100 publications with a readership of well over a million and a half people.

Constructing Your Problem-Solving Process Article

The Problem-Solving Process Article is composed of a series of bullets. These bullets are packed with information and clearly directed to a precise buyer population. They indicate to them that you understand what their problem is and provide information on how to solve it. Sound familiar?

It should, because the Problem-Solving Process Article is directly related to the Précis. Indeed, you can look upon the Précis as a Problem-Solving Process Article that you distribute yourself, directly to buyer prospects. You can consider the Problem-Solving Process Article as a Précis that a publication distributes to your buyer prospects for you.

The success of this article begins with its headline. You already know how to create the perfect headline, (or if you don't, you should go back to Chapter 3). It must target the group of prospects you are aiming at and scream to them "This article's for you!". It must also indicate that you have the solution to one of their pressing problems.

Personally I like two-part headlines and use them a lot. "Collecting The Money You're Owed: Ten Things You Can Do Right Now To Get Your Creditors To Pay Their Debts." The first part of this headline is called the "grabber", for very good reason. It grabs the person who has the problem, the person who also happens to be your prospect. The second part is called the "descriptor". It tells the reader (your prospect) precisely what he can expect to get from this article, and (although he doesn't know it yet) from your product or service.

If you have written the proper headline, you are going to snag the exact right prospect for what you are selling. *No other reader matters.*

Now your job is to convince him that you can help him solve his problem. This is the purpose of the Problem-Solving Process Article.

Many people have a hard time figuring out how to construct these articles. I can't understand why. Here are two ways to quickly do so.

Use The "What Next?" Technique

To solve any problem, the prospect must follow a logical series of steps. The Problem-Solving Process Article is built on a series of logical steps. The article opens with an anxiety paragraph. Here's an example: "If you're like most small business people, you give away thousands of dollars of free products and services each year. Not because you're a philanthropist either, but because the people you've sold them to don't pay for them. No, you're not a philanthropist. You're a sap. That's why you need to know what you can do to collect the money you need, because not knowing how to do so is cutting your profit and threatening your business."

The anxiety paragraph must speak directly to your prospect and must hit his anxiety, in this case, the slicing of his profit and the imperilling of his business. It might also touch his aspiration, in this case, getting the money he's owed and altering his behavior from sappy to savvy.

Having begun with this anxiety opening (the opening that speaks directly to your prospect), then logically follow with the question, "What do I, the expert, recommend my client, the reader, to do first to solve this problem?"

Let me tell you this: if you haven't written one of these articles before (and I'll bet you haven't), you'll have trouble opening with the very first logical thing the prospect must do.

The second problem you'll have is that your opening will be too vague.

The essence and power of the Problem-Solving Process Article is that it convinces the prospect you know what you are talking about and provides him with useful information, the kind of information he'll want to keep on hand. It lowers his resistance to you to the exact degree that you show him you know what you are talking about.

But at the same time, you can't give away the store. That would be suicidal. No, you need to tell him (does this sound familiar?) what he needs to accomplish, but not how to accomplish it. The same as with the Précis. Because if you tell him how to do it, he doesn't need you, now does he?

Here's a paragraph that could follow the opening (anxiety) paragraph of the article above. "How can you avoid this unsatisfactory situation and get the money you're owed? Begin by an act of will. Most people find the business of collecting the money they're owed onerous. Often it makes them physically sick. The reason for this is they hate confronting people who owe them money and feel, at a psychological level, that these people are not going to like them any more if they push them to pay what they owe. Successfully getting the money you're owed starts with your becoming mentally resolved to get the money to which you're entitled, to get people to pay for what they've bought from you and to do it as quickly as possible."

Now consider. I have told the reader, my prospect, *what* he needs to accomplish ("become mentally resolved to get the money to which you're entitled"), but I have not told him *how* to do that. For that he needs me and my product or service.

But even though I haven't told him how to do what needs to be done, I've still supplied him with a very useful bit of information. A bit that (if he's smart) he'll keep on hand and refer to each time he faces the unpleasant business of collecting the money he's owed. Because I've told him something he can use.

The extent to which he believes that what you have told him is true and useful and the extent to which he keeps it on hand to refer to when he has the problem you're in business to solve, is the extent to which this marketing article has been successful.

Write the article by asking at the end of each paragraph "Now what? What should the reader, my prospect, do now to solve his problem?"

The Problem-Solving Process Article is composed of up to 10 paragraphs which have specific answers to the "Now what?" question.

And how does this article end? It actually has two endings, which I collectively call The Marching Orders. The actual article itself ends with a paragraph telling the prospect that he can make progress solving his problem if he takes action now, if he follows the steps you have just outlined. All Problem-Solving Process articles are action-oriented. They aim to move the reader, your prospect, from where he is now (in the midst of a problem) to where he should be (at the point of solution as aided by your product or service).

Here's an example of what I mean:

"So you see, you can get more of the money you're owed, faster, with less psychic distress to yourself. It's not easy. But it is possible. It's up to you. You can keep acting like an unwilling John D. Rockefeller, doling out products and services to people who are only too thrilled to take advantage of you and your generosity, or you can begin to function like a business and get fair payment for the product or service you've already delivered. You decide. But take my word for it: you'll be a lot happier if you follow these steps and get your money. Then you can give it to the charity of your choice, which might just be you!"

This ending does a couple of things. First, it connects the conclusion with the beginning of the article. The original paragraph of the collections article talked about the person owed the money as being an unwilling philanthropist. The final paragraph reminds him he can avoid this fate by following the steps already presented. Stylistically the final paragraph connects with the original paragraph and makes the article a neat package dedicated to a single point: in this case, how a person owed money can get it.

At this point the person with the problem is ready to take action. Therefore, you must make sure the first action he takes is in your direction, towards buying your product or service.

Here is the final brilliance of the Problem-Solving Process Article.

The Action Conclusion

You've probably noticed that at the ends of most articles there is a brief biographical tag about the author. It usually says something like this: "Nancy Smith got her Ph.D. at Oklahoma State University in Astro-Physics and is currently an Assistant Professor at The State University of Lower Maine." In other words, from a marketing standpoint, it is completely useless.

Think! You've now got the reader, your prospect, to a critical point. He knows that you understand his problem. He appreciates that you've given him helpful ways to solve it. He's ready to take action to go further in solving it. And at the moment he is ready for action, you desert him. THAT'S MIND-BOGGLINGLY STUPID!!!

You need to give your prospect his marching orders. Your conclusion (which actually follows the article and is often printed in italics) should read, "If you want to get the money you're owed, contact Dr. Jeffrey Lant, the author of this article. Dr. Lant is a specialist in getting creditors to pay what they owe. He's also the author of the helpful pamphlet, 'Getting Your Money: Exactly What You Need To Know To Get The People Who Owe You Money To Pay It'. You can contact Dr. Lant and order his book ($10.95 postpaid) by calling with your MasterCard or Visa at (617) 547-6372 or writing him at 50 Follen St., Suite 507, Cambridge, MA 02138."

Sure, it's longer than the usual blurb. Sure, some publications won't want to give it to you. But fight for it. This blurb is what the Problem-Solving Process Article is all about. If you don't get it, the article will fail. Because, you see, the essence of marketing is getting the prospect to trust you and to make it easy for him to take action when he does. Which is precisely why these marching orders are so important.

Another Way Of Structuring Your Article: The Problem-Solving Process

An alternate way of crafting your article is by using the problem-solving process. In this case here's what the skeleton of your article would look like:

- Grabber-descriptor headline

- Paragraph 1: anxiety opening paragraph

- Paragraph 2 tells the prospect what mental attitude he must have to solve the problem. It basically asks the prospect, "Are you mentally prepared to solve the problem you have? If not, you will fail."

- Paragraph 3 deals with whether the prospect is technically prepared to solve his problem. Often there are things one must know or personnel one must have to solve a problem. You, as the problem-solving expert, tell the prospect what these are. Thus, tell the prospect:

  - what specific things he and his staff need to know to solve the problem;
  - how to recruit the people for his staff who do know these things if he isn't going to train existing staff; and
  - how to find and work with independent consultants, if he doesn't want to add full-time staff.

- Paragraph 4 tells the prospect how to ascertain what his real problem is. Too often people assume they know what their real problem is when, in point of fact, their actual problem is quite different. This paragraph tells the prospect how to find out what the real problem is, so he is not fighting ghosts.

- Paragraph 5 tells the prospect how to sell the need for a new approach to the actual decision makers. If you are trying to sell your product or service to people who are not themselves the decision makers, you had better tell them how to deal with the people who are. Otherwise, all your marketing will be for naught.

- Paragraph 6 tells the prospect what documents he needs to solve his problem and how to prepare them. This includes not only written materials but also software.

- Paragraph 7 advises on what kind of implementation strategy the reader needs to move towards success. This deals with questions like who he needs to meet with, how often he needs to meet, how meetings to solve his problem should be arranged, and how follow-ups to these meetings should be handled. In short, it provides the reader with change-oriented suggestions that will lead to the beneficial result he wants.

- Paragraph 8 deals with how he should deal with success (if there are people to thank, for instance) and how he should cope with failure, if it occurs, when he'll need to alter his strategy.

- Paragraph 9 tells him how to review his situation after he has altered his habits. Are things working as well as they might? Now that the new system has been in place for a time, can it be improved? Has it, in fact, become a new problem that calls for a new solution?

Your conclusion tells the reader to get started now in solving his problem. It tells him candidly to use this information and get the solution process underway, or else continue to suffer from the problem he now has.

After this conclusion, don't forget the final Marching Orders in which you provide information on how the prospect can contact you and either buy your product directly or get further information.

Either of these alternatives is acceptable for creating a truly useful Problem-Solving Process Article.

Further Details About The Problem-Solving Process Article

This article may be any length between 1000 words and 2500 words. Indeed, properly understood, the form may be used for problem-solving audio and video cassettes, newsletters, booklets, books, workshops and talk programs of every kind. If you want to learn how to do so, read **TRICKS OF THE TRADE: THE COMPLETE GUIDE TO SUCCEEDING IN THE ADVICE BUSINESS,** which tells you in excruciatingly thorough detail how to do just that. But as an article, 1000 to 1500 words is probably about right.

You should send this article to every conceivable publication that reaches your buyers. Don't send it out one at a time either. Send it wholesale to as many as may want it and which connect with your prospects. This course causes many people to quail. Why?

The object of writing this article is to attract buyers, to get people to write or call you with their direct order, or to request further information. I print up over a hundred copies of each article I write and send them out — on the same day. Moreover, I send it later as I either find other publications which reach my prospects or which write me and ask for something of mine to publish. It is understood that I maintain all rights, including the right to use this material later in other formats, including books and tapes. Each publication gets one-time-use rights only.

Why do they accept this? Because, ladies and gentlemen, we live in the Great Age of Information. With the advent of desk-top publishing more and more people are publishing books and newsletters, and the need for top-quality material has grown astronomically. Put yourself in the shoes of the publisher. He has lots of problems to solve. One of them is lack of good editorial material, material that speaks to and interests his readers.

Then you come along, offering him precisely what he most needs and requesting nothing more from him than that he run what I call a Resource Box at the conclusion of the article. The Resource Box tells people in precise detail how they can get access to you. If he blanches at that thought, you're easy. Swap the articles for ad space, requesting twice as much ad space as the dollar value you have assigned for each article. A good rule of thumb is to price each 1000 word article at between $100 to $200.

What's the publisher to say? You are solving one of his major problems. You are not asking for any of his slender cash reserves; and you are offering material of interest to his readers. Is it any wonder, dear reader, that publishers come clamoring for my material and that they will do the same for yours, giving you in the process continuing access to your prospects? Under the Rule of Seven this translates directly into dollars in your pocket and a glorious reputation as one of America's premier and most-loved problem solvers. What could be better! *N.B.* Don't expect your competitors or others who might have gotten this space to love you quite as much.

Using, Reusing, And Updating Your Problem-Solving Process Article

Let me put it to you this way: if you get this Problem-Solving Process Article published once, you can get it published again. Go back to my article on collection techniques. (Don't, by the way, call me to order the pamphlet I cited. I haven't written it yet!) How many people have collection problems? Every one who sells products and services. Thus, there can be a collection tips article for pizzeria owners, for innkeepers, for llama breeders, for home-based business people, for independent publishers. Get the idea? And each of these groups has its own specific, targeted publication, often a newsletter which is a superb place to put this kind of article. What did I tell you before?

Change the place where you use the material. Don't change the material itself, except as you need to to develop your reputation as a credible problem-solver for the precise group you are targeting.

What this means is that so long as your prospects have problems (in this case, collecting the money they're owed), you can use and reuse the same material over and over again. Of course, you are going to update it as circumstances warrant, and of course, you will put in new information as it becomes available. But so long as your prospects have the problem and so long as the information you have is valid, you'll use it.

Need I say that what I am telling you now is entirely different from the way most people approach the business of using articles? I want to stress that the purpose of the article is not to impart information. If you do that, and that's all you do, you're a swell person, but a dumb marketer. No, the purpose of the article is to alert your targeted buyer prospects that you understand their problem, that you are going to give them information on how to solve it, and that you are available, through a product or service, to work with them to conclusively solve their problem.

Becoming The Recognized Expert In Your Field And The Inevitable Source For Your Prospects

I hear lots of nonsense by people in a similar field saying they are not in competition with each other and how they should share and share alike. What idiocy! Let me tell you something: if people buy a book on marketing from one of my competitors, they aren't going to buy another book on marketing for awhile (even though they'll need it). I'll be the poorer for it. People in the same field are competitors, and this competition is in deadly earnest.

Thus, in your marketing, you must aim to obliterate your competitors. Fortunately, unabashed promotion can help you do just that. If you are the expert in collection techniques and your "tricks of the trade" articles are generally available, there isn't going to be room for anyone else's. Just yours. If *Innkeeping* newsletter runs your article on must-use collection techniques, that's it, at least for now. You have therefore preempted a slot that a competitor could have used. And you have done it in such a way that your own image and availability as the recognized collection expert are enhanced. Pretty neat. Which means that your competitors will have to work around you. Which is just how you want it to be.

Pressing Your Advantage

Once you've got the slot as the problem-solving expert, keep it. Do a "Son Of Problem-Solving Process Article." This means, come back at regular intervals with more information, more tricks of the trade, including newly-available information on how people can solve this problem. Once you have the slot, don't lose it to another, more unabashed promoter. Remember, such people do exist: look at me!

Go back to the Rule of Seven. Once your original Problem-Solving Process Article has appeared, you know you're going to want to hit your prospects again and again and again. Therefore, let the editor know that you'd like to be kept in mind the next time he'd like a collection tips article. But don't rely on the memory of a fallible mortal. After six months suggest a sequel, or suggest another article that deals in detail with a part of the subject you addressed in your original article. Perhaps your sequel could be, "Tracking Down Skips: Tips For Finding People Who've Gone Away And Left Their Bill Behind." You get the idea.

The important thing is to make sure that you are again hitting your prospects. That they understand, clearly understand, that you are The Inevitable Expert in your field. That you have what they need. And that you won't go away but intend to keep on beating, beating, beating away at their sloth, lethargy, slowness, and, yes, stupidity until they take the action which is very much in their own best interest. This is what marketing is all about.

A Word On Following-Up The People Who Respond To Your Problem-Solving Process Article

The people who respond to your Problem-Solving Process Article are qualified prospects. They have told you (directly or in effect) they have the problem you can solve. They have some idea you can solve it. They have taken action to put themselves in touch with you. They are now yours to win. And if you don't win them, it's your fault, not theirs.

If they write to you, follow up with:

- your Précis;
- information that indicates you clearly understand their problem and have developed means of solving it;
- full order information if you are selling a product;
- your client-survey assessment questionnaire, to find out more information about what they want to accomplish.

Or call them. It's perfectly appropriate now. The only consideration is whether it makes better economic sense to follow up by letter or by phone. If you're selling a service, call. If you're selling a product, let its price be your guide.

In other words, build on your fine beginning. Continue to let them know you understand their problem and that you, your product and your service exist to solve it. Again, if the price of your product or service warrants, let them know you'll be following up this packet in a few days to see how else you can be of assistance. In other words, let them know help is at hand. Be assertive, by all means, but be assertive within a helpful context. There is absolutely no reason at all for holding back now. These prospects have told you they have the problem. You clearly have the solution they require. You lucky dog.

Moving Into Electronic Media

I've concentrated so far on print media for a very good reason. Print media lasts. Sure, your prospect may skip over your article the first time he leafs through the publication. But unless he throws it away, it is still there. Not so with the electronic media. If he misses the show you're on, he misses it. And that's that. That doesn't mean you shouldn't think about using radio and television. Given certain preconditions, you should. But it does have its limitations.

I've concentrated on print media, too, for another reason. Once you appear in it, it's easier to get the attention of the electronic media. Once the print media finds you "media-worthy," you're going to be able to get the electronic media coverage you want much, much more easily. So, start with print, and make sure you are always appearing regularly in print. You don't need to be the fanatic about this that I am; (I *am* exceptional). But remember: your objective is to hit your client prospects at least 7 times in 18 months. Factor in the print media getting to them accordingly.

Do You Want To Use Radio And Television?

You want to use radio and television programs if they reach your targeted prospects in sufficient numbers to justify the time you must put in to get on such programs. Like all media, television and radio programs are targeted to specific audiences. There are programs for senior citizens, for young people, for women, for newlyweds, and for investors. If your product or service solves the problem of one of the media's targeted groups and if your buyers are present in significant numbers within this group, then, and only then, should you target radio and television shows for unabashed promotion.

What the radio and television program personnel want to know is: are you offering their specific audience a solution to a problem that interests them right now. If the answer to this is yes, then they want you and, more to the point, you want them, too. If not, then concentrate on the relevant print media, and leave the electronic media alone.

Let me give you a for instance. I publish a book by Debra Ashton entitled **THE COMPLETE GUIDE TO PLANNED GIVING**. It's a highly-specialized book on an important but technically difficult subject of particular interest to nonprofit organizations building endowment funds. As far as I know, there isn't an electronic media program in the country that is directed to this group, (please let me know if I'm wrong!). Therefore this book is not appropriate to offer to them. So we concentrate on getting print media attention for it.

On the other hand, I'm the author of a companion volume that tells nonprofit organizations (of which there are about a million) how to raise money from individuals. This subject is sufficiently broad and sufficiently important that I can, without difficulty, get regular electronic media attention. The thrust of the program I offer is, "How you can help your favorite charity raise the money it needs."

The question I have to ask myself is: are there enough people in this particular audience interested in this topic (and hence in my problem-solving products and services) to justify my time in doing the program? That to me is the more important question than whether the media source will put me on to discuss the subject in the first place.

Getting Media Program Directors Interested In What You Are Talking About

I'm not going to spend a long time discussing this subject, because you should have more than a glimmering now about what I am going to say. Media program directors are interested in problems and in the people who can solve them. Thus, to get on an electronic media program you have to do the following:

- Convince this person that what you are talking about is an important problem needing a solution;
- That people in his audience have this problem and so need to hear what you're saying;
- That you can put your message across convincingly, intelligently, and entertainingly;
- That you'll be easy to work with.

In short, you need to convince the program planner of two things: that you'll interest his audience and that you won't be any problem for him. That's what your initial letter to this source should do.

What Your First Letter Should Say

Dear Program Director (by name):

Did you know that one out of every two marriages will fail? That's right, every other marriage will end in divorce. Within five years of the couple's having vowed to "love, honor and cherish" each other in "sickness and in health", half of them will have split up. But fully three out of four of these marriages will already have children!

And that's the problem. What becomes of these children of divorce? Young people who must grow up without being together with father and mother, who must often adjust to complicated logistical situations, spending one week-end with one parent, while living with the other? Children who are so often drawn into the emotional squabbles that so often come with divorce?

That's the problem I set out to investigate 8 years ago in my counseling practice focusing on the problems of the children of divorce. Now I have written what many regard as the definitive book on this subject, a book which helps divorcing parents better cope with this very difficult situation and which contains step-by-step guidelines on how to minimize the emotional pressure and confusion of the children.

Given the fact that four out of five viewers of "Good Morning, Dayton" are women and that a significant percentage of them are divorced and have children, I think this subject — and how to cope with it — would be of particular interest to your audience.

As a guest on "Good Morning, Dayton", I can discuss:

- The four things every parent should know about how children under 10 regard divorce;
- How to break the news to children that the parents are getting divorced;
- How to minimize the stress on children who alternate spending time with parents who are still in the process of divorcing;
- Helping the children of divorced parents deal with their friends whose parents are still married.

I also deal with how the children of divorced parents feel about these parents when they themselves become adults, and how they can get over the anger and humiliation they still so often feel.

And much, much more.

I have had much experience dealing with both the children of divorced and divorcing parents and the parents themselves. I also regularly make presentations on this subject. Should you care to hear it, I can make available an audio cassette of my last presentation on this subject to the local Rotary Club.

With this letter I am enclosing further information about my long-established counseling practice and my new book *The Children Of Divorce*. I shall call in a few days to see if you might like to have me on your show or if you need further information.

There is so much pain involved in divorce for both parents and children that I look forward to being with you to do what I can to lessen it.

Sincerely,

Possible Television Guest

A Closer Look At Your Introductory Letter To The Program Director

- Begin with a problem statement, information about the seriousness of the problem. In short, your opening paragraph should be the hook that snags the interest of the media source. Don't make this technical. Do make it conversational. Notice in my illustration that I bring in the marriage vows themselves. Your job is to indicate to the media source that you know what the problem is and can put it (and solve it) conversationally. Remember: the electronic media programs of the kind which feature experts rely on these experts being conversationally adept.

- Follow by stating the problem the people you are trying to reach have and which you can solve. "What becomes of these children of divorce?" This is the essential question, the question on which the program is based (and which you are in business to solve).

- Now provide the media source with information that establishes that you are an expert in solving this problem. Use whatever evidence is necessary to convince him that you understand this problem and can solve it.

- Tell this source why you think his is the appropriate program for you to discuss this problem and your solution to it. Don't rely on the intelligence of the media source. Make the best possible case as to why you think his program slot is the best possible slot for what you are talking about, for the solution you are offering.

- Give information on the kinds of subjects you will discuss. The host wants to get a feel for what kind of program you can offer. Give it to him.

- Provide evidence that you will be a good guest. This means evidence that you can talk well and empathetically. The program planner wants to know that you know what you're talking about and that you can relate well to his audience. You must convince him on both counts.

- Send further information which establishes your credibility and underscores the importance of the topic you want to talk about. A reprint of a recent article on this subject is perfectly acceptable.

- Indicate how you'll be following up this letter. Stay in command of this process. You are offering the program director something of value. It is important that he know, too, that you are organized, disciplined and can follow through and do what you say you're going to do. He'll reckon that this is the kind of guest you'll be. Don't spoil things now.

Remember, send this letter and your materials to any media program that reaches the kinds of people who (in this case) could buy your professional service and problem-solving book. Getting on the electronic media when you don't know that the program reaches the people who can buy what you're selling may be good for your ego but makes no financial sense whatsoever.

When The Program Director Proves Difficult To Reach

Count on it: you are not always going to be able to get through to the program director you need on the first try. Not even when you're a star. So you need to master some techniques to work with the media and maximize your chance to get the coverage which is in your interest, and in the interest of both the program director, and the people whose problem you can solve with the product or service you are selling. Here's what you do:

- If you call and the program director is out, leave a detailed message. Say, "This is Dr. Jeffrey Lant. I'm following up my recent letter on a program on how nonprofit organizations can raise the money they need under the new tax laws. Would you please ask Mr. Program Director to call me at (617) 547-6372 this afternoon, if possible?"

He won't return your call.

- Call again. Leave the same message, but tell the secretary to mark it "Second call."

He won't return your call.

- Call again. This time explain to the secretary that Mr. Program Director hasn't returned your call, and you don't know whether he's interested in your program. Tell her what it is. Could the secretary ask him? You'll call back the next day and (if the program director is not available) ask the secretary for a response. In other words, use the secretary to make the connection you need.

This could work.

- If it doesn't, write a message to the media source saying that you regret you haven't been able to connect and enclosing a self-addressed post card. On this post card give the problem you are solving and two lines of information about the program you are proposing. Ask the Program Director to check one of two boxes. "Yes, I am interested. Please call me to schedule." "No, I am not interested at this time, but I would like you to keep in touch with further developments in this field and other ideas. Please keep in touch."

This could work. Even if the program director is not interested now — but does return the card — you have an opening for the future. In the second case, return a short note saying, "I'm sorry your schedule is too full to have me on right now. I know you appreciate the timeliness and importance of the subject 'The Children of Divorce' and hope you will consider me for a later time. I'll keep in touch with further information about this important subject, but you can always reach me at (specifics)."

In other words, let the media source know that the subject is important and that you will keep in touch. Being relentless is a necessary part of marketing success.

Then make sure you really do keep in touch.

When You Get The Program Director On The Telephone

- If you get the program director on the telephone, and he hasn't read your materials (as is usually the case), don't attempt to explain them on the phone. Arrange a convenient time to call back.

- If, when you call back, the program director sounds uncertain, ask why. Don't rush ahead. Find out what may be bothering the director. When you find out, then make your best case. Don't feel you have to make it only on the telephone. A further letter with additional information may be warranted.

- If the program director turns you down, send a thank-you note! That's right. Thank him for having considered the program, and let him know you are available to discuss this and such other topics as you may suggest whenever he has the need. Indicate that you are available on a twenty-four hour basis. Say that all he has to do to get you, if, say, one of his guests cancels, is call. Media plans change constantly. Don't be surprised if this results in the invitation you couldn't get in the first place!

Using Your Air Time Profitably

The reason you are going on this radio or television show is not to impart information. It's to sell products and services. But there is a fine line to toe. The ostensible reason you have been invited is to discuss a problem that has interested the program director and which concerns numbers of the audience. But your primary task is to let them know that you have a product or service which can help them. Fortunately, the objectives of all parties can be met.

To prepare for your appearance, do the following.

- Send the program director the introduction you want the host to use. "Dr. Jeffrey Lant is a graduate of Harvard and author of many books," is far less useful than, "Dr. Jeffrey Lant has been helping nonprofit organizations raise the money they need for many years. The Cambridge-based management consultant to nonprofit organizations now presents his step-by-step methods in his new book **DEVELOPMENT TODAY: A FUND RAISING GUIDE FOR NONPROFIT ORGANIZATIONS.**"

You'll notice the words "nonprofit organizations" are repeated several times in this introduction. Why's that? For targeting. You want the people whose problem you solve to be made aware that you are talking to them. The best way to do that is to say, over and over again, "Hey, I'm talking to you!" Hit 'em once. Hit 'em again. And then hit 'em again.

- Send the program director a list of questions to ask you. Twenty is ordinarily sufficient for a thirty-minute show. The first ten should be designed to elicit basic information about the subject you're discussing, "Tell us, Dr. Lant, what's the situation like for nonprofit organizations under the new tax law?" The final ten should offer you outright promotional opportunities. "Why did you write **DEVELOPMENT TODAY**, your fund-raising guide for nonprofit organizations?"

- Bring to the studio a complete set of any materials you may have sent. Media people are notorious for losing things. Anything that you want with you, you had better bring yourself. Count on them having nothing.

- When doing television, make sure you arrange in advance for them to run your address and/or telephone number on the screen while you are talking. You should be set up so that people wanting to follow-up this program can do so while you are still on the air. I often remind people that there may be a busy signal when they call, and if this happens to them to please call back. You can rest assured that your telephone line(s) will be clogged, and you might as well notify your prospects accordingly. *N.B.* If you wait until you get to the studio to arrange to have your telephone number run, it will probably be too late.

- When you've booked a radio show, tell the program director you would like a copy of it. Ask him if you need to bring your own cassette (you sometimes do with smaller stations), or if they will supply one (occasionally, for a price). You want a copy of your program both to hear how you did (and to learn what needs improving) and to make available to other program directors who may wish to have you.

On The Air At Last!

At last you'll be on the air, ready to connect through the host with your prospects. This is a critical time. You must be prepared to make the best use of it. Here are some rules so that you will:

- Talk conversationally. Don't pontificate. Talk as naturally as possible. Regard the host as a surrogate for the kinds of people (your prospects) you are really trying to connect to. "Mr. Program Director, are you connected to any nonprofit organizations? Do you ever get fund-raising letters in the mail? What do you think of them?"

- Don't use complicated language. Media language must be short, crisp, concise and action-oriented.

- Don't use statistics. Never say "50%". Say, instead, "One out of every two people listening to this show... "

- Don't use pronouns that stand in place of the full proper names of your products and services. Never say, "My new book... " Instead say, "My new book **DEVELOPMENT TODAY: A FUND RAISING GUIDE FOR NONPROFIT ORGANIZATIONS.**" Remember, you must hit your targets and hit them and hit them again.

- Make sure the host provides your prospects/his listeners with your telephone number during each segment of his show. This will be every 8 to 10 minutes. Tell your prospects what they'll receive when they call. It should be the précis, of course. "Tom, when your listeners call me today I'll send them a handy 10-point guide to raising money for their nonprofit organization under the new tax laws. You can call me right now at (617) 547-6372 to leave your name and address, and I'll send it out today."

- If the host gets off the subject, bridge to get it back on track. This is your time. Not his. It is your job to connect with your prospects. The garrulous host threatens your ability to do that. Don't let him!

- If you don't know something, say so. It's okay. But remember: you know more about your subject than the host probably does. If you're doing your job right, no one will know that you don't know absolutely everything about your topic, but that, instead, you know enough so that the people who have the problem you solve will want to contact you.

At The End Of The Show

When you're still on the air, thank the host for having you on to discuss your important subject. Name that subject again. And again invite the audience to contact you. Be warm. Inviting. And close with complete follow-up information. If the host doesn't give you the opportunity to provide it (he usually will), take the initiative. The people in your audience need to hear it again.

After you're off the air, again thank the host. Find out if he'd be interested in hearing about other topics from you. If you've been a good guest (or just out of a sense of courtesy), he'll probably say yes. That's your opening for your next approach. Make sure, too, you thank the program director. He's a critical link in the chain leading to your next appearance.

Now go back to your office, where, if the program was live, you should have a tape full of messages, all left by qualified prospects for what you are selling. If the program was taped, make sure you are set up to handle their calls, even if the program airs at 4 a.m. Sunday morning. I am. Are you?

Last Words On Properly Using The Media To Get Clients And Sell Products: Becoming The Recognized Source

As you've surely noticed, some people are invited on the media over and over again. Their names appear in stories over and over again. (I am one of them.) Ever wonder how we pulled this off? I can tell you. We are the Recognized Sources. And you can become one, too.

There are lots and lots of advantages to being a Recognized Source. It's a sure sign that you've arrived. That's soothing to a demanding ego. But more importantly, it assures you of getting continuing publicity without having to seek it out. This really means you are being invited by the media source to get access to your prospects, while being perceived as doing a favor for the source. Very neat, indeed.

What Is A Recognized Source?

A Recognized Source is an individual the media calls upon for information or a point of view or to comment on breaking news developments. But more than that, the media knows that this person is available to them at a moment's notice and will give them precisely what they want, precisely when they want it. In return, the media source is glad to give you what you want: another opportunity to hit your prospects and to gild your reputation as an individual who's worth doing business with.

On Becoming A Recognized Source

How do you become this sought-after creature? Do the following:

- To begin with, identify every conceivable media source who handles the kinds of subjects in which you are interested. By this I mean every media source who can connect you to your prospects. This means coming up with a list of people who write about the subjects in which you are interested. As you find such people (for you will never stop looking as long as you are in business), contact them with a Recognized Source Letter.

This letter simply says that you are available to help them when they are next working on the subject of your expertise. You can even provide them with leads to "hot topics" in this area. These topics, of course, ultimately relate to one of your products or services. Such a letter can and should be sent the minute you read a story or hear a program about something about which you are knowledgeable. Let the reporter or program director know you are available should something similar or related be done on the topic later.

- Don't expect this letter to be answered. It doesn't need to be. But do expect to follow it up in the future with further suggestions and information on what you are doing to solve the problem you want the media person to handle. Have you written a Problem-Solving Process Article? (You should have!) Send it! A book? Let the media source know it's available. Are you giving a speech on the subject? Even if the media person can't come, you'll have a tape in case he wants to hear it. Get the idea?

The whole idea behind the Recognized Source concept is that there are only so many ideas under the sun. A reporter who has just done an article on growing tomatoes is probably going to do another at some point. And if he doesn't, he'll know someone who will. Either way, the chances are good that you'll get called to participate in this, and so be able to promote what you are selling.

When The Media Calls You

You'll often get these calls at odd hours. I seem to get mine late Friday afternoon. These are the hours, however, the media source is on deadline, and when they haven't got time to run around seeking new sources. They have to rely on the ones they already have.

When the media source calls, drop everything. This is the moment to show what a trooper you are. Don't say you'll call back. Don't say you're busy. Even if you're with a client, ask the client if he minds if you give the media source ten minutes. If you don't give it to him now, when you call back he may not need you. Furthermore, you've given him the wrong signal about your ability and willingness to solve his problem.

Even though you weren't expecting this call, be prepared for it. Make sure you know in advance how you want to be identified in the article or on the tape. "Dr. Jeffrey Lant, management consultant, " isn't as useful as "Dr. Jeffrey Lant, Cambridge, Massachusetts-based management consultant to nonprofit organizations and author of **DEVELOPMENT TODAY: A FUND RAISING GUIDE FOR NONPROFIT ORGANIZATIONS.**"

At the very least, anyone interested in this subject can follow up by calling directory information in Cambridge. Which is just what you want. But if you're not clear with the media source about the kind of identifying information they should print about you, you're going to have to take whatever they give you. I can assure you, when a media person is under pressure and on deadline, he can be remarkably sloppy!

Thanking The Media Source

When you get this kind of call, be grateful for it. But don't be silently grateful. Whenever you're given attention by the media, thank the person who gave it to you. That's still true, even when you're a Recognized Source. There are lots of people who crave this title. Few get it. When you are used, let the media person know that you're glad to have the opportunity to be of service and will always be available when needed. Then reaffirm what you wrote by continuing to send in suggestions for topics and information of interest to the media source. That way they'll know you are really serious. It really does pay off.

Last Words On Using The Media To Get To Your Buyers

I'm a fanatic about using the media. And why not? These radio and television stations and print media outlets have the ability to get your message to millions at trifling expense. Moreover, I confess that I still feel thrilled to sit in my office in Cambridge (or even my bedroom!) knowing that my words, sometimes bounced off the nether side of the moon on a radio wave, will cause my targeted prospects thousands of miles away to sit up, take notice, and send in a check to this total stranger without the slightest misgiving, because they now feel I can help them solve their problems. Yes, this is a thrill and rightly so. And it will happen to you, if you follow the suggestions in this chapter, including using these recommendations which will be of the utmost assistance in this publicizing process.

Resources

If your audience is national, use these two wonderful resources:

- Broadcast Interview Source. Editor Mitchell P. Davis prepares a regular "Guest Directory" which he sends to radio station program directors nationwide and other journalists. You can get a simple listing of your specialty free. Providing more extensive details about you and your subject costs a reasonable sum. Contact him at 2233 Wisconsin Ave., N.W., Suite 930, Washington, D.C. 20007 or call (202) 333-4904.

- My friend Bill Harrison runs one of the most cost effective means I know of connecting with radio station program directors. Called *Radio-TV Interview Report*, Bill mails his monthly newsletter with 75-250 word write-ups on available guests and how to contact them to the people who need experts like us! His price is very reasonable. For $2 he'll send you a sample issue and information about his other publicity vehicles. Contact Bradley Communications, 135 East Plumstead Ave., P.O. Box 1206, Lansdowne, PA 19050-1206, (215) 259-1070.

Between these two sources, you'll connect for the most reasonable price with about every radio program director in America.

Finally, use my own book **THE UNABASHED SELF-PROMOTER'S GUIDE: WHAT EVERY MAN, WOMAN, CHILD AND ORGANIZATION IN AMERICA NEEDS TO KNOW ABOUT GETTING AHEAD BY EXPLOITING THE MEDIA.** This book is now rightly regarded as a classic on promotion, on getting your message to the right people for the least possible price. If you don't have it yet, get it. It's a prejudiced recommendation, to be sure, but I have succeeded to the extent that I have largely because of the unrelenting promotional techniques laid out in this volume.

CHAPTER 7

Profiting From Classified And Small Space Ads

You already know I'm keen on publicity. For what is publicity, after all, but being able to reach your buyers on other people's money? That, of course, I find a most satisfying concept.

The alternative is to buy paid advertising. That is the subject this chapter takes up.

Paid Advertising Can Be Risky To Your (Financial) Health

I've been in business long enough to know the allure — and the risks — of paid advertising. It's so seductively easy.

You pick up a rate card from any publication and see these exciting words jumping out at you; "Your ad in *The Fatuous Fortnightly* reaches over 8,000,000 customers — for pennies." Sounds good, doesn't it? But it's a snare, folks, a costly, possibly disastrous snare. Just like so much of advertising can be.

Let me say this as strongly as I possibly can: for most people advertising doesn't work. It doesn't put you in touch with people who can buy what you're selling. It isn't an investment. It's an outright expense. And a complete waste of money.

The next time you consider buying an ad of any kind, read these words. I am probably describing precisely what will happen to you. If you want a better way of wasting your money, open the window in your office and throw out your wallet. It comes to about the same thing.

But this needn't happen. Most of the mistakes made in advertising are predictable. They ordinarily fall into one of several areas, areas which are addressed right in this chapter.

The Reasons Why Most Ads Fail To Make Money

- The ad isn't targeted to the right people. You don't know who you are trying to reach. So it doesn't much matter where you put your ad. Thus, you tend to put it in the wrong publication.
- The timing of what you are offering is wrong. Face it. It's too late to advertise Christmas products in the December issues of monthly publications.
- The offer is wrong. You've got the wrong product for the group reading the publication. Or you're offering the right thing, but have supplied the prospect with inadequate information so he cannot decide to go ahead. Either way, the offer is wrong.
- The offer has not been repeated sufficiently often. You've forgotten the Rule of Seven, which, of course, applies to advertising, too.
- You haven't given the prospect an inducement for taking action NOW!
- The ad's layout is unfocused. The prospect's eye doesn't rest naturally on the two most important aspects of the ad: the benefit he gets by acting now and his marching orders which tell him what to do and how to do it.
- You haven't stressed the Benefits and the Ultimate Benefits which really cause people to buy. You are promoting features, not benefits.
- The ad copy is boring, imprecise, untargeted. No one knows you're talking to them, and no one cares because what you have to say is so dull and unspecific.

- You don't know what to do with the prospect's name after you've got it and mailed to him once. The prospect, a typical Flatworm, needs to hear from you again, but you stop after a single mailing.

- You count on too great a return too quickly, applying direct mail guidelines to advertising. They aren't the same.

The reason ads fail is usually found to be one of these points. That's why I intend to go into them in detail.

The Ad Isn't Targeted

I've said it again and again in this book. And now I'll say it yet again. If you want to succeed in profitably marketing what you are selling, then you have got to target the *exact* people who have the problem you are solving and hit them again and again and again. Targeting is an essential condition of successful marketing.

This means you have got to know as much as you can about your prospects and buyers. This includes knowing the precise publications they read.

Fortunately, the publications and electronic media outlets make this relatively easy for you. Most do care that your advertising works. This isn't just altruism either. If advertising through their medium pays off for you, you'll be back to spend more dollars. So it is very much in the interest of the media source to provide you with precisely the information you need.

This information is contained on the rate card. The rate card tells you essential demographic information about the media source you are considering; the age, sex, household income, education and other information which will enable you to precisely answer the question, "Does this media source connect with the people who have the problem I am solving?" You must have this information to decide whether this is the right source for you. If you are uncertain, don't go ahead. It'll be a costly mistake.

How do you get this information?

- Start with *Standard Rate And Data*, 3004 Glenview Rd., Wilmette, IL 60091 (708) 256-6067. It's available in most libraries and will provide you information about the publications in which you're thinking of advertising.

- Always write to the advertising department of the publication in which you're interested and request a sample copy and their rate card. Be as specific with them as you can. Tell them precisely what you are offering (provide information on your problem-solving product or service). Tell them exactly who has this problem and exactly whom you are trying to reach. Then ask for their suggestions on what you should do.

- Never stop looking for good places for your ads. Ask your prospects what they read. Then write for a sample copy. You'll find that if you intend to use paid advertising to reach your prospects, your research into the means to connect with them never stops. This is also true, of course, with the media sources you intend to use for unabashed promotion.

The Timing Is Wrong

As one of my college professors used to say, in this world timing is everything. I've decided that this cliché was probably worth the price of my graduate education.

Your timing can be wrong for any number of reasons:

- What you are offering is not in sync with the season at which the ad appears. Offering Christmas merchandise in July probably won't work.

- You've got the right season but have allowed inadequate time to follow up the inquiry or sale properly. Unless you have merchandise on hand and immediately available for shipment, you can't ship items for Christmas after December 10th and expect them to get to their destinations before the big day. Thus, advertising holiday goods in a monthly December publication makes no sense whatsoever.

- You're not ready to follow-up the inquiry immediately. We Americans want everything immediately. If you are not immediately able to follow-up your inquiries, you have a problem. Thus, you must ensure that you have the following available at the time your ad runs:

  - the product itself;
  - an accompanying letter which thanks the customer for buying (if you have used your ad for a direct sale), or a sales letter which provides him with the detailed information he needs about product/service benefits (if you have solicited an inquiry);
  - ride-along offers; that is, offers on related products and services which may be of interest to the buyer/inquirer.

In other words, you must have those materials available which will either move your new buyer on to the next sale or persuade him to make the one he is now contemplating.

The Offer Is Wrong

Please understand what I mean by offer. An offer can consist of your attempt to sell a product directly from an ad, or it can consist of your invitation to the prospect to contact you for further information.

Ordinarily the offer is incorrect if you attempt to sell a product for over $3 directly from the ad itself. People will risk sending $3 for something they want. Before they make any greater expenditure, however, they want to know more about what the product can do for them.

Thus, your offer is wrong if you are trying to sell your prospect something about which he needs more information before you have in fact given it to him.

Your offer is also wrong, of course, if you are offering the people reading, seeing or hearing it the wrong thing, something that solves a problem they don't have or which you have failed to communicate adequately to them.

The Ad Has Not Been Repeated Sufficiently Often

Advertising is a subset of marketing, and as such the Rule of Seven applies. Thus, running a single ad will probably be insufficient. Your prospects don't know enough about you (the trust-factor). Even if they have the problem, it may not be at the very top of their priority list for solving now. In other words, they are not ready to buy when you are ready to sell. That's why you have to repeat.

I've been stressing throughout this book that you put into gear a mix of methods to target your prospects. This mix rightly includes advertising, (although you already know that I, as a good Yankee, will try to find other, less expensive, and equally- or more-effective alternatives first). The question you have to answer for yourself is not *whether* you will repeat your advertising (for you must do so), but how often you repeat it to the same group and in what sequence. How many issues of a monthly publication, for instance, can you safely afford to skip without undercutting your effectiveness in reaching prospects? That is the $64,000 question.

You Have Not Given The Prospect An Inducement For Taking Action NOW

When you are advertising, you are competing against the thousands of other messages that the prospect is seeing weekly. No one knows how many of these there are. One study I recently read said that we may be subjected to as many as 7,500 advertising messages weekly! In any event, it's a staggering total.

Why should your prospect take action now, as opposed to waiting? The prospect, you see, knows that the likelihood is high you'll be back again with another offer. At some level, he reckons that he can wait until then — perhaps even longer — to take action.

You always have to work against this tendency. You must always answer the prospect's certain-to-be-there question, "Why should I do it now?". If you can't, you've essentially said to the prospect, "It's okay to wait, because I can't think of any reason why you should do anything now, except for the fact that I need the money." This isn't a very good reason to act from the prospect's point of view, is it?

The Ad's Lay-out Is Unfocused

There are only two things of real value in an ad; the Ultimate Benefit the prospect gets when he has your product/service and is using it and the marching orders which explains what he needs to do to get this benefit. Getting the prospect to focus on these two items — as opposed to the many other items which may in fact be present in your ad — is the job of the graphic designer.

If your designer knows his stuff, the prospect's eye should move effortlessly to these two key points. First, it should focus on the Ultimate Benefit. If you have offered a meaningful benefit, the prospect will want it. Really, who can resist the possibility of having more money, being healthier, sexier, having more friends, and all the other Ultimate Benefits that those of us selling products and services really offer people? No one. And that's the point.

Yet who can resist the products and services that bring about these benefits?

Lots of people. In fact, most of the people seeing your ad and both wanting and needing the Ultimate Benefit your problem-solving product and service make available will not take action.

Therefore, when we have the very fleeting attention of the prospect, let's focus it on two things and two things only; the Ultimate Benefit he really wants and the way he can get to us — this minute! — to get it.

Give your ad to other people. Watch the way they look at it. If you're not sure, ask them what they see first in your ad. Ordinarily they look for the Ultimate Benefit first. Then, if they want this Ultimate Benefit, they want to know how to get it from what you're selling. Then they look for the marching orders, what they need to do to take action and so get what they want.

Thus, make sure your designer concentrates on the Ultimate Benefit deriving from the use of your product or service and then moves the prospect to the marching orders which, when followed, ensure he'll get it. Any other information in your ad should be regarded as of secondary importance and handled accordingly.

You Haven't Stressed The Benefits And The Ultimate Benefits

Too often ads fail because they tell you about the product. As I write I'm reviewing such an ad. It leads with detailed information about the number of pages in the book being offered, the book's size, even the book's color. But this is a book about saving money on your taxes, a subject of interest to all of us. Only after the product details are given does the advertiser begin to provide information about the benefits to be derived from using what he's selling.

This example occurs all too often. Of course, you are interested in your product or service. Of course, you are fascinated by how it works. But don't expect your prospects to share your enthusiasm. What they want to know is very simple, "What's in it for me?" They want to know this as soon as possible and in the most compelling way possible. Why do people with products and services to sell find this lesson so difficult to learn?

Remember what I've been saying throughout this book. Products and services are made up of features. These features relate to benefits. In other words, if you are selling a tax-saving guide, its features consist of a certain number of pages, a certain kind of format, tables, and charts. These features must connect to benefits.

For example, if you use the step-by-step technique provided on getting money out of your closely-held corporation, this will lead to a benefit. That benefit is money. But money is rarely an Ultimate Benefit. It is an intermediate benefit. The real benefit of money is that you can spend it the way you want, when you want, for what you want. So that the Ultimate Benefit of following the technique actually is to have spendable money in your pocket when you want it.

Let me say this as clearly as I can: unless the buyer actually feels that money in his pocket, the creator of the tax-saving guide won't be able to sell his product. Because that feeling of money in his pocket is most important to the prospect, the advertiser needs to lead with this and stress this Ultimate Benefit over and over again. Other features can follow later when the prospect, heeding the advertiser's marching orders, asks for more information. As he will — if the Ultimate Benefit has been put sufficiently compellingly.

The Ad Copy Is Boring, Imprecise, Untargeted

Too many ads are dull ads. But this needs explanation. Exciting ads do not necessarily feature slinky women in provocative clothes draped around the bumper of a luxury car. Not by a long shot. Dull ads are ads that:

- don't use action words. The best ads, like all marketing devices, take the prospect from where he is now to where he wants to be. By definition, these ads are made up of action words.
- don't scream desirable benefits at the prospect. Often the prospect doesn't know what he wants until he's told what he wants. An ad, any ad, should make these wants palpable.
- don't involve as many of the five senses as possible. If you want to get a person to take action, involve all the senses.
- don't make it easy for the prospect. Americans are lazy. Smart advertisers know this and make it unbelievably easy for the prospect to take action. They either create or stimulate the want in the prospect's mind and make it incredibly easy for that prospect to take action to get what he wants, without so much as moving from the chair he's sitting in when he first becomes aware of what you've got for him.

Furthermore, the copy is boring if not selfish copy. By this I certainly do not mean selfish from the advertiser's perspective either. Because that's precisely what's wrong with most ads. They tell you about the advertiser. This is okay if advertising is a form of ego gratification for you. But it is a disastrous miscalculation if you expect to sell products and services to your prospects.

Boring copy fails because it doesn't say, "Mr. Prospect. This ad is for you. It's written with you in mind. It's written precisely for you. And I don't mean someone like you. I mean YOU. You know that's true because you can agree with every word in the ad. You know we've done our homework, and you can therefore conclude that the product/service we are talking about is just right for you."

Let me say this: when someone writes something nice to you (think of the last love letter you got, the epitome of marketing copy), you don't care if there are mistakes in it, that the grammar is wrong, that diction has been thrown out the window. What you do care about is that it is especially for you. You must achieve the same result with your ad copy.

You Don't Know What To Do With The Prospect Name After You've Got It

Too often, once an advertiser has got your name, he doesn't know what to do with it. Yet getting the name either of a qualified prospect or of a certain buyer is a triumph. If you cannot convince these people that your products and services are for them, frankly your business is going to fail. However, convincing them means having a plan for regularly following up the prospect once you know who he is.

Don't buy an ad unless you know precisely how you are going to follow up the buyer/prospect now. Moreover, don't buy an ad unless you know how you are going to follow them up over the next year.

Face it. The prospect is not necessarily going to take immediate action, even though he has the problem you can solve. Even though he needs the Benefit and Ultimate Benefit you offer. Even though you've given him an inducement to take action now.

Face it. Your buyer is not always going to want to buy something else immediately after having bought another of your products or services. Perhaps he's simply not able to. Perhaps he needs time to use what you've already sold him.

For whatever reason, you need to have a strategy for reapproaching these people — and reapproaching them —until such time as you decide they are not really qualified prospects (or further buyers) but only window shoppers.

This means that your ad can be a financial success even if it doesn't draw large numbers of people with check in hand. Such success can only occur, however, if you are prepared to keep telling those who did respond (however few they are), in crystal-clear detail, that you understand their problem and can solve it, if only they have the good sense to take action now, when you have made it easy for them to do so. If they don't take this action now, you must be prepared to approach them again later with the same pressing message.

This process of reapproaching prospects must be regarded as an essential part of what makes your ad profitable. If you have not thought through a series of steps designed to get you back in touch with your prospects and buyers, then you might well ask yourself if there is any point in doing the ad in the first place. I can assure you, that given this standard, for most advertisers there is no such point.

You Count On Too Great A Return

While I was writing this chapter, a friend wrote me with a suggestion that he buy some paid advertising in a publication to run ads promoting my books. He'd calculated that he'd get a 1.5% response based on the number of subscribers to the publication and that we'd soon be on Easy Street. What did I think of his swell idea?

Well, picture the situation. He wasn't asking me to pay for the ads. Only supply the products. Certainly, I must have gone along with his thinking, right?

Wrong.

I told him his idea was lousy. Even though I personally had nothing to lose (since I wasn't paying for the ads) and some sales to gain, I advised against it. Why?

It is part of the seductive myth of advertising that an ad, any ad, will pull responses from a vast number of people seeing it. Actually the reverse is true. People these days are hit with so many offers and can respond to so few, that a response of 1.5% to your ad is highly unlikely, even if you have correctly targeted the right people, presented them with the right offer, given them a reason for acting now, and done all the other things I've suggested.

Oftentimes the advertising novice will confuse what may well happen in direct mail (the 1.5% response) with what is possible with advertising. They are vastly different.

If it were possible for me — or any other potential advertiser — to target our audiences through print and electronic media, select the right ones and count on a 1.5% response, none of us would ever have a financial problem, ever. But it just isn't possible.

Advertising is a slow, methodical, calculated process. And as should by now be clear, it demands not merely putting your ad in the right place but following up the people who answer it again and again and again, until such time as it no longer makes economic sense to do so.

Thus, if you expect to be successful as an advertiser, you must learn to accept a small response and to make your money by working to convert those who do respond from prospects to buyers. This is the real secret of successful advertising. Not getting bales of dollars in the mail daily because of one sizzling ad or another, but making money slowly, steadily, surely by hitting the right people and hitting them again and again and again until they regard you and what you are selling as the Inevitable Solution to their problem.

The First Step Towards Advertising Success: Mastering The Lowly Classified Ad

In business there's a lot of snobbery and when people get snobbish, they get stupid. Thus, many businesses who could benefit from classified ads reject them as somehow unbefitting the status of their superior company. What idiocy!

The classified ad always has been and always will be a superb vehicle to connect certain types of businesses offering certain types of products with their qualified buyer prospects. The classified, which all of us know, has many advantages:

- It's cheap. On a cost-per-word basis, classified ads are probably the cheapest advertising vehicles you can buy.

- Properly written, it will target the exact buyers you want to reach and get them to take the exact action you want them to take (namely, contacting you for further information).

- It can provide, within the compass of a very few words, information on both the Benefit and the Ultimate Benefit you are providing.

- It is action-oriented. It moves the prospect from the place he is now to a place he wants to be, and it does so with graceful economy of language.

- It's a good learning experience. My rule of business has always been, since one is going to make mistakes anyway, to make them at the cheapest possible rate. Classified ads allow you to do just that. Rather than risk thousands of dollars, risk tens and learn from the results. If you succeed in writing profitable classified ads, which cost a relatively few dollars, then you will be successful in writing small space ads, too.

Allow me a personal story at this point. While I was lecturing recently at Southern Methodist University in Dallas on "Creating A Profitable Mail Order Business," there was a young woman in my workshop who had just sunk over $3,000 into a one-shot space ad in a major publication. It was all the operating capital she had, and she did it because she thought she was supposed to do it.

When I saw her, her ad had only drawn three responses. Just three. She was sure going to have to sell a lot more $20 fruit baskets to pay for the ad, much less for the product itself!

Ladies and gentlemen, listen to this! During the 12 years I've been in business, I have never spent more than $250 for an ad. And even that expenditure was probably unnecessary. Remember: if you want a quick way to throw your money away, advertise unwisely. Just ask my friend from SMU, every one of whose worst fears about advertising was vividly realized.

I told her that for what she had paid for one single space ad, she could have had over 30 minimum-rate classifieds in major publications. Over 30! I also told her I would guarantee she'd have more than 3 responses, or off with my head! She looked at me sadder but measurably wiser. Unfortunately, this kind of wisdom comes all too often after an expensive — and unnecessary — mistake.

Writing Winning Classified Ad Copy

There are secrets to writing profitable classified ad copy. Here they are.

Being the good Yankee I am, I like to write ads that are the minimum length the publication will allow. This is usually 10 words. When you're buying a single word, you're buying 10, so you might as well use the number you get for the minimum price and see if this won't do. If you write the right kind of ad, it will.

To write your ad, do the following:

- Begin by writing it out in complete sentences.

Let's say I want to get my Sure-Fire Business Success Catalog into the hands of a small business owner like you. My complete-sentence offer might read: "Our Sure-Fire Business Success Catalog has over 140 ways to help make your business more profitable. Order your free copy from Jeffrey Lant Associates, Inc., 50 Follen Street, Suite 507, Cambridge, MA 02138." This ad is called a two-step, because I am not trying to sell directly from it. Instead, I am attempting to elicit a response from a qualified prospect who wants what I am really selling ("Sure-Fire Business Success", a/k/a money).

- Then start slicing (remember, you're paying by the word!), attempting to reach your objective, which is targeting the right prospect, presenting him with a meaningful benefit and marching orders — all in 10 words. No, Virginia, this is not a trick question. It is possible. You can do it!

Start from the address, an easy and essential part of your ad. Reduce your address to the fewest number of words which still ensures that you will receive the response. In this case "JLA, 50 Follen, Cambridge, MA 02138". This counts as 5 words for most publications, since the state and zip code usually are counted as a single word. Usually but not always.

Each publication has different standards, and they stick to them rigidly. When you contact the publication for the rate card, make sure you ask for their classified ad guidelines and procedures. If you've miscounted even by a single word, the publication will probably bill you and not run your ad until the invoice is paid. This obviously takes time and sets back your whole advertising process.

You've now "spent" five words, and you've got five words left.

- Target. Who are you speaking to? Remember, all ads must be addressed to the most specific audience possible. Sometimes the targeting has been done by the publication. If I am running my classified in *Innkeeping* newsletter, which is exclusively read by innkeepers, I don't need to use the word "innkeeper" in my copy. The publication has, in fact, targeted for me. If, however, I am running my ad in *Popular Mechanics*, which has an extraordinarily wide reach, then I most surely want to have a targeting word. So this factor will change. For this illustration, let's say I am using *Popular Mechanics*. I therefore need to have the words "small business" included.

- Now I need an immediate-action word. From the prospect's standpoint what's important about my offering? Well, two things actually. First, it promises a clear benefit ("Sure-Fire Business Success"). Second, the prospect can learn more by hazarding nothing more than a 25-cent stamp. In other words, my information is FREE. FREE is one of the key words in constructing meaningful classifieds.

Other compelling words include these 100 compiled by Judy Blake of *The Stamp Collector*:

absolutely, approved, attractive, authentic, bargain, beautiful, better, big, colorful, colossal, complete, confidential, crammed, delivered, direct, discount, easily, endorsed, enormous, excellent, exciting, exclusive, expert, famous, fascinating, fortune, full, genuine, gift, gigantic, greatest, guaranteed, helpful, highest, huge, immediate, improved, informative, instructive, interesting, largest, latest, lavish, liberal, lifetime, limited, lowest, magic, mammoth, miracle, noted, odd, outstanding, personalized, popular, powerful, practical, professional, profitable, profuse, proven, quality, quick, rare, reduced, refund, remarkable, reliable, revealing, revolutionary, scarce, secret, security, selected, sensational, simplified, sizable, special, startling, strange, strong, sturdy, success, superior, surprise, terrific, tested, tremendous, unconditional, unique, unlimited, unparalleled, unsurpassed, unusual, useful, valuable, wealth, weird, and wonderful.

Resource Note: If you can't find the word you want on this list — and FREE doesn't seem to work either — try a book like J. J. Rodale's *The Synonyn Finder*. It's a superb resource offering over one million synonyms. You can get it through Rodale Press, 33 East Minor St., Emmaus, PA 18049 (800) 441-7761.

- Now you need the benefit word. You must provide a word that tells the prospects you have targeted and whom you want to take action, what's in it for them. I like the word "success".

- The code. You need to know which of your ads is drawing and which is not. A code enables you to do this. But why use up part of your word allotment with a code? It's not necessary, as you'll see.

Here then is the structure of your ad:

(immediate inducement for acting) + (precisely targeted prospect group) + (benefit for acting) + (what prospect will receive from you) + (address) = profitable classified ad.

Following this formula and the information I gave you above, here's what one of my ads might look like:

"Free Small Business Success Catalog. JLA/a, 50 Follen, Cambridge, MA 02138." (*N.B.* The "/a" at the end of JLA is, of course, the code which indicates the publication and/or month your ad ran.)

Ten words which I have used successfully many times.

Writing Ads, Testing Ads

The trick, of course, is not just to write a single ad, but to write many ads and test them. This testing process begins before you submit the ad to a publication. Start with your prospects. Ask them to give you a reaction to a few ads. But don't give them the ads all at once. Dole them out one at a time and see what the reaction is.

Of course, this is a time-consuming process. But it is also an inexpensive process. Why find out that your ad is a stinker after you've paid for it? Find out beforehand, and go back to the drawing board. Yet how few people actually do this!

Running Your Ad

Every publication that prints classified ads has a special price for volume advertising, usually over three runs. Looks good, doesn't it? But beware. Until such time as you know that your ad is going to draw, there's no point in taking advantage of these offers no matter how advantageous they seem. Remember the underlying philosophy of this book: spend as little money as possible, spend it as slowly as possible, and test, test, test to make sure that the money you do spend is wisely spent.

The publication may prove to be a superb source for your ads. But then again, it may not. If it is, and you don't buy the discount rate, then the decision has indeed cost you money. But if it isn't a good place for you — a far more likely alternative — then you'll be better off waiting. The Lant Rule is that it's always better to be safe than sorry. Don't you agree?

Determining If Your Ad Is Successful

An ad is successful if it either makes money for you outright or begins a process which will produce money in due course and after successive approaches to the prospects who have initially responded and those who have bought what you're selling and can buy again. If you have any other reasons for running your ad, they are not sensible.

Let's not waste any time on the first alternative. It should be obvious to you when your ad has made money outright. The difficult — and more common — alternative is when it doesn't make money right away, and you have to figure out what to do next.

Let's say you run a 10-word ad in *Popular Mechanics*. The current cost of this ad is about $70. Let's say your product sells for $30. Even given the gigantic circulation, only about 30 people may respond. You have to send out 30 sales packets which each cost, say, 30 cents; (the first class postage stamp being the largest single cost of communicating with your prospects.) Say one of them buys the product. Yes, one! You need at least three more sales to make a profit (even a tiny one), given the fact that your product costs money, too.

Given that your product costs $30, you can afford to add these names to your mailing list and to send subsequent mailings. If they are truly qualified prospects, you have every likelihood of making these names profitable. If your product sells for under $10, however, you probably won't. There just isn't enough money in this deal, and therefore every time you mail to these prospects you are actually digging yourself further into a hole.

This suggests, therefore, that to make classified (much less any other) advertising successful, the following conditions must exist:

- You must be selling an item for at least $25.

- You should move as quickly as possible into other, related items (see my previous discussion about creating the profitable catalog). Doing so will distribute the cost of your advertising investment because you'll be solving many prospect problems.

- You must follow up all the prospects several times and, of course, all your buyers. Remember the Rule of Seven applies here. Ideally, you would be getting to them through some combination of paid advertising, free publicity and direct mailings, so that they would come to see you as the Inevitable Solution to their problems.

- You must be doing a sufficient amount of advertising so that you can send out your responses by bulk rate, not first class, thereby slicing your postal bill, one of your major expenses.

The Bad Things About Classified Ads

Not surprisingly, there are negative things to keep in mind about classified ads:

- They attract a lot of "freebie seekers". There are people who must spend all their time answering ads and seeking free information. Use your discretion about sending your information to them. My rules are:

  - If the request is obviously mass-produced (like a photocopied letter), consider whether you want to send your information.

  - If the request is from a prisoner, consider whether you want to send it. (You'll know because most prisons stamp the envelope with an indication that it is coming from a prison, or because there is a multi-digit number that follows the prisoner's name. Prisoners ordinarily try to make this look like part of the address, but it is, of course, actually their identification number.) *N.B.* Prisoners can buy products. I have received checks from prisoners drawn on their prison-run accounts!

  - If the request is sloppily handwritten and comes from a post office box, I usually don't send my material. I sell professional and business advancement books. People who can't type, who write on the back of an old envelope and who send me a letter loaded with misspellings, are probably not a good candidate for what I'm selling. You must create your own standards.

  - If the request comes from a child. You'll know because you used to write that way, too, when you were 15. A dead giveaway.

In other words, use your discretion. Just because a person has answered your ad is not sufficient reason for you to send your material. You'll develop a sense for when a prospect is really a prospect and not just a window-shopper anxious to get mail.

If you follow these rules, the process which begins with printing your classified ad will be profitable. Furthermore, by reinvesting a percentage of the money you make into buying more classified ads both in the publications which you know now work — as well as those which look likely for what you're selling — you will make more money still. And so be able to pay for your small space ads.

Resource

Two booklets by classified advertising authority Bernard Lyons provide further information about profitably using classified ads. These booklets are entitled *The Mail Order Ad Clinic* and *How To Make More Money From Your Mail Order Ads*. Lyons' booklets have lots of good ideas about classifieds, even though they tend to be repetitive and are very poorly put together. You can get them through Owen Publishing Co., Box 771, Battle Ground, WA 98604.

Preconditions For Running Successful Small Space Ads

There isn't a businessperson in America who doesn't like to see himself in print. Since most haven't read my books and aren't using the principles of unabashed promotion to get free publicity, they are left to buy paid ads to get this thrill. But for most people, that's the only thrill they get, since their ads don't produce dollars, which is for me a much more substantial cause for excitement.

Before you lay out a dime on any space ads, ask yourself the following questions:

- Am I targeting a precise group of people who have a precise problem which my product/service can solve?
- Am I really going to reach these people through the advertising source I have chosen. How do I know?
- Have I made the commitment to hit this precise, targeted group at least 7 more times in the next 18 months?
- Am I attempting to coordinate my approaches to them through free publicity, paid ads, direct mail advertising, and workshops and talk programs? In other words, are they likely to hear about me and my problem-solving offer(s) in several different ways?
- Am I putting too much reliance on a single ad? Do I expect it to do the work of seven?
- Have I written action copy packed with benefits and indicating precisely what I want the prospect to do?
- Am I prepared to handle the prospect if he does what I want him to do?
- Am I prepared to follow-up the prospect time and time again if he doesn't take advantage of my offer the first time he hears about it? If he doesn't take advantage of my offer the first time he hears about it, will a sale (when it ultimately occurs) generate enough money to pay for all my attempts to convince this prospect to take this beneficial action, as well as all those who don't?
- Have I tried to swap for the ad by bartering it for my services/products or by exchanging it for one of my problem-solving process articles? Am I absolutely sure I need to spend my good old Yankee dollars? Or is there another way of getting what I want? Could I barter my mailing list? Or insert advertising information about the publication in my outgoing information, getting an ad in return? Or get the ad as partial payment for one of my speeches or workshops?

If, and only if, these crucial questions have been entirely satisfactorily answered should you go ahead and buy your space ad. Even if you do this, you should always work your way through these questions each and every time you consider spending your money this way. Remember: in the Lant universe, spending your money is the last thing you do, and you do it only after you have investigated all the other alternatives, and you have considered long and hard how you can minimize the risk for the expenditure you are about to make. Is this how you do business? Well, it ought to be!

More Things You Should Know About Successful Small Space Ads

Remember what I keep urging you to do: take your ego out of the reckoning. Of course, it's simply spiffy to see yourself and your products and services in print or beamed over the electronic media. But does it make money? Does it reach the right people? Does it reach them a sufficient number of times? This is what's important.

Small space ads will be more likely to make money if you:

- Keep your costs down when buying them. One good way of doing this is to target the publications which reach your prospects. Then let them know you are interested in buying remnant space. And what, pray tell, is that?

All media sources are made up of severely time-bound valuables. That is, once the magazine or newspaper has been printed, the publication can't make any more money from selling advertising in it. The same applies for television and radio advertising. Thus, as the publication- or air-date gets closer, the value of the commodity the media source is selling may drop. This is your chance to get the advertising you want at the price you really want to pay: less.

Of course, in such instances you will not get first choice. That's always left for the people who pay their money upfront and first. However, if you play your cards right, you *may* be able to get *precisely* what they get — and pay much less for it. This happens if you can buy remnant space, the space that's left over, that no one has bought and that the publication would rather take some money for than get nothing for at all.

To get this remnant space, write the director of advertising at the source you have targeted, and indicate you are interested in buying remnant space. Tell him you have camera-ready artwork of a particular size which you can send to the publication with 24-hour (overnight) notice. Indicate what price you are willing to pay for this space. It is certainly permissible to ask for a 50% discount. You may also do better, if the space you are buying is oddly-shaped because of the make-up of a page.

Now be ready to take advantage of these calls when they come. They most assuredly will, since very few publications are ever fully sold, whatever they say to the contrary.

First, however, you may get a call from the person you've written to explaining that they don't sell remnant space, that they hope you'll still buy paid ads from them, and that you'll get a good deal if you buy a series of ads. Stay cool. Be equally polite. But don't change your position.

Indicate that you are certainly interested in doing some ad business with this publication. That you respect it highly and know it reaches your prospects, but that you have a policy, and you're going to have to abide by it. (Yes, even if you work alone like I do, you can still have a policy!) Ask him to keep your specifications on file. Definitely let him know you would be interested in buying a small space ad under the terms outlined in your original letter when such a buying opportunity becomes available. Then end the telephone call amicably.

And wait.

Someday your price will come.

Twenty-four hours before the publication closes its issue, you'll get a frantic and oh-so-friendly call from the advertising director letting you know they accept your terms, if you can have your camera-ready ad to them by overnight mail.

Will you be ready?

Steps Towards Developing Your Camera-Ready Copy

At this point, you should know whether you are a good advertising copy writer or not. If not, hire someone to help you write your ads. You can even hire me. Modestly, I tell you I am faster and less expensive than your average copywriter despite the extra services I offer.

The average copywriter is just a wordsmith, someone who's good with the language but doesn't help much with conceptualizing your ad. By conceptualizing, I mean helping you with:

- whom you are trying to reach;
- why you are trying to reach them;
- what benefits they want from you;
- which features of your product/service they are interested in.

Copywriters write. I strategize — and write, too.

Preparing Yourself For A Copywriter

Unless you are a strong writer, you are going to need a copywriter. Even very slight changes in language can make all the difference in whether your ad is successful, or just another boring interruption between juicy editorial content. Advertising authorities I respect like Robert Bly in his book *Create The Perfect Sales Piece* and Edmond Bruneau in his book *Prescription For Advertising* do not merely advise you to get a copywriter. They are adamant about your getting one. And I know why.

If you're like most people taking my marketing workshop (and the run of them are very bright people), you are a lousy writer with no gift for language. This may not matter much around your office, but it is a prescription for disaster when you write advertising copy. Such copy must be clean, crisp, action-oriented, featuring the elegance of economy. In short, the simpler it appears, the more difficult such copy is to write, whatever you may think to the contrary.

Hence, you need a copywriter.

Before you go looking for one, however, prepare yourself so that you get the best use from the one you select. Do your homework, and give the copywriter precise answers to the questions which constitute the heart of marketing and hence the heart of successful copywriting:

- whom are you trying to reach?
- what benefits are you offering them?
- what Ultimate Benefit(s) are they getting from your product?
- why should the prospect buy now?
- what will happen to them if they wait?
- what obstacles are preventing the prospect from acting?
- what do you want the prospect to do?
- how do you want him to do it?
- where do you want your advertising to run?

Don't even think of talking to a copywriter until you have made your best possible effort to answer these critical questions.

Then, do the following:

- Get a copy of the publication where you'd like your ad to run. In fact, get several. Go through every small space ad, and select the ones you like, the ones which have got you excited about the product and ready to spend your money to get it. By the same token, select the ads that do nothing for you. Prepare to give both examples to your copywriter.

- Once you've identified an ad you really like, call the company (particularly if it's local) and ask to speak to the copywriter. See if he does free-lance work. Most copywriters moonlight. You might as well seek one out whose work you like, and by this I mean one who has motivated you to buy.

- Or see if your area has a publication like we've got in New England. Here there's a directory of graphic designers, copywriters, photographers, illustrators, video and film producers, printers and other suppliers of graphic and creative services. It's called *Worksource*. Buyers of creative talent and services can get a copy free by contacting Worksource, 15 Mt. Auburn St., Cambridge, MA 02138 (617) 864-1110. If you're not in one of these categories, this excellent book costs $50 postpaid. *N.B.* If you provide one of these services, you can be listed free. Contact them for details.

- Comtact your local Ad Club. All major cities have an ad club composed of people in the advertising business. A look in the Yellow Pages under "Organization" usually does the trick to get their telephone number. Find out if they have a list of copywriters, or what they suggest to get hooked up. It's very much in their interest to help you. Remember that, if they are vague, rude, and disorganized.

- Check the Yellow Pages, too, under "Copywriter". Sometimes the telephone company is more organized than we think.

- Large cities also have specialized publications directed at people interested in advertising and featuring ads by copywriters hawking their services. *Ad East*, headquartered in Boston, covers all of New England. *Ad Week* from New York does the same there.

- Check your local business publication. Copywriters regularly advertise their services in the *Boston Business Journal*. You'll find an excellent list of them in the *U.S. Regional Publications Directory* (which also features many other kinds of publications). Get it through Bradley Communications, P.O. Box 1206, Lansdowne, PA 19050 (215) 259-1070.

- Check, too, with local advertising agencies. They all have copywriters, and most of them moonlight. Do be discreet when calling. Ask if they'll give you a referral to one or more of the free-lance copywriters they use. Or ask if someone on their staff does occasional free-lance assignments. Don't just ask for any copywriter, however. It's useful to provide some guidelines which will make it easier to the agency —or whomever else you contact — to give you the proper referral.

Give them information about the copywriting category in which you're interested. It is technical? Retail? Service? Nonprofit? Does it involve an emotional pitch? Or a more logical one? The more information you can provide about your project to the person from whom you're soliciting the referral, the better the chances you'll get the right person for your job.

Now Go Scots

The Scots (not, Scotch, please, that's a libation, not a people) are a remarkably canny and parsimonious people. I know. By heritage, I am one myself. Now I am asking you to join the clan. In contacting a copywriter, remember you are about to make an investment. You want to make sure the copywriter can help you get the proper return on your dollars. Thus, be all hardheaded business about your contact with your prospective copywriter.

- Advise your copywriter about what you are trying to do. Don't hesitate to send samples of the ads you like. Do ask to see samples of his work that is comparable. Never hire a copywriter until you see his work. Never.

- Ask the copywriter how he charges. The copywriter will probably want to charge you an hourly rate. You'll want a project rate which ensures you'll not be charged for a dilatory copywriter or for the changes which I guarantee you're going to want. Particularly when working with a new copywriter who doesn't know you or your product or what you are trying to achieve, I can assure you it will take time to bring about a meeting of minds. Don't let this process be on your tab.

- Get references. Sure copywriters are artists. But they don't have to behave boorishly as a result. Find out from someone who has worked with them if they meet deadlines and try to understand what you as the client are trying to do. Remember, this is your project not the copywriter's. This is a piece of advice you'll need to remember when you see the copywriter's work for your ad. It's your product or service. Not his.

Additional Things The Copywriter Needs To Know

The copywriter will also need information on:

- the contemplated size of your ad. This, in turn, relates back to your advertising budget. Unlike other authors who write about advertising, I am not going to suggest what percentage of your budget you should allocate to advertising. My answer to that is, "It depends."

It depends, that is, on your ability to use other means of getting to your targeted buyers. If you're not going to use the many other suggestions I'm making throughout this book, you are going to have to allocate a greater percentage of your budget than those of us pursuing other alternatives. It's up to you.

Either way, you need to give your copywriter an idea of your ad budget, including the number of different kinds of ads you'll be needing, whether these ads must be entirely different or whether they'll follow sequentially from each other, and the size ads you want. Please note, "The cheaper, the better" is not a guideline.

What do I mean, then?

Let's say you only have enough money to run a single ad in a single publication four times in 18 months, and that you are going to get to these targeted buyers in other ways to make up the minimum of seven times necessary under the Rule of Seven.

It would be foolish to have your copywriter write four different ads. Foolish and too expensive. Two would be the most you'd need. Two which alternate or which, perhaps, follow in logical sequence, depending on what other means you are using to reach your targeted prospects. But the copywriter needs to know what you're going to do, for it is infinitely easier for him to write both your ads at once than it is to do one now and one six months from now.

What Must Always Be In Your Copy

You've seen ads — lots of them — that don't seem to be selling anything. They don't even have specific follow-up information. Nothing. I'm sure some genius somewhere thinks these ads are brilliant, as art perhaps. I strongly disagree. They are a complete waste of money.

The ads you write must always have certain pieces of information, and you must work with the copywriter to make sure that the more important of these are properly highlighted:

- benefits. Lead with benefits. Follow with features. The benefits must be in the ad. You can send the features of your problem-solving product or service in your follow-up letter.

- marching orders. Very specifically, what do you want the prospect to do? When do you want him to do it? How do you want him to do it? You must include all the information he needs, including a specific person to contact, a 24-hour telephone number, and an address. Information about the specific person to contact is most important. We live in an impersonal and alienated age. People rightly feel intimidated dealing with institutions. They want to have the name of a specific person to contact, a person they have some reason for feeling will be able to deal with them effectively.

- a guarantee. If you are selling directly from an ad, you have to include your money-back guarantee, or you will be handicapping sales. Even if you are using your ad as part of a two-step sales process, the guarantee is still important. I use something like this, "I guarantee these books do what I say they can do. If you don't agree, return them within 30 days for a complete money-back guarantee. Jeffrey Lant." This kind of statement combines the benefits of the guarantee and the personal commitment, both key aspects of a successful ad.

- an easy way to buy what you're selling. To have an ad and not tell people how they can buy with their MasterCard or Visa is a mistake. You not only need a twenty-four hour order center (which you can have with even the simplest answering machine) but also the ability to take credit cards. Don't run an ad without it.

Ads should always be built around what must be in them and then, depending on space, on what you might also like to have in them. But the "musts" must always be there.

A Few Words About Working With Your Graphic Designer

Copywriters write words and make suggestions about lay-out, but designers actually design the ad. The designer you work with, whom you can find in the same way you find your copywriter, should be doing one thing and one thing only: focusing the prospect's eye on the two key constituents of your ad. These are the benefits the prospect's getting from what you are selling and how he can take action to get it.

The designer is worth his salt if he helps snag the prospect's attention and directs his eye to the right place in your ad. There is no other reason for having a designer.

The designer (who'll charge you between $20 and $40 per hour) should work the finished copy into at least two designs. You always need to have a choice of what ad to use, and the chance to test the different possibilities on some of your prospects. Don't hesitate to make suggestions about how the ads should be improved, but do listen to what the designer says in response.

My experience in working with designers is that each has a style which he will try to impose on you. That's okay if it accords with what you want to do, with the look you want to project. But you need to put your foot down if it doesn't.

I remember when I worked with a designer for the cover of one of my books. He brought me a series of designs that seemed inspired by "Miami Vice." I knew they weren't what I was looking for, but I let the designer have his vigorous say about why he thought they would work. I considered what he said. Then I sent him back to the drawing board with a very specific indication of what I wanted. Remember: you have to live with the design and its consequences far longer than the designer. Never forget this.

Once you, the copywriter and the designer have all agreed on the finished product, the designer should create both a mechanical and a photostat or, simply, stat. The mechanical is the original artwork. Any publication can shoot from this. However, you're probably better off not sending the mechanical. Leave that on file with your designer (as I do), or keep it in your own possession in a safe place.

Instead, have the designer make a stat for you and send that. Publications are not always gentle to your artwork. Instead of risking that your original will be damaged or lost, it simply makes more sense to send them a stat. This will, however, cost an additional $10 or so.

Remember, however, the important thing is to be ready when the publication calls you and says that, yes indeed, they have inexpensive space available, if you can get them your artwork immediately.

More Advertising Do's And Don'ts

- Much has been written about the advantages of opening up your own in-house advertising agency so that you can save the 15% agency commission. This isn't a bad idea if you follow some simple guidelines.

You're not an advertising agency just because you say you're an advertising agency. While the amount of work in setting up such an agency is not great, there are certain things you need to do:

- Get yourself some letterhead, and set up your company. Put words like "Advertising," "Public Relations," or "Communications" in the title. "Lant Communications" would do nicely, although not if you're selling a product or service with your name in it. If you are, select something different.
- Buy yourself cards with your company name, your title, address, and telephone number.
- Develop a standard form on your agency letterhead for submitting your ad copy. This form should include:
  - the name of your firm;
  - the kind of product or service being sold;
  - the name of the publication where you are placing the ad;
  - the number of times the ad is to be run ("till forbid" are the words you use if you want it to keep running until you tell the publication to stop);
  - the date of the first insertion (and the dates of subsequent insertions if not sequential);
  - the copy you want run (if you are submitting your camera-ready art attach the artwork to this form with a paper clip. Do not staple!);
  - the rate you are paying;
  - the overall amount of your order;
  - the agency commission you are getting (15%, unless otherwise noted);
  - the cash discount you get for paying at time of order (usually 2%);

- the net amount of the order;
- the number of your check enclosed.

Indicate at the bottom of this sheet that you would like this submission to be acknowledged, and to be sent tear sheets of your ad.

This is very straightforward, and so long as you pay cash with your ad, you won't have any problems. What's important to keep in mind is that advertising rates are not cast in cement. Sure, someone at some publication is likely to say something to you at some point about whether your advertising agency is "real". Don't get into an argument about it. Just say yes.

Keep in mind that the publication is giving discounts to others, whether they have their own agencies or not, and that if you just stand firm and are polite, you'll get your discount, too, even if the publication isn't exactly wild about it.

The problems begin when you request credit. Publications are rightly worried about the ability of particularly small firms to pay their bills, and no publication wants to become your banker. So, if you want credit, expect problems.

- You'll be asked to fill out a form and provide credit references. Even so, you may be turned down, because you won't be listed in any of the major directories of advertising agencies. This usually determines who can get credit.

If this happens to you, try guaranteeing your order with a credit card. That may work if the publication is set up to take MasterCard or Visa. Moreover, you may actually want to pay with a credit card anyway. I do.

Eastern Airlines has a special Gold MasterCard under which you get 1 mile of frequent flyer credit for each dollar you charge on this special card. As a result I use this card every chance I get. (*N.B.* Even the Cambridge Post Office now takes MasterCard, so I earn nice overseas vacations when I answer your letters to me!) So long as you don't lose control and pay your bill promptly so there is no finance charge (for the rates on this special gold card are higher than currently prevailing credit card rates), you'll be better off using it. Moreover, you may be able to get around the problem many small businesses have of opening credit accounts.

By the way, for information on how you can qualify for the Easter Airlines Gold Master Card, contact Eastern Airlines, Inc., Frequent Traveler Program/MIACP, P.O. Box 02-8525, Miami, FL 33102-8525 or call (713) 952-1630. Several other airlines also offer similar cards.

Still, if these things don't work, you can always stick to cash and take the 15% agency discount and the 2% cash discount (since you're paying with your order) for a grand total of at least 17% off the rate card price for the ad you're buying. Not bad.

And, as you already know, you can probably do even better if you stick to buying remnant space.

On Size, Time, And Position

The problem each of us has when using advertising is to determine how frequently we must advertise, how large our ads need be, and where in the publication they should go. These will always be problems. Here are some guidelines:

- Don't think of buying a full-page ad. Get a half page instead. It loses some of its impact, to be sure, but not enough to justify the extra money. By the same token, it's better to buy two quarter-page ads than one half-page ad. Always. Lant's Rule says it's always better to buy more smaller ads for the same price than one big ad.

- Spend time finding out the best months for you to advertise. If you're selling something to be used indoors you'll do well in October, November, December, January, February and March. These are the months when you should do your maximum advertising and also, of course, when you should be making your major effort to contact your buyers in other ways.

- Remember: the right side of the page is better than the left. The top of the page above the fold is preferable to the bottom. The front of the publication is better than the end.

- Don't use daily newspapers if you can avoid them. Use longer-lasting publications like monthlies and quarterlies, particularly specialty publications especially created for your targeted buyers.

- Finally, think real hard before you even consider using radio and television as advertising sources.

What I've tried to impart in this chapter is how ephemeral advertising is, and how much competition you face when you begin to market your products and services. Television and radio advertising is among the most ephemeral. Hence among the most dangerous. Don't consider using it unless:

- You are prepared to deal with your prospect the minute he sees your ad. To deal with television and radio effectively you must have a number (and an "800" number at that, if you are asking the prospect to call beyond his local telephone area) where they can call the minute they are interested in the solution you offer him. And I mean the *minute*.

If you are not prepared to do this, don't even consider using television and radio to advertise. You won't be surprised to hear that I feel the same about how to profit from your free public relations exposure.

- You either are selling a product that runs out and can generate brand loyalty (thereby amortizing the cost of getting this customer over several purchases), or you running a retail establishment, where your new customer may also buy other things once he arrives.

Unless these conditions apply, don't even bother to consider radio and television advertising. If these conditions do apply, then check out these references for further information.

Resources

For information on using radio to advertise your products and services, study *Production In Format Radio Handbook* by Michael Keith. It's available through the University Press of America, Inc., 4720 Boston Way, Lanham, MD 20706.

For information about producing television commercials, consult *How To Produce An Effective TV Commercial* by Hooper White. This solid, how-to book is published by Crain Books, Div. of Crain Communications, Inc., 740 Rush St., Chicago, IL 60611 (312) 649-5250.

Also, see *Or Your Money Back* by Alvin Eicoff. This book is packed with the tales of a direct-response television entrepreneur, but it also contains solid information on how to advertise on the medium. It, too, is published by Crain Books.

I'll tell you one thing: before I'd spend any money advertising on either radio or television I'd study what the experts have to say real hard. Furthermore, I'd explore the other, less costly advertising and public relations options, testing all the while to see if they drew responses. Then and only then would I commit the more substantial dollars you need to succeed in radio and television advertising — and only with the help of seasoned professionals.

More Resources

This chapter has covered a lot of ground, and yet there is much more to say about successful advertising. Thus, see my book CASH COPY: HOW TO OFFER YOUR PRODUCTS AND SERVICES SO YOUR PROSPECTS BUY THEM... NOW!

Also consult Eugene M. Schwartz' *Breakthrough Advertising; How To Write Ads That Shatter Traditions And Sales Records*. It's published by Boardroom Books, P.O. Box 1026 Millburn, NJ 07041 (201) 379-4642.

And check out Edmond Bruneau's short and provocative book *Prescription For Advertising: Understanding The Complex And Confusing World Of Advertising*, Boston Books, P.O. Box 9909, Spokane, WA 99209-0909 or call (800) 735-1116.

CHAPTER 8

MMMM

Phone Profit: Keeping Existing Customers Happy And Getting New Ones By Telephone

Every day the telephone brings annoyance into my life.

I'm working away when a total stranger calls and without so much as a "by your leave", launches into a spiel about some product or service. I haven't asked this person to call. I'm always involved in something else when he does. Moreover, I am usually appalled by the way he handles the conversation. And if I am appalled, I don't buy. That's that. The experience is a waste of time on the part of the person making the call and a waste of my time, the person who received it.

I wrote this chapter both to cut down on such needless waste and to increase the profit potential of your telephone.

Let me!

Why The Telephone Doesn't Work For Most People

I can say without fear of contradiction that most people using the telephone use it poorly. Indeed, they are actually worse off after they have made their call than they were before doing so. If they haven't succeeded in reaching their objective for the call (to set up an appointment or to sell their product or service), a little more of their self esteem has been whittled away. Moreover, because of the way they have handled the call, they may actually have made it impossible to do *any* business in the future with the individual they called. So the call, which takes time and money to make, actually is their nemesis.

This doesn't have to happen to you.

Just following a few sensible rules will reduce the chance that it will.

- Don't call someone and immediately launch into your spiel. Of course you are primed to go ahead. But the person you are calling was presumably not sitting around waiting for your call. He's doing something else. This may not be a convenient time for him to talk. Ask him.

- Don't presume on an intimacy that doesn't exist. *Without fail* every telephone salesman calls me "Jeff." It's a name I loathe. When they use it, I resolve to punish them by getting rid of them quickly and certainly by not buying the product they are selling, whether I need it or not. If you've ever called me, you know I invariably answer my telephone, "Jeffrey Lant speaking."

Invariably.

Why then does the salesperson immediately say, "Jeff?" It immediately distinguishes him as an oaf. And as President of the Oaf Eradication Society, I do what I can to get him out of my life and get him out fast.

What the salesperson has done, I call the Rechristening Syndrome. This is where the person making the call gives you the name he thinks you ought to have, not the one you call yourself. It is an outrageous abuse, and one that all too many telephone salespeople perpetrate with seeming oblivion.

N.B. While writing this book, I published an article on the Rechristening Syndrome and its destructive consequences for salespeople. I told about my own irritation when salespeople call me "Jeff." A fellow from Oklahoma called up to compliment me on the article (remember, my telephone number ordinarily runs with whatever I write). His comment? "I liked your article. It made a big impression on me, Jeff." I could tell.

- They don't listen to what I have to say in response. I recall a recent situation where a telephone salesperson called to sell me a place in an advertising postcard deck. I told him politely that I would be glad to participate, dividing the retail price of my products on a 50-50% basis. I told him that was my policy.

The seller didn't hear, certainly didn't acknowledge. He said that that wouldn't do at all and continued, without pausing, into his spiel. I said, a little more firmly, that I had a policy. That I would be delighted to do business with him and his company but on the basis I had outlined. Again, he said "No!" and continued with his spiel.

I could see this was getting nowhere fast and told him to present my proposal to his boss, and if there was any interest to get back to me. He called me the next day and instead of addressing the proposal I had made, again launched into his spiel!

Was this person dumb or what? Needless to say, he didn't get what he wanted.

- They try some phony opening on me like, "Hi, Jeff, this is Russ Smith. I'm returning your call!" This actually happened to me while I was writing this chapter! I assured the caller I hadn't placed any call to him. Then, instead of bridging to his subject, the salesperson had the audacity to tell me I was wrong, that of course I had called him!

Ladies and gentlemen, things like this happen in the telephone sales market every day. That's why most of what people do in telephone sales in futile, why most telephone sales people are despised and looked down upon, and why there is a terribly high turn-over in this kind of telephone work.

No wonder.

Most people using the telephone:

- Don't use it in the right way.
- Don't use it at the right time.
- Don't know what it can do.
- Don't know what it cannot do.

They, therefore, succeed in shooting themselves in the foot time after futile time.

That's why this chapter had to be written.

Getting Ready to Profit From Your Phone

This chapter essentially deals with five situations:

- Using your telephone to keep in touch with your current clients and buyers. It is important to use the telephone to check in with both users of your products and your clients and make sure they are still happy.

More than that, it is important to talk to them about upgrading the product they are using and the service. The telephone is helpful in making sure you are solving, either through products and/or services, as many problems of your current buyers as you can. It is a huge mistake to assume that somehow, through osmosis?, these people will know what problems you can solve and present themselves without prodding (although, gratefully, this does happen every now and then!).

- Using your telephone to keep in touch with people who already know you, particularly your past customers and clients, (but not excluding those to whom you have previously talked but were not then ready to buy).

One of the greatest marketing mistakes continually made is the failure to keep in touch with people who already know who you are and (we hope!) like your product or service. If you're like most marketers, you are more interested in finding new buyers than recapturing past buyers. This is a mistake. The telephone can help you overcome it.

- Using your telephone to connect with people who have expressed an interest in what you are selling. These are the people who have taken the initiative to get in touch with you, either by returning some type of interest document or by telephoning you. They have qualified themselves as prospects. Your job is to follow up this interest expeditiously and give them the solution they want (which just happens to be what you are selling).

- Using your telephone to follow up your targeted mailings to selected buyer prospects. You have sent these people information which indicated you understand their problem and let them know you can solve it. You are now following up by telephone to make appointments and direct telephone sales.

- Using your telephone to call people who know nothing about you and have not indicated an interest in you or your problem-solving product or service. I put this last for very good reason. It is the most difficult kind of telemarketing. Sadly, it is the one on which most other books on this important subject concentrate. Quite wrongly.

Lant Sounds Off About The Other Telemarketing Literature

If you review the telemarketing literature as I have done over the last months, you might well come to the conclusion I have. Namely, that these books and articles are written by sadists who enjoy putting their fellow humans into the most difficult situations, situations, I might add, which the authors of these materials avoid like the plague. I mean making cold calls to people who have expressed no prior interest in what they are selling.

Let me assure you of something: this kind of work is hard, grueling, often frustrating, and has a very high burn-out factor for those doing it. Yet it is the kind of telemarketing that all the other books concentrate on. Quite, quite mistakenly in my humble opinion.

If you learn nothing else from this chapter, you will learn that calling people cold who have expressed no interest in what you are doing, without first preparing them for the call, is a form of insanity that you should avoid whenever possible. This chapter offers you a step-by-step plan so that you'll put your time and effort into those situations where you can reasonably expect the best possible return, only doing cold calls when there is absolutely no other alternative and when you have exhausted all other means of both contacting your prospects and preparing them for your call. Is that understood?

Using The Phone To Keep In Touch With Users Of Your Products And Clients of Your Services

Let me say this as strongly as I can: a current user of your product or client of your service is a qualified prospect. Indeed, I'd go further. This person is a Top Prospect. Why?

Because, unless you have grievously mishandled the relationship by selling him a product that doesn't do what you say it can do or by engaging in a relationship that is not assisting him to reach his problem-solving objective, this individual knows you and trusts you. Moreover, since the trust of the prospect is one of the things you must have before you can sell him anything else, you are in a wonderful position both to ascertain what problems the client/buyer wants to solve and to offer to solve them in such a way that he is likely to allow you to do so.

In short, this is the most desirable sales situation there is. Here's the way I'd handle it.

Making Your Current Buyers Feel Warm And Wonderful

Everybody likes to be loved. Of all the universals, this is probably the most powerful. So use it to your advantage. Make the telephone your love instrument. To do so, several conditions must apply:

- Either you must sell a product that runs out and/or a service that the customer needs to have over and over again.

- The dollar value of the product or service you are selling must be high enough to warrant this kind of sustained customer contact. Sure enough, bags of chocolate kisses run out, but it just doesn't make good economic sense for the grocery store to call you up and remind you that you're going to need some more.

If these two conditions are met, however, you must use the following guidelines with your existing customers and clients:

- Foster a sense of belonging. Let your customers and clients know that when they buy from you, they are joining a family. That you are there not to sell them something, but to work with them to meet their needs.

- This sense of belonging begins the minute they buy from you. You will help your later contacts (both when they are buyers and if they stop buying), if you send a welcoming letter with the product either when the customer buys it or immediately thereafter.

This letter should:

- Confirm that they made a wise decision. (Buyers often doubt their own judgments. Quite rightly, too!)
- Let them know how glad you are that they chose to do business with you.
- Let them know you will do what you can to make sure they are happy.
- Tell them that if, at any time, they are not happy they are to telephone you directly. (Provide them with your telephone number right in the body of the letter).
- Stress that you are serious when you tell them their happiness and well-being is paramount in the way you do business.
- Tell them, too, that you will be bringing special "family" offers to their attention from time to time and that you are looking forward to getting acquainted.

There isn't a business in America, tiny or gigantic, that wouldn't be better off using this strategy, even if because of the volume of products being sent out, each letter cannot be personally signed, as, in theory, it really ought to be. The point is not to forego using a beneficial customer-contact device because you cannot make it perfect, but to do the best you can given your circumstances.

Phone Profit: Following Up Your Initial Letter

To use the telephone effectively in these situations, you need to get the telephone numbers of your customers and clients. This is not difficult to do even when you are selling low-cost items.

When you buy one of my books directly from me, I ask you for your telephone number. That number is immediately entered into my computer, usually while you are still on the line. No one has ever asked why I'm taking this information! But if they did, I'd be candid.

I'd say that I often have "buyers only" specials, rigidly restricted to people who have bought my materials and whom I can contact quickly. Who can resist this? These buyers get the excitement of participating in something that everyone cannot have and know that they are part of a special group. Wouldn't you give your phone number in such a case?

If you're running a retail outlet, you can always have a drawing. Don't even bother to say that participants must give their telephone number. Say instead, "Winner will be notified by telephone." People will then automatically include their phone number.

Now Create Something Special For Your Customers And Clients

Now that you've got your data base, for that's what you are assembling, use it. Remember the Rule of Recency. People who have bought from you recently are your best buying prospects. The more recently they have bought, the better a prospect they are, because they know who you are. They have just received a warm, welcoming letter from you, and they are happy. Never forget this!

So create a "special" for them. Make something available to them before it's generally available. Make it available to them for a special price. Make it available in a special way. **But make it special.**

Then use the telephone.

Ring. Ring. Ring.

"Hello."

"Hello, is Betty Smith there?"

"Yes. **This is Betty.**"

"Betty, this is Jeffrey Lant calling. **You remember** I'm the author of **THE CONSULTANT'S KIT** which you bought from me a couple months ago."

"Oh, yes, Jeffrey. How are you?"

"Fine, thanks. And you?"

"Very well, thank you."

"Betty, I'm calling for a couple of reasons. I wanted to know how you're coming along with your consulting practice, and **if you've found THE CONSULTANT'S KIT helpful?"**

"**Yes**, I have, Jeffrey. **I'm glad you called so I could tell you.**"

"Well, then, Betty **I think you're going to be equally happy about my new book on marketing**. I call it **MONEY MAKING MARKETING: FINDING THE PEOPLE WHO NEED WHAT YOU'RE SELLING AND MAKING SURE THEY BUY IT.**"

"Sounds interesting."

"It's packed with ideas about how to handle your marketing most efficiently for the least possible expense. **I felt sure this would be something you'd like.**"

"Yes!"

"Betty, what's exciting is that for the **next two weeks** I'm making **MONEY MAKING MARKETING** available at a **special price for people who are already using one of my books**. That's why I wanted to call. I wanted to let you know you are one of these people so you could get your copy and start using it to **make your marketing even more effective.**"

"That's thoughtful of you, Jeffrey. How much is it?"

"You know my books sell for $30 each, Betty. But you can get MONEY MAKING MARKETING for just $25.50, and I can send it out to you right now if use your MasterCard or Visa. Would that be convenient for you?"

"Sure, let me get my card number."

Preparing To Analyze This Fruitful Conversation

Lots of things are going on in this conversation, and it's important to point out what they are. Key sections are marked.

- To begin with, I have an objective for the call. Every call you make must have an explicit, defined objective. In this call, I want to do two things, actually: I want to make sure my past buyer is happy. And, if she is, I want to get her to buy from me again and work to solve another of her problems. If I can convince her that I can solve her problem, I will solve my problem: the need for the sale.

- I am confident I will make the sale. If the customer is happy, then I have every right to believe she will buy from me again. Remember, my constant motto, "Don't Sell. Solve." Consultants have marketing problems. Betty Smith probably has them, too. Therefore, I am doing her a kindness in bringing to her attention something that is going to help her solve one of her pressing problems. You must believe this. It's true!

- Assuming the customer is well satisfied with the last solution I sold her, I expect to be well received. I expect to be greeted not as a friend (for I am not that) but as a respected and valued connection, as someone who doesn't call frivolously but always with something worthwhile and important to say. Remember, "I don't sell. I solve." Once the customer knows this, you should be greeted civilly, even warmly. After all, how many people are there in one's life who take an intelligent interest in what you are doing and can actually make a positive impact and help you reach your objectives?

A Closer Look At This Conversation

- The name question. Most people telephoning others make an egregious error with the name. I don't. As you may recall, I have my Ph.D. in 19th century English history and happen to be a specialist in protocol. I am very sensitive to the nuances of how to use names, what to call people, and how to make sure I am treating people the way they want to be treated. You must become adept at these subjects, too.

To get a handle on the name your customer wants to be called:

- Ask. Don't fall victim to the Rechristening Syndrome, and give your customers and prospects the name you want them to have. Ask them what name they want to use. People are always happy telling you precisely what they want to be called. Then enter this information in either your card file or on your computer.

- If you don't have this information, wait for the customer to give you your cue. In the above illustration, it is the customer who quite properly tells me what she wants to be called, "Yes, this is Betty."

- Use intelligent guesswork. If the individual you are talking to is your age, he will be more receptive to your using his first name. If you are 10 or more years younger, always start with the appropriate honorific: "Mr.", "Mrs.", or "Ms." Then take your cue from what the person calls you.

- This is perhaps the best way to do things. I try hard not to make any assumptions about people's names. If I'm not sure, I wait until I get a hint from the other person. Or I simply say, "What do you prefer to be called?" Simple politeness is infinitely preferable to unbearable assumption.

- Assume the person remembers you. Don't ask whether they remember you. Just assume they do. But don't make it difficult for the customer. Give them the handle they need to be able to remember. "I'm the author of **THE CONSULTANT'S KIT** you bought from me a couple of months ago."

- You'll know right away whether you are going to be warmly treated or kicked. If you don't hear something like, "Oh, yes, Jeffrey. How are you?", then there is a problem. This is your opportunity to solve it. You must find out whether they are happy with the product they bought or the service they are getting.

A Note About Complaints

Every business these days says it is customer-oriented. It's a standard phrase and like most such phrases, it's usually meaningless.

When you call people to find out if they are happy with your product or service, sometimes they are going to say they are not. This is, however, not a moment to panic. This is an opportunity for you. You've got to see it as such.

What if Betty had said, "Oh, Jeffrey, I'm glad you called, because I've been meaning to tell you how useless your product is." What then?

It is important to clear this problem up for two reasons:

- It is well known that people who have complaints tell more people about them than people who are happy.
- You have already invested a lot of time and effort in this person (remember the Rule of Seven), and you both want and need to amortize this investment over the course of several more purchases.

For both reasons, you have to solve this problem. The telephone allows you to do just that.

Dealing With Complaints

- Don't be defensive. Of course, the person's complaint is going to hurt you. Especially, as in the example above, if you are the person who invented the product or delivered the service. But you cannot take this complaint personally.
- Ask what the problem is. You need information before you can say anything else. "Jeffrey, I felt **THE CONSULTANT'S KIT** was just too elementary given my experience in business."
- If the complaint is (mostly!) reasonable, validate the complainant. "I can certainly understand with your background, Betty, how you'd feel that way. What you need is a book that helps you refine the techniques you already know."
- If the problem can be corrected, indicate immediately that it will be corrected. Say how it will be corrected, when it will be corrected. Also say you are glad to correct the problem (even if you're not!).
- Then do it. But don't just send a new product. Include a short note saying you are sorry there was any problem. Say that you want to keep this person happy and that you would be grateful if they'd bring any further problem to your attention. *Then* give them a discount on another of your products or services as compensation for the inconvenience they have suffered. In other words, let them be compensated for past inconvenience by buying another solution from you!

Remember: Don't sell. Solve! Always let your customers, even the previously disgruntled ones, know there is another solution especially available to them and that, because of their previous problem, you aim to give them a special deal on getting it. Good business. Good sense. But please do not attempt to sell this customer anything else, until you have taken care of his problem. Please!!!

More Analysis

- As soon as you know the customer is happy, move the conversation ahead to the second reason why you've called: the upgrade reason. Don't be sheepish about this. You have nothing to be sheepish about if you understand the prospect's problem and know you have a *bona fide* solution to it.
- Once you've presented the benefits of what you are offering, don't hesitate to say something like, "I felt sure this would be something you'd like."

You're entitled to say this if you have done your homework. If this Top Prospect is happy with what she's already using and if you have good reason for thinking what you are suggesting would be useful, don't be hesitant! Be a problem-solver. Not a product-seller.

Besides, most people are not very good at making up their minds. They mistrust the decisions they make. They want to rely on someone else to help them. Be that helpful, authoritative individual they so desperately need.

What If There Is Hesitation?

In some instances even this Top Prospect may be doubtful about whether he wants to go ahead. Plan for this. Make sure you have your motivation and persuasion tools lined up before you need them. Say that Betty had said, "Sounds good, but I don't know, Jeffrey."

- First, don't criticize what the prospect has said. Say instead, "I can understand how you feel, Betty. I'm like you. I like to be real sure before I spend my money!"

- Do reassure the prospect and make the decision less threatening."You remember, Betty, that all my books come with a complete 30-day money-back guarantee. If this book doesn't help improve your marketing and save you money, then I want you to return it to me."

Please review the structure of these sentences. You are not selling a book. You are selling a solution. What you are saying is that if the product doesn't provide the solution the prospect wants, you want it returned to you. Moreover that you take full personal responsibility for ensuring the prospect is happy.

Imagine what a relief this is to people who fear the burden of making decisions and are looking desperately for others to assume the responsibility for them!

- "That's thoughtful of you, Jeffrey." Expect the prospect to be grateful. Each day people tell me they are grateful for what I do for them. This is more than mere politeness, beyond a figure of speech. I know they mean it. If you take an interest in the welfare of your buyers, they will be grateful to you. This gratitude and the sense of security they feel about you are the basis of your prosperity.

- After you have heard all this, it's time to move the sale to its logical conclusion: buying the product or service you are recommending. Get the prospect to commit to buying that very minute. People always want new things. Always want the possibility of getting a solution to their problems. Let your prospect know he can have just that by making a commitment now, and that you'll do your part to making his life better.

Thanking Your Customer —Again!

Each time someone buys something from you, you are in a position to congratulate him for the decision he has just taken, and to position yourself for the next solution purchase he will make from you. Don't miss it.

Here's your opportunity to send him another note reaffirming he made the right decision, stressing that it will help him solve the problem he wants to solve, and that you are there to help him realize their objectives both now and in the future. Remember: the business of getting a buyer doesn't stop when you have that buyer. It continues. What is nice about this process, however, is that if you are doing it correctly, it not only gets easier, it gets downright pleasant.

For when you are dealing with your existing clients and customers, you are dealing with people who are usually happy with you, who know who you are and are really glad you are taking a sustained interest in them. If they know this, they'll do what they need to do — keep buying! — to make sure you'll keep helping them. Take my word for it!

Using The Phone To Retrieve Former Clients And Customers

There may come a day when people who have used your products or services will stop doing so. Sometimes there's nothing you can do about this. Say you're offering a local service and the user moves away. That's that. Sometimes, however, the lapse is entirely avoidable and can be overcome by instituting a rigorous policy of keeping in touch with your past buyers and asking them to come back.

Frankly, here's how I'd handle this situation.

Luring The Lapsed

Leaving aside past buyers who have some logical reason for no longer buying from you (though I reckon anything less than death nothing more than an excuse!), I say that getting back former customers is a pivotal part of succeeding in business.

Why? Well, for one thing you've invested a lot of money in these people. It took time, trouble, and cash to get them to be buyers in the first place. If you lose them now, you are admitting that they were right to leave and that your problem-solving products and services weren't really up to the mark. If this is true, you have a terminal problem and ought to admit it. If it isn't true, then you better do everything you can to get these former customers back.

Here's how you can:

- Create a special offer for them. Let them know that, like the prodigal son, they are still part of the family and that you intend to do something special when they return.
- Send them a mail piece incorporating your special offer and let them know, because of the high esteem in which you hold them, that you'll be calling shortly to regain their confidence and reestablish your relationship.

Make sure this letter breathes a warm, enthusiastic desire to have them back. This letter should not only sell the recipient on the benefit of the problem-solving product or service you are selling but on the value of reconnecting with you. Again, you are selling belonging.

N.B. If you know the customer well enough — or feel comfortable enough with your telephone skills — to jump over this stage, do. There's nothing wrong with calling your former customer directly and working to reestablish the relationship, if you feel you can do so. If you're hesitant, however, send the advance letter.

Now get on the telephone and fight to get them back.

Bringing Betty Back

Let's go back to our consultant Betty Smith. Suppose she hasn't bought in a while, and I want to get her back. After the phone rapport preliminaries, here's what should happen:

"Betty, I'm calling for a couple of reasons. I haven't heard from you in a while and **wanted to reestablish contact with you. How's your consulting business coming along?"**

"Things are a little slow just now, Jeffrey."

"I'm sorry to hear that, Betty. What's the problem?"

"I'm trying to figure out how to cut my marketing expenses and increase the number of clients."

"Well, Betty, that's a problem consultants always have. But **I think I can help you."**

"Really, Jeffrey. **How?"**

"I've been working for the last year on developing a series of inexpensive and very effective marketing techniques which I've incorporated into my new book **MONEY MAKING MARKETING. It sounds like this would be real helpful for you."**

"Probably, Jeffrey. But **money's low right now."**

"No, problem, Betty. **You're a good customer, and I want to reestablish the connection with you. I'd like to offer you a special price**. Just $25.50 with the shipping, instead of $38.50. How does this sound? And you know that if you don't find it helpful, I'll be happy to take it back."

"Sounds good to me!"

The Analysis

- You need to let the lapsed customer know you want her back. You have essentially three objectives for this call:

  - You want your former customer to know she's wanted. There can be nothing impersonal about this call. You've got to transmit over the phone circuit a strong sense that you care to have this important person back.

  - You need to find out whether the person is still in the condition she previously was in so that buying your problem-solving product or service makes sense. "How's your consulting business coming along?" You need to find out whether she is buying products and services from others, or whether she has lost interest altogether in what you can do for her. Or simply if she has been so slothful that she's done nothing, which, of course, is a most common scenario.

  - You want her to make a commitment to buy.

Each of these objectives is important.

- If your customer has had a problem, empathize. The fact that Betty's business isn't going well does call for an expression of your concern. Make it. If you connect with Betty on the human level, it's going to help you achieve your objective.

- Ask what the problem is. Your job is to empathize with what's happening to the former buyer and see if what you offer can be helpful. Remember: "Don't sell. Solve!" In this case, once Betty has stated her problem, she provides me with the perfect introduction to what I'm selling.

- Find out what your former buyer is trying to do. If you can link what you are selling to the problem the former buyer wants to solve, you are well along towards the sale you want to make.

- Let the prospect know you can help. This is the essence of successful sales. If you can help, there's nothing wrong with saying so, as strongly and enthusiastically as you can.

- Tell the past customer you want to reestablish the relationship you had. Make sure she knows, because you stress, that she is important to you. Tell her, too, she is getting a special offer, an offer reserved for her. And, as always, lessen the anxiety of buying by including whatever guarantees you ordinarily give.

The "Welcome Back, Prodigal Son" Letter

Many of your past customers, approached in this warm, enthusiastic way, will come back. After all, it's nice to be wanted! It's nice to be sought after! It's nice to be included in a special group and to be sought out by someone who can help solve your problem!

Follow up this renewal in a special way, by sending the "Welcome Back, Prodigal Son" Letter.

- Tell your old buyer you are glad, really glad!, to have him back. Make him feel your enthusiasm. For like renewing ties with an old friend, this is an important moment, a moment for celebration.

- Let him know you want to keep these ties strong. That you'll be keeping in touch with him. And that you want him to keep in touch with you, especially if there are any problems. Provide your direct-dial number so he can reach you personally.

Don't send this letter alone, either. Make sure there are ride-alongs with it, information about the other products and services you provide. Remember the Rule of Recency: the person who has bought from you most recently is among your best prospects. Let him know all the other ways you can help him.

N.B. Use this technique, too, to connect with people whom you previously contacted but were not then ready to buy from you. Overlook the fact they didn't buy from you then. Proceed on the assumption they will now. Write and/or call to reestablish the contact, to find out the problem they are currently interested in solving, and to see if your product or service is what they need now. Remember the Rule of Seven. Any previous contacts you had with them, even though they were unsuccessful, count. So now do what is necessary to complete the job.

Using Your Telephone To Connect With People Who Have Expressed An Interest In What You Are Selling

People interested in what you are selling may either contact you directly by telephone, or they may mail you an expression of their interest which you can follow up by phone. Either way, you're going to be using the telephone. So you might as well find out how to use it correctly.

When The Prospect Calls You

If you conscientiously follow the guidelines in this book, people are going to call you. Often lots and lots of people. I know. My telephone number appears in millions of documents each year and is provided to millions more on television and radio shows. As a result I get telephone calls around the clock. That's the way I like it. Therefore, I'm ready for them whether it's teatime or daybreak. Just as you should be. To make these calls productive for both you and the prospect, you need to know how to handle them.

- Be prepared to help the prospect when the prospect is ready to be helped. Of course you are doing something else when the prospect calls. This is an unscheduled call, to be sure. But it should not be an unexpected call. After all, you set in gear the marketing steps that produced it. So when it comes (as it will come), you should not be surprised and should be prepared.

Even if you are not in your office, have an answering machine that lets your prospect know you want to help him solve his problem. Don't just run one of the all-too-typical inane messages that says you're not in your office. That's stupid! Instead, say "This is Jeffrey Lant. I'm out of my office just now helping people improve their marketing. I want to do this for you, too. Please leave me your name, telephone number and a brief description of what you'd like to accomplish and how you'd like me to help you. I'll call you back and start helping as soon as I can."

Now that's a proper marketing message! Do you have one?

If you are present, act like it. Remember, your job is to solve the prospect's problem, not to sell anything.

Begin by taking a human interest in the person calling. Oftentimes they will not introduce themselves. So behave civilly. Say, "To whom am I speaking?" Make sure you get the name and the pronunciation right. You are, after all, trying to build a relationship.

Ask how you can help. Your job is to find out not so much what the prospect wants to do right now but the problem he wants to solve.

- Once you've discovered the problem, restate it so that you are certain you understand it. "You're calling to improve your marketing skills. Is that right?" In other words, get confirmation from the prospect that that is indeed the problem he wants to solve. No sense trying to solve the wrong one, is there?

- Tell the prospect you're glad he's called you about this problem, because you can help him solve it. "I'm glad you called me about this problem, Mrs. Smith. I can help you solve it."

- If the prospect needs to learn more about how you operate, the products and services you have available, before making the commitment, keep control by saying, "Let me send you some information about how I can help you solve that problem. I'd like to send it to you today." When you know the prospect is going to need more information before making a decision, then don't wait for the prospect to ask for it. Volunteer to send it and keep the initiative. Then ask for the correct spelling of his name, the address, and the telephone number.

- Tell him how you are going to follow up. Say, "You'll get this information in about three days, Mrs. Smith. I'd like to call you then to see if you have any questions about it. Will you be available Friday?" In other words, make a real appointment to follow up. The prospect who calls you is an interested prospect, and it's your responsibility to pursue this interest to the logical conclusion where the prospect becomes a buyer.

The Add-On/Upgrade

Suppose the prospect calls and wants information about a certain product or service. Suppose he even wants to purchase it right then and there. Do you simply sell it to him?

Certainly not!

Again, you must remember you are in the solution business. Not the selling business. "Jeffrey," the enthusiastic prospect says, "I'm calling to order a copy of **THE CONSULTANT'S KIT.**"

"Thanks so much for calling. I've got a copy for you! But are you aware that this book is part of a seven-book series that helps consultants solve a series of problems?"

"No, I'm not. What are the other books in the series all about?"

The Analysis

The stupid salesperson, the person I call the order-taker and who uses the telephone passively, simply responds to what the prospect wants. This is a terrible mistake. To respond in this way assumes that the prospect not only knows what he wants but knows all the ways we have of satisfying his desire. This is, of course, ridiculous.

Thus, instead of responding directly to the prospect, we must find out the problem the prospect wants to solve and make sure he knows all the ways we can help him solve it. I call this the Add-On/Upgrade.

Is the prospect put off by this tactic?

Certainly not.

The prospect who calls you is an interested prospect. He has a problem, and he wants help in solving it. He wants to find in you an interested and knowledgeable person capable of giving him the help he needs. If you don't give it to him now, he may well buy what he is calling to buy, but he will not be the beneficiary of all the help he needs and will certainly not purchase more from you right now to solve his problem. Thus, you both lose.

Hereafter always make sure you:

- Find out from the prospect what he is trying to accomplish.

- Let him know the various ways you can help him do what he wants to do.

Then provide him with your expert advice on what you think he should do, given the need that he has and the products and services which you have available.

Let me tell you something: if you do things this way your prospects will buy more, and they will be happier about the purchases they make.

Sadly, this sensible technique is very rarely used. Find out for yourself. The next time you call someone for information, even with the desire to purchase a product or service immediately, does the seller merely act as an order-taker, or does he function as your problem-solver? I think we both know the irksome answer. However, now that you have these new phone-profit techniques, you won't make the same mistake. Will you?

Responding To A Written Expression Of Interest From Your Prospects

If you're following the techniques in this book and sending out client-survey instruments, people are going to be writing to you regularly telling you what problems they have and what objectives they want to reach. You'll be using the telephone regularly to follow up these prospects and work with them to solve their problems.

You already know about how to create these client-survey documents, but if you need a refresher, see Samples, page 261. As long as you're in business, you'll be distributing them:

- at conferences you attend and at talk sessions you provide;
- with each package you send, including all your outgoing products; and
- in response to people calling you after hearing you on radio or television.

In short, you'll find yourself distributing tens of thousands of these inexpensive forms which, you'll remember, ask prospects to tell you what they want to achieve, thereby allowing you to tell them how your products and services can help them achieve it. It's a wonderful, wonderful system.

Following-Up Client-Survey Documents

People who take the time to fill out a questionnaire indicating what they want to achieve are people who want to buy what you're selling. Don't blow it!

- Before making the call to these prospects, review the questionnaire they've submitted. I'm looking at one as a I write in which the prospect has indicated 10 objectives she would like to achieve — 10! Fine. I must know what these ten objectives are and must be clear about how my products and services can help her achieve them. Only once you are certain in your own mind that you know this should you even contemplate making the call. Otherwise, you'll be exposed as someone wanting to make a sale, rather than solve a problem.

- Now make the call. Remember: by filling out the questionnaire, the prospect has not only indicated he is interested in solving a problem but has actually given you permission to recommend the appropriate solution and sell it to him. Imagine! You have been invited to make the sale. You must keep this in mind as you make this call.

Ring. Ring. Ring.

"Hello. Is Betty Smith in?"

"Yes, this is Betty."

"Betty, this is Jeffrey Lant. I'm calling to help you master profitable telemarketing techniques. You remember you told me you were interested in doing this. Am I calling at a good time to discuss how you can?"

"Yes, Jeffrey. Thanks for calling. Now's a good time to talk."

"Can you tell me a little bit about your business, Betty. Then I can be sure I'm making the right recommendation for your situation."

"I'm a fund-raising consultant, Jeffrey. I want to use telemarketing techniques both to attract new nonprofit clients and to help them create effective telemarketing fund-raising campaigns."

"I'm glad to know that, Betty. As a result, I can make four recommendations to you. In my one-day workshop on effective fund-raising, one of the subjects I deal with is how to effectively use telemarketing to raise money for nonprofit organizations, including how to work with volunteers. Is this the kind of thing that you're interested in knowing more about?"

"Yes, Jeffrey. It's hard to work with volunteers, and I could use more information about how to find them and how to work with them."

"You'll get that in the workshop and also in my fund-raising book **DEVELOPMENT TODAY: A FUND RAISING GUIDE FOR NONPROFIT ORGANIZATIONS.** It has detailed guidelines on effective telemarketing."

"Sounds good. What are your other recommendations?"

"For the nitty-gritty of effectively using the telephone, I recommend my telemarketing guidelines in **MONEY MAKING MARKETING: FINDING THE PEOPLE WHO NEED WHAT YOU'RE SELLING AND MAKING SURE THEY BUY IT.** You can use them to make your own telemarketing efforts more profitable and can train your own clients in these techniques. Am I right in thinking you'd like to know about materials that make your practice more profitable?"

"That's right. I want to help myself and my clients, too!"

"Then you'll find my practice-building techniques in **TRICKS OF THE TRADE: THE COMPLETE GUIDE TO SUCCEEDING IN THE ADVICE BUSINESS** useful, Betty. It's very detailed, advanced practice-building information. I'd like to put you down for a copy of this, too."

"I'm not sure I can afford to get all these things right now. What do you think I should start with?"

"Well, let me ask you a few questions about your practice and what you are trying to do right now... ."

The Analysis

Look what's going on here. The poor salesperson using the telephone would call up Betty and sell her a telemarketing workshop or a book. Then he'd begin looking for another client. That's using the phone passively — and foolishly.

Not me!

I want to solve Betty's problem. She's perfectly happy to tell me what it is. She needs help attracting her own nonprofit clients. She wants to achieve a greater mastery of telemarketing techniques for herself and those her nonprofit clients can use on their own behalf. She also wants help building a stronger consulting practice. All these are aspects of her problem, not just what she ostensibly called about.

My job is to provide her with recommendations about how she can solve *all* these problems.

What you've got to keep in mind is that Betty may not be financially able to pursue all these solutions at a single time. That's life. Nonetheless, just because she is not necessarily able to proceed now with everything she needs, doesn't mean you drop the contact after she buys part of what she needs. No way.

She's a qualified prospect. She has indicated an interest in pursuing a solution. Your task is to find out how much of the solution she can reasonably pursue now and how much must be deferred until another time. Don't make that decision for her, at least not right away. Wait until she says something.

The Conversation Continues

"Let's see if we can work together to see which of these problems is most important to you to solve just now."

You now need further information. What if you discover she doesn't have a nonprofit client right now needing a telemarketing campaign, but that she is working hard, and somewhat futilely, to get more clients? What then? You'd make your recommendation accordingly.

What is important is that you not be perceived as a seller but as a solver. Sellers sell, whether the prospect needs the item or not. Solvers work for long-term relationships, understanding that it takes time to find qualified prospects, and that once they have they want to, indeed need to, maintain that relationship.

Thus, once you know what Betty, that qualified prospect, needs to achieve and in what order she needs to achieve it, you can make suitable recommendations and sell her the right thing. But don't stop there. Sell her what she needs today. Also let her know that you'll be back, in say 30 days, to see how things are coming along and to sell her the product or service which will continue to help her move ahead. Whatever you're selling, you're building a relationship. The telephone allows you, without moving from your desk, to maintain the active intimacy and movement of a mutually beneficial relationship.

A Few Hints

- Follow up the questionnaires promptly when you get them. If you can, do it the same day you get them. Prospects need to catch your enthusiasm, and you need to benefit from theirs. The day they fill out the questionnaire is the day they have the most enthusiasm. Thereafter it dwindles day by day until there is none left, until they don't even remember completing the questionnaire. Thus, act promptly.

- Don't say you are following up the questionnaire. Say you are calling to help make their telemarketing more profitable, or whatever benefit you are really selling. Your prospects don't care about questionnaires. They do care about achieving the objective they checked on the questionnaire. Never forget this.

- If the prospect sounds less than enthusiastic when you call (yes, this happens, even after they've indicated their interest in achieving an objective), ask why. It's perfectly acceptable. Find out whether the prospect has decided to go elsewhere to solve his problem. Prospects don't so much lose interest in solving problems, as they lose interest in solving them using your products and services.

Once a prospect has indicated he wants to achieve an objective, solve a problem, he's probably going to move towards doing so. But it may not be with you. Keep this in mind, because if you don't sell this prospect and solve his problem, somebody else is going to. That's basically what he told you when he completed your questionnaire.

One Final Word

Using these techniques, you should shortly after you follow them up close about one in three of the prospects who completed your questionnaires. Don't drop the other two, however. Remember the Rule of Seven! Follow them up at regular intervals. At that time find out how they are coming along in achieving the objective and solving the problem they told you on the questionnaire (and in subsequent telephone conversations) they wanted to achieve.

If they're not doing very well achieving what they still want to achieve, that is the moment to make a very strong recommendation, as their concerned problem-solving colleague, that they do what you urged them to do in the first place. "I hope, Betty, you'll get **TRICKS OF THE TRADE** now. It'll be most useful in helping you build your practice. Won't you at least try it?" In the end, in using the telephone successfully, persistence is more useful than brilliance. Genuine care and your continuing attempt to solve the prospect's problem are more important than any amount of glib words. Never forget this!

Using Your Telephone To Follow Up Your Targeted Mailings To Selected Buyer Prospects

Here's where the going begins to get rougher. And it can be very rough, indeed, if you don't clearly think through whom you are trying to reach and the prospect problem you can solve with what you are selling.

No telephone call to a prospect, whether qualified or cold, should ever be done without preparation. You should always:

- have a precise objective for the call. Why are you making this call? What do you expect to achieve?

- keep notes of what happened during the call. You should write down both what the prospect bought, and why. And why the prospect didn't buy, including his objections and how you responded to them, or could respond to them better in future.

- follow up each call with a note to the prospect or new buyer. Even if the prospect doesn't buy just now, write to thank him for his time. Let him know you are available to help solve selected, enumerated problems. You cannot get discouraged just because the buyer didn't buy when you thought he should. However, you must let him know you are available to serve him when he wants to be served. And, of course, you already know how to communicate with your new buyers. Don't you?

When you are dealing with a precisely-targeted group of prospects (as you should be), there are other ways to get prepared, too. Have you:

- used the steps of unabashed promotion so that these buyers have the chance of knowing who you are?
- been featured in an article in their trade publication?
- submitted such an article?

In short, have you tried to make the Rule of Seven work for you, instead of against you? I strongly believe you should do whatever it takes to acquaint your prospects with who you are and what you can do for them before calling them. Face it. Calling people on the telephone, no matter how adept at telemarketing you are, is difficult. Therefore, you owe it to yourself as well as to your prospects to do whatever you can to make it easier for both of you.

That's one reason you send them something before calling.

Profitably Using Telemarketing With Targeted Prospect Mailings

Resolve to make your life easier by including a prospect-survey questionnaire in every targeted prospect mailing you do from now on. This won't necessarily obviate the need for calling your prospects, but it will increase the number of qualified prospects who write or call you.

Okay, what about the rest, the multitudes who don't take the trouble to fill out the questionnaire, but who may very well need what you are selling? Here's how to deal with them.

N.B. I'm assuming you have done your homework. That you know what problem you can solve for the person you have contacted, and that you have some very good reason for contacting this person. This means your mailing needs to go to someone specific. Someone whose situation you understand and can help with.

- Send your letters out in small batches, a dozen at a time, tops. Given the vicissitudes of telephone-tag, it'll probably take you five telephone calls and call-backs to connect with these people. Because people have very short memories, don't send out more letters than you can reasonably expect to follow up in a week.

- Make the letter you send personal and professional, warm (but not intimate), and enthusiastic. Indicate that you will be calling by telephone with a definite objective. This objective should be either setting up a meeting or selling your product or service directly over the phone.

- Then make sure you call when you say you are going to call. If you fail to follow through here, the prospect has good reason for assuming you aren't really the helpful, organized, problem-solving person you say you are.

When Your Prospect Isn't There Or Is Difficult To Smoke Out

- By all means leave a message. But don't say you are following up a mailing, or responding to a questionnaire the prospect filled out. Say instead, "I'm calling with recommendations on how Mr. Prospect can make his telemarketing more profitable." Or (if he did return your prospect survey), "I'm calling because Mr. Prospect asked for my recommendations about how to make his marketing less expensive." These, after all, are the things you really are selling!

Indicate when you are available to receive the prospect's call. Also indicate that if the prospect is not able to return your call during this time, you'll call back tomorrow.

- If, after leaving two of these messages, you have still not connected with the prospect, ask the secretary to help you. "As you know, I've left two messages with Mr. Prospect about making his telemarketing more profitable. We haven't been able to connect yet. I wonder if you'd help us both? Could you find out from Mr. Prospect when he would like my recommendations on how to make his telemarketing more profitable? If he's not here when I call tomorrow at this time, perhaps you could let me know what he says, what he'd like to do, and when he'd like to do it. Could you do this for both of us?"

N.B. Secretaries are taught to block. Unfortunately, they are not always taught how to effectively screen calls, to assist with the calls that could be helpful to their bosses and the companies they work for. You've got to impress the secretary with the importance of what you are doing (which is solving, remember, not selling), and enlist her support to move the sales process along. This can all be comfortably done on the telephone.

Still, let's say you call back, and the secretary tells no more than "Mr. Prospect says he'd be interested in reviewing some literature." What then?

Say, firmly but politely, "Ms. Secretary, I sent Mr. Prospect some material last week. I am very anxious to help him improve the profitability of his telemarketing efforts, but before I can do anything else, I really need to have more precise information on what he is doing now, what he would like to do, and what he needs now. Perhaps you can supply me with this information?"

"I'm afraid I can't."

"Then please schedule a telephone meeting with Mr. Prospect so I can give him what he wants, information on how to make his telemarketing more profitable."

In other words, persist.

Never tell the secretary she cannot make the decision. That's an insulting assumption. Just ask her questions it is most unlikely she can answer, so that she'll be forced to work with you to schedule at least a telephone meeting with the prospect. "Tell me, what exactly are your telemarketing plans for this fall?" Who is more likely to know this, the secretary or the person you really want to talk to?

Smart Follow-Up

After you get the telephone meeting with the prospect, send the secretary (you have asked her name, haven't you?) a thank-you note, or at least call and express your gratitude. She may not have done much. But I'll tell you something. The next time you call and want to be put through, she'll remember you were the only salesperson all year who actually went out of your way to thank her for what she did. Don't you think this'll help your cause when you need to get through the next time?

The Prospect's On The Phone

Of course, you won't always be blocked. Sometimes you really will get the prospect on the phone. For such situation, don't forget what every Boy Scout knows: "Be prepared." Be prepared, that is, to reach the multiple objectives every call has:

- You want the prospect to like you and think you professional, competent.
- You want to find out (or confirm) what the prospect's problem is.
- You want the prospect to know your product or service can solve that problem.
- You want to move to the next logical step in the sales process, scheduling a meeting, sending out more detailed information, or closing the sale right on the telephone.

Here's how to handle this necessary four-part sales sequence.

Moving The Prospect To What's Good For You Both

You begin to achieve this result by calling the prospect to follow up your letter.

- If the prospect indicates he didn't get what you sent, don't attempt to explain what you are offering. Say instead, "The material I sent contains specific information about how you can improve the profitability of your telemarketing, Mr. Prospect. Since you didn't get it, I'd like to send you the information again. I'll do that today. You should have it on (three days from time you are speaking to the prospect). I'd like to call you then to discuss these suggestions. Could we schedule a convenient time for you that day when I can call back?"

- If the prospect has received the information but hasn't read it, don't explain it over the telephone. Say, "Mr. Prospect, I'm glad you received the information. It contains specific suggestions about how you can increase the profitability of your telemarketing. Would it be convenient to discuss these suggestions in (forty-eight hours from the time you are speaking to the prospect)? Can we schedule a telephone meeting now for 11 a.m. Thursday morning?"

Then follow up accordingly. Savvy prospects test salespeople regularly. They want to know whether you are just full of hot air, or whether you do what you say you're going to do. My sad experience is that more than half the salespeople I deal with have no follow-up skills, and that I am right to dismiss them as incompetent.

Other prospects, of course, just hate saying no to anyone and use the "haven't received it yet" or "haven't read it yet" responses just to put you off. To find out whether the prospect seriously wants to solve his problem or just wants to waste your time or avoid hurting your feelings, say (even if the prospect doesn't have your material or hasn't yet read it) "Mr. Prospect, if I could show you how to increase the profitability of your telemarketing, would you at least consider doing business with me?" You'll know from the answer the prospect gives you whether this is a qualified prospect or not.

If the prospect isn't interested, what then? Simply say, "It doesn't look like I can help you today, Mr. Prospect. But I'd like to keep in touch with ways to improve the profitability of your telemarketing. Would this be acceptable to you?"

True, some people who are not really prospects will falsely encourage you to stay in touch. (Remember, there are people in the world who cannot bear to hurt anyone else, even though an honest answer at this point would be much more useful to you than a misleading indication of seeming interest). Fortunately, most of those who say yes now are at least sufficiently interested to warrant your continuing effort.

Follow up accordingly.

Write the prospect a note saying you are grateful for his frankness, and that you'll be equally frank in turn. Say you want to help him increase the profitability of his telemarketing, and that you will be in touch from time to time in the future with specific ways about how he can reach his objective.

In other words, persist. All these contacts are covered by the Rule of Seven.

Qualifying The Prospect: Finding Out If The Prospect Has The Problem You Can Solve And If He Wants To Solve It

Just because someone has received your information doesn't mean much. The first thing you need to do is to find out whether the individual has the problem you solve with your product or service. In other words, you need further information.

Will the prospect take the time and trouble to supply you with it? He will if he can be made to see that there is something in it for him, that you can help him achieve his objective. So, the first thing you need to find out is whether he wants to achieve the same objective your product or service helps deliver.

"Mr. Prospect, this is Jeffrey Lant calling. I wonder if you received the information I sent about how your nonprofit organization can increase the number of dollars you raise from corporations, foundations and individuals?"

"I did."

"Have you had the chance to review this material?"

"I have."

"Are you interested in raising more money from corporations, foundations and individuals for your capital, project, operating and endowment needs?"

"We could certainly use the money!"

"Well, Mr. Prospect, I think I can help you. I am in the business of helping nonprofit organizations like yours raise the money they need from corporations, foundations, and individuals."

I'm going to discuss what happens next in the following chapter, Solution Selling. Suffice it to say that by following these steps you have properly positioned yourself for success. You have acted in a competent, professional manner; have begun to find out what the prospect's problem is; and have told him you can help solve it. Now it remains for you to realize the objective for this call: either scheduling a meeting or selling your product or service right now. The important thing is that you stand a very good chance of doing this.

Cold, Cold Calls

As you already know, I am not a big advocate of cold calls. I'll tell you why. They are very, very difficult. For those of us who are shy (and, yes, I do include myself!), they can be very troublesome indeed. It is very difficult to pick up the telephone and intrude without warning into someone's life and manage, in a few sentences, to transform that person from a total stranger into a buying prospect. Of course it happens, but it is difficult. I'll never be convinced it isn't.

Fortunately, if you follow the guidelines in this book, you will increase the likelihood that the prospect knows you and that you have an indication of what the prospect wishes to achieve before you have to make telephone contact with him. That's the way I prefer it. I suspect you feel the same way.

Nonetheless, I feel obliged to provide guidelines on how to handle cold calls, calls where the prospect doesn't have any inkling you will call and is entirely unprepared for you.

Pre-Qualifying Techniques

Your problems as a telemarketer will be substantially reduced if you make contact with the right person, the person who has the problem (or at least the responsibility for solving it) and who has the authorization to purchase the solution. Thus, begin by identifying the people you need to contact. You need to call and find out the following:

- proper name
- pronunciation
- title
- prospect's function
- whether he is the right person to deal with for the product or service you are selling.

When calling your prospect's office, you can get all this information without even giving your name. However, if you need to provide a name, consider giving yourself a telephone name, a name you use when making these kinds of calls. "What's this in reference to?" the secretary asks. "I'm calling for Dr. Jeffrey Lant. He will be submitting his profitable telemarketing recommendations to Mr. Prospect and wanted to make sure they are sent to the right person." This should suffice.

I have to tell you that at this point, I'd send this prospect a letter with information about my products and services. However, given your deft telemarketing techniques, you can pick up the telephone and begin to move towards scheduling a meeting or selling your product or service right over the phone.

Cold Call Prospecting

"Hello, is Mr. Prospect in?"

"Whom shall I say is calling."

"Kindly tell him it's Jeffrey Lant with his profitable telemarketing recommendations."

This may be enough to get your call through. The secretary won't necessarily know whether you are expected or not. Importantly, you are certainly not being deceptive in any way. Your telemarketing recommendations are profitable, aren't they?

However, say you've got a real obstructionist at the other end. "Is Mr. Prospect expecting your call?", she'll say.

"No, he isn't. If this is not a good time for me to talk to him about increasing the profitability of his telemarketing, could you kindly find out from him whether he would be interested in learning how to increase the profitability of his telemarketing. If he is, would you please find out how he would like me to submit my recommendations on this subject? I'll hold."

With these sentences, I've parted company with many other writers on telemarketing. I don't believe in trying to trick your way through the secretary to her boss. I don't believe in presenting yourself to the decision-maker when he doesn't know you, doesn't expect your call, and isn't prepared. When this happens to me, I am invariably curt, and I'm not surprised others are, too. Plan accordingly.

It's certainly acceptable to get information about which person is the right person for you to call. It's equally acceptable to try to make contact with that person. But, by all means, leave yourself an out. In the example above, if the prospect cannot talk to you now (a very real possibility), you've at least positioned yourself to find out two key things:

- whether the prospect is interested in the solution you have for him, and
- how he would like you to handle the matter.

Please take note. By presenting yourself in this way *you* have kept the initiative and can continue to keep it — as you should.

"Mr. Prospect tells me he can't speak with you right now. He says he is interested in learning more about how you can help us increase the profitability of our telemarketing. Would you please send him your material so he can take a look at it?"

Now What?

Have you lost? Certainly not. By following up this promising beginning (for you at least know that he is interested in bettering his present telemarketing position, if you have the means of doing so), you can let the prospect know in no uncertain terms that you are organized, professional, and client-centered. There's nothing wrong with that!

To begin this process, thank the secretary for helping you. You enlisted her support, and she gave you useful information. You're going to be needing her again soon (you do have to follow up what you are sending, after all), so you might as well make friends with her.

Secondly, build on the team relationship you have just begun with the secretary. Tell her to let your prospect know when your material will be going out, and when they can expect to receive it. If there is information on the prospect that will help your cause and that the secretary can send you, ask to have it sent. Remember: you are not in the business of sending literature. You're in the business of building profitable relationships. Too, let the secretary know when you'll be recontacting your prospect. Ask her now if it would be convenient for you to schedule a telephone meeting with your prospect. The key word here is "schedule."

Now do what you said you were going to do. Use the Principle of Assertive Courtesy to build your very embryonic relationship with this prospect. What is the Principle of Assertive Courtesy?

Presume that the prospect is interested in hearing from you. Presume that he is interested (as he said he is) in solving the problem your product or service can solve. Presume that he will be grateful for the relationship which you are moving to create. Remember: presumption is the root of success. Keep in mind, however, if you can solve the problem he wants to solve, what is now presumption will soon be fact!

What must you do?

Writing To Your Newest Prospect

- Thank the prospect. He has agreed to something you want.
- Follow with the benefit you provide ("increased profitability for his telemarketing")
- Provide illustrations of other companies, like his, if possible, which have used your services profitably.
- Let him know that you will work as hard to provide him with a beneficial result.
- Confirm that you will be calling him in three days' time. (Or reconfirm the time you have already arranged with his secretary.)
- Say what you now want. Either let him know you'll be seeking a meeting, or that you can provide sufficient information when you call him so that he can make a decision on the telephone.
- Let the prospect know how this telephone meeting can be made even more effective and efficient. If you are seeking to improve the prospect's telemarketing, ask the prospect to prepare a list of what is working with his telemarketing and what is not. Ask what the prospect would like to do and when he would like to do it to improve matters. *N.B.* If you can get the prospect involved in the solution of the problem, you are well along towards making him a client.

Using these techniques will ensure that much of what is difficult about telemarketing (for, of course, there is much that is difficult) will be minimized, and your chances of using the telephone profitably will be enhanced. The key, as always, in successful marketing, is not only focusing your entire interest on the prospect, his problem, and what he wants to achieve, but being perceived as so focusing. Then you must persist until such time as you enter into a constructive relationship with this prospect.

Call Reluctance And How To Overcome It

Sadly, however, there are other problems which interfere with successful telemarketing. The most serious of these is a deep anxiety about approaching prospects by telephone, the kind of anxiety that literally makes it painful, if not impossible, to pick up the telephone and make the call.

Yes, there are people who are literally afraid to pick up the telephone and make contact with people they can help with their products and services. They suffer from what is called "call reluctance." Fortunately, help is at hand.

Specialists George Dudley and Shannon Goodson have identified 9 types of call-reluctance behavior and have created step-by-step guidelines on how to help these people overcome what can be not only an unnerving but a crippling problem. If you don't have it, you may wonder at just how terrifying this problem can be. I've been aware of it for some time because of a friend who literally breaks into a sweat if he has to call any stranger on the telephone, obviously a serious problem in our society.

If you fear picking up the telephone (or know someone who does) and are subject to acute anxiety attacks when doing so, you need help. You'll find it in *The Psychology Of Call Reluctance: How To Overcome The Fear Of Self-Promotion*, the most thorough guide ever written on how to handle a problem which could destroy your career in telemarketing and effectively prevent you from using the telephone to help your prospects.

Resources

In addition to *The Psychology Of Call Reluctance*, three other books will help you become the success in telemarketing you want to be:

- Dr. Gary S. Goodman's *You Can Sell Anything By Telephone*! This is a short book, but packed with lots of helpful ideas.

- James D. Porterfield's *Selling On The Phone: A Self-Teaching Guide* is thorough and systematic.

- George R. Walther's *Phone Power: How To Make The Telephone Your Most Profitable Business Tool* contains information about handling every kind of telephone call.

Last Words On Becoming A Successful Phone Profiter

It would be wrong to end this chapter without giving you a few principally physical tips about using the telephone. So here they are:

- Always work from a call objectives sheet. Sit down at your desk with the sheet in front of you, copies of the materials you sent the prospect, and any materials you may have received back. I work in the kind of efficient space which allows me to sit at my computer and get to my telephone without moving. I've found this effective.

- Make sure you have extra pens at hand to take notes. Take these notes during the call or immediately thereafter. Especially write down everything you promised to do and when you promised to do it. I find taking notes on my computer also very helpful.

- Smile when you're talking. Your friendliness will be noticeable. Consider having a mirror on your desk so that you can see your facial expressions. *You* may think you're being friendly. Your face — and hence your conversation —may not show it.

- If you don't project well while seated (and most people don't), then make your calls from a standing position. You always project more power and authority while standing.

- When receiving calls, try to answer them by the second ring. My telephone is so situated that I can get it on the first. I want my customers to know I am right here for them!

- End every telephone call by saying thank you. Whatever they've done for you (no matter how meager it is just now), you have something to be grateful for. Furthermore, by always ending a conversation by saying thank you, you'll develop the reputation of being the most considerate person in your business. Which is no bad handle for you.

CHAPTER 9

Solution Selling: What You Need To Know And Do To Close Your Sales

I have a friend who is bright, energetic, and knowledgeable about his field. Yet he is among the world's worst salespeople. Why? Because he's terrible with people.

He always comes across as superior, grouchy, surly, and difficult. Whatever idea you have, he always manages to put down as somehow inadequate. He constantly belittles your initiative and continually carps that what you have just done is flawed and could have been much better, if only you had called him in.

Despite his many gifts (which are considerable) and a heart which I feel sure is really in the right place, his consulting practice never does more than limp along. Moreover, until he masters the art of selling it always will. His failure to be a better, more client-centered salesman ensures that most of his prospects will have to do without his problem-solving skills, and that he himself will be financially poorer and less influential, a terrible waste all round.

This chapter is dedicated to him — and to the millions like him who for dozens of often very simple reasons make it impossible for themselves to succeed in sales.

The *Sine Qua Non* Of Successful Sales: Belief

Face it. Everything you have done up till now is utterly pointless unless you close the sale, unless you actually get the prospect to buy what you are selling or get your current customer to buy again. If you cannot do these two things — and keep doing them — you had better find another kind of work, for you are doomed to failure here.

Face this, too: salesmanship is a game. It is, however, largely a game without mutually-understood rules. The prospect doesn't announce, "Here's the type of buyer I am. Here's how you should handle me," so that you can act accordingly. No, it's a situation the French call *nuancé*, meaning that you have to be very alert to both ostensible and subtle factors which influence both you and the prospect and which determine which way your dealings will go.

Sales is never merely logical or rational. It always involves a psychological, even emotional, aspect. But one thing is clear: you can never succeed in sales unless you really care about people and want them to be better off; and unless you do what it takes to let them know this is how you feel. For if they sense that you are bored, or uncaring, or that your heart is elsewhere, you will surely be a failure. So before you read another word of this chapter, ask yourself these questions:

- Do I really believe in the product or service I am selling?
- Do I think that the people who use it will be better off, that they will be more able to reach their objectives if they use this product or service than if they don't?
- Am I confident that my product or service can do what I say it can do?
- Would my prospect really be better off going elsewhere to get his problem solved, or am I (with my product or service) the best one to solve it?
- Do I still feel enthusiastic about the product or service I'm selling? Or am I just going through the motions?

Unless you can answer yes to each and every one of these questions, you are going to have a very hard time in sales. Furthermore, the problems you are undoubtedly experiencing in selling now are not problems of technique, but rather problems of belief.

Be honest with yourself. If you do not believe, either improve your product or service to the point where you can believe in it. Or if you cannot make these improvements yourself, suggest them to the appropriate personnel in your company. If this fails, go somewhere else where you can answer yes to each of these questions.

Technique, no matter how polished and professional, will never compensate for the lack of an honest and informed belief that your prospects will be better off using what you are offering them. The methods of this chapter are designed to help you communicate this informed belief (and the key word here is "informed") to the people who need what you're selling.

I can say without fear of contradiction that if you radiate confidence that what you're offering your prospects will help them achieve their objectives, you will (at the very least) plant a seed of interest that they need what you are selling. You will also make them doubt whether they really wouldn't be better off getting it than not getting it. Building on this interest and this doubt, you will ultimately make the sale which will benefit both of you.

In a world of indifference, apathy and crippling uncertainty, these prospects must be impressed by your confidence, your enthusiasm, and your based-on-the-facts certainty that what you are offering will help them. Even if they do not buy the first time they hear about what you are selling (and you already know they may not), your repeated efforts to bring your knowledge of their problem and your confidence in your solution to their attention, must succeed.

During the period, however, before the prospect shares your enthusiasm and commitment to your problem-solving product or service, only your own belief in its value will sustain you. It is this belief which must come before any sale you make, and if you don't have it, you will never be anything other than an order-taker instead of what you should be: a problem-solving, client-centered sales specialist.

First Step Toward The Close: Know Thy Prospect

To make sales means to know as much about your prospect as you possibly can. Before you can possibly think about closing your prospect, you must have the following information about him:

- who is he?
- what is his problem?
- what does he want to do?
- why does he want to do it?
- when does he want to do it?
- what obstacles are there to his doing it?
- what is his ability to pay for it?

Whenever possible, gather this information about your prospects before you meet with them. Indeed, particularly when you are selling a service, it is a wise idea to keep a Prospect Log. Keep the following information in this log:

- name of prospect
- title
- company name
- address
- telephone number
- person you were referred by
- problem you are seeking to solve for prospect
- evidence that prospect has this problem
- date of initial contact with prospect
- how made
- result of this contact
- if a meeting is planned, what you asked prospect to do to prepare for it
- what you promised prospect you would do
- date by which you promised prospect you would do it
- date you will re-contact prospect

- other (personal) information about prospect helpful in establishing your relationship
- once prospect buys, date you expect to be back in touch (particularly important where item prospect has bought needs to be replenished).

Print up some of these log forms, and enter them into a three-ring Prospect Log binder. Then set out resolutely to gather this information. You must have it to make the sale!

If a prospect asks, "Why are you asking me so many questions?", be honest. "I want to give you the best possible recommendation I can about how I can assist you in achieving your objective. The information you give me will enable me to do just that. Please bear with me just a little longer. I assure you it is for your own good." Who can resist such a plea?

Getting The Prospect To Prepare For The Meeting

Whenever possible, ask your prospect to prepare for any meetings he has with you, particularly the first one.

As you know, one of the services I sell is expertise in getting corporation, foundation, and individual donations for nonprofit organizations. Before I meet with my prospects (executive directors of these organizations), I ask them to prepare for it and so make the meeting more productive. I ask them for:

- current proposals they are using;
- an annotated list of their Board of Directors;
- information about the level of their Board support;
- sample fund-raising letters they are using;
- a list of corporate and foundation sources where they currently have proposals under consideration;
- a list of how much money they would like to raise for their capital, project, and operating objectives in the next year, *etc.*

If you allow prospects to do so, they will, like the Caterpillar in "Alice In Wonderland", turn your meeting into an interview. "Who are you?" they will ask. You'll be forced to trot out your credentials. In such situations, the decision-maker will inevitably ask for more time to make up his mind. He'll feel obliged to shop around to see if there are others better prepared than you are. The entire sales process will come to a screeching halt.

Good salespeople, therefore, work hard to ensure that the meeting focuses not on them but on the prospect's problem. Now think! Is the prospect really worried about you and your credentials? Or is he concerned and anxious to get his problem solved?

As soon as you can, focus the prospect on his problem. Get him talking about it, and the entire matter of your credentials will be postponed until a later time, when the prospect has already made up his own mind about you, favorably, if he sees that you can solve his problem. Remember: always lead with the prospect's problem. Later you can follow with your formal credentials for solving it.

What If The Prospect Won't Prepare?

I get telephone calls and letters regularly from people who say they want to solve their problems. I treat these introductions with a grain of salt. I get right back to these people and tell them, very directly, very professionally, exactly what they need to do to enable me to help them solve their problem. I always ask them for a 250-word (single page) précis with answers to these kinds of questions:

- what do you want to do?
- when do you want to do it?
- what have you tried so far
- what are your obstacles to doing it?

With this questionnaire I am accomplishing several necessary things:

- I am getting the information I need to determine if they really want to solve their problem, or whether they simply say they want to solve it.

- I am controlling the sales process. Once you are certain you have a quality product or service that can solve the problems of your targeted prospects, to let these prospects ask you elementary questions about whether what you are selling will work for them is a waste of time. Far more important is your knowing whether this prospect will do what it takes to solve his problem. This you can only find out from the prospect. It is essential that you find out as soon as possible.

If the prospect merely wants to talk about solving his problem instead of taking the necessary action to solve it, then you must terminate this relationship as soon as possible, as cordially as possible.

Letting The Unprepared Prospect Go Gracefully (While Putting The Hook In Him For The Future)

Most sales people make a critical error when they discover that a prospect has been "just shopping". Instead of trying to leave an impression of being helpful and ready to assist when the prospect is really prepared to proceed, once they discover the prospect isn't going to buy right away, everything about them breathes disinterest, unconcern, and an air of "get out of my life immediately."

Don't think the prospect won't notice this. Prospects treated like this are prospects you will never sell to.

When you discover that a prospect is not a prospect right now but merely a shopper, do the following:

- If you are dealing with this person by letter, write him and advise the prospect on what he needs to do to prepare to become a client. Do not say that you cannot help. Say, instead, that there are certain things he must accomplish before any interaction with you can be profitable for him. Be clear about what these things are.

- If you are to deal with the prospect on the telephone, send a letter first outlining what he needs to do. Then follow-up with the telephone call, making sure that the prospect understands what needs to be done and why these things need to be done before you can enter into a profitable relationship.

- If you are dealing with the prospect in person, be very careful. Unless you train your body in these techniques, you are going to have a problem carrying them out. You must practice these techniques so that you get them right when you need them:

Look directly at the prospect and in a calm, unhurried voice say, "I'm afraid I can't help you right now. But I would like to help you in the future. May I make a couple of suggestions about how we could make such a contact profitable for you?"

Wait for the prospect to give you permission to proceed.

Then take out a piece of paper, and write down your recommendations. Then hand them to the prospect with any additional sales and marketing literature which would be helpful for him to have.

Finish this conversation by again indicating that you would like to help and by providing the prospect with your name and address so that he can contact you directly.

Why The Fuss?

Being in business means selling products and services now and preparing to sell them in the future. It's as simple as that. Depending on the kind of product or service you sell and its specialized nature, there will either be few or many people unable to use it profitably right now. Don't discourage them, however.

Advise them on what they must do to profitably use your service or product in the future. Let them know as directly and warmly as you can you'd like to help them.

But don't terminate the contact until you get their name, address and telephone number. These people, after all, know who you are and know that you can help them. They have been given their "marching orders" about what to do. Now you need to follow them up at regular intervals to see if they are moving towards becoming clients.

Let me tell you: this approach works. Over time, using this approach, you will get new clients, and you will be able, without guilt, to prune from your prospect-list those who are not willing to follow your professional recommendations. You will get the buyers you deserve and not have to deal with the people who won't do what they must to succeed. What could be better?

N.B. When you follow up these prospects, don't just ask them how they are coming along. Be specific. Say, "How are you coming along on developing your new fund-raising proposal?" Their answer will enable you to advance the product or service you are selling. "Not very well," the prospect may say. "I've had a lot of other things to do."

Now check and see if they still have the original problem you discussed with them. "Do you still need extra money for your meals-on-wheels project?" "We do." Then proceed to a trial close. "Well, Mr. Smith, I'd like to help you raise the money you need." Then wait. Either the prospect will indicate he wants to buy your product or service, or he'll raise an objection you'll have to answer before closing the deal.

The important thing to remember is that once you have spent time with a prospect, you must follow this contact through to its logical conclusion: either becoming absolutely sure this was never a prospect in the first place (which means that you have made a mistake) or consummating the sale.

A Few Words About How You Need To Look, Act & Be

I always talk about sales being a two-tier process. First, the person you deal with has to feel good about you. Then, he has to feel sure your product or service will give him the results he wants, the way he wants them. If the prospect feels unsure about either of these matters, you will not make the sale.

Getting The Prospect To Feel Good About You

What I am about to tell you may seem obvious and unnecessary. Let me assure you it isn't. But first a story.

While writing this chapter I took a friend out for cider in Harvard Square. It was Christmas Eve, and we went to the counter of a coffee house to make our selections. After we stood for too long, though the place was nearly empty, a young woman approached us to take our orders. She didn't look at us. In fact, she allowed another employee to interrupt the order and made us wait some more. "Do you have any lemon pound cake?" I asked. "We're out of it," she said tartly. She didn't make any other suggestions. She didn't even bother to look at me. She acted as if the entire process of serving her customers was beneath her notice. And this was Christmas Eve, no less! To make it worse, my friend's father had just died the day before, and I had taken him out to cheer him up a little.

I sat down feeling somehow dehumanized, more like an interruption than what I actually was: the lifeblood of that business. I had never been in this particular coffee house before and will never go back again. But I shall always remember the look of indifference, boredom, and even resentment on the employee's face as she served us, the people who were clearly a blot on her Christmas Eve.

What bothers me is how different it might have been.

The Ghost Of Christmas Future

Jeffrey and friend approach the counter of a quiet Harvard Square coffee house on Christmas Eve and **shortly after** an attractive young woman appears to take our order. **She's happy, enthusiastic — or at least**

we think she is. She steps up to the counter and **with a bright smile says, "Merry Christmas! What can I do to help you!"**

Jeffrey and friend smile back, saying "We'd like some hot cider and lemon pound cake."

"I'll get you the cider immediately,"our helpful employee says, "but **unfortunately the lemon pound cake is all gone. It's so popular**! Fortunately, **we've got these delicious brownies. I recommend one of them."**

"Thanks, I'll try one... They look good."

Young woman, as Jeffrey pays the bill, **"Since you liked the brownies so much, maybe you'd like to take some home for your family. They're just the thing for Christmas."(She pauses.)**

"Okay. I will."

Employee looking me right in the eyes and smiling, "Merry Christmas now! And **when you come back in the New Year, don't forget to try the lemon pound cake. You'll love it, too!"**

Some Analysis

Do you think my story far-fetched? It isn't. It happens millions of times daily, and as a result businesses lose customers and revenue. Perhaps you'd feel I was giving you more for your money if I came up with a complicated theory to explain how sales are made, but we don't need that theory. We need more time spent on the basics.

So let me walk you through my "Ghost Of Christmas Future" story, and show you how simple things make all the difference. I've marked the key phrases in the text for your convenience.

- The good salesperson doesn't make the prospect wait. Of course, you can't always deal with the prospect now. Perhaps you're waiting on someone else. But you can say when you will be free to wait on the new prospect. "I'll be right with you." You can also be considerate of them while they are waiting, "Is there something you would like to see while you are waiting?" Furthermore, you can bestow this consideration with a smile.

- The good salesperson realizes that sales is theatre. You may not always feel happy, enthusiastic. But you can always make the customer believe you feel this way. If you can't, then strive for empathy, the human connection. The young woman could have said, "I'm fresh out of enthusiasm right now. You know how it is this time of the year. But I'm going to give you all I've got left." It'd be a hard-hearted person who couldn't respond to that opening!

- What the prospect wants may not always be available. That's life. The good salesperson cannot always ensure that his product or service will be available. He can, however, always empathize with the prospect.

If you find yourself in this situation, first give the prospect the part of his product or service you can deliver as soon as possible. Only then tell him you cannot supply the rest. If you cannot deliver what the prospect wants, make sure you let him know how popular it is. Plant the seed of desire in the prospect. People want what's popular.

- If the good salesperson cannot supply everything the prospect wants, he is prepared to make a recommendation. Indeed, I go so far as to say that this recommendation can even be for something you don't sell. If you don't have what the prospect wants, then in your friendliest and most helpful manner direct the prospect to a place where he can get what he wants. In future, there is at least a chance the prospect will return to you, because of the professional way you handled his situation. After all, he knows you are client-centered!

- The good salesperson always seeks to serve additional needs of the customer. Since I liked the brownies, the employee reckons I may want to get more. But consider this line, "Since you liked the brownies so much, maybe you'd like to take some home for the family. They're just the thing for Christmas!" In reality, what is she selling? Brownies? Or a better family experience? She's letting me know very, very subtly that brownies are a way to show my love. What a knock-out punch! Although I probably had absolutely no intention of buying additional brownies, I'll have to buy them now.

- The good salesperson invites you to come back — but not in a general way. Instead, he invites you to enjoy something specific. The one in my fantasy plants the seed of desire in me for that very popular lemon pound cake. She's so confident I'll return that — I must.

The Benefits Of This Approach

Surely you must see the very tangible benefits of this approach?

- The customer (me!) will spend more on his initial visit. Instead of buying no cake at all (as happened in real life), I bought the first brownie and then additional brownies to take home. This translates into more revenue for the storeowner. Multiply this by the hundreds of people who come into the establishment, and it means significantly higher earnings.

- Instead of feeling that I never want to come back (as happened in real life), I am much more likely to become a customer, someone who returns regularly. After all, I've got to try that popular lemon pound cake!

- When I come back, I'll probably come with friends to whom I'll transmit my own enthusiasm for the place. Thus, the store will have the best, the most powerful advertising working on its behalf —word of mouth marketing. Moreover, if my friends are impressed (and I'm going to help them be impressed!), they'll return, thereby keeping the growth process going.

- Finally, I'll feel better as a person. I'll feel wanted. The strongest human feeling. Yes, I'm sure to return to a place that does that for me and to a person who fusses over me. The irony is this profit-making sales approach takes about the same amount of time as the other defeating one.

The Moral

What I'm trying to point out to you, using this all-too-common illustration, is that *every* contact you have with a prospect is an opportunity for you. You can either do what it takes to ensure that this crucial individual will speak well of you and your business (even though he may not have bought anything yet!), or vow never to have anything to do with you. Sales is the art of ensuring the one and avoiding the other. Your profit is a tangible indication of the extent to which you have succeeded.

Quick Rules To Ensure Your Prospect Feels Wanted

- When dealing with a prospect or customer, deal only with that individual and with no one else. Do not allow yourself to be interrupted by another employee. Employees can wait. Prospects cannot. The only exception is when another prospect comes in. Give that person a moment of your time to let him know when he can expect to be dealt with. Do this whether you are speaking to your prospect in person or on the phone.

I have, for example, a call waiting device on my telephone. When I am dealing with the prospect or customer on the first line and the other line rings, I say, "This is Jeffrey Lant speaking. I am taking another call right now. It will take me about 5 minutes to conclude. Would you care to wait, leave your name and number, or call back in 15 minutes?" In other words, let the prospect make the decision. Then you follow up accordingly.

- Before dealing with any prospect, throw your shoulders back, face the prospect, and smile. Then walk slowly to the prospect. Quickly approaching a prospect you don't know may make him anxious. Walk slowly, focusing on him, and smiling.

- Shake his hand, if possible. This contact is important. Make the handshake a firm one but no bonecrusher. If you cannot shake the prospect's hand, then lean into the prospect, or bow your head. In other words, give him the greeting to which he is entitled.

- If you're sitting with the prospect, always have the prospect on your right hand side. If you cannot arrange that, then make sure you are on the prospect's right hand side.

- When a meeting concludes, look the prospect (perhaps now your customer) right in the eye and smile. Shake his hand again. Tell him you are pleased to have this opportunity to serve him.

And mean it. Sincerity is one of the most powerful sales tools.

Dealing With The Ardent Prospect

In preparing this book, I had occasion to read a good deal about sales and to listen to some leading audio cassettes on the subject. One thing particularly surprised me. The experts all acted as if every sale was a difficult one, needing vast strategic planning. Nothing could be further from the truth. If you use the marketing techniques in this book, you'll find yourself confronting prospects again and again who are anxious to buy.

In your delight over this situation, you may very well fail to gain the maximum advantage and to help your prospect to the furthest extent. Don't let this happen to you!

As I've said before, "Don't sell. Solve!" Whether the prospect is enthusiastic to buy or not, find out first what problem the prospect is trying to solve. "Jeffrey, I've heard about your book **THE CONSULTANT'S KIT,** and I want to get a copy right now!", the enthusiastic prospect will say. This happens to me regularly. But do I sell it to him?

I could simply function as an order-taker and take the order. Or I could be the problem-solver I am and try to solve as many problems as possible for the prospect, benefitting the more in doing so.

In this situation:

- Let the prospect know you have what he wants. Do this immediately. "I'm glad you called. I have a copy in stock just for you."

- But don't stop there. Find out what the prospect is trying to do. "Would you mind if I asked you a couple of questions, so I can serve you better today?"

Now find out what you need to know to recommend the appropriate products and services given his problem and objectives. "How long have you been in business?" "How do you handle your marketing?" "Are you planning to do any seminars or talk programs?"

What's important to point out is that each of these questions is connected to a product or service I offer. Your questions must elicit information that enables you to recommend the right products and services, given the prospect's situation and objectives.

"Oh, so you'd like to create workshops which you could use to attract new clients, get publicity, and make money in their own right? I think you'll find my book **MONEY TALKS** is just what you need to reach this goal. Let me tell you a little about it."

The Ardent Prospect Talks

As the ardent prospect talks, take notes. He is telling you what problems he wants to solve. Perhaps he can't afford to solve all of them now. But position yourself so that you'll be the one he deals with when he is ready and does have the money.

A very good way to handle this matter is through the Continuing Service Letter. A word-processing system makes this a snap to do, although you should do it even if you have only a traditional typewriter.

This letter lists all the objectives the prospect wishes to reach and should let the prospect know you can help him get what he wants. As the prospect buys certain items — or as his desires change — other objectives move up in priority. It is your job to continue to bring these items to the prospect's attention so long as he's interested. In the process, you should be discovering what new problems the prospect is interested in solving. In short, the selling process never ends so long as you have solutions to the client's problems.

Finishing With The Ardent Prospect

Before you let the ardent prospect leave, do the following:

- After you have found out what other problems the prospect wishes to solve, direct his attention to the appropriate product or service. Never say, "Is there anything else I can do for you?" Say instead, "Given your interest in creating profitable workshops in your field, I have something here which I feel sure would be useful to you. Come take a look."

- If the ardent prospect cannot buy any more now than he originally planned to get, let him know you'll stay in touch with information about the other subjects in which he's interested. If you can, let him know when you'll be in touch again. In this way, you are using anticipation on your behalf, since the prospect will be expecting you to call. This will help you make the sale.

- Even with an ardent prospect, tell him what a wise selection he has made, and that it will do what he needs to have done. It is always a wise idea to reconfirm for the buyer the fact that you have provided something which will help him get what he wants. So long as the buyer knows you can solve his problems, he'll come back to you. Never miss an opportunity to let him know you can.

- Once the prospect has become a buyer, move the process to its logical conclusion — moving the happy buyer away from you. But don't do so in the casual, neglectful way most salespeople use. Use appropriate ceremony. Shake the buyer's hand. Walk him to your door. Give him your most brilliant smile. Tell him you are grateful for his business and will strive to continue to earn his respect. All this takes very little time, but it is the essence of good salesmanship, for it cements the current transaction and makes the customer feel good about the relationship which you want to develop. Yet how few salespeople do this!

Over the next few days, each time you buy anything, note how the transaction ends. Do you have a feeling of dismissal, or a feeling that the transaction has ended cordially, authoritatively, with suitable expectations for the future and the development of a relationship? You'll find that most salespeople, being nothing more than order-takers, do not give you this feeling. The extent to which they fail to create it is the extent to which they have failed as sales specialists, failing in the process the customer, their employers, and themselves.

Dealing With Less Ardent Prospects: The Objections You'll Hear And How To Overcome Them

As you already know, not all prospects are ardent. Some, in fact, are downright antipathetic. Not to worry. If they have the problem your product or service can solve, you can close the sale. Never forget this!

As you move towards this closing, however, you are going to hear some of the most banal — and a few of the most original— excuses for not buying you can imagine. Your task is to be prepared to answer these excuses as you hear them, so that the sales process moves towards its necessary, inevitable conclusion: the prospect buying what you are selling.

Here are seven of the most common objections to buying you'll hear and how to successfully cope with them:

- "I have to ask someone else. I can't make this buying decision myself."
- "I have enough of this already."
- "I buy from someone else, and I'm happy with our relationship."
- "It doesn't meet my needs."
- "I'm just looking."
- "It costs too much!"
- "I have to think it over."

Excuse #1 "I have to ask someone else. I can't make this buying decision myself."

Shame on you! You should never hear this objection. You should know in advance if the person you are dealing with has authorization to buy what you're selling. Thus, find out before any dealings with the prospect whether he can buy. Ask, "Will you be making this decision yourself, or are there others you need to consult before taking action?"

If others must be consulted, then suggest a way of getting them the information they'll need to make an informed decision:

- Propose a joint meeting.
- Suggest you call or meet personally with the other decision-maker to bring him up-to-date on developments.
- Send the other decision-maker appropriate literature, including copies of any letters or documents that the original decision-maker has already seen.

In short, do what is necessary to ensure that the other decision-maker has what he needs.

Still, let's say you do hear this objection. What should you do? Say to the person you are dealing with, "I can certainly understand you have to check with your colleague before going ahead. But I'd like to ask you a couple of questions before you do so." Then ask, "If you had the authority to buy this independently, would you go ahead today?"

It's very important to smoke out any objections your prospect may feel about your product or service. Look for signs, both bodily and in the language he uses, that he isn't entirely sold on what you are offering. If you see these signs, don't be afraid to say, "Am I wrong in thinking you still have some doubts about what I'm suggesting? If you do, I'd like to give you the information you need." Then pause.

The prospect will probably bring up other objections that need to be dealt with. Indeed, having dealt with these objections you may find that the person who just a moment before told you he didn't have the authority to proceed, suddenly discovers that he does have it after all!

If this can't-make-the-decision-himself prospect doesn't want you to meet with his colleague and doesn't want you to send any material independently, make sure the prospect knows enough about your product and service to make a good case. In this case, it's perfectly acceptable to ask *him* to summarize for you the benefits of your product or service to the prospect. He, after all, is going to have to make the next sales presentation.

If the prospect isn't presenting the benefits properly, advise him on how to do so. In other words, work with the prospect, in this case, as you would with one of your own co-workers. I'll tell you one thing: if the prospect really isn't interested in your product or service, he isn't going to take the time to learn how to present it properly to anyone else. This is when you ask him if he himself needs further information on the benefits it offers.

Excuse #2 "I have enough of this already."

This one sounds impossible, doesn't it? I mean, if a person's got enough he's got enough, right?

Not quite.

When your prospect says this to you, don't panic. Instead, remember:

- If he's got a lot of this product, he likes what it does for him. This, then, is obviously an account worth working for.

- If he's got a lot, he probably uses a lot and therefore will run out at some point.

Thus, to sell this prospect, you need to:

- Find out how much of this product he uses.

- Discover whether he expects to be ordering soon.

Then you need to find out if he is entirely happy with the product or service he is currently using.

As you approach a competitor's product, never disparage it. Of course, it's not as good as yours is (is it?). However, it's better to let the prospect find this out on his own (though with a little help from you!). Therefore, say the following:

"You obviously use a lot of this product."

"We do."

"How much do you usually order at a time?"

He'll tell you.

"When do you plan on reordering?"

He'll tell you.

"Are you entirely satisfied you're getting the results you want with the product you are now using? Is there anything about it you'd like to have improved?"

These are crucial questions, and the answers to them will enable you to move towards a relationship. For consider, there isn't a person in the world who is entirely satisfied with every product he's currently using. Your job is to find out what's bugging him without in any way directly criticizing the product he is now using.

"Well, we do like the product, but I have problems with how long it takes to get delivered to us."

"How long is that?"

"It takes over 10 days to get it to us. This means when we get a big order we often run out and cannot fulfill it. That's why we have taken to ordering more of the product than we really need. Of course, we do get a better price."

"But it probably takes up a lot of storage space, doesn't it. You're obviously spending more money on the product at any one time than you were previously."

"Yes, that's the problem all right."

Now you know enough to be able to make a constructive proposal to the prospect. He's not overstocked simply because he loves the product but because he hates costly delays. Therefore, if you can offer your product at the same price-level but can ensure prompter delivery, you are on your way to getting an important new account.

"Jim, I think I can help you with your problem. But let me make sure I understand what you'd like to accomplish. As I understand it, you'd like to get a competitive price for this product, avoid having to store it, avoid having to commit too much money upfront at the time you order, and get faster delivery. Am I right?"

Before you make any offer to the prospect whatsoever, not only get the facts but have the prospect confirm their accuracy. If the prospect confirms your understanding of his problem, you are on the verge of an agreement. If he doesn't, you'll have to integrate the information he gives you (the new objection) into your thinking and proceed accordingly.

What is important to point out is that many customers are using a product or service that doesn't entirely meet their needs. They may not be sufficiently dissatisfied with it to go out and actively look for a substitute, but they would be open to change if a reasonable alternative presented itself. Your job is to make sure it does.

Excuse #3 "I buy it from someone else, and I'm happy with our relationship."

As you now see, this is merely a variation of the situation presented above. Thus, as above, your job is to find out what the prospect doesn't like about his current situation, and present him with an alternative that gives him all (or at least most) of what he currently has, while adding other things he is not currently getting.

Remember, price may not be an issue in this situation. The prospect may be willing to pay more money to get the additional service he desires. Your job is to find out how aggravated he is about the things he doesn't have. Depending on the degree of his aggravation and your ability to get rid of it, he may feel quite happy about paying *more* for the product or service than he is now.

Excuse #4 "It doesn't meet my needs."

This prospect is asking you to pay closer attention to what he wants to accomplish. Here's what you need to do:

- Go back and confirm what the prospect wants to accomplish. Be as specific about what the prospect wants as you can be.

- Ask the prospect to confirm that, yes, indeed, these are the things he wants.

- Then show the prospect how your product or service gives him explicitly what he wants. But do this by focusing on only one feature at a time and confirming that the prospect understands that he is getting what he wants from it.

"Mr. Prospect, I'm sorry you don't think this product meets your needs. Let me make sure I understand what you want to accomplish. I understand that speedy delivery is something you want. Is that true?"

"Yes, we need to be able to order and get the product within two days."

"Well, with our product I can guarantee you two-day delivery if you place your order before 5 p.m. That means that if you order Monday afternoon, you can have the product Wednesday morning. Would this meet your needs?"

"Yes, it would."

"Mr. Prospect, I also understand that you need 30-day credit to pay for the product. Is this something you need?"

"Yes, it is."

"Fortunately, you can get these credit terms with us. We do require the first order to be paid in cash at the time you place the order. But with subsequent orders, you'll get the 30-day credit terms you need. Is this what you want?"

See how this works?

If you have done your homework and made certain that this prospect really has the problem your product or service can solve, then it is your obligation to make sure the prospect understands precisely what you can do for him. Your job is to discover each of the objectives the client wants and to point out, in simple, compelling detail, precisely how your product or service gives it to him.

As you'll notice, what you are offering may not be exactly what the prospect wants. (In the illustration above, the prospect must pay for his first order in cash). But the salesperson in this example rightly concentrates on the fact that the prospect will thereafter get precisely what he wants. Your job is to show the prospect to what extent you go to satisfy what he wants.

When you have at last demonstrated that your product or service does in fact meet the prospect's objectives, then you are ready to look him straight in the eye and say, "I think you'd agree, Mr. Prospect, that your interests will be well met doing business with us." This is a statement, not a question. Is he really in any position to disagree?

Excuse #5 "I'm just looking."

This one's a killer! What I interpret this to mean is "I've got some money to spend, but I haven't decided yet what I want to spend it on." Your job is to help the prospect spend it on what you're selling. But how do you do this without offending him or making him feel pressured and rushed? Do the following:

Begin by walking slowly up to the prospect, looking at him directly and smiling. Say, "My name's Jeffrey. May I help you find something special today?"

"Oh, we're just looking, thank you."

"Well, we do have some particularly beautiful things right now, and if you'd like any help or information about them, I'll be right here ready to assist you."

Now step back and pay attention to your next customer.

Remember, don't leave a prospect alone too long. He is shortly going to need your attention, and if he doesn't get it, he'll either lose interest or get irritated. If you are particularly busy when the prospect comes in say, "We're awfully busy today as you see, but I hope you'll let me help you." Do it as if you're asking the prospect for a favor. It's a hard plea to resist when said with charm and evident sincerity.

When the prospect needs you, walk up slowly and smiling. "Have you found something that interests you?"

"Yes, I want to get my son a sports coat for college."

"Well, we have a particularly good selection right now. Have you found something you like?"

You need to ask this question before proceeding. If the prospect has found something he likes, sell it to him. Then, using the add-on sales techniques previously discussed, suggest he buy the appropriate accessories. If the prospect hasn't made a selection, however, be prepared to offer your expert advice and move the prospect to a buying decision.

If the prospect needs assistance, give it by asking questions. On the basis of what you're told, direct the prospect accordingly. "Well, given what you told me, I think your son would like this classic blazer. It's stylish and always suitable." If the prospect is hesitating, it may be for one of two reasons. Either he wants something different, or he is uncertain of whether what he is (in this case) considering makes him look good. Get the prospect to provide you with information. You are not ready to close until you have all the information you need to make certain you are selling the right thing.

"I can tell you're a little hesitant about the blazer." Pause.

The prospect will either say, "I think I'd like something a little more trendy." Or "I like it. But what do you think?" In either case, you'll know how to proceed. In the first case, you'll direct the prospect to something else (already knowing that he wants to buy it). In the second, you'll confirm the prospect's own opinion and thus confirm his desire to buy. In either event, you are well along towards your next sale!

The essence of selling to the "we're only looking" crowd is:

- introducing yourself and letting them know you want to help and are available to do so — when they are ready;
- not leaving lookers alone for too long, but being ready to walk up and take control as soon as they light on something that interests them;
- finding out what problem the looker is trying to solve and discovering whether he has already found the solution or is still in need of selection assistance;
- confirming that the prospect has made a good choice ("It looks great on you!"), or, by using information questions, directing him to what he'd rather have.

How different this is from the usual way the order-taker functions after discovering the prospect is just looking. "Okay. Just let me know when you need me." That's order-taker thinking all over. It's passive, unhelpful, and downright stupid. Yet it's the kind of technique I see every day.

Excuse #6 "It costs too much!"

Now we get to the biggie, the one you'll probably hear most often. It's one you must learn to overcome.

"It costs too much" really can mean two very different things:

- "I can't afford it."
- "I don't think this is a good use for my money."

The sales specialist should never hear the former and should be prepared to overcome the latter. Here's how.

"It costs too much." (*i.e.*,"I can't afford it.")

The world is filled with people who want things and cannot afford them. Some of these are certain to find their way to you. You do not want to offend these people, but you can't waste your time with them either. They must be handled in such a way they come to the conclusion that they cannot afford to buy without your telling them as much. If you tell them they are not able to buy, they may well be humiliated. In this case, they'll both never become customers of yours and may well spread negative word-of-mouth publicity about you and your go-to-the-devil business.

Thus, with these people do the following:

- Thank them for their interest in your high-priced product or service.

- Point out its benefits.

- Then qualify them: "Would you agree, Ms. Smith, that this product can do what you want it do to?" Pause for an answer. "Would you agree that it has the benefits you want?" Pause for an answer. "Can you tell me whether you are in a position to go ahead and get one today?"

The person who is not financially able to proceed will let you know. Their voice will break. They will look away from you. They'll falter in some way or another. You'll then know the problem has nothing to do with the product, but with the prospect. In such circumstances, your job is to break off this contact as graciously as possible and as quickly as possible without in any way offending the not-quite-a-prospect before you.

"I can tell, Ms. Smith, that you need some time to think about this. Not to worry! It is a big decision, and I don't want you to feel pressured in any way. Here's my card. Would you please just drop me a note or call when you'd like to proceed? I know you'll be happy with the product or service, and I'm anxious to get you one."

Then end the meeting with ceremony.

Order-takers, on becoming aware they are dealing with a person who doesn't have the money, go out of their way to insult this individual. I never do. When people are affronted they are at least five times as likely to tell people about their experience than if they are happy. Working as hard as I am on my positive word-of-mouth publicity, I cannot afford to launch a negative trend. Moreover, it doesn't take much longer to be nice to a not-quite prospect than merely to dismiss him. I look upon this as a seed planted for the future. These people have friends and colleagues. Even if they don't have the money, their friends might. Keep this in mind.

But it is, of course, on the other objection that I'd really like to concentrate.

"It costs too much." (*i.e.*, "I don't think this is a good use for my money.")

Money is a commodity. People part with it when they want what they can get for it more than they want the money itself. We all know this. Yet too many sales people regularly forget this. We all need to be continually reminded that people don't buy to gratify the seller. They buy to gratify themselves. They buy to get something they want more than the money. When you are told by a prospect who can afford the product or service being presented that, "It costs too much!" what you have just been told is "I'm going to keep my money until I find something which meets my needs better than I think this does."

Under these circumstances, your task is clear. You've got to show the prospect that what you are offering does meet his objectives sufficiently strongly to justify him in spending his money.

Here's how you do that.

- Begin by making common ground with the prospect. "Mr. Prospect, I'm concerned about my money, too. I never buy anything until I am absolutely convinced it meets my needs. So, we're both in agreement on that. I certainly wouldn't want to sell you anything that doesn't meet your needs. That's not the way I do business. But before we break this off, I'd like to show you why I think this product (or service) does meet your needs as I understand them. Please let me."

There is always tension in a sales situation. The prospect is always afraid that high-pressure sales techniques will overcome his natural hesitancy about buying and will leave him with something he really doesn't want. You've got to let the prospect know this is not the way you do business. Your sincerity here is very important. Make sure the prospect understands you are attempting to develop a long-term relationship and that a quick sale that makes the prospect unhappy is not in either of your interests.

When the prospect tells you, "It costs too much!" there is naturally the tendency on your part to shriek, "Listen, you old tightwad. This is the best product on the market. It's priced as low as possible. And it'll meet your needs. What's wrong with you anyway?" This response, however, really wouldn't be too helpful.

Instead, get the prospect to restate the benefits he wants. Then you reconfirm that your product or service delivers these benefits. As soon as you know this is the product or service that can solve the prospect's problem, ask him if he still feels the price is too high. If he does, say "Could you please tell me why you feel the price is too high?" You have got to get the prospect to be as specific as possible about why he feels the price is too high so you can close on what he says.

"Well, Jeffrey, I just think $30 is a lot of money to pay for a paperback book."

Don't blow it now. You've got the piece of information you need to close.

"I can certainly understand that, Tom. If you were buying a romantic novel it certainly would be a lot. But you're not. You're buying proven techniques to build a profitable business for yourself. Let me ask you a question. How much do you charge for your consulting time?"

"$50 an hour."

"Let me ask you just one question. How long do you think it would take you to develop all the sample contracts that you get in this book or to pay an attorney to develop them for you?"

Pause for the answer.

"Well, more than an hour, that's for sure."

"That's the point, Tom. It would take lots more than an hour. But you won't have to spend your valuable time on this mundane task. You'll already have all the documents you need — plus a whole lot more — right at your fingertips. Frankly, Tom, what's more important? Several hours of your time or the $30 price of this book, which you'll be using for years? You really ought to have this book you know."

N.B. Please note you are not asking him if he wants your product or service. You are telling him (in the nicest possible way) he ought to have it, because it gives him what he wants: more of his own time to devote to other, more profitable projects. Since you've answered the prospect's ostensible objection, you are ready to close. So close.

Keep questioning the prospect until you isolate every objection he has. Each time you answer the objection, attempt to close. Once you are absolutely sure the prospect will be better off with what you are selling (you are, aren't you?) and that his having it will launch a successful, long-term relationship, it is your absolute obligation to keep pushing. Each time the prospect objects, answer the objection and attempt to close. Keep letting the prospect know he needs what you're selling and that you're going to smilingly persist until he gets it.

And if this doesn't work?

Try these techniques.

- Do a benefit/liability list. Fold a piece of paper in half. Label the first column "Reasons for using (product or service)." Label the second one "Reasons for not using (product or service)." Do not use the word "buy". It can alarm a prospect!

Now give this paper to your prospect. Let him write in the benefits and liabilities, not you. As often as possible, let the prospect get involved in deciding which way to go. You, however, control the process.

"Tom, you've just told me that it would take you several hours of your valuable consulting time to reproduce the contracts that appear in my book. Do you agree?"

"Yes."

"Well, then, would you agree that one of the reasons for using the book is the fact that you'll save at least several hours of your time in not having to write the contracts?"

Once the prospect agrees, let him write it down in the benefits column.

"How much does your lawyer charge, Tom?"

"$75 an hour."

"How many hours do you think he'd need to draw up these contracts?"

"At least three."

"Well then, since you'll already have these documents readily available and won't need to use your lawyer, you'll save at least $225. Would you write that in your benefits column."

You Relentless Sales Specialist, You!

Using this approach, the prospect may agree to purchase your product or service long before he gets to the "reasons for not using" column. Even if he doesn't, you are certainly not going to be adding reasons for not taking action, are you? They'll all have to come from the prospect, and he won't know as many reasons for not proceeding as you will for going ahead. Moreover, you'll have an answer for every objection, and he'll run out of objections long before you'll run out of persuasive reasons.

How do I know this?

Because one of the things you have to do to succeed in sales is to keep an Objections Log, a list of all the objections which people give you and your answers to them. Most of us are not very quick on our feet. "Winging it" doesn't help us. It hurts. So be prepared. Whenever you hear an objection from now on, write down your best response. If you are working for a company, ask the top salespeople how they respond to this objection. Then use what they say, and refine it until you are sure you have the best possible response.

Excuse # 7 "I have to think it over."

Let me tell you what this means. It means, "I'm not buying." You know that. You use it with this meaning regularly yourself, and to suggest it means anything else is fatuous. Yet all too many salespeople delude themselves that this line is right next to a sale. It's not. It means you are right next to losing the sale.

So what can you do about this pervasive objection?

- First, don't let the prospect get away with this. He's simply indicating to you he's uncertain and needs further information. So, give him the information he needs right now. But not in an argumentative way.

Confirm that the prospect is right to think about this important decision. "Mr. Prospect, I agree with you. Deciding whether to buy this product (or service) is a significant matter. And as we both know a stitch in time saves nine. However, I would like to point out the benefits to you in going ahead right now."

Remember your psychology. People more often buy because of a fear of loss than because of a desire for gain. Now is the time to point out why the prospect should buy today. The reason, of course, is not that you need the business. Never that! Instead, make sure there is a reason:

- a premium the prospect will be able to use;
- a scheduled increase in price;
- declining availability of the product.

The important thing is that this reason must be substantial, and the prospect must feel he is losing something by not acting.

Now go further. Push.

"Mr. Prospect, before I leave, I'd like to ask you a couple of questions. I assume you could go ahead and purchase today if you wanted to." Wait for this answer. Perhaps you will now find out the prospect really doesn't have the ability to buy that you thought.

If the prospect could buy today, then there is a reason he isn't buying today. It may be he wants to shop around. If he wants to shop around, it is because he is not convinced by what you have said. Acknowledge this.

"Mr. Prospect, shopping around means you have some question about my product. I'd like to know what it is and to answer it right now. At the very least, I want to make sure you have all the information you need about what I've been talking about." You must do this to smoke out the objection to what you're selling. Because, mark my words, a prospect who wants time to "think it over" is a prospect who doesn't accept what you've told him and feels sure he can do better elsewhere. He wants to buy. He just doesn't want to buy from you.

Now it's most important to keep alert not only to what the prospect says but how he says it. This may be a person who has no intention of buying but who doesn't want to hurt your feelings, who hates confrontation of any kind. Nonetheless, you need more information. Otherwise, you won't *know* what to do next. You'll only be guessing.

"Mr. Prospect, I think you're trying to tell me there's something about my service you don't quite like. I'd like to know what it is. If my service can be improved, I want to improve it. Please tell me." In other words, try getting the information as a favor to you. Then answer the objection accordingly.

In short, do not leave this meeting until you have again elicited objections from the prospect and had the opportunity to answer them. Moreover, if you find the prospect really does need more time to come to a decision, arrange with him when you can either call or come back. In doing so, keep the initiative and attempt to isolate the area of the prospect's concern. "I can see, Mr. Prospect, you need some more time to discover if you can get faster delivery of the product than the two days I can give you. I'd like to call you on Thursday to see whether you've found it. Say, 11 a.m.?"

End by looking the prospect right in the eyes and saying, "I feel sure my product can give you what you want, Mr. Prospect. And I want to build a relationship with you. I'm looking forward to doing business." You must let him know you want this!

When You Return To Your Office

When you return to your office, send the thinking-it-over prospect a note restating what he wants and how your product or service gives it to him. Also confirm when you'll be calling again. In this situation the momentum can easily be lost. Make sure it isn't!

What To Do When Your Prospect Says No

Face it. It happens to everyone. You've finished your sparkling sales presentation, and now you're ready to write the order. To your consternation and even irritation, your prospect says, "No. I'm not buying what you're selling."

Now what?

How you handle this sure-to-happen-to-you situation will determine whether you'll become a sales specialist, making money with what you're selling, or whether you'll never be anything other than an order-taker, that lowly creature who merely fills out paperwork when people want to buy.

Before You Leave

• Proceeding As If You Were Going To Make The Sale

When your prospect says no, you're going to be hurt, disappointed, even angry. That's only natural. Unfortunately, it's also fatal. When the prospect declines to buy your offer, you need all your wits about you.

If you are sure this prospect has the problem your product or service can solve, you need to ignore the negative you've just heard. You need to act confident the sale will still be made. Furthermore, you cannot terminate this interview before you accomplish two things: try at least once more to sell your product or service, and (if this fails) find out why the prospect has declined to buy.

• Giving It The Good Ol' College Try

The first thing you need to do is try again. This is hard but necessary. You've already put a lot of your time and effort into arranging this meeting. Days, perhaps weeks, of marketing time have gone into getting you where you are now. It would be terrible to leave without trying just once more.

After the prospect declines to buy, pause. Take a minute to get a hold of yourself. Then look the prospect directly in the face and proceed slowly. "Mr. Prospect," you say, "I will certainly respect your decision. But before I leave I'd like to make sure I understand why you have made it, so that I can serve you better in the future."

By using this response, you indicate to the prospect (who may well be defensive about the decision he's just made) that you respect what he's said. Argument is futile here. Good sales techniques are not. While you are letting him know you intend there to be a future between you, take this opportunity to close right now.

"Before I leave I'd like to ask you a couple of questions."

Now find out whether you understand the prospect's problem. State your understanding of it. Ask the prospect to confirm your understanding. If you haven't understood the prospect's problem, it's unlikely he'll want to buy what you're selling.

Once the prospect has confirmed your understanding of his problem, again present the benefits of what you are selling. Do not ask for permission to proceed. Instead, put the prospect in the position of having to stop you. Since you are doing all this for his benefit, why should he want to?

Now show how the various features of what you are offering provide the prospect with what he wants, when he wants it. After you have presented this information, get the prospect's confirmation that this is what he wants done.

Now ask the prospect if there is something about your product or service still bothering him? It is very important that you isolate his objection, so you can answer it.

"Yes," the prospect may say, "as I've already told you, I think your product is fine. It's just too expensive for me."

Now take the offensive. Ask the prospect why he feels what you are selling is too expensive. Often prospects don't know why. They just *feel* it is. It is your responsibility to show him he's getting good value for his money and that what you are selling provides him the benefits he wants.

• Try Closing Again

As the prospect runs out of objections, close again. "Mr. Prospect. You told me you wanted faster delivery. I can provide it. You told me you wanted a competitive price. I can provide that, too. You told me you wanted a service representative to take care of your account. That's what I do. I think it makes good sense for us to do business together. I hope you agree. As Cole Porter said, 'Let's do it!'"

- If The Prospect Still Declines To Buy

Even using this affirmative, goal-oriented, client-centered technique, there will still be prospects who decline to buy. In such a case, before leaving the prospect's office, do this:

- Shake the prospect's hand, and thank him for the time he has given you.

- Look the prospect directly in the eye and say, "I know my product (or service) will help you, Mr. Prospect, and that we'll do business in the future. I look forward to speaking with you again about how I can help your business."

There is nothing to be gained by leaving the prospect's office upset or irritated, and a lot to gain by acting confident that what you are selling will help and that there will be a future relationship. The prospect, being human, may well wonder what makes you so upbeat, enthusiastic, confident. Remembering his Shakespeare ("To err," he recalls, "is human."), he may well wonder if he hasn't let just what he needs walk out the door. That, of course, is how you want him to feel.

On The Way Out The Door

Before leaving the meeting, thank the secretary for helping you. In fact, she may have done precious little, blocking your calls for weeks. But selective memory is very helpful in sales success. Instead of turning your back on this human roadblock, say "Thanks, Mary, for all your help."

Now let her know you'll be coming back and when. "I'll be contacting Mr. Prospect again in about six weeks to follow up today's meeting. Talk to you again then." For all Mary knows, you and the prospect have pre-arranged this time. Because you've already gotten in the door, she'll be more careful about how she treats you in the future, and your calls shouldn't be obstructed. As I've always said, presumption is the root of success.

After The Meeting

All of us in sales need to review our techniques. We need to do it when we succeed, and we especially need to do it when we don't. Of course, being human, we don't do this nearly enough, and so we go on making the same mistakes over and over again.

In reviewing a sales meeting that has so far not produced results, run through the following checklist. Did you:

- Ask the prospect to define his problem for you? Of course, before you get to the meeting you should have some idea of what the prospect wants to accomplish. However it is your obligation to get the prospect to define his problem as clearly as possible. You shouldn't make your presentation until you've gathered sufficient information about what the prospect wants to do to ensure you are properly positioning what you are selling. Did you?

- Ascertain precisely which benefits about what you are offering most interest the prospect? People buy the same thing for many different reasons. Can you honestly say you understood the reasons why the prospect would buy? Or did you impose your reasons on him?

- Check throughout the course of the meeting to make sure the prospect understood what you were saying? The minute you cease to be client-centered is the minute prospects lose interest. Did you make a presentation (a word I loathe), or did you focus on your prospect?

- Isolate each of the prospect's objections and answer them? If you left any of the prospect's objections standing, you gave him a perfect reason for not buying what you're selling.

- Give the prospect a sense of your own enthusiasm about what you're selling and your own commitment to the company selling it? Or did you act like this was your tenth sales call of the day and hence utterly beyond redeeming interest of any kind? The salesperson's lack of interest in what he's selling necessarily taints the prospect's interest in it.

Don't just ask yourself these questions verbally. Keep a log with them, and write down your answers. Over the course of even a few days, you'll discover a pattern about your approaches and your prospects' responses. As a result you may find that you — not your prospect — are the problem.

Now What?

Always assuming the prospect has the problem your product or service can solve (the key factor), do this:

- Resolve to build a relationship with this prospect. Resolve, that is, to do what is necessary for him to see you as the helpful problem-solver you are. You must have a vision at this point, a vision of helping the prospect do what he wants to do even when he doesn't accept the fact he needs your help. This necessary vision logically precedes the relationship, and the relationship cannot take place without it.

- Send the prospect a note thanking him for his time, saying that you want to build a relationship, and telling him you'll be back in touch. It is a wise idea to say when you'll be back in touch. That will, of course, depend on what you're selling, but by all means let the prospect know.

Then write down the date, and make sure you are back in touch at that exact time. Prospects judge our products and services by our sales habits. If you are slipshod about doing what you said you were going to do, they are right to reckon that our products and services are the same way. Make sure at least some of your sales literature is enclosed with this note. People often buy for no better reason than that they know the product or service. Use every opportunity to build familiarity.

- As organizations comparable to the prospect's use your product or service, drop the prospect additional notes letting him know, in the nicest possible way, that others are making headway towards solving comparable problems. Always let him know that you want to do the same with him. Envy, you know, is a terrific motivator.

Call The Prospect Again

Call the prospect when you said you were going to. In calling him do the following:

- Let him know that you are doing what you said you were going to. "When we last talked, Mr. Prospect, I said I'd call you April 20th. Here it is April 20th, and I'm ready to help you."

- Never launch into a sales presentation. Instead, confirm that the prospect still has the problem he had when last you talked. "When we last talked, you said you wanted to raise more money from corporations for your meals-on-wheels program. Is this still what you want to do?"

- If it is, then you are ready to talk about how your product or service can help him achieve his objective. If, however, he's changed his objective, you'll have to change your approach by gathering additional information. "No," the prospect may say, "we're now interested in raising additional dollars from our community for our endowment fund."

Before you can adequately respond to this, you may well need additional information. However before asking for it, let the prospect know you can help him achieve this objective (if, indeed, you can!): "My company can help you do this, Mr. Prospect. But I'd like to know more about what you need to do and when you need to do it. Could you please tell me... ?"

N.B. It is perfectly acceptable in this situation to ask for additional time to consider your proposal to the prospect after you've gathered the new information. Don't rush. If you need time, take it! It is better the prospect get the exact proposal he needs from you, than that you prematurely rush things.

Persisting

How long do you continue to approach this prospect in this systematic, client-centered fashion? The answer, my friend, is simple: so long as he has the problem your product or service can solve. Succeeding in sales is a combination of plodding persistence and rigorously client-centered behavior. These two factors, not high pressure tactics and the boorishness associated with so many in the profession, ensure success. Take my word for it!

Last Words On Becoming A Sales Specialist

As long as you are in business, you are in sales. This means you must become a sales specialist to prosper. This chapter is full of helpful suggestions. To finish it off, here are some more:

- Your job is always to help the prospect visualize how much better his life will be using your product or service than not using it. Effective salespeople are dreamspinners, people who put before their prospects a better world for them, one they can taste, feel, see, smell, experience. Your job is not so much to sell as it is to motivate these prospects to reach out and do what is necessary to get the better life they want.

- Ask the prospect to prepare for meetings with you. Get the prospect involved in working with you to solve his problem. The greater the prospect's involvement before the meeting with you, the more likely he is to do business.

- Get rid of unhelpful sales language. Don't mention “buying”. Instead, say “investing,”or “using”, or “experiencing.” People don't like to buy. But they do like to use.

- When the prospect finally buys, as he will from you more often now, do the following:

  - Look him in the eyes and smile;

  - Congratulate him on the decision he's just made, letting him know it is a sensible one and how it will help him;

  - Let him know how to reach you if he has further questions (or problems);

  - Tell him when you'll be returning so that he's prepared.

Then leave promptly, with only one last word of thanks to the secretary. It's time for you to go on to your next sale, specialist!

Resources

No one has a corner on all the sales wisdom in the world. That's why I want to recommend two additional resources to you.

The Best Seller by D. Forbes Ley is an exhaustively detailed step-by-step guide showing you how to motivate prospects to buy. He rightly reasons no one is ever really persuaded to buy. They motivate themselves.

Secrets Of Closing Sales by Charles Roth and Roy Alexander. If you can't close, you can't succeed in sales. This book has marvelous information showing you how to perfect your closing skills.

CHAPTER 10

More Marketing Methods: Specific Ways To Sell More To Your Existing Customers And To Get New Buyers, Too

This chapter is divided into two parts. The first part deals with specific ways of selling more to your existing clients and customers. The second concentrates on how to put you in touch with new prospects and future buyers. Both are crucial. But there's a reason why I've divided the chapter this way.

As should now be clear, I place a high premium on ways of converting current buyers as quickly as possible into repeat buyers. The reason for this should be obvious. Getting these buyers is an expensive proposition. It takes imagination, creativity, time and money to get a buyer — any buyer.

If you want to improve the return on your investment (and let me tell you something: you do!), you've got to think of solid, continuing ways to renew the connection with your current, especially your new buyers. If you don't, you're merely an order-taker, and you're depriving your customers of the solutions they need and yourself of the revenues you need.

Thus, resolve that you'll do whatever is necessary to reconnect with your buyers as quickly as you can, as consistently as you can.

Selling More To Existing Customers

In this section, I'm going to discuss the following means of selling more to existing clients and customers:

- add-on/upgrade letters
- using credit card confirmation
- premiums and purchase steps
- package inserts
- special "family-only" discounts
- request-letters for your buyers to send
- doodads with your name on them
- catalogs bound into your books and using nonfiction books to sell consulting services, and
- personalized new product and service announcements.

Please note, these marketing techniques overlap. In practice, you'll find yourself combining aspects of these techniques as you work on ways to reconnect with your buyers and get them to buy again — soon.

Add-On/Upgrade Letters

If you're smart, you've grouped your products and services into lines. The most likely business to fail is a business with only a single product or service. Successful businesses create lines of products and services. Some of these are products and services they offer themselves. Others are products and services provided by others but sold by you.

Businesses do this for one very simple reason: a customer who likes one item you've got will probably like related items. Your job is to bring these related items to his attention in a way that makes it easy for him to buy. This is what add-on letters do. Briefly, they inform the buyer (now your Top Prospect) about what related items you've got to solve his problems.

Frankly, having a computer will be immensely helpful in writing add-on letters, although the technique can be used (less successfully) with offset print letters and your typewriter.

Contents Of The Add-On Letter

The Add-On Letter is divided into the following parts:

- personal greeting to your customer;
- your thanks to the customer for having bought one of your products or services, and
- confirmation that this purchase is a sensible one, and that it will help your customer reach his objectives.

Having welcomed the customer to your business family, expressed your appreciation for his patronage, and confirmed that his purchase was a wise one, then continue by:

- Informing the customer that what he has just bought is part of a series or a line of related problem-solving products or services. Assume that the customer didn't know this. Also assume he wants to know this, and that once he knows it, he will want to act.

As usual in a sales situation, it is important that you act like the customer wants to buy. Don't forget your Assertive Courtesy; assume the customer wants to buy and so solve his problem. Assume that you are courteously giving him the information he must have to be able to do so.

Now follow with complete details about what you are selling and why this will continue to help the customer reach his objectives.

Once you have finished presenting this information, close with warm words, your expressed hope for a continuing relationship, and an order blank. Make sure you make it as easy as possible for the customer to buy again. Include your address, telephone number, and credit card information for quick follow-up. A satisfied customer, happy in his new purchase, will often simply pick up the telephone and call you immediately with another order. *N.B.* Time this offer.

Don't simply send an offer to the buyers you wish to upgrade. Send a timed offer. I recommend one expiring two weeks after the customer has received the original order. This is neither too short to seem pushy nor too long so that he forgets how helpful you and your product/service are.

Two weeks gives your customer plenty of time to evaluate what you've already sent. Now it is the product or service itself which will convince him to buy more; that and the prospect of losing something if he doesn't act within the prescribed amount of time. You can even print the date this special offer expires — in capital letters — on the order blank to impress on your customer the need to take action now, or lose something he needs.

Personalizing The Add-On Letter

Here's where a computer comes in very helpful. With it you can easily personalize this letter by:

- adding the customer's name;
- indicating what he has bought and thanking him specifically for this purchase, and
- including the date when this special offer expires.

Even with lengthy add-on letters (like I use) the entire process of writing to your customers shouldn't take long at all.

But what if you don't have these modern conveniences?

My rule of thumb is always make the best of your current circumstances. If you can't use the best alternative, use the alternative that's best, given what you can do. Thus, create an offset-letter with appropriate blanks and check lists.

- Type in the customer's name.
- Include a list of all the products and services you provide, and check the one(s) the customer has bought.

• Buy a date-stamp, and update it daily to show when the special offer expires.

The Personal Touch

Whether you produce the Add-On Letter on your computer or use a typewriter, each letter should be personally signed by you. I often add a personal post script, too. Something like, "Hope to hear from you soon, Mary!" will do nicely; anything that is personal from you to your buyer and which increases the sense of belonging to a select group and doing business with someone caring about you. Now I ask you. Do you talk to your buyers and try to foster a sense of belonging, of friendship, of caring, even with people you'll probably never see? Or do you simply deliver your service or ship your products? Be honest.

Aside from the obvious benefits of this course, there is another important one to be gained: word of mouth publicity. People talk about their friends. As someone who is friendly to your buyers, you'll garner enhanced word of mouth promotion.

When To Use Your Add-On Letter

Insert this letter in *all* your outgoing packages. Then wait for the phone to ring with additional orders. I'll tell you something: it will! Moreover, your buyers will be more enthusiastic about what they buy. They'll approach you as an old friend. They'll buy from you with enthusiasm and seek out your recommendations. The personalized Add-On Letter is a powerful sales tool. *N.B.* When these buyers contact you, they'll act like they know you. Don't blow it now! Be just as amiable and conversational to them as they are to you. (For a copy of one of the Add-On Letters I use, see Samples page 262.)

Using Credit Card Confirmation To Make Additional Sales

These days people are rightly concerned about who gets access to their credit cards and what is charged on them. I have turned this pervasive anxiety into a marketing opportunity in the following way. As you know I use drop-shipping to provide goods to my customers. This means, to remind you, I don't manufacture or store this merchandise. I sell it, often by credit card. Since I don't (usually) ship the merchandise, you might think there is no particular reason for me to be in touch with my buyers again about this particular order. Wrong.

• Buyers want a copy of their charge slip.
• They want to know how long they'll have to wait to get what they've ordered.

Now I could simply send the slip and a note advising them it takes between four to six weeks to fulfill an order using special 4th class (book rate) shipping. But that's inadequate. Use your evident care for their feelings to gain a marketing advantage.

The Credit Card Confirmation Letter

This letter should:

- Thank the customer for his order and confirm that what he has ordered will do what you said it will do. Expressing your appreciation to your buyer and confirming the wisdom of his decision are always necessary in customer communications.

- Tell him you wanted to get him a copy of the charge slip as soon as possible for his records.

- Indicate when his merchandise will be coming and what to do if it doesn't arrive in the usual time. Provide him with your direct-dial number. Customers hate getting the run-around when calling to complain about non-delivery of merchandise, and whatever good will you've built up will be quickly dissipated if you cannot handle this situation!

N.B. It's a wise idea for you to develop a "late delivery" letter with which you can jog a product manufacturer. Such a letter should provide the manufacturer with the name and complete address of your buyer, and the date you placed your order. You should request verification that the order was sent and confirmation that this matter has been resolved. In this situation, always presume the customer — not the manufacturer — is right. There are customers who will abuse your trust. However, manufacturer shipping errors are more common.

- Now advise this customer about one or two (not more) additional items which, given what he's already ordered, would be of particular interest to him. These are, in short, your current recommendations about how he can achieve the objective his previous purchase suggests he wants to achieve. Tell him you've included further information about your recommendation and how the customer can take advantage of it.

Premiums And Purchase Steps

What will help the customer decide to take advantage of these recommendations are special premiums available upon reaching certain levels of purchase. For instance, buyers who buy over $150 worth of merchandise from my catalog get a premium. Until the work overwhelmed me, I automatically enrolled them in what I then called my Article-Of-The-Month Club. As members, each month for a year they received one of my tip-packed Sure-Fire Business Success Articles, ordinarily before any of the publications printing it did. This is a superb premium for several reasons:

- It is something I produce myself, and thus is relatively inexpensive. Nonetheless, it still has a real commercial value, since you can buy this subscription separately.
- It has my name attached to it but is something which, because of the information in the article, is unlikely to be discarded by the buyer/reader. Thus it fulfills an essential marketing condition: it will be kept.
- It offers recommendations on other products to buy. That's because each of my Sure-Fire Business Success Columns concludes with a "Resource Box" listing information on products mentioned in the article and some of the products I produce myself. Needless to say, all of them are available through me, and my address always runs with each article. Therefore, the premium itself offers the possibility of future sales.

Since discontinuing this valuable (if exhausting) premium, I've used many others. Currently, individuals ordering over $150 get one of my 60-minute audio cassettes. Those ordering over $225 get their choice of any one of my 7 Get Ahead books *and* the 60-minute cassette. And I'm always seeking out special premiums from other companies, premiums they offer their buyers that they'd be willing to offer mine, too — without charging me anything. Just recently the National Business Association offered all my catalog buyers a free piece of software that enables people to determine if they qualify for a Small Business Administration loan. The trick is to keep looking for premiums and making them as enticing as possible so people take immediate action to get what you're selling.

Last Words On Premiums

The question arises, of course, as to how one finds suitable premiums and makes premium deals. Frankly, there's no mystery to this. Premiums are quite literally everywhere. Here are the criteria you should consider in evaluating them:

- Is the premium you are contemplating meaningful to your buyers? Is it something they want and find useful?

- Can you get the premium without paying a high price for it?

In other words, will the premium be meaningful to your buyers but not costly to you? If the answer to both questions is yes, you have a premium possibility.

As you consider the question of premiums, think expansively. Literally any product or service can be offered as a premium. But there is one further condition you need to keep in mind: your buyers should not be able to get the same premium offer elsewhere. What you offer must be unique.

This isn't as difficult as you may think. Say you want to offer your buyers a special premium in the shape of a 50% discount on the retail price of a dozen roses. To make this deal, you would have to find a florist with an '800' number (where the order could be placed), the ability to take credit cards (for easy payment), the capacity to deliver flowers nationwide (any FTD florist can do that), one who was not offering this deal generally, and, finally, one who would make a certificate available that you could send your customers (though you can, of course, produce this yourself). As you see, on this basis, *anything* can become a suitable premium. The range of such premiums is limited only by your imagination itself.

What is also important is that this kind of premium costs you next to nothing. Moreover, it firmly establishes you as a caring, client-centered entrepreneur, just the way you want to be seen. Therefore, it doesn't matter a whit whether your customer actually uses the premium offer or not. What matters is that it is available to him. Its mere availability, need I say?, will make you money, for people will buy merely to get the premium. You can, of course, help this process along.

Nearer My Premium To Thee

If you're smart, you'll offer a series of premiums, or at least two at different purchase levels. As you know, I offer mine at about $150 and about $225 per quarter. Let's say an individual buys $100 worth of goods. The average order-taking seller tallies the sale and goes on to the next buyer. Not me. It has taken me much time and treasure to get this buyer in the first place. Now I want to improve the return on my investment, not simply go on to the next buyer. Here's where a premium is particularly helpful.

- Send a letter (again, a computer is most helpful here) informing your buyer about the premiums you have available. Expand upon their importance, usefulness, and desirability. Then point out how close, how very close, this buyer is to getting not just one of them, but everything you have available.

A buyer at $100 is only $50 away from my Premium 1 and just $125 away from Premium 2. The cost of the first premium to me is about 50¢ and the cost of the second about $7. If I can induce the buyer to upgrade to the $150 level, I make $49.50 profit. If I can induce him to go to the next level, I make $118 profit. Not bad for a single letter!

This is why premiums are so helpful. They enable you to be clearly perceived as client-centered, while at the same time nicely improving your bottom line for minimum effort. Still, it's no surprise to me that more supposed marketers fail to employ them, for the bulk of these people are no more than uninspired order-takers. I know, however, you'll be different.(See Samples, page 265)

Package Inserts

Package inserts are simply additional offers inserted into your outgoing packages, or, a simple variation, handed to customers over the cash register or as they enter your establishment. In point of fact, add-on letters are merely a sophisticated version of package inserts. The difference is that in an add-on letter you make a real effort to make the letter personal to the buyer. With a standard package insert, you simply enclose information that may or may not be of interest to the buyer. Why not use both?

When There Is A Package

It is only low-lives with an order-taker mentality who sell a customer simply what he asks for and delivers simply what he has purchased. This will never do for the rest of us! Instead:

- Seek out offers which supplement what you are selling and delivering to customers. In the long run, you may develop additional products and services yourself. However, if you don't have them yet (or even if you do!), make a concerted effort to find manufacturers who have products and professionals who have services which nicely supplement your own offerings. We've discussed this previously in relation to catalogs.

What you need from these manufacturers is:

- An adequate discount. Each field varies, of course, but you should try to get at least 50% of the retail price. After all, you could argue, the difficult part is finding suitable customers. With package insert offers, you can be reasonably sure what you are offering is going to the right person. This is a real boon to both customer and manufacturer. You should be compensated accordingly.

- A photostat with their offer. There is no need for you to create your own advertising materials. The manufacturer should provide them. After all, what you're trying to do with a package insert is simply make a little money, not necessarily become the major distributor of the manufacturer's products that would justify an investment of time and money producing your own materials for what he offers. No advertising materials, in short, no relationship!

N.B. Go even further. Why not ask the manufacturer to provide you with 500 or 1000 (start with this number) of his flyers with your name and address printed on? That way you don't have to put up any money yourself. Be prepared, however, for the manufacturer to turn you down. After all, he doesn't know whether you are reaching the right market for his products or not and will want to wait and see. As you show that you can move their product, however, ask again. If you don't get the cooperation you feel you deserve, look elsewhere. There are plenty of product manufacturers who will be happy to see you!

- If you do print your own flyers, use a bright paper such as canary so that it stands out. Make sure, too, your address and telephone number are clear. So many of the package insert flyers I receive look amateurish and sloppy, thus reflecting adversely on the people producing them.

Once you've got your flyers, simply insert them into all your outgoing mail. Don't despair if the return is low, as it probably will be. This is not your main offer. It isn't taking you much time to bring it to the attention of your buyers or to fulfill resulting orders. Just keep stuffing, and you will see a reasonable return on your investment. That's all you can expect.

When There Isn't A Package. Hands Across The Register!

If you don't ship but offer what you're selling on a cash-and-carry basis, you should still use a variation on the package insert idea. The basic idea, as you should now be aware, is to have your latest customer buy again. The best way to ensure his doing this is personally to bring to his attention other buying possibilities related to what he has already bought and to ask, specifically ask, him to buy again. That's where the Add-On Letter is so useful. It doesn't just bring offers to the prospect's attention. It shows him what he needs, asks him to buy it, and provides him with all he needs to do so easily.

Now try this across the counter.

Each time a customer buys anything, he should be given the opportunity to purchase something else. Those with an order-taker mentality (even though they may have additional sales material) are useless in this situation.

The order-taker will merely stuff the package insert material into the customer's bag and leave it at that, never mentioning it specifically. The marketer, however, hands the flyer to the buyer and *invites* him to take advantage of the offer.

Any product can be handled in this way. Say it's a toothpaste special. The check-out personnel simply say, while flashing a bright smile, "We're having a special on toothpaste today. Here are the details. Hope you'll take advantage of it. You'll find it on aisle 3." Better yet, if you can arrange it, have your customers get this information as they come into the store so that they won't have to go through the check-out lines twice. But either way, do it.

A More Sophisticated Variation

Of course, you want people to spend their money now. You also need them to come back later. So when they are checking out, personally hand them a flyer announcing a special which will take place within the next week. This flyer can have several variations:

- It may offer a discount to the person using the flyer you are handing out, (thus making it essentially a coupon.)

- It may have a mail-in feature as well as a walk-in feature.

Treating your customers like this offers several distinct advantages:

- It makes them feel wanted, always an important benefit. People often do things merely because they are asked. If you are not asking your customers to buy, perhaps they are buying elsewhere.

- It makes a nice personal contact. What is therefore terribly important is how the customer is asked to take the flyer. If the flyer is handed over in an apathetic and disinterested way, the customer will know he is the object of a marketing campaign and will resist accordingly. However, if the flyer is handed over as if it were the Holy Grail, an object of inestimable importance, how can he, really, how can he, resist the opportunity you are giving him?

- It's cheap. Even in my expensive neighborhood you can still get 1000 flyers for around $30-35.

- It makes money. How can it not? You have already identified the customer. He's right in front of you. He's happy with your product or service (or at least you may assume so). Moreover, if you've selected your objects carefully, he'll be interested in what you tell him about, for make no mistake, you don't need to focus merely on one item. You can easily do 8 to 10 items on a single side of a single 8 1/2" x 11" flyer. This variety gives you a very good chance to present something the buyer wants to have.

Now make it easy for yourself. Develop a standard form into which you can insert these special offers. Open it with a warm headline: "You're Invited... " Or "Special To Our Business Family..." You get the idea. Invite your buyers, in short, to connect with you, not just to buy from you.

Selling Products Before They Exist. Specials For The Family

If you're familiar with my operation, you know I sell my books before they even exist. That's right. Before I have written so much as a word of the text, (but only after I have created a scintillating title and set the publication date), I begin to sell the book. You can appreciate the reasons for this decision:

- I raise a considerable portion of the money I need to publish the book from buyers of the book.

- I can begin to promote the book from the minute the title is set, a considerable advantage over mainline publishers.

But, you ask, will anyone buy a product on this basis? Of course they will if:

- they trust the seller and feel the offer will help them meet their objectives, and

- they get a special discount, a "family" discount.

The first of these conditions can be met once you have already sold your customers a product they like. At that point they should believe in your ability to help them. Once such trust has been clearly established, you are ready to sell products which do not yet actually exist. Trust, you see, not necessarily ready availability is what sells products. The second comes through a special pre-publication offer.

To make this offer succeed, prepare a special flyer (or include a section in your add-on letters or catalogs).

- Remind your buyers that what they get from you is a quality product which helps them solve their problems. Don't assume they know this. People often know only what they are told, and only what you remind them about.

- By all means, let them know you have other (already existing) products and services.

• Tell them, too, you can give them a special price on a product or service you are just creating.

The key points here are that people must already be familiar with your problem-solving abilities, and there must be a precise date when your buyers can expect to have the product or service which does not now exist.

N.B. If you delay delivery much beyond this date, you may get yourself into trouble with federal authorities. If you have sold your product nationally, you come under the jurisdiction of the Federal Trade Commission. To be in compliance with its rules, you must ship your product within 30 days of when you said you would. Thus, it's better to tell people your product will be shipped "in May" than "May 15th", since the former gives you an extra two weeks to ship.

If you cannot get your product to people within this time (that is, by June 30 in the illustration above), you must send your buyers a notice telling them when within the next 30 days you will be shipping (that is, by July 30th in my example). You must also offer them the possibility of getting their money back. If you cannot ship in this time, you must return all the money you've collected. So be prompt, and set liberal production schedules for yourself.

I have found this technique most profitable, especially when the not-yet-available product is part of a series which is otherwise ready to be shipped to the customer. The customer feels the less compunction about buying what does not exist to the extent that what does already exist is substantial and impressive. But surely what you are offering is that?

How Much Should You Discount? And When Will Your Customers Buy?

I give 1/3 off the eventual retail price of my products during my pre-publication offers, a substantial savings. Most of those taking advantage of it do so in the final 60 days before the price goes up. That's typical of the human animal. Not to worry. Through all the other seasons you have promoted the availability of this offer, you have also been promoting the benefits of the product or service itself and hence raising its profile, a not unimportant point.

Getting Your Buyers To Help You. Something Really Different!

You know you are in the business of helping your customers. However, have you ever thought they should be helping you, too, beyond giving you a check for your offering? If you haven't, you are not unusual. But listen to this.

As you know, I am a publisher. This means I need to be interested in sales not only to individuals but to libraries and similar institutions. How to get libraries to buy my books is a marketing problem. In my attempt to solve it, I have come up with a unique gambit. When I send out my books to my buyers, I ask them to do me a favor, to send a letter to their local public library recommending that it purchase all my books and so help people in the neighborhood. I bet you've never seen anything like these samples!

Sample Helpful Buyer Letters

JEFFREY LANT ASSOCIATES,INC.
50 FOLLEN STREET, SUITE 507
CAMBRIDGE, MA 02138
(617) 547-6372

January 4, 1991

Mr. Jack Chatfield
875 Comstock Ave., 11-C
Los Angeles, CA 90024

Dear Jack Chatfield,

Thank you for buying at least one of my "Get Ahead" books. As I hope you'll agree after using it, I've worked hard to include a host of specific techniques to build your business. If this is how you feel, I hope you won't mind if I ask you for a favor.

In my attempt to get my books into every library in America, I'm asking my friends and buyers to do me a favor — to write to their local acquisitions librarian and recommend the purchase of my "Get Ahead" Books. These librarians pay close attention to these recommendations, and I therefore hope you'll be willing to send the enclosed letter I've taken the liberty of writing on your behalf. All you have to do is sign it and mail it in!

When you have, let me know, and I'll send you one of my Sure-Fire Business Success Articles. You've probably already seen these articles. They run in over 100 publications nationwide and are packed with profit-making techniques. I'd like to send you one with my compliments for helping me place the best in get-ahead information in every American library.

Need I say that what I'm asking you to do is a most innovative marketing technique? I don't know anyone else using it. It's typical of the kinds of inexpensive, cost-effective, profit-making marketing suggestions you'll find in my new book **MONEY MAKING MARKETING: FINDING THE PEOPLE WHO NEED WHAT YOU'RE SELLING AND MAKING SURE THEY BUY IT**. You can get this huge, oversized and very innovative book for just $38.50 postpaid. I hope you will.

In the meantime, thanks for helping me and thanks for helping bring the best in get-ahead information to your local library!

Sincerely yours,

Jeffrey Lant, Ph.D.
President

875 Comstock Ave., 11-C
Los Angeles, CA 90024

January 4, 1991

Ms. Carol E. Moss, County Librarian
Los Angeles County Public Library System
320 W. Temple St.
P.O. Box 111
Los Angeles, CA 90053

Dear Ms. Moss:

I'm writing today with a recommendation that our library purchase a new book by Dr. Jeffrey Lant. The book is **TRICKS OF THE TRADE: THE COMPLETE GUIDE TO SUCCEEDING IN THE ADVICE BUSINESS**. It's $34 postpaid from JLA Publications, 50 Follen St., Suite 507, Cambridge, MA 02138.

Here's what *Consulting Intelligence*, one of the leading publications in this field, said in its November issue. "This is another of Jeffrey Lant's blockbusters... It is probably the most complete work of its kind and hard to imagine that any reader would not find much that is useful, no matter what his or her specialty is." I think this book would make an excellent addition to the library's collection.

I would also like to draw to your attention other books by Jeffrey Lant for your consideration. They include:

THE CONSULTANT'S KIT: ESTABLISHING AND OPERATING YOUR SUCCESSFUL CONSULTING BUSINESS ($30 retail, $32.50 postpaid. 203 pages.)

THE UNABASHED SELF-PROMOTER'S GUIDE: WHAT EVERY MAN, WOMAN, CHILD AND ORGANIZATION IN AMERICA NEEDS TO KNOW ABOUT GETTING AHEAD BY EXPLOITING THE MEDIA ($30 retail, $32.50 postpaid. 365 pages.)

MONEY TALKS: THE COMPLETE GUIDE TO CREATING A PROFITABLE WORKSHOP OR SEMINAR IN ANY FIELD ($30 retail, $32.50 postpaid. 302 pages.)

DEVELOPMENT TODAY: A FUND RAISING GUIDE FOR NONPROFIT ORGANIZATIONS ($24.95 retail, $28.95 postpaid. 278 pages.) In the February issue, BOOKLIST gave this book a superb review!

CASH COPY: HOW TO OFFER YOUR PRODUCTS AND SERVICES SO YOUR PROSPECTS BUY THEM...NOW! ($24.95 retail, $27.95 postpaid, 480 pages.)

HOW TO MAKE A WHOLE LOT MORE THAN $1,000,000 WRITING, COMMISSIONING, PUBLISHING AND SELLING "HOW-TO" INFORMATION ($35 retail, $38.50 postpaid, 552 pages.)

I think our library's collection would be better off with these books, and I would be grateful if you'd add them.

Looking forward to hearing your decision,

Sincerely,

Jack Chatfield

Think about this and consider the benefits.

I get a local recommendation for my books, a very powerful thing. Local librarians listen to local citizens. This is scarcely surprising given the fact these citizens pay the taxes that keep the library in business. These citizens thus have power. Moreover, it is a power most don't even know they have, since few citizens have ever recommended their library buy anything. That, of course, is the brilliance of the idea. With it I can tap into a hitherto unexploited source of power and profit.

Thus, I not only sell more books but place them where they will be seen by many more people. These others in turn will themselves become future customers, because of the complete order information carried in every book and my request of every reader to make himself known to me so that I can help him achieve his business objectives. In this way, I turn each library into a promoter for my books. For how else should a library be regarded by a publisher but as a showcase for his products?

Why, you ask, would anyone take the time to help me, the publisher, sell my books to others? It's a very good question.

There are four reasons, I think:

- I give them a premium. Anyone sending such a letter to their local library receives a premium from me. You can guess what it is: one of my Sure-Fire Business Success Articles, itself, of course, a marketing device. But they don't get this premium automatically. They must write and specifically let me know they have sent this letter. Not surprisingly, this letter is often accompanied by an order for one of the books they have recommended!

- What I am asking is easy to do. Easy? Decidedly so, because I write the letter to the library, down to and including the customer's name. You see, the letter (produced by computer) is from my customer to the acquisitions librarian or head of the local library. All he has to do is sign the letter, and mail it to get the promised premium.

  Where do I get the necessary information about his local library? As I have preached from the beginning of this book, knowing your market is the essence of business success. In this case, the critical information I need about my library market is contained in *American Library Directory*, published regularly by R.R. Bowker Co. Knowing this book exists is the first step towards creating the circumstances which will result in your buyers' assisting you to get your books into these repositories at the least possible cost to you.

- I ask the buyers to do this. People, as I firmly believe, more often do what they are asked than not. The trick (as Tom Sawyer knew) is to make what you ask easy to accomplish and involve minimum commitment. This marketing technique follows these guidelines. Moreover, if there is more reason to do the task than not, the task will very likely get done. That is certainly the case here, even though I do not supply the buyer with postage. He must use his own envelope and affix his own stamp.

- By helping me, my buyers achieve a greater sense of belonging, of membership in my business family. I insist this sense of customer belonging is important. Would you rather do business with an impersonal institution, or with someone who knows you and is grateful for what you do for him?

Once the customer tells me the letter to his library has gone out, my premium to the customer is mailed. Since my premiums exist in my computer, I personalize them thus, "Special to Pam Smith, with the thanks of Jeffrey Lant for her help!" Now what do you think? Is this likely to be kept or thrown away? Given that the premium itself is packed with information the customer can use and that it begins with a note of appreciation from me, there is a very good chance it will be kept. This, of course, is excellent, since, as you'll no doubt remember, this premium is itself a marketing document with additional offers available to the customer.

N.B. It goes without saying that many buyers will come from the same community with the same public library. What then? I do two things. I make sure the official in charge of buying is the one to whom most of these marketing letters are sent. I also designate other library representatives to receive selected correspondence from my buyers. Not surprisingly, I want to create the impression of an avalanche of public support, thus ensuring that the library will have to act. Moreover, keep in mind that large libraries buy multiple copies of books. Producing a greater measure of public support is necessary in these cases.

Now before you tell me this technique is not suited to your business, think. Isn't there someone you would like your buyers to contact for you? It's up to you to harness this untapped source of support and make it work for you. Do, however, start soon, before the techniques of this book become common knowledge!

Caps, Calendars, Golf Tees, Rolodex Cards, And Dozens Of Other Doodads With Your Name On Them

We've all seen these things. The most famous examples are, perhaps, designer jeans. The best include your name, address, and telephone number, and an indication of your service. I confess I used some (pens) in the past, but I must also tell you I haven't spent my money this way in some time and have no plans to do so. Nonetheless, if you can't think of any more original way to get back to your customers' attention, try the following (admittedly incomplete) list of possibilities:

- A clever wallet-sized card, including a calendar, information on holidays, frequently-called numbers, personal dates to remember, emergency telephone numbers, personal data, and whom to call in case of emergency is produced by Positive Promotions, 222 Ashland Pl, Brooklyn, NY 11217. (718) 858-4199. With your name, company name, address, telephone number, and service data, this makes an interesting premium or package-stuffer for your buyers.

- For the golfers in your life, try imprinted golf tees and markers from Highlander Company, 1072 Jacoby Road, Akron, OH 44321-1799. They have many other products, too. Ask for their catalog.

- Get customized tote bags from Art Poly Bag Co., 140 Metropolitan Ave, Brooklyn, NY 11211. (718) 388-0866. Good for conventions.

- Those ubiquitous caps. Get them from :

  - B & B Advertising, P.O. Box 458-C, Scott City, KS 67871
  - Cardinal Industries, Inc., Highway 83-131, Box 1430, Grundy, VA 24614 (800) 336-0551. They do tee-shirts, too.
  - Custom Caps, P.O. Box 481, Pleasant Grove, UT 84062-9985
  - Montana Athletic Supply, 718 6th St. N.W., Great Falls, MT 59504.

- Purchase pens from National Pen Corp., 9395 Cabot Dr., San Diego, CA 92181.

- Order coins and medals from Hoffman & Hoffman, P.O. Box 896, Carmel, CA 93921-0896.

- Get badges, label pins, and buttons of every kind from Badge-A-Minute, 348 North 30th Road, LaSalle, IL 61301 (800) 223-4103. Also for buttons and rubber stamps, contact Button Mania, 3293 Bacon, Berkley, MI 48072 (313) 548-8352. Tell Rickie Knowles I sent you!

- For a catalog with items ranging from a car vacuum to a Swiss army pocket knife with your imprint (and dozens of other possibilities) try Custom Promotional Merchandise, Sales Guides, Inc., 10510 North Port Washington Road, Mequon, WI 53092-9986 (800) 352-9899.

- Rolodex cards. I've kept until last the item I like best (although it is not inexpensive): telephone file rolodex cards with your picture. I like them for two reasons: they are laminated (and hence will last). Further, because of the stick-up tab which they have, they'll stand out from the other cards in your rolodex. Moreover, because of their size and the fact they are printed, they are big enough to contain not only the basics about your business (name, address, and telephone number) but service line data, too. Try David Scott Industries, Inc., 3910 W. Devon Ave., Lincolnwood, IL 60659 (800) 323-5556.

For Further Information

Obviously this list is very selective, but it will get you started. For further information contact:

- Premium/Incentive Business, 1515 Broadway, New York, NY 10036. It will give you ideas and update information on promotion marketing.

- Specialty Advertising Association International, 1404 Walnut Hill Lane, Irving, TX 75038 (214) 580-0404. They have a catalog with items in it for people interested in specialty advertising. Unfortunately, they didn't send me any of the materials I asked for, so I'm unable to attest to their value. You may have better luck.

A Special Note To Book Publishers On Getting More Sales From Your Customers

I have often said - and frequently published my belief — that most book publishers are most interested in producing books than in selling them. If you are an author yourself or a publisher, and you are really interested in selling more to your readers and customers, do this:

- At the very least include an order-blank at the back of your books for all the books you publish. Include precise information on the books, why the customer should buy them, and how the customer can buy them. Then make it easy for the customer to buy them by taking orders twenty-four hours a day and using credit cards.

- If you are selling nonfiction books, offer other books on similar and related subjects. In short, create a catalog with offers which you'll ship directly or fulfill through drop-shipping. Bind these catalogs right into your books. This is smart for the following reasons:

  - People who are interested in a subject want to know more about that subject. Provide them with the information they need, and profit accordingly.

  - By putting a catalog in the back of all your books, you'll cut the cost of the catalogs (especially if you find your books being produced with extra, unused pages at the end), while getting connected to the people who buy your books in bookstores or read them in libraries. In this way, you identify future customers and build a lucrative mailing list. Most publishers have no connection with these readers, and they are therefore losing a valuable source of revenue. Don't make this mistake!

Finally, if you are either the author or publisher of a nonfiction book, make sure you are getting your share of the consulting revenues that should be created by such a book. Remember: people who are interested in the subject of your book may also want a more direct consulting relationship in which the author works with the reader to solve his problems. Thus:

- Nonfiction authors: make sure you have proposed to your publisher that one of the end-pages of your book be given over to a full-page ad touting your direct problem-solving services and asking the readers to contact you through your publisher. You can use a client-survey questionnaire to ascertain what problems they'd be interested in having you solve.

- Publishers: enter into an independent contractor relationship with your nonfiction authors. Such an arrangement deals with such matters as the division of fees and how inquiries from readers/prospects will be handled. My suggestion is that you get not less than 20% of the gross value of any contract resulting from the lead generated through the book you publish, and that all inquiries be sent to you first. Then you may send them to the author/consultant, who can fashion the appropriate contract, send you a copy, and pay you your percentage of the resulting fees. For further information, see my books on succeeding in consulting, **THE CONSULTANT'S KIT** and **TRICKS OF THE TRADE**.

If you are not using your books as a prospecting device, you're mad. For the reader, having finished this book, should trust the author and know he could be helpful working with the reader/client on a one-to-one basis. If your books and authors don't generate this feeling, publishers, you are publishing the wrong nonfiction authors. In which case, you should let me help you.

Personalized New Product And Service Announcements

All businesses make announcements about new products and services. There's nothing different about this. If you aren't doing so, you should. However, I'm recommending creating a special personalized letter particularly about your new services and especially alerting your buyers to it. This letter should:

- be sent directly to your buyers;
- give them the sense of being let in on an important secret known only to a few. My announcement letters say, "Because you're a good customer of mine, I particularly wanted to bring to your attention… ";
- include complete details about the offer, and
- provide them with an incentive to take immediate action. A "buyers'-only" discount is recommended.

As variations of add-on letters, you can send these personalized new product and service announcements to selected buyers as you fulfill their orders or answer their queries. The trick, however, is to make these buyers feel they are getting something other people are not and are being treated in a special way. Your personalized attention to them demonstrates just that. (See Samples, page 267.)

More Ways To Connect With New People Interested In Your Products And Services

As you already know, there are essentially two major problems in business: finding buyers initially and selling to these buyers again and again. If you can solve these two problems satisfactorily you will be the business success you deserve to be. In this section I shall be helping you solve the first of these problems through a thorough understanding of the following topics:

- cross-promotions
- card-deck advertising and bingo cards
- co-op advertising, and
- trade shows.

Creative Cross-Promotions

There are businesses whose customers should know what you are selling and who, by the same token, would like to get access to your customers. I sell to independent professionals. Thus, a person selling disability insurance would be interested in getting access to my customers. By the same token, as the publisher of the Sure-Fire Business Success Catalog I'm interested in getting access to his crop of independent professionals and small business owners.

Once you have made the assessment that your business and another, with which you'd like to do business, hit the same prospects, it's time to create a cross-promotion. What this means is that each of you help the other reach your prospects on a strictly reciprocal basis.

Here are some ways of doing this:

- Swap mailing lists on a straight name-for-name basis. The minute you have even five hundred names is the moment to start swapping.

- Ask another business to distribute your literature to its customers and prospects, and do the same for them. This needs a few more words.

You already know about package inserts, but have you ever tried having your material distributed by a retail outlet? For instance, all my customers need photocopying service. Many of the people using my local copy service are small businesses who could profit from my catalog. This is a situation tailor-made for a cross-promotion. I distribute their material; they distribute mine.

N.B. Indeed, even if you don't have something appropriate for a cross promotion, you can still use most of the technique. Simply ask your local copyshop to print, say, 1000 of your basic flyers and distribute them with their compliments. Why would they do this? For at least three reasons:

- You'll purchase the flyers at their shop, so there is a direct economic reason for them to cooperate.

- You'll put the copyshop's name, address, and telephone number on the flyer, perhaps in a special box. As in, "Distributed with the compliments of Smith Copy Center, your business copier."

- The flyers are easy to distribute to their customers. All they have to do is put them on their service counter with the notice "Take one!". Or, if they are rather more helpful, they can give them to all the customers. Within a 30-day period, you'll hit most of the customers at this location, whereupon (if this form of distribution proves successful for you), you can try it again with another likely copyshop. About the same time next year, it'll be time to return to the first shop, and do it again. You see, the process never ends!

Organizing Your Cross-Promotions

There is scarcely any limit to the number of cross promotions you can have going on simultaneously. To get started:

- Write down all the businesses you can think of whose customers are your customers. This should produce a bumper crop of possibilities.

- Develop a standard one- or two-sided 8 1/2" by 11" flyer with your offer, including space for the name, address, telephone number, and logo of the company you wish to distribute your information.

- Write a letter to the presidents of the companies you have selected, including a sample of your marketing piece and showing where the information about them will go.

- Indicate how many flyers you'd like to exchange and how you intend to distribute their materials.

- Indicate when you'll be calling to discuss your suggestion.

Any individual you approach with this idea who rejects it is probably an idiot. Such people abound, of course. However, I think you'll find most of those you speak to will see the advantages to be derived from cross-promotion. If they don't, photocopy this section and give it to them with my compliments. It's a lot more civilized than ridiculing their shortsightedness.

Successfully Using Direct Response Card-Deck And Bingo-Card Advertising

We've all seen both direct response postcard decks and bingo cards. In fact, you can't miss 'em. Card decks are usually 3"x 5" postcards which come in bundles of 50 or more cards and are mailed to a highly-targeted audience, generally in lots of 100,000. They come in a single package bound in clear plastic. I love them so much I set up my own deck, "Jeffrey Lant's Sales & Marketing SuccessDek". It goes out 10 times a year to 100,000 sales and marketing executives nationwide. IF this is the audience you want to reach, you'd better get in touch with me, especially since I've got — by far! — the lowest prices of any card-deck to this audience.

I like bingo cards, too. This is usually a page in a publication or postcard in a direct response deck featuring a number of offers. The reader simply circles the items in which he is interested, returning the business reply card to the company which has placed it. The names are then computerized and sent to the company buying the space. It then forwards its information to the new prospects.

What's important to keep in mind is that both card-deck and bingo-card advertising is expensive. Unless certain precise guidelines are followed, using these alternatives will be an extremely costly mistake. That's where Bill Norcutt comes in.

Bill is a specialist in these fields and has written the most sensible guide to profitable card-deck advertising I know. His lessons hold true, too, for bingo cards. Here's what he advises:

- Don't use a card-deck or a bingo-card until you produce your own catalog of related offers. The cost of name-acquisition through these programs, even though less expensive than others, is not cheap. Count on spending about 50 cents per name.

- If you are selling directly from your card, doing so will probably be a "loss leader" for you, meaning that you won't profit from what you are selling off the card and will have to make up for the loss through other things you'll sell this customer.

- This suggests that you shouldn't try to sell directly from the card but should follow a two-step procedure, whereby the prospect requests information, and you send additional material. You must therefore have a strong follow-up program, one which is designed to hit these targets several times.

- You'll make money, perhaps indeed your entire profit, by compiling the names of your queries and customers and renting them out. This means you must be computerized.

These rules apply, too, to bingo-card advertising. The principal difference between the two, indeed, is that with a bingo card you'll probably get no more than a line or two to make your case while with a card-deck you'll have more space. Too, with a bingo card you usually pay a set amount per inquiry-name received, whereas with the card-deck you pay by the card itself.

Why Some Cards Work, Why Others Don't

Card-decks are dominated by certain companies which advertise in them over and over again. They are the ones who most often fulfill the conditions listed above. They are the ones who have the best cards, too, the ones you should pay attention to in creating your own. Here's what distinguishes these cards:

- a strong headline focusing on prospect benefits;
- horizontal, not vertical, printing;
- an illustration of the product;
- an overwhelmingly good deal, a strong reason for buying now. (*N.B.* This deal is usually a "loss leader" for the company making the offer.)
- plenty of space for the prospect to fill in his name, address, and telephone number.

To Use Business Reply Or Not, That Is The Question

An unrelenting debate rages in the profession about the benefits of using business reply mail. I'm agin' it — for me. I like my leads as highly-qualified as you can make them. Forcing the prospect to use his own envelope and stamp is an indication that he really is interested. In the debate between quality and quantity, I am on the side of quality leads. You may decide differently.

To be sure, for all of us in direct marketing, success is to a greater or lesser extent a numbers game. But I have learned with my products that many are interested to have the information and many fewer to buy. I have therefore made the decision to get my prospects to indicate some interest to me before I take them on. The higher the price of what you're selling, the more successful this technique will be. You have to decide.

So Much For The Basics. How Can You Get The Service For Less Money?

You already know the cost of both card-deck and bingo-card advertising is expensive. The cost for designing your card, creating the photostat (art work) and buying space in a postcard deck with 100,000 circulation (the standard mailing size) can easily be $3000–$4000. It's a lot of money. Bingo card names generally run 40 to 50 cents apiece on pressure-sensitive labels. Can anything be done to cut the cost? Yes, but it means bargaining.

- Identify the decks you want to be in. Make sure they reach the kinds of people for whom your offer makes sense.

- Call and request the name of the marketing director or person in charge of selling space.

- Write him and tell him you are interested in participating in future mailings on a remnant or reduced-cost basis.

Keep in mind that the current cost of producing and mailing 100,000 post cards as part of a deck is about $750. The retail price for an individual card starts at about $3000 for the ordinary deck (the deck, that is, that I'm not producing). There is thus usually a lot of room for negotiation. Here are some possibilities.

- You can suggest you'd like to participate for a fixed, flat fee representing 50% of the card's retail price. State your willingness to participate on this basis and wait for their call. You'll probably get it even where you are told that such a price is "impossible." Sit tight. As the card deck company considers its profit picture for this mailing, your offer should look pretty good.

Here, however, as with other of the possibilities I am suggesting, your art work must be prepared in advance. When you bargain, you often get called late, often the day before the deck is printed. You must be ready to send your artwork immediately, by overnight delivery service. So be prepared.

Is even this a good price? That depends. While I've heard accounts of fantastic response rates from card deck advertising, my own experience suggests that a return of 1/10 to 1/5 of 1% is average. This means roughly 100 people will request information out of 100,000 decks mailed. Of these, roughly 10 will buy an offer of under $50 on the first mailing and perhaps as many will buy on a second mailing at about which time you will have recovered your initial investment, particularly if you have a catalog of offers available as you should. With these mailings, and the wide variety of choice they represent, these names should produce a profit for you over time, especially if you have qualified them by making them use their own envelope and stamp to get in touch with you.

- You can offer to pay the actual cost of the card upfront (about $750.00). The first $750 that comes in would then go to reimburse you for the amount you'd already paid. Subsequent revenues could be divided according to an equitable formula, say 50%–50%. In this case, the publisher will want all revenues sent directly to him. He'll send you your money in the agreed upon percentage as it comes in along with information so that you can fulfill the order or follow up appropriately.

Here, your counter offer should be the producer's actual cost plus a fixed, flat fee per name. You can also pay the actual cost upfront, have all payments sent to you until this amount is reached, and then split the proceeds with the company 50-50%.

- You can also offer to participate on a straight per inquiry basis, say 50% of the retail price of the goods you'll be advertising. In this case, the card-deck company bears the cost of the card and is speculating your offer will draw sufficiently well to make them a profit after costs. Most companies only reluctantly consider these offers and generally accept them only if they need more cards to strengthen their decks. It goes without saying that this is the option I prefer. When I participate in card-decks (which I frequently do) it is often on this basis. So should you.

N.B. After you participate in one card-deck, you'll be contacted by many others. Anticipating this response, you should work out your participation policies in advance so that you're prepared to deal with the salesmen when they inevitably call you.

Further Information About Card-Decks And Bingo Cards

My friend Bill Norcutt knows a lot about how to participate successfully in card-decks. He has produced these two resources to help you:

> *Secrets Of Successful Response Deck Advertising* and *The Direct Deck List & Media Planner*. The latter lists information on over 600 postcard response decks with the information you need to send in your reduced-fee offers. For more information about these useful guidebooks, contact Bill at Thinkbank Publishers, P. O. Box 1166, Arlington, TX 76010 (817) 265-1793.

Here are three other resources you'll find helpful:

- *Beyond Lead Generation: Merchandising Through Card Packs* by Nat G. Bodian and Robert Luedtke. Published by Solar Press, 1120 Frontenac Road, Naperville, IL 60566 (708) 983-1400. Further excellent information on profiting with card-decks. See also their *Card Pack Media Directory: Specifications and Rates*.

- Standard Rate And Data Service, 3002 Glenview Road, Wilmette, IL 60091 (708) 256-6067. This is the standard reference source for most mailing lists and advertising rates. You'll find information about postcard decks in their *Business Directory*. The service is costly (currently around $477 yearly), but any good business library should have it.

- A good deck for those selling products to small businesses is produced by Machalek Publishing Co., 15 S. Ninth St., Minneapolis, MN 55402. Tell them I sent you!

And don't forget, I've written a dandy Special Report on successful marketing in card-decks (see the catalog at the back of this book) and produce card decks myself which may be just the thing for you. If you call me, I'll be glad to get you a sample and further information.

Resources For Bingo Cards

My words of wisdom for negotiating with card-decks apply, too, to bingo cards. Within a single ten-minute conversation I have been able to shave as much as 30% off the initially-quoted price for this service. Advertising rates are remarkably fluid. *You* decide what a fair price is. State it. And stick to your guns. You'll find these companies cooperative — after they know you are serious. Here are some helpful resources:

- American Parade of Catalogs, Division of Nationwide Shopper Systems, Inc., 144 South First St., P.O. Box 3197, Burbank, CA 91504 (818) 846-5576.

- Donald Moger Direct Marketing, P.O. Box 69219, Los Angeles, CA 90069 (213) 852-1154

- Select Information Exchange, 2315 Broadway, New York, NY 10023.
- Venture Communications, P.O. Box 895, New York, NY 10102.
- Visual Horizons, 180 Metro Park, Rochester, NY 14623-2666 (716) 424-5300.

Understanding And Successfully Using Co-Op Advertising

Psst. Want some extra money for advertising? Money you can use to increase the visibility of your retail establishment and enhance your advertising program? If so, you need to explore the possibilities of cooperative (co-op) advertising.

Simply stated, co-op advertising is a system whereby the manufacturer and/or distributor of a product will remit to you, the seller and advertiser of that product, an agreed-upon percentage of the costs of advertising it. The rationale for this policy is simple. Producers reckon that when their product is advertised by a certain retail establishment both the store benefits and they benefit. They are willing to acknowledge their benefit by remitting a percentage of the advertising cost. It's a very neat system.

But surely there's a catch? Not so, according to my co-op advertising information source Karen Taylor of Boston's Landon Associates, a full service advertising company. The only negative she brought to my attention was that product producers can be slow in remitting the agreed-upon percentage to those retailers using their programs. This didn't surprise me. After all, who likes to pay for a meal that's already been eaten?

Taking into consideration Karen's caution about occasionally slow remittances, the co-op system still offers overwhelming advantages to those using it. Here are her suggestions about how to do so:

- First, find out which companies offer co-op advertising programs. Currently there are over 3,500 co-op programs in existence covering over 8,000 trademarks. Ask your vendor if his company offers this service. Don't wait for him to offer the information. After all, he may be nothing more than an order-taker.

- Familiarize yourself with the different co-op plans available. There are at least five:

  - The 100% plan whereby the manufacturer reimburses you for the complete cost of your ad up to the limit of your co-op fund. This fund is created as you buy the manufacturer's products. A percentage of what you buy, as determined by the manufacturer, is set aside for your use in co-op advertising.

  - The shared plan (perhaps the most common) whereby the manufacturer reimburses a portion of your ad cost (say 50%) with you paying the rest.

  - The manufacturer/distributor plan which pertains to selected products purchased through your distributor. Here the manufacturer and distributor each contribute to your ad costs. Generally in this case, you submit your claim for payment to the distributor, who reimburses you.

  - The unlimited or fixed-accrual plan. The manufacturer offers reimbursement at a fixed amount for the year. Your co-op fund is not determined by the amount of product you purchase. This alternative is principally used with products that have a very limited selling season, such as lawn mowers and snow removal equipment.

  - The ingredient producer plan whereby the producer of raw material reimburses the retailer through the manufacturer.

- Study each co-op plan thoroughly. Their guidelines tell you for what time period the manufacturer's co-op offer is in effect; the amount of advertising cost you can expect the manufacturer or distributor to reimburse; the details of how the manufacturer determines the specific dollar amount of your co-op fund (generally a certain percentage of the dollar value of your purchases); and any advertising requirements that must be met to qualify for reimbursement, such as which media you can use, what information the ad must contain, which radio and television scripts are appropriate, and the guidelines for the proper way to submit your claim for reimbursement.

- Plan ahead. As you begin your co-op planning, you must know how large your advertising fund is for each manufacturer's product you intend to promote. If you haven't been told by your vendor what this amount is, ask now!

- Now use your co-op dollars wisely. With them, Karen points out, you'll be able to increase the frequency of your advertising, use different media, and promote products which ordinarily are slow sellers. You can advertise on different days of the week than you do usually and try color, which increase an ad's impact.

Furthermore, don't forget the other services that manufacturers often supply as part of their co-op arrangement. These include providing you with fixtures and in-store display materials.

- Once your ad has been run, file your paperwork (including proof of its cost) promptly and with all the information the manufacturer requires. It generally takes at least 60 days to receive your reimbursement.

Further Sources Of Co-op Information

- Start with my expert Karen Taylor at Landon Associates, 38 Newbury St., Boston, MA 02116 (617) 266-2141. You'll find her both knowledgeable and pleasant about how co-op advertising can become a successful part of your promotional plans. Moreover, Karen advises you to become friendly with the co-op representative at your local media. These people are now trained in all aspects of co-op advertising assistance.

Also check with:

- Federal Trade Commission, Office of Public Reference, Room 130, Sixth & Pennsylvania N.W., Washington, D.C. 20580. Co-op advertising guidelines are spelled out in their Federal Trade Guides.

- *Co-op Source Directory*, another fine publication of Standard Rate and Data Service, Inc., 3004 Glenview Rd., Wilmette, IL 60091.

- *Recas*, a computerized co-op data base. This is a product of MultiAd Services, 1720 Detweiller Dr., Peoria, IL 61615-1695.

Success At Trade Shows When You Have A Booth — And When You Don't

We all go to trade shows. But do we, either as registrants or exhibitors, make the best of them? I wonder. Having attended many, many such shows as registrant, exhibitor and speaker I've developed some handy guidelines which will enable you to make the best use of your time at shows.

Have An Objective For Going

Like everything else in life, you'll get the most out of a trade show if you know why you're there and what you want to accomplish. In marketing terms, here are the kinds of things you want to accomplish:

If you're an exhibitor, you want to:

- attract as many qualified prospects to your booth as possible;
- sell your products and services at the show;
- gather the complete names, addresses and other pertinent follow-up information of prospects who need further attention as well as finding out what they want to do so you can give them the appropriate response;
- get media coverage both before the show and after the show in the publication of the sponsoring organization. This means meeting their media representatives.

If you're a trade show registrant you want to:

- meet people who can sell your products and services through cooperative agreements and look for new products and services that you can sell;
- distribute information about your problem-solving products and services and make sure appropriate people get it;
- meet media representatives of the sponsoring organization to ensure future coverage for your products and services.

If you're a speaker you want to:

- get advance coverage for your products, services, company and problem-solving skills in the sponsoring organization's publication;
- get a complete list of the names and addresses of all the people attending your program;
- speak to the people planning the next convention about what they are looking for in speakers so that you can submit a proposal to participate again;
- identify people at the show (usually exhibitors, but not always) offering products and services you can sell to your customers and which supplement your own line.

Yes, whoever you are at a trade show, you need fixed objectives.

Should You Get A Booth?

I have very mixed feelings about booths at trade shows. While writing this book, I happened to be a speaker at a large trade show in New York at which I speak annually. One lunch hour, supposedly a busy time in an exhibit hall, I wandered through the exhibits. I was mostly appalled by what I saw. Exhibits were left unattended. Many had staff but no visitors. A few were busy. Most were not. Some were badly lighted. Others were bunched together in a corner. Those at the farther reaches of the hall were just too far away and their attendance suffered accordingly.

If you're an employee in these situations, paid hourly, perhaps being stranded in a dimly-lit corner without visitors isn't too bad. But if you're paying the bill, this is a terrible fate!

Given that renting a booth and manning it for the duration of a convention is an expensive proposition, what can you do to see whether this is an investment you should make?

- Find out whether the people expected to attend the meeting are those who have the problem your products and services can solve. If what you're selling is not of direct interest to these people, let me tell you something: there isn't any point in your going. And that's that.

- Ask the organizers how many people they expect to attend. If this is a new show, divide their enthusiastic estimates in half. Then figure that you'll be fortunate if 5% of the people attending drop by your booth, even for a quick look. If the show has been around for a few years, ask for the average attendance of the last three years and the actual attendance figure for the year before. Again, figure that not more than 5% of the people in attendance will actually drop by.

What you're trying to determine is if it is better for you to spend your money for other forms of marketing (the many forms discussed in this book), or if it makes sense to invest it here. That, of course, depends.

There is no question that if you have a product people need to see, feel, smell, or taste to want to buy, you may well find a trade show the answer. If you're selling a service, however, as I do, you're probably better off not spending your funds this way. Never consider participation in a trade show in a vacuum. Ask yourself how else you could spend the money and whether another expenditure makes sense. Remember, just because you don't take a booth doesn't mean you can't be an active trade show participant. You could try to be a speaker, after all.

N.B. I am firmly opposed to participating in a trade show merely to "show the flag." This is a ridiculous misuse of your money and time.

- Get a map of the exhibit area and find out where people get in and where they leave. Find out, too, where popular exhibitors are likely to be placed. Some things to keep in mind about where to be:

  - Place yourself next to a popular exhibitor. You'll benefit by the proximity;
  - Avoid the exit doors. By the time people are ready to leave they are surfeited on information and don't want to look at another thing. Sure you'll see a lot of people. But they'll be tired and wanting to leave;
  - Don't get yourself placed immediately inside the entrance doors. People tend to like to rush in and walk just a bit before lighting. Most won't stop at the first booth they see;
  - Avoid corners. The center of a room is preferable. So is the right side of a room.

- Develop an interactive exhibit. Marketing is not a sport for the passive and unimaginative. Your job at a trade show, as anywhere else, is to attract people to your exhibit. Do that by:

  - stressing benefits, not your company;
  - finding out what problems people coming to your booth want to solve;
  - asking them to get involved in your exhibit and hence in your problem-solving products and services.

Say I was exhibiting at a meeting for consultants. Having discerned that my prospects will be in attendance, people to whom I can sell my products and services, and having made the decision that this is a good use of my money, the next thing I must accomplish is developing a theme that will attract people to my booth.

Let's say the theme I select is "Do you have what it takes to succeed as a consultant?" Note: I am not beginning by promoting myself. I am leading with a question every consultant asks himself. Here are some ways of drawing the people in, making my booth interactive and giving my participation a sense of excitement — all the while gathering leads for both present and future business.

Use Your Prospects For Show Advertising

Step 1 in successfully participating in the show defined above is developing an easy quiz that people coming to my booth are asked to take. The quiz consists of a series of questions (it can even be an easy True/False or Multiple Choice quiz) asking queries successful consultants know the answers to. *N.B.* This quiz must be fun and easy enough for everyone to pass. A typical question? "Jeffrey Lant's well-known book **THE CONSULTANT'S KIT: ESTABLISHING AND OPERATING YOUR SUCCESSFUL CONSULTING BUSINESS** is packed with information on succeeding in the consulting business. True or False?" Why this kind of quiz? Because those passing it are to be given a button that simply says, "I have what it takes." That button is your free advertising that people will wear around the convention.

Note the expression. It has a nice double entendre. Printed on a white background with brilliant red lettering it makes a very effective mobile billboard for your company, even if your name isn't on it, (although if you're smart you can put your name, address, and telephone number on a sticker and put it on the *back* of the button). Why? Because people will notice it. Ask what it means. Talk about it. Laugh about it. And in short promote you each time they do so.

Obviously you'll wear the buttons yourself. But you can be more creative than that:

- Get them to the officers of the association with a note from you, and leave them in their hotel mailboxes.

- Give them to the best looking people in attendance, men and women.

- Make sure popular people in the association have them.

In short, be creative.

These buttons, by the way, are easily ordered through a local supplier or through a large company like Badge-A-Minute, to which I previously referred.

Getting The Information You Need From People Visiting The Booth

You're not giving out buttons just for the fun of it. You need information from your prospects, information which will enable you either to make sales at the show or effectively follow up.

Thus, each person either taking your quiz or getting your button should be courteously asked for his or her card. Or, better, should be asked to fill out a client-survey questionnaire providing information on what he'd like to accomplish, what problems he'd like to solve.

If he won't take the time to fill it out on the spot, don't worry. Simply give it to him. You can even indicate that there is a small premium for completing and returning it. But in this case make sure the back of your survey has detailed information about your products and services, including complete order information. It goes without saying that once people have indicated what problems they'd like to solve, you should talk to them about how you can help them do so, directing their attention to appropriate products (which you may have on display) and services, about which you'll have information.

Booth People Skills

Once you've set your objectives, created a theme and determined how you'll get people into your booth, the essence of a successful exhibit is the way the people manning it meet the visitors and handle them. All of us have dealt with the wrong kind of people running a booth. People who are disspirited, apathetic, who lack information about the products and services being offered by the company and have no idea how to handle your demonstrated interest. People, in short, who expect you to do all the work. I recall a recent instance of this kind of self-defeating behavior.

I approached a woman running a booth at a publishers' trade show. Her company produced a catalog of books which looked like a good opportunity for me and my products. I approached the miserable creature. From the first minute I knew she was nothing more than an order-taker, a lackluster Flatworm.

No, she didn't know anything about how things got in the catalog. No, she didn't know who was in charge of the catalog. No, she wouldn't pass my name on to him. But, thrusting a copy of the catalog in my hand, here's the company's telephone number. Why didn't I call and find out for myself? Why not indeed? And to think that the company employing her was actually paying for the privilege of giving her a forum for such mindless and destructive behavior!

Surely you can imagine by now how I would suggest this scenario be handled.

- Keep a convention log. Have all visitors to your booth log in. Most will give you nothing more than a card. That's fine for your mailing list and for sending them your material. In fact, I recommend that you take very little of your literature to a show. It's not only difficult to move. It's relatively pointless to bring, since everyone passes out material and most people don't have the time to look at it. It's better to follow up the show with a special letter to your prospects and ensure they get the information you want them to have.

If people ask questions that you cannot answer (either because they need a lengthier answer than circumstances permit or because you don't know), write down the question (or, if there are many demands on you just then, ask them to write it clearly in your log book). Tell them how it will be handled. The trade show is not finished until all these queries are successfully dealt with. After all, how can your buyers trust you if you ignore them and what they want from you?

Hint: you should be able to figure out *in advance* what most of your trade show queries involve. So do yourself a favor. Prepare your information packets and letters in advance and spend the day or two after your return from the show getting them out. Your prospects will be rightly impressed by your quick turnaround.

- Be client-centered. That, of course, is the message of this entire book, but rarely will you meet as many possible prospects in so short a period of time as you will at a trade show. These shows test the mettle of the best of us. But the trick is focusing the discussion on the prospect and what he wants to achieve. Then and only then should you tell him what you've got available. Frankly, in my experience this is not the way most show exhibitors handle the situation. They are always more interested in telling you what they've got than hearing what you'd like to accomplish. Such behavior is a huge mistake.

Thus:

- Greet the visitor when he enters your booth, but do so in a way that indicates why you're here and why he's come. "Hello, I'm Jeffrey Lant. Please feel free to see how we help consultants succeed."

- If you have an interactive device to share, do so. "Here's a little quiz we've developed to determine whether people have what it takes to succeed as a consultant. You might like to try it." Don't be pushy about offering this, however. People always need time to feel familiar in a new place and never want to feel pressured. Give them time to light. Then approach and ask what they are trying to accomplish. You can also give them a client-survey questionnaire.

- Some people, of course, are just browsers. When they look like they are leaving say, "I hope you'll stop by again. But in the meantime, here's some information on how we help people solve their consulting problems. I'd like you to have it." Don't ask. Just give. And please note your wording as you do so. You are reinforcing what you said when they entered your territory. People with whom you have had a more substantial conversation should be ushered out substantially, "I've enjoyed our conversation. I'll be getting back to you within a week about how I can help you with your marketing objectives." Then shake hands and walk with them to the edge of your perimeter. In short, show that you are caring and client-centered.

What Else You Need To Do As An Exhibitor

- As soon as you know you are participating as an exhibitor in a show, contact the editor of the association's publication. Try to get a problem-solving process article in their publication. It can even be on something like "How to get the most out of the trade show" with tips for visitors. But the trick is to make sure you are in the convention issue. Conclude your article not only with the usual information (name, address, and telephone number) but your booth number and location, too. Act like you're a person of consequence, and you'll be more likely to be perceived as one.

- If there are people you want to meet at your show, send them a personal note in advance and include the number and location of your booth. If you are passing out buttons and the like, reiterate your invitation in a note that greets them when they arrive. Enclose the button for them to wear. Don't send the button in advance. They'll forget to bring it.

- Alert other trade media (and appropriate reporters at local media) to the fact that you'll be in attendance. Tell them where you are and when you'll be calling. Trade shows are always news to someone. Make sure you're part of the story.

When You're Just A Participant

Most people attending trade shows as participants are extraordinarily passive. They look at things. They listen to things. They eat and they drink. They go home and they forget. Don't be one of these lotus eaters. Consider the following story, and use it to inspire yourself as you plan to attend any meeting in the land.

A few years ago I wanted to attend the American Booksellers Association convention, one of the country's greatest shows. Over 25,000 people attend it. As I pondered these numbers, I tried to figure out how I could be one of the people featured in the articles that always accompany this show. Then I hit on an idea.

Former First Lady Rosalynn Carter was one of the headliners at this meeting. It was the year when her book *First Lady From Plains* was newly out. So was my book **THE UNABASHED SELF-PROMOTER'S GUIDE.** The idea? I sent Mrs. Carter an autographed copy of my book and asked her to swap me an autographed copy of hers. Then I alerted the press that I had sent her my book. The story line was, "Now that Mrs. Carter isn't in the White House anymore she'll have to learn what every successful author needs to know: the tricks of the trade for book promotion." As revealed, of course, in **THE UNABASHED**... I also said that I would be attending the American Booksellers Association, as would Mrs. Carter.

Not much of a story, you say? Wrong! The august *New York Times*, of all places, ran the story on its "Washington Talk" page under the headline "Rosalynn Carter and Jeffrey Lant to attend American Booksellers convention in Washington." I was the only author to be publicized in this fashion.

What else? The story was syndicated through the *New York Times* and appeared in hundreds of local newspapers, each time promoting me and my new book. Then it was sent by the paper to radio stations around North America. I appeared on "All Things Considered" and on the Canadian Broadcasting System. I also was interviewed by dozens of local radio shows across the nation. During the convention itself I was interviewed by the NBC Network. In short, by clever use of the piggyback technique described in **THE UNABASHED SELF-PROMOTER'S GUIDE,** and by hooking my story to both an attending celebrity and a convention that gets lots of attention, I secured an avalanche of publicity for my own book and company.

Did Mrs. Carter mind? Certainly not! Her book was publicized each time the story ran. And she sent me the autographed copy of her book that I asked for. I like to think that I helped her secure her place on the Best Seller List.

Keep all this in mind for what you can accomplish as a mere participant in even the grandest of conventions.

- Review the program of the convention in advance. Identify those speakers, trade association officials and exhibitors you want to meet and contact them. Most people usually find themselves with a little time on their hands at conventions. Seize it. When I was younger I'd write to the executive director of the association saying I was attending and indicating I could be helpful. In return for assisting with many of the small matters which inevitably accompany the opening of a meeting, I was invited to the smaller, more productive functions that the leadership always holds, usually in posh suites with panoramic views. Being thoughtful about what leaders need, being available when leaders need you, and not forgetting charm and consideration will assure you of having a profitable experience.

- Distribute your literature where people will find it. Usually there is a literature table at conventions. Ordinarily it is overflowing with papers stacked on top of each other. Of course, leave some of your material there. But be more creative about where you place the rest.

Arrive early for workshop sessions on topics where those attending would be likely to be interested in your products and services. Walk in. Give your materials to those seated (after all they have nothing else to read and might as well focus on your literature). Ask one of the people to hand out your flyers to latecomers. Then go on to the next likely place. *N.B.* Make sure that what you distribute asks people to contact you. Remember you don't have their names! Put your material next to telephones, on the cigarette machine, and in the bar. In short, make sure your material goes where your prospects are likely to go. Don't just stay in the standard areas.

- Just because you're not an exhibitor doesn't mean you should overlook the media. Remember my Rosalynn Carter story. Find out in advance if there is likely to be a press room. Whether you are an exhibitor, speaker, or merely a participant draw up a media release in advance based on your participation in the meeting. Following the guidelines in this book and **THE UNABASHED SELF-PROMOTER'S GUIDE,** make sure that every press representative in attendance gets your media release and information about your problem-solving products and activities. Include information about how they can reach you while you're at the meeting. Visit the press room daily. Each day different media people may be in attendance. Be certain to do so on a day when a celebrity is addressing your meeting. The association will have gone to great lengths to get media attention. You might as well place your materials in the media's hands, too.

- Attend sessions on topics related to what you are selling in your business. Occasionally you'll be provided with the names and addresses of those in attendance. But not always. In those cases where this amenity is not provided, ask the speaker whether he minds if you pass around a sign-in sheet for participants. Say that you'll make yourself responsible for sending this information to all those attending. This gives you a perfect reason to get back in touch —and include information about what you are selling.

When You're A Speaker

This subject will be handled in detail in the next chapter. Suffice it to say here, your job is to make constructive contact with your audience, contact which enables you to engender trust and which provides you with the information you need to be back in touch. When you read the next chapter, you'll see precisely how you can reach these objectives.

Last Words On Effective Participation In Trade Shows

Whatever role you're taking in a trade show — exhibitor, speaker, or garden-variety participant — your experience breaks down into three parts:

- before the trade show
- during the trade show
- after the trade show.

Merely being there is never good enough. Be clear then about why you are going, what you want to accomplish, whom you want to meet, what you want to do with them once you meet them, what you want them to know about you, and how you will effectively follow up this initial meeting. Unless you have thought through each of these topics and know that you'll benefit from the meeting, do something else. If, as Clemenceau said, wars are too important to be left to the generals, then trade shows are too important to be left merely to those who have no understanding of how they work and what they are meant to accomplish. But this, thankfully, is not you.

Resources For Successful Trade Show Participation

- The best overall book on trade shows (though the author is not a spritely stylist) is Robert B. Konikow's *How To Participate Profitably In Trade Shows*, rightly described as "including step-by-step methods to design, build and staff business-producing exhibits at low cost." It's available from The Dartnell Corporation, 4660 Ravenswood Ave., Chicago, IL 60640. Konikow includes a good bibliography of resources, including materials which list trade shows around the world.

- For information about all aspects of participating successfully in shows, consult *Show & Sell Magazine*, P.O. Box 212, Santa Claus, IN 47579. It offers a directory of trade show resources, including those for air freight, trade show associations, audio-visual suppliers, decorators and contractors, exhibit designers/producers, exhibit installation and dismantling services, exhibit management, exhibit transportation, exhibition halls, fabric exhibits, hotels, independent exhibit designers, inquiry handling, literature displays, magicians, modular exhibits, photo labs, portable exhibits, product models, product presentation firms, puppets/robots, seminars, show and exhibit evaluation, tent structure, trade show marketing firms, and trade show promotions.

CHAPTER 11

Mouth Marketing. How To Use Talk Programs Of Every Kind To Promote And Sell Your Products And Services

Talk programs of every kind — speeches, workshops, seminars, institutes, and conferences — are a superb way to sell your products and services. Most people know this. Yet most people don't begin to make the best possible use of these vehicles.

Let me share a single story with you which seems to me to epitomize the fatuous way most speakers mishandle their marketing opportunities when giving a talk program.

I was giving a speech at the University of Minnesota as part of an annual program it offers to writers. Essentially the program is on marketing, as it seeks to inform local writers, mostly novices, on aspects of how to become a successful writer. Quite obviously, this includes marketing.

I was the keynote speaker of the convention. But there were many other speakers, too, most on panels on various subjects. Many of those on the panels were offering services of interest to the writers, just as I was. But I was the *only* speaker who made any sustained attempt to connect with the audience, the only speaker who tried to understand what problems members of the audience were interested in solving and to let them know I could solve them, the only speaker who came prepared with information about my products and services.

I'll never forget the other speakers. They sat on the platform like tin gods. What they said was disembodied, directed at no one, surely not at the people in the audience. They made no attempt to focus on the problems of the audience. Made no attempt to let the audience know they could solve them. Not one of the speakers brought anything so elementary as a marketing brochure to distribute to the audience. Not one passed out a single piece of paper to the audience, certainly not a paper indicating how members of the audience could get in touch with the speaker.

The sponsoring organization did not provide us with the names of the participants. This didn't seem to bother any of the other speakers. Certainly they made no ostensible attempt to gather the names of the people in the audience for follow-up.

What they did instead was simply make their remarks (most didn't even bother to stand while doing so), reading from their notes, droning on interminably, oblivious to the danger signals of boredom and distress emanating from their audience. They then sat down to the most perfunctory of applause. But at least, they probably reckoned, they had done their duty.

Let me tell you something: if this is what these severely-inadequate speakers felt, they were wrong, entirely, completely, thoroughly wrong. But what was worse, they had bungled a wonderful opportunity both to help members in the audience and to showcase their own problem-solving products and services. For remember this: a speaking engagement, any speaking engagement, is a tailor-made opportunity not just to pass information to an audience but to increase their trust in you, lower their resistance to you, and let them know that you can help them solve their problems after the program is over through your problem-solving products and services. If you don't do this, the experience is wasted, whatever you may think.

The Three Necessary Parts Of A Successful Talk Presentation

Successful speakers are successful marketers. And successful marketers realize that the success of their program is dependent upon what happens before, during and after they speak. It is never enough just to give a good talk. Instead, the success of your talk is directly linked to how successfully you carry out certain necessary success procedures before, during, and after you speak.

What The Successful Marketer Does Before Speaking

When you walk to the podium to give a presentation, you should already know that it will be successful. The way to ensure this result is essentially threefold: by mastering the essentials of what makes a successful talk, by learning how to give your talk, and by properly positioning yourself so that the audience sees you as the solution to a problem they are interested in solving.

Essentials Of What Makes A Successful Talk Program

The message of this entire book is that all your marketing must be client-centered. This applies no less to a situation where you are making a talk presentation. Hence, do the following:

- Discover what questions your audience wishes to have solved. How? Get the assistance of the organization inviting you to speak. Ask the sponsor to provide you with a list of questions the audience is interested in having answered. Ask for — and then read! — a year's worth of the organization's publications so that you understand the issues they are facing, the different points of view on these issues, and the names of the people who are prime movers on either side of an issue. This kind of homework ensures that your talk will be relevant and not dismissed as the observations of an outsider unfamiliar with the problems the audience is facing.

- Ask for a profile of who will be attending the talk you are giving. Find out as much about your audience as you can. Again, it is your sponsor's responsibility to provide you with this information. But it is your responsibility to ask for it and to make sure you get it.

- Decide what kind of talk you're going to give. There are, of course, many different kinds of talks. The one best suited to us marketers is one that seeks to move the audience (our prospect) from where he is now uncomfortably situated to where he will be more advantageously placed. That is to say, the best kind of talk we can give is a talk about movement, an action talk that will push, pull, prod and persuade the prospect to move to another, better place. Why does this talk make the best sense?

Because as marketers we are in the business of changing peoples' lives. We do this in a talk by letting them know we understand their problem and by persuading them that there are things they can do to ensure positive change. And that one of these things includes using our problem-solving product or service.

It is never enough for a marketer simply to tell a prospect what his problem is or to rehash how he came to have this problem. Instead, a marketer must convince the prospect that he understands what is happening to the prospect. He must also let that prospect know that if he takes action — as recommended by you and which also involves using your products and services — he can achieve the beneficial result he wishes. That is the purpose of every talk you give.

Thus, resolve that all your talks will be about movement, about moving the prospects in the audience from a place they no longer wish to be to a place they want. Your talk should be built around a series of action recommendations, of precise step-by-step activities your prospect can do to improve his life and solve his problem. I call this talk the Problem-Solving Process Talk, and if you use it, your recommendation for your prospect to use your problem-solving product or services makes eminent good sense and is not seen as selling but as solving. Just as you wish it to be.

Resource

For further information on how to construct these talks, use my book **MONEY TALKS: THE COMPLETE GUIDE TO CREATING A PROFITABLE WORKSHOP OR SEMINAR IN ANY FIELD**. I believe it to be the most complete book ever written on how to make money with talk programs and, of course, how to successfully use them to sell your products and services.

Delivering Your Talk

Although this is a book neither about the kind of talk you should be giving nor about how to give your talk, I cannot overlook these subjects. If you fail to give the right talk and fail to deliver your talk properly, you will severely limit the likelihood that the talk will be successful for you from a marketing perspective. Hence the necessity for a few words on each of these subjects.

I have already suggested what kind of talk you should be delivering. Now I'll give you a few typically candid suggestions on how to give the talk so that you'll increase both the audience's trust in you and the possibility they will both buy your products and services and use you in the future.

When you are giving a talk from a marketing perspective, you must:

- Be enthusiastic. There is nothing so damning to your chances of being perceived as the client-centered marketer as delivering a talk in a monotone, without evincing the slightest excitement in what you are talking about. If you are not interested in what you are talking about, why should your audience be? Audiences around the nation regularly tell me that what attracts them to me is my enthusiasm, my excitement about the possibilities of what I am talking about.

Let me tell you something: this enthusiasm excuses many errors. An audience will forgive you for scrambled grammar, for mixed metaphors, for sentence fragments and for many other transgressions. But it cannot, should not overlook your failure to be excited by what you are talking about. I say without fear of contradiction that a speaker who cannot generate a sense of excitement in himself about what he is talking about can never be a successful marketer. You will know within the first two minutes of a speech whether you are listening to a client-centered specialist or to someone who is merely going through the motions of speaking, uncaring himself and, as a result, uncared for by an audience which is right to dismiss him without a second thought.

- Talk to the audience, your prospects. However large my audiences are, I talk to them. I do not lecture at them. This is where some of your homework will prove most helpful. After you've read a year's worth of an organization's publications, you'll have an idea who their v.i.p.s are. You'll know the people. You'll know the issues. You'll know what things this organization regards as important and why. Don't merely know this information. Use it. Hubert Humphrey used to say that a great speech to a Democratic audience goes something like this, "Franklin D. Roosevelt!!!... murmur. murmur. murmur. Harry Truman!!!... murmur. murmur. murmur. John Fitzgerald Kennedy!!! ... murmur. murmur. murmur." You get the idea.

People like to hear names they know. People in an organization love to be referred to from the platform. They like to hear their ideas complimented. They enjoy, in short, being recognized and becoming part of the show. If you want to be a successful marketer from the platform, this is how you'll behave, too. You will increase the chances for the audience's liking you as you involve yourself with things they already like and as you seek to connect yourself with what they already know, feel comfortable with and excited about.

- Connect with your audience through words they understand. If you want to communicate, and not just try to impress, use the words your audience understands. If you want them to trust you (and you do) so that they'll buy what you're selling, you have to show them you understand what's bothering them. If you do that, then they'll want what you're offering.

N.B. Once they have this trust in you, you may not even need to say anything to be successful at what you're selling. While I was working on this chapter, I gave a marketing workshop for the Boston Computer Society. The workshop started at 9 a.m. one Saturday morning. Without my saying a word, everything I had brought was sold by 9: 15 a.m. The fact that these people knew me through my articles in *Microeconomics*, a publication of the Boston Computer Society, the fact that several had attended other workshops I had given, the fact, in short, they trusted me sold the products. Not any harangues and frequent commercials. Please learn this lesson!

- Be blunt about the problems facing prospects in the audience. Be blunter about why they must take action. Be uncompromising about your understanding of why they don't take action now to solve these problems and the consequences that will ensue if they continue to remain irresolute. Then be hardhitting in your recommendations about what they need to do.

One reason so many talks fail is because the speaker isn't willing to take a point of view and to level with the audience. This is a mistake. People with problems know they have problems. What they are looking for is someone who understands what is facing them and is willing to talk straight to them about what needs to be done and when it needs to be done. Your talk must be at once sincere, enthusiastic and focused on what the prospect in the audience needs to do to solve his problem. You gain nothing by circumlocution and meandering. Once you have determined who your audience is, what their problem is and where they want to go, your job is to help them get there in the most direct way you can.

- Dramatize the problem. Get them to see the solution. Too many speakers bore their audiences with numbers, statistics, an overabundance of facts, and too much excruciatingly-dull information. As a marketer, you cannot afford to be one of them. When you are giving a talk, any talk, you are necessarily in the entertainment business. Your job is to get through the defenses of your audience, to get inside where they are squirming with discomfort and to make them sit up and take notice. You must show them the weakness and insecurity of their present situation. You must get them to visualize what will happen if they don't take action. You must also tell them what they need to do to get to the better place they want to be. And you must do so in a way that shows them you are both serious in what you say and concerned that they take the action they must take to succeed.

- Use body English. Nothing is more fatal to your chances of succeeding as a marketer from the platform as merely stiffly standing behind the podium, reading your notes, staring at the paper, avoiding physical contact with your audience. If you do this, you have thrown away the marketing opportunity the presentation offers.

As you step up to the podium, remember Michelangelo's Sistine Chapel fresco of God touching life into Adam. So it must be with you and your audience. This means touching them. When a point is important, thrust your body into the audience to impress them with its importance. When you want to indicate an imperative, let the urgency of your message pulsate through your voice while pointing an insistent finger at the people who need to be impressed by what you are saying.

In short, use your body to dramatize and reinforce the points you are making in your remarks. Lean. Push yourself. Jump. Thrust. Pound the table. Do whatever is necessary to leave an indelible impression on your audience. This advice may not please you. But I am not worried that you are going to offend your audience. I know from my considerable platform experience the reverse is true. Instead, I am worried that if you do not do what is necessary to impress them, you will underwhelm them with the importance of what you are saying, and so lose this superb marketing opportunity.

- Train your voice. Much of what makes your talk memorable is the way you deliver it, including the way you use your voice. The day after even the most important talk, most of your audience will not remember more than a fraction of what you said. But they will recall the way you said it and how you said it. This is why you must train your voice. Otherwise, you are handicapping your marketing efforts.

If a point is serious, make it serious through the words you choose and the way you modulate your voice. Speak the words slowly. Space them. Look at your audience. Everything about you must say, "This is serious."

If a point suggests the need for immediate action, speak in imperatives. Put a note of urgency in your voice. Underscore the importance of the point by leaning into the audience, impressing them with the significance of what you are saying.

You can and must do this.

The point of your talk when you wish to market your products and services is never just to transmit information. Nor is it ever to show people how bright you are. That is anathema!

Instead it is to get the audience — your prospects — to trust you and to get them to do what is necessary to begin to solve the problem you have so aptly detailed. This includes using your products and services, about which you will come prepared with ample information and samples.

Resource

My friend Joan Detz has written a handy little book that will improve the caliber of your speeches considerably. It is *How To Write And Give A Speech*, and, as always, you will find further information about it in my catalog.

Properly Positioning Yourself Before Your Prospects — Before You Even Open Your Mouth

If you follow these steps, you'll make your audience excited about what you have to say before they even hear you. They will be convinced you understand their problem and can help them. And they'll know what you've got available for them to use to solve their problems. All this — without so much as a peep from you. If this scenario interests you (and it should), pay attention! Here's what you need to do:

- Work so that you reach all the people in the organization you are addressing, not just those present at the time you are speaking. This means working with those producing its publications.

Whether you are being paid for your talk or not is not relevant. Ensuring that you reach the maximum number of people with your problem-solving information (including information about your products or services) is. Thus:

- When making arrangements for your talk, offer at least one of your problem-solving process articles for publication. If the sponsor balks, tell him the article is packed with problem-solving information of interest to the organization (it is, isn't it?) and that running it will increase interest in the program.

This article should run in the organization's publication before you speak, presumably at the time they are announcing your presentation. Your article will thus reinforce your ability to solve their problem in the minds of those who have it. If you have enough articles (and if not, why not?), offer to have them run, too, after your presentation. Again, this will help your prospects remember who you are and what you can do for them.

It should go without saying (but probably doesn't) that each of these articles will conclude with the usual resource box listing your name, address, telephone number and information about your product or service. Without this resource box the article is essentially useless to you.

N.B. Most publications will want your photograph to run with these articles, too. In such cases a standard 5" x 7" black and white head shot is perfectly adequate. In sending this photograph, make sure the caption you wish to have (yes, even this is your responsibility) appears on the back of the photograph on a sticker. Do not write directly on the photo as it may show through. Also ask to have it returned to you. Otherwise, it probably won't be.

- At the same time, make sure your talk will be reported in the issue immediately following your appearance. Arrange to have a member of the association or publication present to review what you say. Depending on the length of your presentation, one or more articles (in addition to the review) may be taken from your remarks.

- If you are not being paid for your remarks, that is no reason not to benefit. Each talk you give must have an assigned dollar value. If you are just beginning, bill your talk at the rate of $100 per hour. That's perfectly reasonable. If the organization is not prepared to pay this amount in cash, they must compensate you in other ways. If they are not prepared to compensate you along the following lines, it's probably not a good idea for you to go at all.

Such compensation may include ad space in their publication, inserting your information in one or more issues of their publication or including it with their mailings, and swapping you their mailing list on pressure-sensitive or cheshire labels so that you can contact their membership directly. If you are addressing a convention meeting, you can also request that your literature be placed in all the registration packets. Be creative! Your job is not just to give a talk. Your job is to connect with your buyers.

My rule of thumb is that where an organization is not paying in cash, they must pay one and one half times as much in other compensation as the price of my talk. Thus, for a one hour talk at $100 per hour, I would get $150 in ad space in their publication or comparable compensation. Note: I would not use these ads in the same issue as my articles were running. Why should I? At the end of each article, you'll have your complete resource box anyway. Use your ads at another time to keep yourself before your buyers.

Still More To Do

- If you maintain a mailing list, offer to give the sponsoring organization a run of your names. It is very much to your advantage to make personal contact with as many of your buyers and prospects as you can. At the very least, under the Rule of Seven, when they receive a mailing about you it increases the likelihood they will remember who you are and what you can do for them. You must offer your mailing list, of course, if you are benefitting in some way from the gross receipts. Assuming you do not have this kind of relationship with another, competing organization in the same area, there should be no reason why making your mailing list available is not a good idea.

- Wherever you are speaking, ask the sponsor to contact the local business press or other appropriate print media. You can offer:

  - your problem-solving process articles;
  - an interview before your program;
  - to have your program covered by one of their reporters.

- Have them contact, too, local radio stations. These stations can interview you by telephone in advance of your presentation. Such interviews help to increase enthusiasm (and turn-out) for your programs, and also give you the opportunity to promote your problem-solving products and services.

Confirmation

Once you have decided the details of your compensation, what media you will use in what way, and who will do what, confirm it all in a letter. Particularly when you are proposing something the organization doesn't ordinarily do (say an insert of your material in their newsletter), it is most useful to have this letter. Once you have it, it is easier to persuade other organizations that they should do things the same way. Nothing succeeds like success.

Thinking Through Your Presentation With A Marketer's Mind

All that I've been discussing so far takes place before you ever arrive at the scene of your impending triumph. But, of course, the marketing continues once you arrive. For make no mistake about it, you should have the following objectives:

- connecting with as many of your prospects as you can;
- making sure they get information about how what you are selling can solve their problems;
- getting the names and addresses of your prospects, so that the burden of follow-up rests on you (who knows how to do it) and not them (who do not);
- touching them with your action-oriented, problem-solving presentation;
- confirming and broadening your relationship with their media;
- arranging for your next appearance before this body of prospects, which now trusts in you and is eager to use what you are selling.

To achieve all these objectives means continuing thought and alertness while you are on the spot.

The Choreography Of Marketing; What To Do Immediately Before You Talk

Your marketing effort begins long before you make the talk and, of course, continues up to, through, and after your talk. Here's what to do from a marketing standpoint before you speak:

- Give consideration to where and how your products will be displayed and sold before you speak. Depending on how successfully you have promoted yourself and your problem-solving products and services before you speak and how well known you are, people will want to buy what you're selling before you ever open your mouth. Depend on it. Prepare for it.

N.B. Arrange to have your products sent in advance. Carrying them with you makes you feel like a camel. Send your products at least two weeks in advance. Have them sent directly to the place where you'll be speaking, not to the program's organizer. Keep a record of the person to whom they were sent and where you were told the products would be put upon arrival. Call seven days in advance to see if your products have actually arrived. Don't just assume they're there. Don't let the person to whom they are being sent assume either. Have him look.

If they have not arrived, there is still time to send another shipment. Better that you should have two shipments present than none. Too, make sure you carry with you at least two complete sets of everything you'll be selling and additional order blanks. These you should always carry personally as insurance. Of course, people always like to take home what they see, but if worse comes to worst and your materials don't arrive at least you'll be able to show them what they'll get in the mail.

Ask to have a table (either 6' or 8') set up in the back of the room. This table should be ready for business from the time the first people are expected. It should have a complete display of your books, tapes and other products and should be manned continually. Upon coming, people should be invited to look over what you've brought. However, need I tell you?, what you are selling is not products but solutions. Thus, never say, "Please take a look at the products on the table." Rather say, "Please take a look at what we've brought to help you build a more profitable consulting business." Which alternative sounds more appealing to you?

If you are not quite ready when people arrive, be prepared even for this. I recall a convention I spoke to in Chicago recently. The display area was not ready when the prospects were. The manager said, "We're not ready for you. Come back in 15 minutes." The way it was said was downright insulting. Sure, he was harassed. But he should have planned for this mayhem and prepared accordingly. Instead say, "We're not quite ready yet. But here's a list of suggestions about how we can help you build a more successful consulting business. Don't go away. We'll be right with you!" Again, which of these responses sounds more appealing?

The thing to do is to anticipate what will happen and to frame the best marketing response so that you'll have it when you need it. If you don't think like a marketer, you'll think like a harassed human, which is to say selfishly.

Handling Hand-Outs

- If you have not otherwise arranged for your literature to be distributed to people in your audience, consider now how this will be done. Before your talk people in the audience should be paying attention to your problem-solving products and services. To ensure that they do either:

    - place the literature on all the chairs in the room, or
    - stand at the entry door and give it to all the people as they enter.

Make sure that one of the pieces you distribute is your client-survey questionnaire. You want people to tell you — right now! — what they want to accomplish. Tell them you'll be collecting these after your talk. To make this work, you have to have a box of pencils handy for those who came unprepared to write.

- About 15 or 20 minutes before the program begins, have an announcement made from the podium about what information the audience is supposed to have. Hold it up and ask whether there is anyone who doesn't have it. You'll find that a significant percentage doesn't. At this time, too, invite people to the refreshment table if you've provided one and then to review the problem-solving products you've brought.

It is much less effective merely to leave the information on a table at the back of the room and let your audience help themselves. Much less, indeed.

As Your Prospects Arrive

- Greet people, if possible. Meet and talk to some of the people in your audience before you speak to them. It will diminish your sense of nervousness and increase your sense that you have friends in the audience. Moreover, you can find out information from them which should enable you to make your talk more particular to this group of prospects. Get a card from each person you talk to so that you can personalize your response to them when you follow-up their interest in your products and services. People like to be remembered. You'll have a greater likelihood of doing so if you get the information you need so you can satisfactorily follow up.

Marketing During Your Talk

Let me say right from the start that the most effective marketing you can do from the podium is to give a good talk. This means a talk along the lines I've previously suggested. If your talk is poor, it reflects adversely (perhaps unfairly, but nonetheless certainly) on your problem-solving products and services. By the same token, your lively, enthusiastic, high-energy, client-centered talk dramatically increases the likelihood that your prospects will buy what you're selling. Thus, just how successful this talk will be from a marketing standpoint is directly in your hands. Here are some additional things you can do to get the result you want and your prospects need:

- Write your own introduction. Don't leave something as important as your introduction to chance. The introduction should be written from a marketing perspective, not just to tell the audience (usually useless) information about you. Thus, "Today, we have with us Dr. Jeffrey Lant, a nationally-recognized authority on consulting" is not as effective as, "Today we have with us Dr. Jeffrey Lant. Jeffrey has spent the last 8 years helping to build profitable consulting businesses in every field. He's going to share with us information on how we can make our consulting businesses more successful." The introduction should be written with your prospect and his problem in mind, not for your greater glory.

- Stride to the podium. Exude energy. Excitement. Enthusiasm. The objective of a good marketing speech is to transmit a feeling of energy, of action. To let the prospects in your audience know that, whatever problem they have you, their problem-solving friend, can help them solve it. Give them as much information as you can about how to solve their problem. The more they feel you are interested — really interested — in helping them, the more they will buy your products and use your services. I guarantee it.

This means not holding back. Don't say things like:

- "I cover that in my tapes,"or

- "If you buy my books, you'll find that subject discussed."

Remarks like this kill the connection you want to develop with your prospects. Instead, give a short, precise, informative answer. Look the questioner in the eyes. Respond earnestly. Sincerely. Honestly. Let me tell you something: you're not going to give away the store. There is never enough time for that. But what you will do is let the person with the problem you are addressing (be he the questioner or a silent witness) know that you can help.

When And How To Give Commercials For Your Products And Services

- The person introducing you can and should give you a brief (under one minute) commercial. Because it's so important, write it yourself. "Jeffrey is the author of **TRICKS OF THE TRADE** (the introducer holds it up), **THE CONSULTANT'S KIT** (introducer holds it up).... These books contain detailed information to help you build a more profitable consulting business. Please see them during our break." If someone is going to make this commercial for you, make sure you have written it yourself. Moreover, make sure he knows how to pronounce your name. Even short ones like mine give announcers trouble.

- Now give the talk of your life, a talk filled with wisdom, captivating enthusiasm, problem-solving suggestions — and a complete absence of further commercials about what you're selling. That's right, don't say anything else about your products or services until a couple of minutes before the first break. At that point invite people to review the problem-solving products you've brought. Indicate where they are available and your payment and return terms. Don't forget to mention your thirty-day money-back guarantee, if you have one. Tell your audience you will answer their questions from the back of the room, near the product display. Then move to it, carrying your questioners with you.

N.B. Take only checks, cash and credit cards for your products. Don't bill. If you bill, you'll have to generate an invoice, and it is all too easy for even the most well-meaning of people to overlook this, especially when you live far away. Instead, if you are giving a special show price or discount, tell people how long they have to use it. You can even initial their sales literature and tell them that if they get this to you by a certain date (or call), they'll get the special price. But you are opening yourself up to many quite unnecessary problems by billing people.

- If your talk continues, it is perfectly acceptable to begin the next portion by thanking people for buying the products they did at both the break and even before you began. Gentility is always an acceptable mode of behavior!

- Also, if you happen to run out of a product, ask those who have it to kindly let those who don't to see it. People always want something that someone else has, and this kind of sharing works very much in your favor.

Concluding Your Talk Like A Good Marketer

If this is the end of your presentation, do the following:

- Ask your audience to pass your completed client-survey questionnaires to the front of the room where they can be picked up.

- Provide the audience with your telephone number so that if they have any questions, they can call you. Of course, that number should be on the information they have in their hands. Give it to them again anyway. You want them to know (yet again!) you are there to help them solve their problems. This is, after all, what client-centered marketing is all about.

Then tell your audience what they will find in the back of the room and what it does for them. Be brief. Five minutes is all the time you need. Remember: the talk, not your commercial, convinces people to buy what you're selling. *N.B.* You need a quarter of an hour to handle your sales business before the next talk or event begins. Make sure the organizing sponsors understand this.

Do not allow yourself to be trapped at the podium. Move briskly to your product display. You should have mapped the route you'll use before your talk begins. Whether you are handling your product sales individually or with the help of a volunteer from the sponsoring organization or paid part-time employee, your place is next to your products. Make sure you're there.

- If you are selling books, autograph them. People may be too shy to ask for your autograph, but you shouldn't be too shy to assume they want it. If you're like me and include at least one of your books automatically in your programs, you can begin the day by autographing each participant's book the minute he gets it. This enables you to meet the people and help yourself learn their names by writing them. It also increases the perceived sense of value of what you are offering. No wonder. Isn't it a fact that celebrities autograph books?

Two Warnings

Warning I. I repeat, do not go overboard on commercials for your products and services. People have come to hear a talk, to gain your problem-solving insights into their situations. They want that first and foremost. If you provide them with good, solid, sensible information, they'll do what's necessary to acquire your goods and services so long as you make it easy for them to do so. If you provide this information and they don't buy, it is because they are Flatworms. And there are always Flatworms in every audience. But if you don't provide the information, they are just being sensible by not buying what you're selling. A hard sell is not only demeaning but definitely works against you.

Warning II. It's a sad fact that there are light-fingered people in this world and that sooner or later one or more will show up at your programs. Thus, do not put out all your products at once. Put out two samples of each thing you are selling. Make sure you have a complete count of everything you brought and sent, but only bring them out as you sell what's displayed.

If you've given a good talk, there will be a lot of action around your display table. Count on it. In such circumstances, it's easy to get confused and to literally give your products away. Thus, rehearse yourself and any helpers you may be using in what you want done. It's better to go slow and be safe. Take my word for it!

Marketing At Lunch

If your talk is divided by lunch or another meal, don't eat, market. I have found in practice that the best use of my time (after I've taken very little nourishment) is to circulate around the room, meeting as many people (my prospects) as possible. By finding out whether they are happy and have any additional questions, you stamp yourself as the complete client-centered marketer. Your job is to connect with as many people in the group as possible. This is one superb way of doing so.

After Your Talk Is Over — And You Are Still In The Room

Before you leave the site of your triumph, there are many marketing tasks to accomplish:

- Gather all the completed client-survey questionnaires. These allow you to follow up interested parties expeditiously.

- Return to the product-display area. As long as there are prospects present, your "store" should stay open. Only when it is clear that the throng has narrowed to a few hangers-on should you begin to pack up. You will find in practice that the act of packing up will stimulate a few last sales. Oftentimes it comes down to one uncertain prospect, wavering about what to do. Now, I look this prospect right in the eyes and say, "This book will help you. And because I believe in it, I'll give you a 10% discount off the regular price if you take it right now. But if you don't get it now, you'll have to pay the full price when you do decide to get it." As this last book begins to slide into the box, the prospect almost always buys it, and you don't have to take it home!

- Whatever is left, make sure it's packed well. Long years of giving talk programs and selling products have given me a very good sense of how many products I'll sell given the size of an audience. I'm almost always able to pack what's left over in my personal luggage. But if you can't, make sure it's properly packed. After all, soon you'll be selling it to someone else.

After Your Talk Is Over — Before You Return To Your Office

Keep marketing.

- Make sure before you leave personally to thank each of the people who has made your talk a success. This includes any volunteers who have distributed your literature and helped man your product sales table, as well as executives in the sponsoring organization. Never forget the "little people." Most everyone does, but they buy things, too, and have friends who can also use you. Never forget this.

- If you can, arrange to meet with the editor of the sponsoring organization's publication. Find out whether the reviewer of your program (who may well be this person) needs any further information to be able to write a good article. This is your opportunity to refine any of the points you've made. Take it. Find out, too, when the review will be out and whether the editor wants any more problem-solving process articles from you for subsequent issues.

- Now that you are a known quantity, seek to make a sales arrangement with the sponsoring organization. If they have a publication which reaches their members, you must propose such an arrangement. What this means is transforming their publication into your catalog by offering the sponsor a percentage of the sale from your products. Here's how such an arrangement can be structured:

  - You create the marketing copy.

  - All orders will be returned to the organization.

  - They will deduct their percentage (generally 50% of the retail price) of the amount sent.

  - They will send you your 50% of the retail price plus appropriate money for shipping and handling and the customer's name and address. In short, the standard drop-ship relationship.

Offer the following rationale for this suggestion: it will help the organization raise money and will also help solve the problems of members of the organization, who now so evidently appreciate your problem-solving skills and message. Again, if the person in attendance is not the right person to consider this offer, find out who is and pursue the matter vigorously. After all, if you've followed my suggestions the market you'll be approaching already knows and trusts you, so that you're well on your way to a profitable arrangement.

- If this person isn't the editor, ask the reviewer to find the answers to these questions. But remember, if you don't find out what you need to know this way, take it upon yourself to call the editor directly and nail down the details. This after-talk promotion is most useful for you.

- If you have taped your program and intend to sell it (as you should), take this opportunity to add a few words like these to the end of the master. "This is Jeffrey Lant. Thanks for listening to my suggestions about how you can build a more profitable consulting practice. For further information, you may get my book **THE CONSULTANT'S KIT: ESTABLISHING AND OPERATING YOUR SUCCESSFUL CONSULTING BUSINESS** for $32.50 postpaid. Get it by writing me at 50 Follen St., Suite 507, Cambridge, MA 02138, or calling (617) 547-6372. Remember, you can use your MasterCard or Visa. Don't forget to ask for your free copy of my Sure-Fire Business Success Catalog!" Each tape you create should end with this kind of commercial. If the organization is selling this tape to its members (as it should), you must add this information while you are on the spot.

- If a representative from the general media has attended your program, make sure you find out whether he, too, needs further information from you. Before your program takes place, remind the sponsoring organization to invite local media to attend. If they come, make sure you seek them out and discover if they need any additional information or assistance. If they don't come, arrange to call them directly to see if they would care to have a telephone interview with you, especially if you are from out of town. This is a good use of your time at the airport!

- Arrange to meet with the program planner concerned with scheduling future talks. If your talk has gone well (as it should!), has made money for the organization, and/or attracted the attention of the media, suggest it be repeated. Be prepared to give your reasons and indicate when you'd like to repeat it. Also suggest other topics of interest to this organization. Never leave the site of a successful talk without suggesting ways you can continue the beneficial association now begun. Find out when the program planner will be making his decision and what additional information you may have. When you return to your office, whatever has been agreed upon should be put into a letter and confirmed.

- Further, ask for a testimonial letter. You will be making many talk presentations in your life. And why not? You want to go to places where you can be properly presented and where your prospects will be excited to see you and to learn what you can do for them. Testimonial letters help you get these kinds of engagements. Your letter should include information about:

  - the size of group you addressed;
  - the reception you were accorded;
  - typical audience comments;
  - the personal reaction of the person writing the letter;
  - the value of your material, your rapport with the audience, and how easy you are to work with;
  - whether the group would consider inviting you back.

In short, a perfect marketing letter to convince someone else to give you the use of their platform to approach their membership!

Now return to your office. You must finish the work that ensures the success of the talk you have just given and cements the connection you have now made with your prospects.

Back In Your Office

For each talk you give, you should have a dollar objective. You need to keep in mind how many dollars worth of your product or service you need to sell to reach your objective. For me, it is a minimum of $5000 per day, and I work before, during, and after my talk presentation to make sure I reach this objective. So should you. Your final steps towards reaching this objective take place back in your office where there is always much to do after you return from a successful engagement.

The Letters You Need To Send, The Phone Calls You Need To Make

- Send a thank-you note to the sponsor. Of course you've already said thank-you. Now write it. Putting your thanks in writing is important. In this same letter, confirm any of the arrangements you previously made. Also say when you will be back in touch to follow up. It is your responsibility to ensure that the relationship which has now started so promisingly continues to flourish. Don't forget to remind the sponsor about your testimonial letter. You'll be using this later to get other assignments.

- Send appropriate upgrade letters to people who have bought at least one of your products or services. Send these letters promptly. If the people think what you have already sold them is valuable and if what you are now offering will move them further towards solving a related problem, they will want to have it. Whether you are using a computer or not, these upgrade letters must be sent at once. Make sure you are set up to take telephone orders. The person receiving such a letter will often simply pick up the telephone and add to his order immediately. If he's happy with what you've sold him, why should he wait?

N.B. If you offer a premium, tell your buyers how close they are to reaching the level where they get it. Sell the premium in terms of its problem-solving attributes. Let them know how long they have to act. There must be a precise deadline. After that whatever credits they've build up automatically expire. With me it's 90 days. Then they must begin again. The premium information can either be included in the upgrade letter or can be separate.

- Make the appropriate response to people who completed the client-survey questionnaire. These are qualified prospects. They have indicated what they want to achieve. It is now your task to show them you can help them achieve it. You may contact them either by telephone or letter. The more expensive the product or service you are selling, the more likely you will follow up by telephone, attempting to ascertain if the prospect needs further information or if you can close the sale immediately.

- Consider sending a letter to everyone else in your audience, the people who neither bought nor indicated an interest in having you help solve one of their problems. If you gave a thorough problem-solving talk and were completely client-centered, you will be able to transform some of these laggards into customers.

- Now approach other groups who would be interested in the kind of problem-solving information you just presented. Never think in terms of a single engagement. Always consider a speaking engagement in the light of:

  - how you will use it to connect with not only the members of your audience but all the members of the sponsoring organization or all similar people in the area served by the local media, and

  - how you can use it to bring you and your problem-solving products and services to the attention of others who have the same kind of problem.

As I have said throughout this chapter, it is never enough merely to think in terms of the individual talk you are giving and solely in terms of the people who are in your audience. This is a terrible mistake, one a true marketer never makes.

- Finally, go through your log book and answer any of the particular questions that people gave you that needed your further attention. You should always travel with a log book. You should either write down people's questions yourself or have them do so. By following up these queries, you build relationships with your prospects. If people know what you can do for them and trust you to be able to do it, you will make the sale. Proper use of your log book helps you achieve just this result.

When You Consider Yourself The Top Banana

Most speakers sabotage themselves. They don't see their speaking engagement as a marketing opportunity. They don't help promote themselves to their audiences before they address them. They don't pursue the many media opportunities that are always present with any talk. They don't provide the right kind of information to their audiences about what they can do for them, and they don't follow up their prospects well. To be different, to get the utmost benefit from every talk you give, do these things well and you will profit. When you do so, you will be at the top of the talk profession and as such deserving of celebrity treatment. Here's a trick of the trade for you to keep in mind when you get there.

Securing A Day In Your Honor

Every civic jurisdiction of the United States issues certificates of recognition for those who have done well. These certificates are already available with appropriate blank spaces for your name and the achievement for which you are being recognized. The reasons for recognition are as various as the people who receive them. Astronauts who gambol on the moon get them, but so do retiring chairmen of local civic organizations. And you should get them, too.

From now on, whenever you give a speech or talk program (whether the remuneration is princely or penurious) ask to get a civic citation thrown in, hand-delivered by the highest possible official you can get. Here's how to ensure that this happens:

- Identify the civic authority you wish to honor you and your problem-solving message. Do you want the governor of the state in which you are speaking? The mayor of the city? A branch of the legislature? You decide.

- Tell the sponsoring organization that you would like this kind of recognition. Needless to say, they won't know how to get it. You'll use these notes to brief them.

- Write the letter they should send to the appropriate authority. This letter should present reasons why you should get the award, should say when and how you want the award presented and should provide the wording for the award. Yes, you write it yourself. All that remains for the sponsoring organization to do is to send the letter and follow it up, both important activities.

- Make sure the sponsor follows up this letter appropriately. It is very much in your interest to get this award. So, as the person most directly affected, it is your responsibility to make sure you get it. Two weeks before you speak, ask the sponsor how this matter is progressing. It generally takes no more than an hour (at the very most!) to make contact with the authority offering the award, explain why the award should be given, make arrangements for who will present it and when. Two weeks before your talk is a good time to make sure everything that needs to be arranged has been. *N.B.* The most difficult part about getting the award is finding someone to present it to you. In a worst case scenario, the sponsor of the talk can give it to you. It's not as impressive as having some local panjandrum do it, but you still get it and can use it!

- Once the arrangements have been made about getting the award, tell the sponsoring organization how you'd like the presentation to be handled. Most importantly, you'd like a photographer from both the sponsor's publication and the local media to be present. You not only get a record of the event, but the publicity you want. Make sure you arrange with at least one photographer to get several copies of the picture. The best photo grouping is you with certificate, presenter of certificate and high-ranking official of sponsoring organization. A nice grouping.

Getting Your Award

After you've gotten the award (and the nice round of applause from your prospects that goes with it), squeeze it for its marketing possibilities.

- Make sure some notice about it is printed in the publication of the organization you are addressing.

- Send a notice about your new honor and why you got it to your local newspaper and to the publications associated with civic, professional, sororal and fraternal, and alumni publications to which you are connected. Use the possibilities of this award to make yourself not just into a celebrity but into a recognized problem-solver in your field. Obviously, only people with recognized problem-solving skills get these awards. So if you receive one it must mean that you know what you're talking about and that what you are saying (and, by extension, selling) is important. Right? Of course, right!

And you know what? Having gotten this kind of recognition once, you'll find it easier and easier yet to get it again as you become in the process the paragon of problem-solvers, the very person your prospects most want to deal with.

A Small (But Clever) Refinement

One way to ensure you'll get your recognition is to make sure others get some, too. One of the things I have noticed in my speaking engagements before associations and organizations around the nation is how much hard work the organizers put in and how very little recognition they get. As a successful marketer you should be able to solve this problem — and help yourself in the process. Here's how.

In suggesting that you receive your award, also suggest that the one or two most significant organizers of the event get something similar. This will be important to them and secure you a friend for life. This takes very little additional time for the issuing authority. In short, it's an ideal situation.

You'll find that the organizers will be deeply touched by this mark of respect. Almost inevitably (without your saying a word) they'll find out it was your idea and therefore when it comes time for you to discuss future programs and additional publicity they can only be amenable. This is just the kind of situation a marketer loves. Create one for yourself!

Last Words About Talk Programs And Marketing

There are many other, better ways to transmit information than through a talk. But there are few situations better for marketing your products or services than a talk program properly handled. I know. That's why I regularly use them to connect with my prospects and transform them into customers. You must do the same; not with the fear that characterizes most people approaching a podium but with a sense of captivating enthusiasm that must distinguish your performance.

Why shouldn't you be so enthusiastic? Nothing, after all, is quite as thrilling as being in a situation where your prospects, primed by your advance marketing into being adherents of your problem-solving products and services (despite the fact you haven't opened your mouth), are about to give you their trust. Having heard your stirring talk and had this feeling confirmed, they will thrust dollars towards your smiling face with the utmost belief that you and what you are offering have come into their lives at precisely the right moment with precisely what they need. To think that all this is done not grudgingly but with the happy music of their applause and admiration excites me every time it happens! And it happens often, as it must happen to you, too, if you follow these steps, you brilliant marketer, you!

CONCLUSION

By now you probably feel like my friend Mary Davies, the former publisher of *Innkeeping* newsletter, who recently wrote, "I am willing to admit I don't know it all, but cannot hide my secret hope that there's not too much more to learn." Well, we all know there is more to learn. But for the moment, if you have made every effort to understand the techniques offered in this book, you have learned enough.

Now you are indeed ready to go out to begin the sweet, if often tiring, task of connecting with the people who need what you're selling.

As you begin to do so, let me tell you something: your customers need you and are waiting for you to enter their lives and make them better.

There will be days, however, many days, that you may doubt this. There will be days when the money dribbles in, or doesn't even dribble at all. There will be days when the telephone doesn't ring, except to bring a renewed plea for payment from some pesky creditor. There will be days when you can't get past the obstructionist secretary for love or money. There will be days when you damn the customer, his obstinacy and short sightedness, and wonder if all your efforts will ever be worth it.

Yes, there will be days like this.

When they happen, you cannot get discouraged. You must remember two thing: first, even the most sublime and polished marketers have them, whatever they may say to the contrary. Remember the Edsel! Second, you have a solution readily available to transform matters. You are, indeed, holding it in your hands right this minute.

On Being The Consummate Marketer

What distinguishes the practiced marketers from the order-taking drones that abound is this. The consummate marketers understand and constantly work to perfect their techniques. They:

- focus on the most precisely-targeted group possible;
- perceive the pain their prospects are in and link their own product and service to eliminating it;
- let their prospects tell them what their problems are, and only then offer to provide the appropriate solution;
- connect with these prospects not once but over and over again so that they know that what is being offered can help them;
- use every available inexpensive marketing opportunity before they use any expensive one;
- attempt to get a buyer to buy again as soon as possible before attempting to connect with new prospects;
- work to retrieve lost customers before spending their money seeking new ones;
- avoid launching marketing methods that bring them to the attention of a group of prospects only once in favor of beginning sequences of contacts that connect them to their prospects over and over again;
- market every day, whether they feel like it or not;
- never impose their values and beliefs on their market, but always seek to understand what their market is feeling and doing so that they can reposition themselves accordingly and speak to the needs of their prospects.

In short, they are always refining their methods so that they connect with their buyers as precisely as possible, as knowledgeably as possible, as often as possible, and as inexpensively as possible.

Now this is just what you are prepared to do.

You now know that marketing is not just a function of presenting the right offer to the right people but having the energy, determination and persistence to present that offer again and again and again, using a variety of means, until that prospect finally takes action and buys what you are selling, the thing that you have always known will improve his life.

As such, marketing is not for the apathetic, the slothful, the meek, or the disorganized. It is an art and a science in which those who succeed exhibit all the skills and deliberation of a finely-trained researcher and the overbrimming exuberance of a passionate lover who will do whatever is necessary to connect with his beloved.

Is it any wonder then that this demanding task of marketing, one of the critical fundamentals of business success, can be regarded, in and of itself, as a wonderful, thrilling, captivating activity, the ultimate game?

If you forget this, get discouraged, or overwhelmed, or just need a refresher, return to this book, to me, for here may be the answers you need either to transform the doldrums of your business or to gild your prosperity with still more luster. This book was not written to be read once and put aside, but to be kept near at hand, ready to help you when you need it.

Marketing is not effortless. It is an often arduous process. Here, right in your hands, are its essential procedures. Use them to your profit, as I use them myself.

For keep in mind that I am working along with you, refining these techniques, creating new ones, all designed to connect me with my buyers more economically, more gracefully, more lucratively, as you wish to connect with yours.

To this end, I salute you. Though our customers may not know it just now, though they may never express their appreciation directly to us, they are counting on us to master these techniques, and thus bring our helpful remedies to their attention. Only in this way will their lives be enriched. It is for this enrichment that you must become the consummate marketer and never give way to the momentary despair that assails all of us who live by business.

Vow that insofar as your offer is significant and helpful to others, you will work to perfect the means of marketing. If you do, you must succeed, knowing in the process that you are doing well by doing good, the very touchstone of a life well lived. As you reach this exhilarating plateau, let me know that I have had some tiny part in assisting you, for nothing pleases me more than to know that you and I have significantly connected both for the benefit of your customers and of yourself.

I await this significant news, feeling sure it will come from you soon.

Jeffrey

APPENDIX

When You Need A Marketing Consultant, How To Find One, And What He'll Probably Do After You Get In Touch

I'm of the firm opinion, as should scarcely come as any surprise to you now, that people should learn how to help themselves and so solve their business problems. I have always believed that if you provide a person with the information he needs to solve his problem, in most instances he can solve it.

Thus, before rushing off to retain a marketing consultant, look for the solution to your problem right here.

As you know, I invite all my readers to contact me for assistance with their problems. I'll tell you straight, however, I get most irritated when they haven't done their homework before contacting me, when they haven't bothered to study the solutions to the problems with which I've presented them in my books. So, do yourself a favor. If you've got a marketing problem, return to this book and see if you can't find the answer here.

Once you've done so, determine what kind of marketing problem you've got:

Problem 1: You don't know what you want to do or what needs to be done.

Problem 2: You know what you want to do and what needs to be done, but you do not have the necessary skills to do it and cannot take the time right now to acquire them.

Problem 3: You know what needs to be done and can do it, but you have other things on your plate, and wish to delegate the task to a specialist.

These are three very different problems.

Towards Solving Problem 1

To solve Problem 1, a consultant will work to help you define what needs to be done, including a complete break-down of tasks to be completed, people to be involved in completing them, and dates by which they need to be accomplished. In this situation, you are purchasing several things:

- help in clarifying what you are trying to do;

- a complete list of what makes sense to do given your goal and limited resources;

- an education, so that in future you can either do some of these things yourself or be clearer about what the consultant needs to do and how he should do it.

This process is expensive. Here you are paying both for an immediate benefit and for education from which you will benefit later. Thus, make sure you understand what the consultant is doing and why he is doing it. Ask lots of questions, pay close attention, and take notes. If you don't, you are not getting your money's worth.

Towards Solving Problem 2

If you lack certain skills and are retaining a consultant with these skills, ask yourself whether you'll need such skills in the future. If this is a one-time only problem, by all means retain a consultant who can solve it, learn what you can, and follow his directions to achieve success.

If you'll need the skill again, however, (but cannot spend the time fully to acquire it now for yourself), regard your work with the consultant as educational as well as immediately problem-solving. Acquiring this knowledge is expensive to the extent that you do not pay attention now. So, do.

One of my complaints about my much-valued clients is their frequent failure to pay close attention not only to *what* I am suggesting or doing but to *why* I am suggesting or doing this. Every consultant is by definition an instructor.

Once you see the importance of what the consultant is doing for the success of your marketing, you may want to invest some of your precious leisure time in upgrading your skills in this area.

Towards Solving Problem 3

Here is where you are best equipped to get the most from your consultant. Why?

You already know what the problem is and how to solve it. You will therefore be able to approach the consultant with at least some understanding of his problem-solving skills. You will be able more accurately to assess what he says and why he says it. As a result, your decisions (for remember, the consultant is only an advisor) should be correspondingly better, more precise. Too many people do not get the best results from their consultants because of their own lack of knowledge about what the consultant can do, too much vagueness about their own needs, and a lack of understanding of the consultant's problem-solving skills. This won't happen to you!

What Next?

Once you've decided *what* you need, you must find the person *who* will do it. Here are some suggestions:

- Call me. I am a marketing consultant. I specialize in the following areas: developing marketing plans, document development, copywriting, direct mail, and getting free publicity. If these interest you, start here. Even if these are not the marketing problems you need to solve, call me anyway. I have a national marketing network of experts in all marketing fields. *N.B.* If you want to be a part of this network, let me know what you can do and what success you've had doing it.

If you want to be difficult and perverse, try the following:

- Contact the marketing department of your local college. Oftentimes students are looking for projects and will help you with yours. In Massachusetts we have a state internship office which will send information to all the colleges in the state about the project you've got. There's no charge, and students will contact you. You can offer a variety of internships: volunteer, volunteer plus expenses, or paid. See whether your state has something similar. For information about our program, contact the Massachusetts Internship Office, 150 Causeway St., Room 600, Boston, MA 02114 (617) 727-8688.

A Word About Working With Students

Today's students are not as responsible as past generation's (like mine!) were, although saying this does remind me of the father's line from "Bye, Bye Birdie" when he sings, "Why can't they be like we were, perfect in every way." Still, having worked with many interns I have reason for saying this. Thus, be clear about what you want. Never assume even the brightest intern understands what needs to be done or how to do it. Monitor their work. And if they disappoint you regularly, politely end the association.

As my father always says, you get what you pay for. Still, even if you're not paying cash, you are paying the intern in other benefits, particularly much-needed experience. The intern has a right to get this. And you have the right to get the best possible effort from the intern. That's the whole rationale for the program. Thus, make sure you structure the situation so that each of you benefits.

More Ways To Find A Marketing Consultant

- Ask local marketing professors if they do consulting. Many moonlight. But be wary of professors. Academic personnel often lack practical problem-solving experience. Ask for evidence of what they've done (and how it worked), not just what they've talked about in class. My recent encounters with marketing professors have only confirmed my belief that most have severely-limited experience.

- Use SCORE, the Service Corps Of Retired Executives. This program of the Small Business Administration matches retired executives with people with business problems. There is no limit on the number of times you can return with your problem, and you generally do not need an appointment in advance. You can just walk in. Check with your local SBA office for the nearest SCORE counselor.

- Monitor your friends and colleagues, particularly those in a comparable business. Find out who's doing well. Ask if they use marketing advisors. Write down the information as you discover it. People, particularly in a competitive industry, can get tight-lipped about who's helped them climb the greasy pole to success. When they are more communicative, take advantage of it.

- Ask your professional association for the names of marketing consultants active in your field.

- Note the names of marketing professionals whose articles appear in your professional publications. Scarcely an issue of a business publication goes by these days without the obligatory marketing article. If the advisor hasn't been smart enough to run the article with complete follow-up information, ask the editor for it.

- Ask your other business advisors. All consultants maintain contact banks and are constantly swapping client leads.

- Consult *Bradford's Directory of Market Research Agencies and Management Consultants In the United States And The World*. Box 276, Fairfax, VA 22030

What To Do After You've Got Some Leads For Potential Marketing Consultants

- Begin by calling the consultants in whom you are interested. Before going further, you need to find out if they are taking on new clients and if they work in the area of your interest. Only if these two conditions are successfully met should you bother with them further.

If they are, you need to send a letter designed both to provide information about you and your project and to elicit further information about the consultant and his work. Remember: good consultants are judging you as much as you are judging them. I know, for instance, just by looking at the way the envelope is addressed and *how* the letter appears (to say nothing of what's actually in it) whether this is a serious client-prospect or a time-wasting Flatworm. Prepare your approach accordingly. Good consultants are very persnickety about whom they work with.

Here's what should be covered in your letter:

Part 1: Information About You And Your Problem

- Be clear about what you want to achieve.

- When do you want it?

- What factors differentiate your situation from others? Are there, for instance, certain constraints that apply in your situation?

- What have you so far done to deal with the problem? Consider including selective supporting documents.

Part 2: Information About The Consultant And His Track-Record

- Ask if the consultant has helped other similar organizations and with what results. Ask the consultant to send you relevant information on these successes or at least references for you to contact.

- Ask how the consultant handles a new client in terms of meetings, information needed, and fees.

A good consultant expects you to be prepared on the points in the first part of this letter. A good consultant is prepared for your questions in the second part.

Evaluating The Responses

Let me tell you something about how to evaluate consultants: it begins *the minute* you contact the consultant, both by telephone and letter. Keep notes about the following:

- How long did it take for the consultant to respond to your call or letter?
- How did the consultant respond to you and in what way? Was he clear about what he needed from you and why he needed it? Does what he said make sense to you?
- Did you get the success-verification information you requested?
- Did the consultant respond to you in a reasonable, professional and timely fashion?

Rest assured that if you are disappointed on any of these points (when the consultant is presumably on his best behavior), things will get worse later. If you have a bad feeling, politely terminate the connection. A short note to the consultant saying that you are not going to proceed now is genteel.

What The Consultant Should Be Doing With You

Here's how your would-be consultant should be handling this contact. He should:

- promptly respond to your request for information;
- reassure you (with hard data, not words) that he has experience solving problems like yours;
- give you precise information about how he handles client-assessment;
- ask you questions to determine *what* your problem is and how seriously you want to solve it. He'll want to determine if you will do what is necessary to solve it and if you have the requisite means, including money.

Expect your would-be consultant to be courteous, but pointed. His questions may appear brusque to you, but I can assure you the consultant needs detailed information to make a realistic assessment about whether yours is a problem:

- he can solve;
- you want to solve;
- you have the means to solve.

He wants to know if this is a situation which will give him at its conclusion a success he can market, or is merely one fraught with frustration and aggravation which he doesn't need, whatever you're paying.

If and only if these questions are satisfactorily answered will the good consultant work with you. After all, he wants you to succeed as much as — if not more — than you do. *N.B.* Pay close attention during this in-take process. Just going through these steps you'll learn a good deal about your problem and your likelihood of solving it.

Will You Pay For The Initial Meeting And Assessment Process?

Let's put it this way: whether you pay for this process before or after you become a client, you'll probably pay for it.

For my own lengthier (one-year) retainer contracts, I give one free hour to client prospects but even the cost of this time is built into the subsequent contract. For shorter-term engagements I charge for all the time I use. This is common.

If the consultant is rendering judgment on issues of interest and value to you, he has a right to charge for his time. Expect it.

Making Your Decision

You know what the consultant is looking for in assessing you. So, what do you do now about deciding if it would be beneficial for you to work with him? That's where the following questions come in:

- Did you like the consultant? He will be working closely with you. He will be candid and may occasionally seem abrasive. It helps if you feel amicably towards him.

- Did you trust him? Did you understand his professional judgment? Did his recommendations and comments seem reasonable to you?

- Have you the capabilities to do what the consultant advises? Perhaps his advice is good in the abstract but not given your circumstances. Is this consultant understanding about you and your situation? Is he client-centered? Is he speaking *to* you?

- Does he inspire you with a sense that this job can and will be done? Is he realistic about the obstacles and knowledgeable about what you can do, in your unique situation, to overcome them?

- Is he trying to impose a structure on you, or is he tailoring his methods to your situation?

If you are uncertain about the consultant in relation to any of these points, raise them at one of your meetings and assess the answers. If you are still uncertain, this is probably not the consultant for you.

Understanding The Good Advisor

Good advisors are seasoned. They understand that solving a problem is not only a question of utilizing technical information. It may also call for psychological skills, political adroitness, persuasion techniques, flexibility, and the constant ability to assess a situation, take into account what is happening, and change his advice as needed. Such skills do not come overnight.

There is much more to a good advisor than merely knowing where to find and how to use problem-solving information. Are you confident that the marketing consultant you are considering bringing into the heart of your business is so seasoned and that he wants you to achieve success as much as you do?

If so, engage him. You are, of course, taking a risk, but it is one that should pay off with a stronger organization bringing your service or product to the attention of your prospects or buyers in new and better ways to the advantage of both you and the people who need what you're selling.

And if you don't feel this way about this consultant?

Keep looking. Marketing is too important to entrust to a consultant who doesn't share your dream or is unwilling to work hard with you in achieving it — as I know you will.

SAMPLES SECTION

Sample Prospect-Survey Questionnaire
(Also called Client-Survey Questionnaire)

Jeffrey Lant Associates, Inc.
50 Follen Street, Suite 507
Cambridge, Massachusetts 02138
(617) 547-6372

Note: In this document, you are trying to ascertain what problems your prospect has. Once you know, you follow up with information on the precise products and services you are selling which solve them.

From: Dr. Jeffrey Lant
To: His Get Ahead Friends and Colleagues

I want to help you make your business more profitable, more organized. Let me!

Take a minute — right now — to check in which of the following areas you'd like to make improvements, become more proficient, and make more money in the NEXT YEAR. Send this form back to me, and I'll return my suggestions as to how you can achieve precisely what you want to achieve. Number the categories in the order in which you'd like to proceed, and I'll recommend books, cassettes, newsletters, associations, and other experts to help!

RESPONSE COUPON

Jeffrey, thanks for your offer to help. I'd like to improve my business or professional practice in the following ways (number in order of priority):

- ❑ deciding whether to go into my own business (do I have what it takes?)
- ❑ profitably self-publishing booklets and books
- ❑ successfully handling my own public relations
- ❑ creating profitable talk programs, workshops and seminars
- ❑ handling my financial planning
- ❑ successfully setting and getting my fees
- ❑ running a successful sideline (part-time) business
- ❑ giving effective speeches and presentations
- ❑ mastering telemarketing techniques
- ❑ creating a profitable, effective newsletter
- ❑ developing effective brochures, catalogs, flyers, *etc*.
- ❑ effectively closing sales
- ❑ setting up a successful one-person, professional corporation
- ❑ becoming a more effective business writer
- ❑ getting the right computer
- ❑ learning how to use on-line computer data-bases
- ❑ cutting my office supplies bill
- ❑ becoming a more successful consultant or advisor in any field
- ❑ learning to cut my stress
- ❑ getting the right kind of disability insurance coverage
- ❑ setting up and managing a successful business partnership
- ❑ winning small claims cases
- ❑ collecting money people owe me
- ❑ finding a good multi-level marketing opportunity
- ❑ developing a profitable home-based business
- ❑ building a profitable mail order business
- ❑ patenting my bright ideas
- ❑ developing an effective logo
- ❑ developing a successful marketing plan
- ❑ raising money for my nonprofit organization or charitable group
- ❑ helping my secretary get more done, better
- ❑ overcoming procrastination
- ❑ other (please be specific)

My Name ______________________ Business Name ______________________

Address ______________________ City/Town ______________________

State __________ Zip Code __________ Telephone ______________________

Return to above address!

Sample Add-on/Upgrade Letter

Jeffrey Lant Associates, Inc.
50 Follen Street, Suite 507
Cambridge, MA 02138

April 3, 1991

Mr. Jack Chatfield
875 Comstock Ave., 11-C
Los Angeles, CA 90024

Dear Jack Chatfield,

Thanks for ordering **THE CONSULTANT'S KIT**. You'll find this book specific, detailed, precise and thorough. I know these techniques work because I use them myself. Day in, day out.

But did you know that this book is part of a seven-book set?

Perhaps not.

The complete set includes:

- **THE CONSULTANT'S KIT: ESTABLISHING AND OPERATING YOUR SUCCESSFUL CONSULTING BUSINESS**. It's designed to get you off to a fast start in a part-time or full-time consulting business. And it's so well regarded that it is recommended by both the U.S. Small Business Administration and by Dick Bolles' in his book *What Color Is Your Parachute?* By the way, it's the only consulting book that is so recommended.

- **THE UNABASHED SELF-PROMOTER'S GUIDE: WHAT EVERY MAN, WOMAN, CHILD AND ORGANIZATION IN AMERICA NEEDS TO KNOW ABOUT GETTING AHEAD BY EXPLOITING THE MEDIA**. Face it. You are going to want to get your message to the people who can buy your products and services, and you're going to want to do so in the least expensive way. That's why this book will help. It's packed with technique after technique to get you to your buyers —for the least possible cost.

- **MONEY TALKS: THE COMPLETE GUIDE TO CREATING A PROFITABLE WORKSHOP OR SEMINAR IN ANY FIELD**. This is now regarded as the definitive book on creating profitable talk programs — of every kind. It gets constant publicity as the one book you need if you want to create a workshop, seminar, lecture, conference, or institute — and make money. One of the nation's largest magazines — *Changing Times* — warmly endorsed it in the November issue. I think you'll find it is absolutely essential reading on how to make money, get clients and build name recognition through talk programs.

- **TRICKS OF THE TRADE: THE COMPLETE GUIDE TO SUCCEEDING IN THE ADVICE BUSINESS**. It's absolutely packed with information on how to profit from problem-solving information. Take my word for it. The book is relentlessly detailed. In fact, I think I may now say that it is the most detailed book ever written on how to make money with information, from being an advisor or consultant of every kind.

- **MONEY MAKING MARKETING: FINDING THE PEOPLE WHO NEED WHAT YOU'RE SELLING AND MAKING SURE THEY BUY IT.** There is nothing like it on the market. Over the past several years I've made a specialty of developing means of ensuring that I get my products and services to the attention of the right people and make sure they buy them. In this relentlessly detailed book, I'm sharing the secrets I know and use daily.

- **CASH COPY: HOW TO OFFER YOUR PRODUCTS AND SERVICES SO YOUR PROSPECTS BUY THEM...NOW!** You're spending a bundle on your ads, cover letters, flyers, brochures, proposals...and all your other marketing communications. This resource tells you what to say so people do what you want them to do...immediately!

- **HOW TO MAKE A WHOLE LOT MORE THAN $1,000,000 WRITING, COMMISSIONING, PUBLISHING AND SELLING "HOW-TO" INFORMATION.** My newest book shows you exactly what you've got to do to make a million dollar+ fortune with books, booklets, audio cassettes and Special Reports. It's the most detailed volume ever created on how to develop the truly profitable information empire.

I'm writing to you today because you now own part of this series. And I want to make sure you get the rest — and profit from what I know.

Ordinarily you have to buy the complete set at one time. If you don't buy it then, you have to pay full price for all the other books you want. The price for all seven is $200 postpaid. Individual titles run from $27.95 postpaid for CASH COPY to $38.50 for MONEY MAKING MARKETING and HOW TO MAKE A WHOLE LOT MORE THAN $1,000,000...

I'm betting that you didn't know about the series discount and that if you did you'd certainly want to take advantage of it. Therefore, if you fill out the coupon below and **get it back to me within two weeks**.of your receiving what you've already bought, I'll happily sell you the entire series for just $166. Which I've got to tell you is a superb deal. And is **not available anywhere else**.

Moreover, you have nothing to lose because all these books — like everything I write — is covered by my 30-Day Money-Back Guarantee. If for any reason you don't think these books will help you, return them to me for a complete refund.

As a good customer, I wanted to make sure you knew about all the Get-Ahead Books and had the opportunity to get them for the special price. Now that you do, I'm looking forward to hearing from you very soon — and to helping you build the strongest possible business at the least possible cost. Won't you let me?

Sincerely yours,

Jeffrey Lant, Ph.D.
President

Order Coupon

❑ Yes, Jeffrey, I want to take advantage of your special five-book offer. (**The title you already have is checked!**).

❑ **THE CONSULTANT'S KIT: ESTABLISHING AND OPERATING YOUR SUCCESSFUL CONSULTING BUSINESS.** $34 postpaid

❑ **THE UNABASHED SELF-PROMOTER'S GUIDE: WHAT EVERY MAN, WOMAN, CHILD AND ORGANIZATION IN AMERICA NEEDS TO KNOW ABOUT GETTING AHEAD BY EXPLOITING THE MEDIA.** $34 postpaid

❑ **MONEY TALKS: THE COMPLETE GUIDE TO CREATING A PROFITABLE WORKSHOP OR SEMINAR IN ANY FIELD.** $34 postpaid

❑ **TRICKS OF THE TRADE: THE COMPLETE GUIDE TO SUCCEEDING IN THE ADVICE BUSINESS.** $34 postpaid

❑ **MONEY MAKING MARKETING: FINDING THE PEOPLE WHO NEED WHAT YOU'RE SELLING AND MAKING SURE THEY BUY IT.**$38.50 postpaid

❑ **CASH COPY: HOW TO OFFER YOUR PRODUCTS AND SERVICES SO YOUR PROSPECTS BUY THEM...NOW!** $27.95 postpaid.

❑ **HOW TO MAKE A WHOLE LOT MORE THAN $1,000,000 WRITING, COMMISSIONING, PUBLISHING AND SELLING "HOW-TO" INFORMATION**. $38.50 postpaid.

Please send your check for $166 for the complete set (or the amount as marked for the individual book/s you want) to Jeffrey Lant Associates, Inc., 50 Follen St., Suite 507, Cambridge, MA 02138 or call with your MasterCard or Visa (617) 547-6372.

Check ❑ MasterCard ❑ Visa Card# ____________________ Expiration ____________

Signature ____

Send Books To: ____

Name ____

Address ____

City ____________________ State __________ Zip ____________

Telephone ( ) ____

Remember: This special offer expires 2 weeks after you receive your book. If you don't take advantage of it during this period, when you want to order other books in the series, you'll have to pay the full retail price/s as marked. So, please, act NOW!

Sample Premium Letter

Jeffrey Lant Associates, Inc.
50 Follen Street, Suite 507
Cambridge, MA 02138
(617) 547-6372

To: The Reverend David Smith
From: Jeffrey Lant

Thanks for ordering from my Sure-Fire Business Success Catalog. I'm proud to offer this unique resource chock full of ways to improve the profitability of your business.

If you've ordered one of my books, it is enclosed. If you've ordered by credit card, your receipt is enclosed.

The books and materials I sell (but do not produce) are sent directly from their producers. In this case, I must advise you to be patient. If your materials are coming Fourth Class/Book Rate it could take up to 6 weeks. Usually, shipment is faster, but don't be surprised if it takes the full amount of time. If it doesn't come thereafter, please let me know. Occasionally things do get lost in the mail! If your things are coming First Class, you'll get them sooner!

As a buyer from my catalog, this quarter you are eligible for two very exciting premiums. Indeed, you are now well on your way to getting them. For $150 in purchases before April 15th, you will receive one of my three 60-minute audio cassettes. A $14 retail value, you can select from among "How To Get Free Time On Radio And T.V. And Use It To Get Your Prospects To Buy What You're Selling"; "How To Create Marketing Documents That Get Your Prospects To Buy What You're Selling...Now!"; and "Essentials Of Money-Making Marketing: What You've Really Got To Do To Sell Your Products And Services Every Day!" Just tell me which one you'd like.

Furthermore, if you spend an additional $181.53 on any products or services from my catalog, you'll receive — in addition to the audio cassette of your choice — any one of my 7 Get Ahead Books including THE CONSULTANT'S KIT, THE UNABASHED SELF-PROMOTER'S GUIDE, MONEY TALKS, TRICKS OF THE TRADE, MONEY MAKING MARKETING, CASH COPY or my latest book HOW TO MAKE A WHOLE LOT MORE THAN $1,000,000 WRITING, COMMISSIONING, PUBLISHING AND SELLING "HOW-TO" INFORMATION. Your selection is worth up to $38.50 and is my free gift to you for shopping in the Sure-Fire Business Success Catalog.

You are now on your way to getting these premiums. So please take a minute to look again at my catalog to see what else you need. The tally of the amount you've spent with me so far this quarter appears below. When reordering before April 15th, simply return this page (which has your name and address on it) along with your order. The appropriate premium will be immediately sent.

You are very close to getting two wonderful premiums. But you must order again before April 15th to get them.

Name: The Reverend David Smith
Company Name: St. Luke's United Methodist Church
Address: 100 W. 86th St.
City/State/Zip: Indianapolis, IN 46260

Purchase amount in this quarter to date: $110.00

Amount remaining to your selection of one of my three 60-minute audio cassettes: $40.

Which audio cassette would you like? When returning your order, just check the one you'd like:

- ❑ "How To Get Free Time On Radio And T.V. And Use It To Get Your Prospects To Buy What You're Selling."
- ❑ "How To Create Marketing Documents That Get Your Prospects To Buy What You're Selling... Now!"
- ❑ "Essentials Of Money-Making Marketing: What You've Really Got To Do To Sell Your Products And Services Every Day!"

Amount remaining to get your choice of any one of Jeffrey's 7 Get Ahead books: $115.

When returning your order, just check the one you'd like. Remember, when your order totals over $225 you get both a free audio cassette and free book!

- ❑ THE CONSULTANT'S KIT
- ❑ THE UNABASHED SELF-PROMOTER'S GUIDE
- ❑ MONEY TALKS
- ❑ TRICKS OF THE TRADE
- ❑ MONEY MAKING MARKETING
- ❑ CASH COPY
- ❑ HOW TO MAKE A WHOLE LOT MORE THAN $1,000,000 WRITING, COMMISSIONING, PUBLISHING AND SELLING "HOW-TO" INFORMATION

Please return this form and payment to:

Dr. Jeffrey Lant
JEFFREY LANT ASSOCIATES, INC.
50 Follen St., Suite 507
Cambridge, MA 02138

Or call with your MasterCard or Visa (617) 547-6372.

❑ MasterCard ❑ Visa Card # ______________________________ Expiration ______________

Signature ____

Where you want materials sent if different from above:

Name ____

Company ____

Address ____

City ______________________ State __________ Zip ______________

Thanks for being part of America's most comprehensive and useful business development information center: The Sure-Fire Business Success Catalog!

Sample New Service Announcement Letter

JEFFREY LANT ASSOCIATES, INC.
50 FOLLEN STREET, SUITE 507
CAMBRIDGE,MA 02138
(617) 547-6372

January 4, 1991

Mr. Jack Chatfield
875 Comstock Ave., 11-C
Los Angles, CA 90024

Dear Jack Chatfield,

As a good customer of mine, I wanted to take this opportunity to announce my latest service: providing brighter-than-bright copywriting.

For years now, I've been writing action-oriented, profitable copy for my own books and services. Frankly, I took this skill pretty much for granted.

But while I was working on the new Revised Edition of my book **MONEY MAKING MARKETING: FINDING THE PEOPLE WHO NEED WHAT YOU'RE SELLING AND MAKING SURE THEY BUY IT**, I've had occasion to look seriously at what other firms — of every kind — are using. And I've been appalled.

I've seen every kind of copywriting mistake — in spades.

Copy that's boring.

Copy that offers the reader no benefits — but only talks about the features of whatever is being sold.

Copy that makes it difficult for the buyer to buy.

Copy that meanders.

Copy that is unspecific.

Copy that is not centered on the buyer but only on the seller.

And on and on and on.

Until I could stand it no more.

And apparently others couldn't either. Because while I was discovering, to my horror, the terrible waste of money that constitutes most business' brochures, pamphlets, mailing pieces, business cards, flyers, order blanks, *etc.*, I was being approached by businesses that didn't want to waste their money like this.

So I inadverently became a consulting copywriter.

I had some doubts about whether it would be possible to offer this service long distance. But now I know.

Working with my IBM-compatible Epson Equity II, the telephone, post and overnight mail services, you can get the kind of top-quality, profit-making copywriting for your own business, product, service or organization that I give myself.

Here's how it works.

1. You let me know you're interested in developing new written marketing materials or improving the ones you already have.

2. You tell me what you want to produce (the kind of document) and when you need it.

3. I let you know if I can produce what you want, when you want it.

4. If the answer is yes, I ask you for samples of your existing documents, information on your product or service, on the benefits people get from it, and other pertinent information. I review them, make an estimate of how long it will take me to create what you want. I then ask you if you'd like to proceed.

5. If so, I begin to write, sending draft material to you for your approval and for my further editing. (Then, of course, we fight, er, discuss, which draft is better for your purposes. It is interactive communication at its finest!)

And how much does all this cost? I charge $350 per hour plus expenses (usually telephone calls and mail service). One third the money is due when we agree to start working together. If you consider this expensive, I'll be happy to refer you to other copywriters and will be happy to look over the final result to make sure you're getting what will generate the most sales for you.

Either way you get fast, accurate, persuasive copy at a fraction of the cost you'd pay elsewhere — and I will work until we both agree that your new marketing documents are markedly superior to the ones you now have. Until, that is, you feel they'll admirably represent you and cause your customers to sit up, take notice, and spend their money with you.

If this sounds interesting, you let me know. Call me at (617) 547-6372 or write with a brief description of what you'd like and when you'd like it. I'll get right back in touch.

And don't forget my book CASH COPY. It's packed with copywriting suggestions in case you want to do it yourself. It's available for $27.95. Take my word for it, this book will help with all your marketing efforts!

Yours For More Profitable Copy,

Jeffrey Lant, Ph.D.
President

ABOUT THE AUTHOR...

Over the last several years, Dr. Jeffrey Lant has emerged as one of America's most well-known business authorities. His provocative and information-packed articles on a wide variety of business development topics (under the title "Sure Fire Business Success") are now carried by over 100 publications nationwide and abroad. Major electronic databases like CompuServe (U.S. Entrepreneurs Network and Working from Home), GEnie (Ephote), and Delphi also carry his articles. Well over a million and a half people monthly get their business get-ahead information from Jeffrey this way! Another million get their information from him on The Business Radio Network. Jeffrey can be heard on 55 radio stations nationwide every week!

Unlike most writers, Jeffrey's telephone number runs along with his articles, so that his readers can call for additional information, hints, and the "kick where it helps" that all of us occasionally need.

A practicing marketing consultant for the last 12 years, Jeffrey is president of Jeffrey Lant Associates, Inc. Based in Cambridge, Massachusetts, he works internationally. Some of his work includes creating marketing plans, developing information products, and writing brochures, cover letters, ads, and response coupons for a wide variety of both individuals and organizations wanting to sell their products and services faster. He also provides fund raising assistance to nonprofit organizations and public relations consultation. His practice is distinguished by his own distinctive brand of enthusiasm, excitement and positive problem-solving skills.

A well-known speaker on such topics as establishing a successful consulting practice, effective marketing, publishing profitable books, succeeding in your own mail order business, running a profitable home-based business, and many other topics, Jeffrey ranges the country giving speeches, workshops and conference presentations. An animated and often electrifying platform speaker, Jeffrey never merely talks to an audience, but also seeks to involve them in his presentation. Intellectually demanding of himself, Jeffrey demands no less of his audiences!

Over the past 10 years, Jeffrey has written a book each year. His titles include the seven volumes in his well-known "Get Ahead" Series, including THE CONSULTANT'S KIT: ESTABLISHING AND OPERATING YOUR SUCCESSFUL CONSULTING BUSINESS (now in a 9th printing); THE UNABASHED SELF-PROMOTER'S GUIDE: WHAT EVERY MAN, WOMAN, CHILD AND ORGANIZATION IN AMERICA NEEDS TO KNOW ABOUT GETTING AHEAD BY EXPLOITING THE MEDIA; MONEY TALKS: THE COMPLETE GUIDE TO CREATING A PROFITABLE WORKSHOP OR SEMINAR IN ANY FIELD; TRICKS OF THE TRADE: THE COMPLETE GUIDE TO SUCCEEDING IN THE ADVICE BUSINESS; MONEY MAKING MARKETING: FINDING THE PEOPLE WHO NEED WHAT YOU'RE SELLING AND MAKING SURE THEY BUY IT, and CASH COPY: HOW TO OFFER YOUR PRODUCTS AND SERVICES SO YOUR PROSPECTS BUY THEM... NOW! His latest book is HOW TO MAKE A WHOLE LOT MORE THAN $1,000,000 WRITING, COMMISSIONING, PUBLISHING AND SELLING 'HOW TO' INFORMATION. Major media sources nationwide and critics regularly hail these books as unrelentingly thorough, models of what a "how-to" book should be. This thoroughness and the complete practicality of the information he provides have become Jeffrey's trademarks.

His other titles include DEVELOPMENT TODAY: A FUND RAISING GUIDE FOR NONPROFIT ORGANIZATIONS (now in a 4th Edition); INSUBSTANTIAL PAGEANT: CEREMONY AND CONFUSION AT QUEEN VICTORIA'S COURT; and (as Editor) OUR HARVARD: REFLECTIONS ON COLLEGE LIFE BY TWENTY-TWO DISTINGUISHED GRADUATES.

Jeffrey has also produced a series of 60-minute audio cassettes on topics like "How To Get Free Time On Radio And T.V. And Use It To Get Your Prospects To Buy What You're Selling" and "How To Create Marketing Documents That Get Your Prospects To Buy What You're Selling... NOW!" Books In Motion of Spokane, WA has produced Jeffrey's books MONEY MAKING MARKETING and CASH COPY in multi-cassette albums. Jeffrey is also publisher of "Jeffrey Lant's Sales & Marketing SuccessDek," a card-deck reaching 100,000 sales and marketing executives 10 times a year. With the publication of this card-deck, Jeffrey revolutionized this advertising specialty by offering by far the lowest prices in the nation!

Jeffrey, his work, and innovative ideas are also featured in many books including *What Color Is Your Parachute?*, *The Harvard Guide To Careers*, *1001 Ways To Market Your Books*, *Create Your Own Career Opportunities*, *How To Succeed As An Independent Consultant*, *The Complete Guide To Self Publishing*, *Maverick: Succeeding As A Free-Lance Entrepreneur*, *Playing Hardball With Soft Skills*, *Cash In On Today's Educational Market*, *Win Them Over: A Survival Guide For Corporate Consultant Relations Programs*, *Marketing To The Fortune 500*, *How To Get Happily Published*, *Homemade Money*, *The Consultant's Guide to Winning Clients*, *The Do-It-Yourself Publicity Kit*, *Writing For Fun And Money*, *How To Get The Prospects You Need So That You Make At Least $100,000 Every Year Selling Real Estate!*, *How To Make Money Buying Pre-Foreclosure Properties Before They Hit The County Courthouse Steps*, *148 Great Ways To Make Money On The Side*, *Street Smart Marketing*, *How To Double Or Even Triple Your Sales*, *Information Marketing: How To Profit Selling Information In The 1990's*, *Book Publishing Resource Guide*, *Secrets Of A Freelance Writer Book II*, *The Guide To Selling Advertising Space*, *Mind Your Own Business*, *Pursuing The $10,000,000 Dream*, and many others. His credentials and achievements are also featured in over 18 different biographical guides from *Who's Who In Finance & Industry* to *The International Who's Who Of Intellectuals*.

His achievements have been recognized by many organizations, including the Boston and Cambridge City Councils; twice by the House of Representatives of the State of Massachusetts, by two Governors of Massachusetts, by the State of Texas, and by the cities of Charleston, South Carolina; Cape May, New Jersey; Virginia Beach, VA and Eureka, California. In 1987 he received special recognition from the Governor of Massachusetts upon the completion of the first five volumes of his "Get Ahead" Series.

Jeffrey is a graduate of the University of California, Santa Barbara (B.A. *summa cum laude* '69); Northeastern University, Boston (Certificate of Advanced Graduate Studies in Higher Education Administration, '76); and Harvard University (M.A.'70 and Ph.D.'75). He has never had a business course in his entire career!

Among Jeffrey's many official positions are: member, National Advisory Board, National Association of Independent Publishers and Editorial Advisory Board Member, *Limited Partnership Investment Review*.

Jeffrey is 43 years old and currently lives in Cambridge, Massachusetts, surrounded by mountains of paper, an underused exercise machine, and a computer and telephone which connect him to millions of people striving to build strong businesses of every kind. You can reach him at 50 Follen St., Suite 507, Cambridge, MA 02138 or by calling (617) 547-6372.

#C1

CASH COPY AUDIO CASSETTE AND BOOK PACKAGE. Get the complete CASH COPY package, including 480 page book and 18 hours of audio tape. Just $140. Save $12.95! If you expect to become a millionaire by selling products or services, get this package today. Years in the making, it tells you just what you need to do to get people to buy… NOW!

#B7

HOW TO MAKE A WHOLE LOT MORE THAN $1,000,000 WRITING, COMMISSIONING, PUBLISHING AND SELLING "HOW-TO" INFORMATION. People just love this book... and no wonder. It's the most complete ever written on how to make money from "how-to" information with profit-making books, booklets, audio cassettes & special reports. It's relentlessly detailed and tells you how to:

- create the information products people want to buy;
- produce the kinds of products you'll make money from for years;
- produce your products fast and accurately;
- make tens of thousands of extra dollars from end-of-product catalogs;
- save money — and avoid problems — by following Jeffrey's product production guidelines;
- turn your personal computer into the most effective customer service center ever imagined;
- get other people to produce products for you so you can make your million-dollar+ fortune faster;
- get all the free publicity you want... so you can reach your buyers on other people's money;
- master the essentials of direct response marketing so you bring your message to just the right people and get them to buy your products NOW;
- make big money through talk programs, bookstores, libraries, overseas rights, exhibits... and more. *Yes, you learn how to make thousands of dollars a day regularly!* Dozens of alternatives fully presented so you can start making money immediately.

552 pages. $38.50.

#B5 *New!*

Revised Second Edition!!! Just Published!!!

MONEY MAKING MARKETING: FINDING THE PEOPLE WHO NEED WHAT YOU'RE SELLING AND MAKING SURE THEY BUY IT. This classic book is packed with the information you need to establish and run a profitable marketing program. Jeffrey doesn't fool around. If you want to learn precisely what it takes to turn your marketing into money, here's the information you need. Get the details on how to:

- identify the right people for the product/service you're selling;
- position yourself so you outsell your competitors;
- formulate just the right message that stimulates immediate action;
- create the right kinds of marketing documents;
- learn how often to hit your prospects with your message;
- set up and run a client-centered business.

You learn about telemarketing, direct response marketing, co-op marketing, free publicity, paid ads... and much, much more. Jeffrey is known as one of America's most unrelenting marketers. Here he tells you exactly what you've got to do to sell more of your products and services. 285 pages. $38.50

#T2

MONEY MAKING MARKETING AUDIO CASSETTE PROGRAM. It's all here — 18 hours of fast-moving, profit-making information. Now, sit in your car or relax at home, and let Jeffrey share his money-making marketing secrets with you. This is the complete book on tape... perfect for the "scrap" time you want to put to good use. These tapes are packed with information and impart, as only an enthusiastic human voice can do, just, the right note of "up and at 'em" that we all need to get started. Just $125

1.5 million people monthly now read Jeffrey's Sure-Fire Business Success Columns in over 100 publications and electronic databases! Another million a week hear him on The Business Radio Network!

#C2

MONEY MAKING MARKETING AUDIO CASSETTE AND BOOK SPECIAL OFFER. Now get both the 285-page MONEY MAKING MARKETING book and 18 hours of audio cassettes for the very special price of just $144.95. You save over $20... and get just what you need to implement the profit-making marketing program you've been looking for.

#B2

THE UNABASHED SELF-PROMOTER'S GUIDE: WHAT EVERY MAN, WOMAN, CHILD AND ORGANIZATION IN AMERICA NEEDS TO KNOW ABOUT GETTING AHEAD BY EXPLOITING THE MEDIA. A recent review said this may be "the most important single book on promotion ever written." We agree! Stop paying money for paid ads. Find out how to get as much free publicity as you can, whenever you need it. This book is exhaustive. You'll use it for the rest of your business career whatever you're selling: product, service, organization or idea. Step-by-step guidelines for getting you and what you're promoting continuing media attention. *The Levison Letter* calls this "The best business book ever written." If you're really interested in getting free media time and space, we think you'll agree. 366 pages. $34

#B3

MONEY TALKS: THE COMPLETE GUIDE TO CREATING A PROFITABLE WORKSHOP OR SEMINAR IN ANY FIELD. Brand new edition!!! Just out!!! If you want to make money with talk programs of any kind, find out how to use these programs to get clients and publicity, then you need the new Second Revised Edition of this well-known book. It's got everything you need to start making money — really big money — on the talk circuit with workshops, lectures, seminars — every kind of talk program. Find out how to get sponsors — or sponsor programs yourself; make money from "back of the room" sales, even when you don't have a product. And when you do. **The Most Complete Book Ever Written On This Subject.** Yes, you can follow these guidelines to make up to $25,000 or even $30,000 *a day!* 308 pages. $34

#C4

Combined offer for the future information millionaire...
Four fast-paced, densely detailed books by Jeffrey give you a fast start towards becoming a million dollar+ producer & seller of books, booklets, audio cassettes and Special Reports. Whatever your field! Get **HOW TO MAKE A HOW LOT MORE THAN $1,000,000 WRITING, COMMISSIONING, PUBLISHING AND SELLING "HOW-TO" INFORMATION; CASH COPY; THE UNABASHED SELF-PROMOTER'S GUIDE** and **MONEY TALKS.** Just $115. You save $19.45!

#C6

Combined offer for the people who want to sell more of their products and services faster...
Now benefit from Jeffrey's step-by-step marketing advice and learn how to sell more of your products and services for the least possible cost. Get a deal on **THE UNABASHED SELF-PROMOTER'S GUIDE, MONEY MAKING MARKETING** and **CASH COPY**. $80 for all three. You save $20.45.

#B1

THE CONSULTANT'S KIT: ESTABLISHING AND OPERATING YOUR SUCCESSFUL CONSULTING BUSINESS. The one book specifically recommended by the U.S. Small Business Administration to new and aspiring consultants in *any* field tells you exactly what you need to know to make a success of your new consulting business. If you're thinking about consulting or have been in business under a year, this is the resource you need. It's the only resource on consulting recommended by *What Color Is Your Parachute*? (the best-selling career guide of all time) because it provides you with exactly what you need to launch a profitable consulting business. 203 pages $34

ACT NOW! THE PRICE OF *THE CONSULTANT'S KIT* IS GOING UP SOON!!!

#B4

TRICKS OF THE TRADE: THE COMPLETE GUIDE TO SUCCEEDING IN THE ADVICE BUSINESS. This book is designed for people who will not be content until they make *at least* $100,000 every year from their consulting practice. If you follow the guidelines in this book, you will! Here's where you get complete details on the Mobile-Mini Conglomerate: 10 steps that you'll use to get the utmost benefit from your problem-solving information. Tells you how to get clients, how to work with clients, how to get the results you want, how to build long-term relationships, even how to work with Flatworms, people who say they want results, but really want to obstruct. It's all here. Herman Holtz, himself a master of the consulting genre, said this may be the most important book ever written on consulting. 315 pages $34

#C5

Combined offer for the success-minded consultant...

Want to succeed as a part-time or full-time consultant in any field? Get a deal on **THE CONSULTANT'S KIT** and **TRICKS OF THE TRADE**. $55 for the pair. Save $13.

"I have just begun to use your books. Your useful information has advanced my learning curve (so far) by at least a year. And I've just scratched the surface! It's nice to have good, practical advice and not have to re-invent the wheel."
Pamela Murray, Kirkland, WA

#C7

... when you want to master all the master's profit-making techniques.

Get all seven books in Jeffrey's "Get Ahead" Series, including **CASH COPY, THE CONSULTANT'S KIT, THE UNABASHED SELF-PROMOTER'S GUIDE, MONEY TALKS, TRICKS OF THE TRADE, MONEY MAKING MARKETING** and **HOW TO MAKE A WHOLE LOT MORE THAN $1,000,000 WRITING, COMMISSIONING, PUBLISHING AND SELLING "HOW-TO" INFORMATION.** Well over 2,000 pages of detailed step-by-step guidelines on achieving success by creating and selling products and services. No other specialist — anywhere — has ever written such complete instructions on what it takes to make money — lots of money. We'll be flabbergasted if you don't make back the cost of this package many hundreds of time. Get all seven for just $200. Save $40.95! You automatically qualify for a free 60-minute cassette with this order!!!

The free "First Step Review" diskette you get by ordering $25 or more from this catalog by 02/01/92 is a user-friendly program designed for IBM-PC and compatible computers. Developed by the Small Business Administration and the National Business Association, it's provided to you compliments of the NBA. With it, you'll be able to figure out if you quality for an SBA-guaranteed loan before you get to the bank!!! Each diskette comes with details about how the National Business Association can help you. Pay real close attention.

60 Money-Making Minutes With Jeffrey (on tape)

#T3

HOW TO GET FREE TIME ON RADIO AND T.V. AND USE IT TO GET YOUR PROSPECTS TO BUY WHAT YOU'RE SELLING. Listen as Jeffrey gives you the secrets of getting valuable free time on radio and television so you can sell your products and services without spending any of your money. Getting on *just one* program could return your investment dozens of times! $14

#T4

HOW TO CREATE MARKETING DOCUMENTS THAT GET YOUR PROSPECTS TO BUY WHAT YOU'RE SELLING ... NOW! Since you spend thousands of dollars on your marketing documents, don't you think you should know what will get people to respond to them faster ... to buy what you're selling **NOW**? Here's just what you need to know. $14

#T5

ESSENTIALS OF MONEY MAKING MARKETING: WHAT YOU'VE REALLY GOT TO DO TO SELL YOUR PRODUCTS AND SERVICES, EVERY DAY! Jeffrey shares his secrets of successful marketing, what you've got to do, when and how you've got to do it to sell your products and services. $14.

#C3

ALL THREE OF JEFFREY'S 60 MINUTE AUDIO CASSETTES. Get all three of Jeffrey's 60 minute audio-cassettes for just $35. Thousands of these have been sold. Why? Because you get three hours of precise profit-making consultation for a ridiculously low price. Just $35. REMINDER: If your order totals at least $150, you get any one of these cassettes absolutely free!

Interested in reaching 200,000 people with your product? I'm mulling over adding extra pages to this catalog and selling them very near cost price. On these pages, orders would go directly to you. If you've got products or services that you'd like to reach a national audience for absolute rock-bottom price, call me immediately.

Special Reports

We've already sold tens of thousands of these quick and dirty profit-making reports (#R1 – #R62). They're densely written five-page, single-spaced computer print-outs personalized with your name so you know you're supposed to follow the good-for-you directions. Don't expect fancy packaging. Just solid, up-to-date information you can use right now. Each report is packed with use-it-now details so you can achieve what the title promises. No one else in the country offers this kind of instantly available, eminently practical information in this form or gets them to you this fast. Stock up on 'em. Just 5 bucks each, 3 for $12.

All prices include shipping!

#R1

THE SECRET TO BECOMING A MILLIONAIRE SELLING "HOW-TO" INFORMATION: 10 STEPS FOR CREATING, COMMISSIONING, PUBLISHING AND SELLING PROBLEM-SOLVING BOOKS, BOOKLETS, SPECIAL REPORTS AND AUDIO CASSETTES. In honor of his new book **HOW TO MAKE A WHOLE LOT MORE THAN $1,000,000 WRITING, COMMISSIONING, PUBLISHING AND SELLING "HOW-TO" INFORMATION,** Jeffrey lays down the rules for profitably selling problem-solving information. $5

#R2

SIX STEPS TO MORE SUCCESSFUL NEWSLETTERS. If you're putting any money into producing either a free or subscription newsletter... or even thinking about it... don't do *anything* until you get Roger Parker's steps for designing the product so it accomplishes your objectives. Roger's one smart cookie, and he knows what it takes to get people to pay attention to your newsletter. Here he shares this vital information with you. $5

#R3

WHICH 2% WILL YOUR AUDIENCE SIT STILL FOR? In honor of the publication of her new book of the same title, Jeffrey interviews author Marian Woodall on how to find the focus that is appropriate for each audience. Too many speakers try to cram everything they know into their talk... and end up alienating their audience. Not you. Here you learn exactly what you've got to do to give the right talk to the people you're speaking to. $5

#R4

HOW TO ELIMINATE JOB STRESS AND INCREASE PROFITS AND PRODUCTIVITY THROUGH STRESS MANAGEMENT. Jeffrey interviews author Dr. Andrew Goliszek about what you can do to cut stress in the office. Stress doesn't just debilitate and even kill you... it cuts your profits! Here's what you can do to help yourself and break your stress habit. $5

#R5

MEGATRAITS: 12 TRAITS OF SUCCESSFUL PEOPLE. Jeffrey interviews Doris Lee McCoy, author of a new book based on interviews with several hundred successful people, and identifies the crucial traits, the "megatraits", they possess in common that helped get them where they are. $5

#R6

HOW TO MAKE YOUR PR MAKE MONEY. For most businesses, public relations is a useless activity that is not tied to the profit picture. Now Jeffrey tells you how to turn your expensive public relations into a money-making activity that will sell your products and services faster. $5

#R7

(Note: if you're a not-for-profit organization, here's the non-profit version of the above report.) $5

#R8

OVERWORKED ENTREPRENEURS' GUIDE TO LUXURIOUS CRUISE DISCOUNTS. Jeffrey interviews Captain Bill Miller, author of the superb new book *Insider's Guide To Cruise Discounts,* and provides you with specific information on how you can take some of the world's best and most luxurious cruises for ridiculously low rates. $5

#R9

WHAT EVERY INVENTOR ABSOLUTELY MUST DO BEFORE CONTACTING ANY MANUFACTURER. Jeffrey interviews consultant Arnold Winkelman, author of the new book *The Inventor's Guide To Marketing,* about precisely what you've got to do before you show any manufacturer your creation so that your rights are fully protected. Must reading if you're an inventor! $5

"I own two of your books — CASH COPY and MONEY MAKING MARKETING. These books are a must for everyone in the business world. My 'work copies' are not for sale!"
Walter Metzger, Grand Rapids, MI

#R10

EIGHT SELF-DEFEATING BEHAVIORS PREVENTING YOU FROM BECOMING THE MILLIONAIRE YOU *SAY* YOU WANT TO BE... AND WHAT TO DO ABOUT THEM! Here Jeffrey lays out eight significant behaviors making it difficult, if not impossible, for people to become millionaires and tells them just what to do to overcome them. If you keep talking about wanting to be a millionaire but just can't seem to get started... or keep failing along the way... these behaviors are probably bedevilling you. Learn what they are... and how to get rid of them. $5

#R11

EVERYTHING YOU NEED TO KNOW TO PREPARE YOUR OWN WILL — WITHOUT THE EXPENSE OF A LAWYER! Eight out of ten people in America die without a will, throwing their accumulated possessions and savings into the hands of the court system which then allocates what's available. To stop this idiocy, Jeffrey interviews Attorney Daniel Sitarz, author of the new book *Prepare Your Own Will And Testament — Without A Lawyer.* Here's exactly what you need to do to prepare your own legal will without a lawyer, securing your estate and saving the lawyer's fees. $5

#R12

WHY MOST CONSULTANTS CAN NEVER MAKE AT LEAST $100,000 A YEAR... AND WHAT TO DO SO YOU WILL. Jeffrey shows you why most consultants fail to make at least $100,000 a year... and provides specific steps to follow so you will. $5

"I give lectures and do programs to people beginning their own businesses and would like to make your materials available to them since I think they are *outstanding*!"
Martha Snee,
Wood-Ridge, NJ

#R13

HOW TO GET FREE AND LOW-COST SOFTWARE FOR YOUR IBM AND IBM-COMPATIBLE COMPUTER. Jeffrey interviews John Gliedman, author of the new book *Tips And Techniques for Using Low-Cost And Public Domain Software*, on how to get your hands on some of the stupendous amount of free and low-cost software currently available for IBM and IBM-compatible personal computers. Gliedman provides the names, addresses and phone numbers of just where to go to save big money on your software and techniques on how to use it effectively. $5

#R14

HOW TO CREATE CLASSIFIED AND SMALL SPACE ADS THAT GET YOUR PROSPECTS TO RESPOND... AND WHAT TO DO WHEN THEY DO! Jeffrey gives you the low-down on how to create classified and small space ads that get people to respond... and how to create an effective, profit-making program so you can turn your new prospects into buyers... fast! $5

"I've really enjoyed HOW TO MAKE A WHOLE LOT MORE THAN $1,000,000 WRITING, COMMISSIONING, PUBLISHING AND SELLING 'HOW-TO' INFORMATION, as I did CASH COPY. It's really amazing what passes for marketing/advertising once one adopts the 'think like a client' Lant viewpoint ... What I really wonder is how on earth you get everything done that you apparently do get done. Amazing."
Jim Gibson, Atlanta, GA

#R15

SETTING AND GETTING YOUR FEE. Jeffrey interviews author Kate Kelly upon the occasion of a new edition being published of her well-known book *How To Set Your Fees And Get Them.* People selling a service either run the risk of pricing themselves too low (and working for too little) or too high... and losing the business. Kate tells you just what you need to do so you price your services just right... for fast sale and maximum return. $5

#R16

HOW TO MAKE MONEY BUYING PRE-FORECLOSURE PROPERTIES BEFORE THEY HIT THE COURTHOUSE STEPS. Jeffrey interviews property investment advisor Tom Lucier, author of the new book *How To Make Money Buying Pre-Foreclosure Properties Before They Hit The Courthouse Steps,* on just what it takes to make big money in pre-foreclosure properties. New workshops have sprung up recently charging as much as $5000 for a week-end providing this kind of advice. Why pay 5G's when specialist Tom Lucier provides the detailed steps right here? $5

#R17

HOW TO DEVELOP AND USE A CLIENT-CENTERED QUESTIONNAIRE THAT GETS YOUR PROSPECTS TO TELL YOU WHAT THEY WANT... SO YOU CAN SELL IT TO THEM. In this report, Jeffrey helps people who hate making cold calls... and can't figure out how to get their prospects to tell them what they want. If you can solve this problem, you can sell *any* product or service. Here are the guidelines you need to create this unique client-centered prospecting questionnaire... and how to use it. When you do, your prospects start telling you precisely what they want... all you have to do is give it to them. $5

#R18

HOW TO DO "HOW-TO" (BOOKLETS AND BOOKS, THAT IS). Here Jeffrey tells you exactly how to produce a how-to booklet or book that really tells your readers how to do what your title promises. Most how-to products are dismal failures, because they don't provide the details your readers need to achieve what they want. Don't let this happen to you. Learn how to create a truly useful how-to. $5

#R19

HOW TO MAKE OVER $100,000 *EVERY* YEAR WITH YOUR OWN CATALOG SELLING PROBLEM-SOLVING INFORMATION PRODUCTS. Most people in mail order try to make a big kill from a single problem-solving information product... or just a few. Here Jeffrey shows you why that's futile... and how to go about establishing a client-centered catalog selling how-to information products that will make you at least $100,000 every year... and maybe a whole lot more. $5

"After reading (maybe devouring is a better description) CASH COPY, I reviewed our marketing communications and was appalled at how ego-centric and, hence, ineffective they were. As a result of the insights and easy-to-understand techniques in CASH COPY, we're improving our copy and strengthening our messages considerably! My sincere thanks for a great work!"
William Doerr, Newington, CT

#R20

HOW TO USE JOB ADS TO LAND THE JOB YOU *REALLY* WANT. If you've ever tried to get a job using classified job ads you know how time consuming and frustrating it is. Here Jeffrey interviews jobs-finding specialist Kenton Elderkin, author of the new book *How To Get Interviews From Job Ads: Where To Look, What To Select, Who To Write, What To Say, When To Follow-Up, How To Save Time.* With these techniques answering job ads *can* lead to the interviews you need... and the good job you want. $5

#R21

YOUR WORST FEARS REALIZED, OR WHAT TO DO WHEN THE CORPORATION OR FOUNDATION DECLINES YOUR PROPOSAL. The competition for corporate and foundation dollars for non-profit organizations has never been greater... and will get worse. You can count on getting turned down, often. What you do next determines whether your organization will ever get the money it needs from these sources. Here are Jeffrey's guidelines for turning a no into a yes, for doing what it takes to build a lucrative relationship with a funding source that has just turned you down. Since this will happen to you (if it isn't happening already), prepare for it now. $5

#R22

IT ISN'T JUST SAYING THE RIGHT THING THAT MAKES A SUCCESSFUL PRESENTATION... OR WHAT YOU'VE REALLY GOT TO DO TO CONNECT WITH YOUR AUDIENCE AND PERSUADE THEM TO LISTEN TO YOU. This isn't a report about speech content... it's a report about how to deal with your audience so they like you and want to listen to what you have to say. Verbal presentations aren't just about imparting information; they're about persuading people to do things. Here's what you've got to do to achieve this crucial objective. $5

#R23

HOW TO CREATE A BROCHURE AND COVER LETTER YOUR PROSPECTS WILL RESPOND TO... NOW! In honor of the new second printing of his book CASH COPY: HOW TO OFFER YOUR PRODUCTS AND SERVICES SO YOUR PROSPECTS BUY THEM... NOW!, Jeffrey tells you how to solve one of the most basic marketing problems of any business: what it takes to create a brochure and cover letter that gets people to respond, instead of being tossed. $5

#R24

HOW TO RAISE MONEY FOR YOUR NON-PROFIT ORGANIZATION WITH AN ANNUAL PHON-A-THON. Jeffrey tells you what you've got to do to use telemarketing to raise money for your non-profit organization... when you've got to work with community volunteers and can't afford professional help. $5

#R25

HOW TO BRING ORDER TO DESK CHAOS, OR ESSENTIALS OF ORGANIZING YOURSELF. Jeffrey talks to organizational specialist Kate Kelly, author (along with Ronni Eisenberg) of the best-selling book ORGANIZE YOURSELF!, about what you've got to do to control clutter and get all those papers in your business life under control. $5

#R26

HOW TO AVOID DESKTOP DISAPPOINTMENT, OR WHAT YOU'VE *REALLY* GOT TO KNOW TO MAKE DESKTOP PUBLISHING WORK FOR YOU. Jeffrey interviews desktop design specialist Roger Parker, author of *Looking Good In Print,* on what to do to avoid the pitfalls of desktop publishing and use design to create compelling marketing communications. $5

#R27

HOW TO USE HUMOR TO MAKE YOUR NEXT BUSINESS SPEECH A SUCCESS. Jeffrey teams up with communications specialist Michael Iapoce to give you tips on how to use humor to make your business presentations successful. The information provided here won't turn you into a Las Vegas comic, but it *will* help you break down your audience's barriers, get them to like you, and help you make more sales faster. And isn't that just what you want? $5

"I find real value in the information you offer! In fact, I recommend your books and tapes to people I meet. Anyone who is open minded to what really works. And believe me, a lot of 'professionals' don't want to know. They want to continue to pump out the same garbage ... Jeffrey, you're bold, you're bright, you're honest. You're genuine. Thank you for sharing yourself, your talents. I'll tell a lot of people about you. You deserve prosperity in abundance." Ronald Ball, CalComp, A Lockheed Co., Anaheim, CA

WE NEVER CLOSE!!! Place your order 24 hours a day 365 days a year by calling (617) 547-6372 (have your VISA or MC — and expiration date — handy). Or send it to Jeffrey Lant Associates, Inc., 50 Follen St., #507, Cambridge, MA 02138.

#R28

HOW TO CREATE A MARKETING PLAN THAT SELLS YOUR SERVICE... WITHOUT COSTING YOU ALL YOUR MONEY. Most people selling a service are "winging it" with predictable results: their marketing is episodic, spasmodic... unproductive. Jeffrey tells you how to create a marketing plan that will sell a service for the least possible cost and greatest results. $5

#R29

TELESELLING: HOW TO GET THROUGH THE SCREEN THAT'S KEEPING YOU FROM YOUR PROSPECT. Jeffrey talks to Art Sobczak, editor of *Telephone Selling Report,* on what you've got to do to get through your prospect's screens... switchboard operators, secretaries... anybody who stands between you and your next sale. $5

#R30

HOW TO OPEN A TELEPHONE SALES CALL WITH EITHER A PROSPECT OR A CUSTOMER... SO YOU GET THE BUSINESS. Jeffrey again talks to Art Sobczak, editor of *Telephone Selling Report,* on what to say during those crucial opening moments with a telephone prospect... and how to build profitable relationships by phone with existing customers. $5

#R31

HOW TO CREATE A PROPOSAL THAT A CORPORATION OR FOUNDATION WILL FUND. Jeffrey tells you and your non-profit organization what it takes to create a proposal that a corporate or foundation funding source will give money to support. $5

#R32

WHAT YOU HAVE TO DO TO SELL YOUR PRODUCTS AND SERVICES THROUGH A FREE CLIENT NEWSLETTER. Jeffrey tells you how to produce free client newsletters that get your prospects to buy your products and services. $5

#R33

HOW TO CREATE INEXPENSIVE, EFFECTIVE AUDIO CASSETTES TO GET MORE OF YOUR PROSPECTS TO RESPOND FASTER... AND MAKE EXTRA MONEY, TOO. Jeffrey tells you how to create inexpensive 60-minute audio cassettes in your home or office that you can use to induce more and faster sales... and sell profitably, too. $5

#R34

HOW TO PROFIT BY INVESTING IN USED AND BRUISED HOUSES. Jeffrey gets step-by-step advice from Florida author and investor Thomas Lucier on how to make money in real estate through affordable used and bruised houses, one of today's smart investments for people with a moderate amount to spend. $5

> ***"As a young entrepreneur, I have really enjoyed your insightful reports in the Working from Home Forum in CompuServe. You don't know how much your information has helped me in a variety of ways."***
>
> Tim Tucker, Micanopy, FL

#R35

HOW TO USE WORKSHOPS AND OTHER TALK PROGRAMS TO GET CLIENTS. In honor of the publication of the new Second Edition of his well-known book MONEY TALKS: HOW TO CREATE A PROFITABLE WORKSHOP OR SEMINAR IN ANY FIELD, Jeffrey tells you how to use lectures and talk programs to get clients. $5

#R36

THINKING ON YOUR FEET, ANSWERING QUESTIONS WELL WHETHER YOU KNOW THE ANSWER — OR NOT. People who can't deal effectively with questions present a poor self-image and can harm a company. Here Jeffrey interviews Marian Woodall, author of a popular book on the subject, about how people can master the crucial "thinking on your feet" strategies. $5

#R37

HOW TO GET FREE TIME ON RADIO AND T.V. AND USE IT TO GET YOUR PROSPECTS TO BUY WHAT YOU'RE SELLING. Jeffrey gives you the secrets of getting valuable free time on radio and television so you can sell your products and services without spending any of your money. $5

#R38

WHY YOU NEED SPECIAL REPORTS: HOW TO WRITE THEM, USE THEM TO GET PEOPLE TO BUY WHAT YOU'RE SELLING NOW, TO PUBLICIZE YOUR BUSINESS, AND MAKE MONEY! The secret to successful marketing is making people take action NOW to get what you're selling. Jeffrey shows you how to create inexpensive but powerful Special Reports and how to turn them into compelling marketing tools that get your prospects to respond NOW, and that you can also sell profitably. $5

#R39

COPY FLAWS THAT DOOM YOUR EXPENSIVE MARKETING DOCUMENTS TO LINE BIRDCAGES IN SAINT LOUIS. Jeffrey tells you just what you need to know to write marketing copy that gets people to buy. Key rules of profit-making copy. $5

#R40

YOUR GRAND OPENING: HOW TO START YOUR MARKETING DOCUMENTS SO PEOPLE *BUY* WHAT YOU'RE SELLING. If your marketing documents don't draw people in immediately, you — and your next sale — are lost. Jeffrey tells you precisely what to do to begin documents so your prospects read what you

F#11

Jeffrey's New National Copywriting Center

You're regularly producing ads, cover letters, flyers, brochures, annual reports, proposals, business cards ... dozens of things costing thousands of dollars. They're all designed to get you business. Sadly, most of what you write is trashed immediately by your prospects. Now you can stop this idiocy by improving the drawing power of what you're producing ... thanks to our new National Copywriting Center. You get what you want from our expert copywriters ... people trained in the seductive arts and hard-nosed science of motivating your prospects to take immediate action. Call (617) 547-6372 now or write for absolutely free details on how we can help. Don' t keep wasting your time and money producing marketing documents that just don't work. (And don't forget, my book CASH COPY contains just what you need to write the kind of copy that gets people to buy NOW!)

have to say — and buy what you have to sell. $5

#R41

COMPUTER-ASSISTED MARKETING: HOW TO INCREASE YOUR PRODUCTIVITY AND MAKE EVERY PROSPECT AND CUSTOMER FEEL YOU'RE DELIVERING *EXACTLY* WHAT HE WANTS. People have computers but aren't using them effectively. Now learn to turn the computer into your best marketing tool. You'll read things here you've never seen before and increase your marketing productivity astonishingly. $5

#R42

MONEY MAKING MAIL, OR HOW TO AVOID THE TEN BIGGEST MAIL ORDER MISTAKES. Every day I get deluged with mail order offers that make me weep for the trees that have died. What rubbish! There are rules to succeed in mail order. Here's what you should avoid — and what you should do. $5

#R43

HOW TO CREATE AND USE OFFERS YOUR PROSPECTS FIND IRRESISTIBLE. The trick to marketing is to create and sell offers — not products and services. Here's what you need to know about offers, how to create them and use them so that your prospects will buy. $5

#R44

KNOWING WHAT TO DO WHEN PEOPLE OWE YOU MONEY, OR HOW TO GET PAYMENT IN FULL. Don't give way to the rage and frustration of being owed money by deadbeats. Get what you're owed. Here's what you need to do in practical detail. $5

#R45

HOW AUTHORS AND THEIR PUBLISHERS MUST WORK TOGETHER TO SELL MORE BOOKS. Follow these precise steps to construct a profitable author-publisher partnership, so each of you makes money from the book. $5

#R46

YOUR IRA: WHY YOU *STILL* NEED IT, WHAT YOU NEED TO KNOW ABOUT INVESTING IT. If you've lost interest in the IRA, think again. Tax-free compounding of earning's no joke, and millions can still take their contribution off their taxes. Here's the low-down. (By the way, last year IRA contributions were substantially up. This report no doubt helped!) $5

#R47

TELESMARTS: EFFECTIVELY USING TELEMARKETING TO SELL YOUR PRODUCTS AND SERVICES. Most people are hideously ill-equipped to use the phone to sell anything. Here's the basics (and some advanced tips, too) on how you can turn the phone into a profitable business tool. Have I reached out and touched you? $5

#R48

HOW TO OVERCOME SALES OBJECTIONS, INCLUDING THE BIGGEST ONE OF ALL: "YOUR PRICE IS TOO HIGH!" If you're in sales (and if you're reading this, you are), you've got to learn how to deal with objections. Here's what you need to know so that you can. $5

#R49

HOW TO STOP BEING THE LOWLY ORDER-TAKER, BECOME THE CONSUMMATE MARKETER, AND GET MORE SALES FROM NEW BUYERS. The dumb marketer simply sells a prospect what that prospect wants to buy. The expert marketer learns the prospect's problem and persuades him to take an upgraded solution. Here's how to do that. $5

#R50

TESTIMONIALS FOR YOUR PRODUCT OR SERVICE: WHY YOU NEED THEM, HOW TO GET THEM, HOW TO USE THEM. If you aren't using testimonials now, you are missing a prime marketing device. If you are, make sure you're doing it right! $5

#R51

UNDERSTANDING AND PROFITING FROM THE RULE OF SEVEN:

"Your book MONEY MAKING MARKETING is awesome! After getting your book from the library and reading the first 3 pages I knew I had found exactly what I had been looking for for the past two years. Very seldom do I ever write to an author to express my gratitude for the product they have produced, but you deserve such a letter."

Dan Dubé, Puyallup, WA

CONNECTING WITH YOUR BUYERS AND CONNECTING WITH THEM AGAIN UNTIL THEY BUY WHAT YOU'RE SELLING. Most marketing gambits don't work. In part this is because you don't hit your prospects sufficiently often to interest them in what you're selling. Now learn how you can. The Rule of Seven is the prime rule of marketing. $5

#R52

MARKETING YOUR BOOK BEFORE IT'S PUBLISHED. Stupid authors and publishers wait to begin marketing and making money from their books until they are physically available. Don't you be one of them. Follow the detailed guidelines in this report and make money long before your book is even printed. $5

#R53

WHAT TO DO WHEN YOUR PROSPECT SAYS NO. We all get turned down. Now what? Tears? Rage? No! Use Jeffrey's step-by-step guidelines to get the sale after all — or do what it takes to get the next one! $5

#R54

ESSENTIALS OF MONEY MAKING MARKETING. Successful marketing is the key to business success. Now learn precisely what you have to do to improve your marketing. Follow these steps; sell more. $5

#R55

WHY YOU NEED A BUSINESS PLAN, WHY YOU RESIST CREATING ONE. Makes a clear case for why you must have a business plan to succeed, how to overcome your resistance to creating one, and what should go in it. A must, particularly for new and struggling entrepreneurs. $5

"I've read CASH COPY through once (couldn't put it down, actually!) and am more than pleased with it. It will get many readings and will be used to make our marketing efforts 'cash copy'." Edward Lee, Honolulu, HI

Look what you get when you place your order from this catalog.

1) If your order is over $25, you get — absolutely free — "First Step Review", a new business software program (IBM compatible only, sorry) enabling you to find out if you can quality for an SBA-guaranteed loan before going to the bank to find out!

2) If your order is over $150, you get your choice of any one of three of Jeffrey's 60-minute cassettes (#T1,2,3) — plus the "First Step Review" software — absolutely free

3) If your order is over $225 you get any one of Jeffrey's "Get Ahead" books including CASH COPY, THE CONSULTANT'S KIT, TRICKS OF TH E TRADE, THE UNABASHED SELF-PROMOTER'S GUIDE, MONEY TALKS, HOW TO MAKE A WHOLE LOT MORE THAN $1,000,000 ..., or the new edition of MONEY MAKING MARKETING — plus the "First Step Review", and audio cassette!

#R56 *New!*

HOW TO GET THE LOWEST CARD-DECK ADVERTISING PRICES AND MAKE THE MOST MONEY FROM CARD-DECK ADVERTISING. Card-decks can get you maximum response for the least price. Now in honor of Jeffrey's new Sales & Marketing SuccessDek, you can learn the secrets of how to get the lowest prices and biggest response. $5

#R57 *New!*

TEN THINGS YOU CAN DO RIGHT NOW TO GET MORE MONEY FROM YOUR NEXT FUND RAISING LETTER. If you're running a non-profit organization and expect to raise money using fund-raising letters, read this report first. Jeffrey's been writing profit-making fund-raising letters for non-profits for over a decade. Here's what he's learned to make you more money. $5

#R58 *New!*

HOW TO GET THE MOST BENEFIT WHEN WORKING WITH CONSULTANTS: THE 10 BIGGEST MISTAKES YOU'RE NOT GOING TO MAKE. All too often organizations hiring consultants don't get their money's worth. This won't happen to you if you follow the guidelines in this sensible report. $5

#R59 *New!*

WHAT YOU THINK MAY BE A COPY PROBLEM MAY REALLY BE A STRATEGIC MARKETING PROBLEM ... HERE'S WHAT YOU CAN DO TO SOLVE IT. All too often what people think is a copy problem is actually a strategic marketing problem. Your marketing strategy has got to be right before you can create the most effective copy. For just $5 you learn how to create the strategy that gets people to buy what you're selling. (Then you can use CASH COPY to create the copy itself!)

#R60 *New!*

HOW TO HAVE AN EFFECTIVE MEETING, OR WHAT YOU'VE REALLY GOT TO DO TO STOP WASTING YOUR TIME AT NON-PRODUCTIVE BUSINESS GET-TOGETHERS. Before you waste another senseless minute in a pointless meeting (or, God forbid, chair such a meeting) get this report and learn how to structure meetings so you get what you want — the only reason for having a meeting in the first place. $5

#R61 *New!*

HOW TO TURN YOUR (PREVIOUSLY UNREAD) ANNUAL REPORT INTO AN ACTION

"Thanks for writing such excellent how-to guides on marketing and information products. Without your assistance, I wouldn't be nearly this close to achieving my goals." Dr. Michael Anderson, Albuquerque, NM

ORIENTED MARKETING DOCUMENT THAT GETS PEOPLE TO DO WHAT YOU WANT THEM TO DO! For most organizations — profit and not-for-profit — annual reports are a complete waste of time and money. Who reads them? But properly created annual reports can become powerful marketing documents that get you new business. Here's what you need to know about creating them. $5

#R62 *New!*

HOW TO GET YOUR CLIENTS TO GET BUSINESS FOR YOU. There are tricks for getting your existing (and past) customers to get new business for you. Here they are. When you have a customer you get not only current income but future business ... if you use these techniques. $5

Money-Making Resource For Non-Profit Organizations

#B8

DEVELOPMENT TODAY: A FUND RAISING GUIDE FOR NON-PROFIT ORGANIZATIONS. April 15, 1990 *Booklist,* the prestigious publication of the American Library Association, again recommended that every U.S. library get the new Revised 4th Edition of this book — just like they did the last edition. Why? Because it has just the information you need to raise capital, project & operating money for your non-profit organization from individuals, corporations and foundations. This classic book is now used by thousands of non-profits to raise the money they need. It covers everything you need to know to raise money as quickly as possible and, like all Jeffrey's books, is packed with a Samples Section containing ready-to-use documents, letters, log forms, prospect background information, *etc.* Money tight? Take this write-up to your local library and tell them about the *Booklist* article... if your library doesn't have the book, they'll get it and you can be the first to check it out! 282 pages $28.95.

Make Money Selling My Products

#F1

Dealers: if you're already selling my products, write when you want the new sales materials covering the CASH COPY cassettes, HOW TO MAKE A WHOLE LOT MORE THAN $1,000,000 ... and the new Revised 4th Edition of DEVELOPMENT TODAY. They're ready for you now! **Everybody else**: if you're not a dealer yet and want to make money from selling all my products, write and request the Free Dealer Information Kit.

Get Your Business Started The Right Way

#B9

You know you need a *written* business plan, and you know you don't have one. That's why you need **THE BUSINESS PLANNING GUIDE**. It's not just a book. It's your basic business tool and roadmap. Packed with forms, checklists and immediately usable examples, this will give you exactly what you need: a specific, written business plan. In about 130 pages, you'll get your MBA in small business management. Over 200,000 businesses already have. Now it's your turn. $21.45

Sell Your Service, Not Your Soul

#B70 *New!*

CONTRACTING YOUR SERVICES. Attorney Robert Davidson's new 256 page book gives you the crucial information you need for selling your services to others: what/who is an independent contractor; should you become one; the right form for your business; where to get financial backing; the marketing & business plans you need; the right kinds of insurance and how to get them; how to find customers and sell your service; how to create winning proposals; how to find the right lawyer; the IRS versus you; contracts ... and much, much more. Davidson knows becoming an independent contractor isn't the money-making ticket for everyone and knows how you can succeed when you take the plunge. Just $30

#B31

One of the most perplexing problems business people have is how much to charge for their services. Wonder no more. Kate Kelly tells you **HOW TO SET YOUR FEES AND GET THEM.** Her guidebook is filled with information and examples of how to charge the right rates for your services. $20.50

Important Insurance Information

#B53 *New!*

HEALTH INSURANCE MADE EASY. Author Sharon Stark subtitles this dandy 102 page guide "The step-

The very late, awfully rich John D. Rockefeller, Sr. used to hand out shiny new dimes to the needy as a charitable donation. Personally, I like giving out checks that generally run between $1000-$3000. And I'm waiting to give you one. All you do is recommend me to any corporation, professional or trade association, government body, or organization as a speaker. After they hire me to give a speech or other program, you get 10% of my fee and gross product sales that day. I'm now regularly dishing out checks this way — great big checks, not just dimes. If you'd like to make the easiest money of your life, call me for complete details at (617) 547-6372 and get a list of my topics. Your "work" is ridiculously easy. Tell a friend, meeting planner or program organizer about me. Tell me you've told them so I can follow up. And sit back and wait for your money. Special note for meeting planners: I'm hopping around North America at a furious pace giving programs. If you'd like me to be at your meeting, call me ASAP. Books, testimonials, audio & video cassettes available.

by-step guide to saving mo ney, saving time, choosing a health plan, submitting insurance claims properly, AND making sure your benefits benefit you." I agree! Get the low-down you need on claim forms, surgery, hospital charges, HMO's, PMO's, Medicare, Preadmission Review, Second Opinions, Deductibles, Preexisting Condition, Chiropractors and a whole lot more. Very, very cheap at just $17.95.

Down On Your Luck? Make Some!

#B54 *New!*

HOW LUCKY CAN YOU GET. I don't know about you but it infuriates me when I hear people talk about "luck". I believe you make your own luck ... and so does author Willis Munson. This deceptively simple little book (just 175 pages) tells you "How you can attract good luck by responding to everyday opportunities." The holidays are coming and you need to give this book to all the people in your life who feel "down on their luck." With this book — and a good swift kick in the pants from you — you'll turn their lives around. And if you're not so "lucky", get yourself a spare copy, too. Underpriced at $19.95.

> ***"Just finished reading CASH COPY. This publication should be Required Reading for all career realtors."***
> Charles Flannigan, Pensacola, FL

Computer Smarts

#B74

Okay, I hate the title of Norma Leone's **MOTHER'S GUIDE TO COMPUTERS,** but I love the book itself. If you're still a computerphobe — or know someone who is — or have children to teach about computers, you need this soothing and useful little book with all its information on learning how to use a computer ... and knowing how to buy the right computer for you. A perfect book whatever your age, and if the title embarrasses you, Big Guy, cover it in brown paper. Just get the book. Every time I've recommended this resource in one of my articles, I get a flood of orders from soon-to-be satisfied customers. You'll be the next. $7.95.

Don't Just Talk, Persuade

#B55 *New!*

SPEAKER'S & TOASTMASTER'S HANDBOOK. If you speak ... if you introduce speakers ... you need Herbert Prochnow's pile of 500 humorous stories, 500 epigrams & quips, 100 stories and comments, 292 humorous definitions, 190 statements on important subjects by great thinkers, 209 wise & witty proverbs, 160 unusual quotations from world leaders, etc. You'll be a lot smarter (and get better speaking reviews) if you send me $22.95 for this book.

#B71 *New!*

THE PRESENTATIONS KIT. Author Claudyne Wilder subtitles her new book "10 Steps for Selling Your Ideas", and if you use her sensible suggestions, you certainly will! This 294-page paperback has guidelines for defining your objectives; organizing your presentation; creating and using visuals; eye, voice and language tips; motivating your listeners; managing and overcoming objections; obtaining group agreement; negotiating and much more. If your profit is dependent on making successful presentations — like mine is — let Claudyne help you! $17.95

#B35

HOW TO WRITE AND GIVE A SPEECH. Joan Detz' book is the best short book I've ever seen on how to give effective speeches ... without falling apart. If you want to know what it really takes to give a good speech, read Detz. She knows. $12.

#B37

THINKING ON YOUR FEET: ANSWERING QUESTIONS WELL WHETHER YOU KNOW THE ANSWER OR NOT. This is exactly what you need if you know someone who can't 'think on their feet', can't answer questions appropriately, and is always embarrassing himself ... or your company. Or perhaps that's you! Either way, you need Marian Woodall's excellent little 100-page book. Stay poised and in control. And answer the question — the way you want it answered. Just $12.95.

> ***If you're ordering materials produced by multiple publishers, they will come in multiple packages. So don't call if you only get a partial shipment. The rest is on its way...***

Protecting Your Ideas & Inventions

#B56 *New!*

THE INVENTOR'S NOTEBOOK: HOW TO DEVELOP, PROTECT, & MARKET YOUR INVENTION. Robert Park's excellent 230-page book tells you inventors exactly what you need about creating the invention process, the options you've got for commercialization, how to create prototypes, calculating costs and selling price, intellectual property protection, how to evaluate a new product's feasibility, investment capital, manufacturing, marketing and much much more. Comes complete with a host of useful forms including invention disclosure, license & royalty agreement, business proposal, etc. This book will save you a lot of aggravation, time & money. Just $15.95.

#B66 *New!*

PATENTS, COPYRIGHTS & TRADEMARKS. If you're going to use any of these three forms, you need this useful 236 page paperback by Foster & Shook. Crammed with useful information about what's patentable, how to conduct a patent search, apply for a patent; what's copyrightable, your copyright rights; how to register your work; how to protect your trademark; frequently asked questions and their answers; myths, etc. Save yourself a bundle by sending me $22 for this exhaustive resource.

Printing Information

#B57 *New!*

DIRECTORY OF BOOK, CATALOG, AND MAGAZINE PRINTERS. Author John Kremer is an astonishing resource. Here he gives you the low-down on 1000 printers of annual reports, books, catalogs, magazines

Could you use an extra $2 million this year? I'm now regularly passing on suggestions to U.S. and Canadian infomercial producers as we continue our search for programs to be played on cable t.v. stations in both countries. We're looking for projects in all fields, including (but not limited to) health, beauty, money making, business opportunities, better living, travel, etc. If you've got a product with broad audience appeal that can be sold through such a program and want to make up to $2,000,000 in one year, send me a long self-addressed stamped envelope (LSAE) and get the details. By the way, you aren't asked for one dime to develop and promote these programs. The producers put up all the capital. But you've got to have the product!!!

and other bound publications. Gives you details on their main focus, print runs, sizes, bindings, equipment, sales, employees, turn-around time, customers, terms, user comments. etc. Even includes a helpful section on how to save money on your printing. Kremer's books are always good value. This one is no exception. $18.

#B20

LOOKING GOOD IN PRINT: A GUIDE TO BASIC DESIGN FOR DESKTOP PUBLISHING. After you've mastered my book CASH COPY (so you've got the right *content* to attract buyers), you need Roger Parker's ultra-intelligent book on desktop publishing design. Use it to turn your spiffy copy into compelling newsletters, ads, brochures, manuals, letters ... and all the rest of your marketing materials. I love this book ... and your new buyers will be glad you used it! 221 pages $27

#B72

DESKTOP PUBLISHING SOURCE: FONTS AND CLIP-ART. Okay, Macintosh users, here's something especially for you. It's Jami Lynne Borman's new 395 page paperback chock full of fonts & clip-art compatible with Adobe Illustrator; Microscoft Word; PageMaker; Quark Express; DesignStudio and Ventura Publisher, among others. Borman knows how you can improve the look of everything you produce on your Macintosh and her book is crammed with the fonts & clip-art you need. Recommended at $28.95.

How To Make Money In Distressed Property

#B58 *New!*

THE SMART INVESTOR'S GUIDE TO DISTRESSED PROPERTY. Distressed property specialist Tom Lucier strikes again with this great 192 page paperwork he rightly calls "The Complete Guide To Finding, Researching, Negotiating, Optioning, Buying, Fixing, And Selling Distressed Property." Get the details you need on DVA, foreclosures, HUD, U.S. Marshall's Sale, Pre-foreclosures, RTC, Probate, Tax Sales, bankruptcy, GSA, FHA, REO's, IRS and eminent domain. The way to make money in real estate these days is to invest in distressed property. Tom knows how. He's the leading expert in this field. Take advantage of what he knows to make big bucks. An investment at $32.95.

Getting a Merchant MC/VISA Account

#B10 New Edition!

STRATEGIES FOR GETTING CHARGE CARD MERCHANT STATUS AT YOUR BANK (EVEN IF YOU'RE A MAIL ORDER DEALER). This new 49-page booklet tells you how and where to get a Merchant MC/VISA account and how to handle your credit card sales. Particularly mail order merchants (who know just how difficult it is to get MC/VISA status these days) will want to get this very useful booklet. I referred one friend to it who had had incredible difficulty in getting such an account. By following the steps in this booklet, he had one in just five days. Cheap at $20.95.

Musts For Your Efficient Office

Revised & Better Than Ever!!!

#B59

THE OFFICE MANAGEMENT MANUAL. Look, if you've got a secretary in your office, you need Anne Morton's "guide for secretaries, administrative assistants, and other office professionals." I can't say enough good things about this 312-page paperback. So useful with details on so many important office activities. Plain, simple, sensible suggestions on the correct use of all office machines, meeting planning, travel, routine correspondence, the telephone, production and editing of all materials, etc. If you've got office help, help them with this! $13.95

#B21

OFFICE PURCHASING GUIDE. Tod Snodgrass' handy little book tells you how to buy better, easier, and save up to 50% on office supplies and furniture, business forms and printing, office machines and equipment. This book has just been revised, and I can't think of an office in America that wouldn't profit from having it. Most people just buy office supplies and equipment without a second thought. But I started giving Tod's techniques a lot more thought when my own bills started soaring. Now I do just what he says. I still pay a lot ... but a lot less than I was before. So will you. Just $32.50

"I ran across your book in the library while looking for some information on writing selling copy. CASH COPY has changed my whole way of thinking in regard to selling."

W. Douglas Pomroy,
Odessa, TX

For Selling More ...

#B60 *New!*

MAJOR ACCOUNT SALES STRATEGY. I don't know about you, but I make a big chunk of my money through a relatively few national accounts that buy heaps of what I'm selling. I work hard to find these people — and keep them happy. And now Neil Rackham's 218 page hard-back book will help you do the same. Here are the precise details you need for finding how customers make decisions to your advantage, getting to the decision makers and getting them to do what you want, how to make your customers need you, influencing the customer's choice, differentiating yourself from the competition, resolving customer concerns so you don't lose the sale ... and much, much more. If you want to get and keep big accounts, spend just $25 here.

#B61 *New!*

SERVING THE AGELESS MARKET: STRATEGIES FOR SELLING TO THE FIFTY-PLUS MARKET. I suspect this new book by David Wolfe will become a classic. Why? Because the fifty-plus market is growing and is affluent. Here are people who can buy what you're selling. Are you prepared to sell to them? This 301-page book is stuffed with useful techniques about how to get older, richer people to buy your product and service. Stuff like the seven key factors in the maturity market and how to profit from them; the six principles that dictate marketing to this market; what sells best; what marketing methods to use. A very timely book. Just $29.

"I purchased several of your 'Sure-Fire Business Success Publications and Audio Cassettes.' They are valuable information sources for anyone starting a new business venture. The information is easy to follow and provides suggestions, strategies and the 'how-to's' of starting and managing a business." Barbara Hacker, M.S. Ed., R.N., Allentown, PA

Back Again!!! #B64

CLOSING THE SALE. I can't think why I ever took Joel Martin's superb little booklet out of the catalog. Every time my article based on his book runs in a newspaper or magazine, I get deluged with orders for this gem. So, here it is again with a mea culpa from me that I've kept it out for even a minute. In Martin's smart booklet you get every objection your prospect could possibly make for not buying what you're selling ... and how to answer. And you get it all for just $8.95. Never wonder again what to say, use Martin.

Broke? Or just very thrifty? That's still no reason why you can't profit from Jeffrey Lant's books. Check your local public library. If they don't have what you want, ask the local acquisitions librarian to get it. Remind the librarian Jeffrey is regularly recommended by *Booklist*, the American Library Assoc's publication. Librarians know Jeffrey's books and will order what you want. But be first to check them out, or someone else will! (Special note for folks in Connecticut & Ohio. Jeffrey was keynote speaker for both the CT & Ohio Library Association meetings this year ... so these librarians all know Jeffrey personally and will be especially happy to order books for you!)

#B65 *New!*

HOW TO SELL AGAINST COMPETITION & WIN. Nobody reading this catalog is without competitors. To succeed in business, you've got to know how to beat them ... and get the money from your prospects they may have been thinking of spending elsewhere. This is where author Bill Subers and this must-read 229 page hard-back come in. Bill cut his teeth at IBM & Burroughs and now gives you great idea after profit-making idea about how to use your competitors' best ideas to work against them; how to discover the "magic" in a product, a word or a customer that enables you to make the sale; refining your personality so you have the winning edge; giving your self and your products the right appearance to make the sale ... and much, much more. You might not have heard of Bill Subers yet ... but take my word for it. This guy's ideas will be golden for you. $22.95.

How To Use The Phone To Sell More

#B12

SELLING ON THE PHONE: A SELF-TEACHING GUIDE. James Porterfield's book has always been a good seller for me, and it's no wonder. So many people in this supposed age of telemarketing savvy are downright primative on the phone. Porterfield's is the best beginner's book I've seen and will start you in the right direction to making more sales by phone faster. $19.95

#B45

Millions of people suffer from call reluctance. I got a vivid picture of just how bad this problem was when I ran an article about it and about this book's excellent suggestions on how to overcome it. My telephone rang for days. If you suffer from call reluctance and sometimes just cannot bring yourself to make that next important sales call, suffer no more. Get **THE PSYCHOLOGY OF CALL RELUCTANCE: HOW TO OVERCOME THE FEAR OF SELF-PROMOTION.** $22.45

"Good Help, My Dear, Is So Hard To Find"

#B62

HELP WANTED: HOW COMPANIES CAN SURVIVE AND THRIVE IN THE COMING WORKER SHORTAGE. If you're from New England you're already vividly aware of the worker shortage problem; it's one of the reasons our economy is a mess. That's why I enthusiastically recommend this new 244 page hardback by Hopkins, Nestleroth & Bolick. You need to know about how to attract the help you need, including more women; how to open the doors to the disabled, recruit older workers, manage the new work force and how to position yourself so that you get the help you need when you need it. Or are you prepared to keep doing everything yourself? $26.50

Living Well Is The Best Revenge

#B63 *New!*

THE WINES OF AMERICA. Why is this new updated 4th edition of Leon Adams' classic book here? I'll tell you why. Because at the end of one of my characteristically long days in the office, I like to spend some of my gains on the best possible wines … and I like American vintages. You get everything in this 528 page stunner of a book … the wines of New York, California … even Washington, Oregon, Idaho … and, yes, Michigan! I've got this book stashed right next to the fine American wines in my collection and refer to it constantly. You will, too. Bottoms up! $17.95

#B73 *New!*

SPA-FINDERS GUIDE TO SPA VACATIONS AT HOME & ABROAD. You know what the "in" vacation for the '90's is going to be: a trip to a spa where you can get pampered — and healthy at the same time. Even "Designing Women" did an episode about this lately! Author Jeffrey Joseph has all the details you need about every kind of spa vacation … and his 285 page backback has details on who pampers you best, spa cuisine & nutrition; spas for fitness and beauty, luxury, weight-loss, new age, spas abroad and more. He's even packed his book with stacks of discount coupons that'll slice the price off your next spa vacation. I'll be seeing you in the herbal wrap room! $17.95

#B67 *New!*

NO MORE SLEEPLESS NIGHTS. Okay, if you can't get to sleep, you're not your best the next day and your income — as well as your personal relations — are suffering. Here's what you need; 262 pages dedicated to conquering insomnia through a natural, drug-free program, stress reduction techniques, improved diet, exercise and environment. Written by Dr. Peter Hauri, Director of the Mayo Clinic's Insomnia Program, it includes a list of sleep disorder centers, one certain to be close to you. Stop counting sheep. Just $24.95

Making Money From Home

#B69 *New!*

101 FRANCHISES YOU CAN RUN FROM HOME. This new, easy-to-read 110 page paperback by my friend Lynie Arden is jammed with over 100 opportunities including tax/financial services; real estate & property investments; desktop publishing and employment services and more. You get the specific low-down you need on each opportunity and follow-up details. If you want to have the benefits of a franchise but still work at home, Lynie's new book is a must. $19.95.

#B43

If you're running a home-based business and you don't have Barbara Brabec's superb book **HOME MADE MONEY,** shame on you. Barb's the national expert on the topic and was recently featured 5 days running on ABC dishing out info about how to profit from home. Her book's the best there is and covers *everything* about home-based businesses, including zoning, licensing, marketing, the good businesses to be in and the ones to avoid. What's more there are literally hundreds of specific follow-up sources in this book which connect you to anyone who's anyone in the home-based business world — including me! You'll have to leave home without it! $20.95

Making Money In Mail Order

#B68 *New!*

STARTING & BUILDING YOUR CATALOG SALES BUSINESS. This is Herman Holtz' latest volume, and you'd better get it if you're not already making millions in the catalog sales game — but want to. 271 pages tell you what types of merchandise sell well by catalog; how to write catalog copy that sells; necessary elements in any catalog mailing; what you need to know about mailing lists; pricing details and much more. You can lose a bundle fast with a money-losing catalog. Use Herman's latest to make sure ***you*** profit. A steal at $33.

I'm looking for new books to publish. What have you got? Topics include making money, business opportunities, better living for upscale people. Surprise me. But if you haven't read and really followed my book HOW TO MAKE A WHOLE LOT MORE THAN $1,000,000 WRITING, COMMISSIONING, PUBLISHING AND SELLING "HOW-TO" INFORMATION, I don't see how you can produce the kind of book that I want. I pay no advance against royalties but do pay royalties monthly, the only person in the business who does this! Write me with your ideas.

#B33

Then get Julian Simon's superb book **HOW TO START AND OPERATE A MAIL-ORDER BUSINESS.** This is frankly the best book ever written on mail order, and wherever you are — beginner or guru — you are going to profit from it. It's exhaustively detailed. $55.50 New Edition!

Publish Your Own Newsletter

#B19

Howard Penn Hudson is America's newsletter guru. If there's something to be known about newsletters, he knows it. That's why you should use **PUBLISHING NEWSLETTERS: A COMPLETE GUIDE TO MARKETS, EDITORIAL CONTENT, DESIGN, PRINTING, SUBSCRIPTIONS, AND MANAGEMENT.** Take my word for it: this is the best book on newsletters ever written. $15.95

Finding Facts And People Fast

#B29

All of us are dependent on information, knowing where to find it and where to find it fast. That's why you need **FINDING FACTS FAST,** the best little book ever written on quick, economical information gathering. $7.45

#B30

If you've lost touch with a loved one or friend or just want to track down the animal who's skipped town on your bill, use Eugene Ferraro's book **YOU CAN FIND ANYONE: A COMPLETE GUIDE ON HOW TO LOCATE MISSING PERSONS.** $17.45

Help From Your Uncle

#B24

FREE HELP FROM UNCLE SAM TO START YOUR OWN BUSINESS (OR EXPAND THE ONE YOU HAVE). William Alarid's 158 page book is packed with ways for you to get money for your business from the government ... 20 loan programs, 14 loan guarantees, 8 direct payment programs, 20 grant programs, 26 information services, 11 counseling services ... and much, much more. This book is so inexpensive and so packed with information, you'd be crazy not to use it to see how much you can get your hands on. Just $14.95

Making Money Exporting, Importing

#B27

THE OFFICIAL U.S. DEPARTMENT OF COMMERCE GUIDE TO EXPORTING FROM THE UNITED STATES. This 148-page book is billed as "The indispensable handbook for selling products and services abroad." I agree. It's got the low-down on how to assess your product's export potential; where to receive free expert advice; how to conduct market research abroad; methods of exporting; how to adapt your product for an overseas market, how to brand, label and package ... and much, much more. Don't wait until the dollar goes sky-high again. Learn how to export now!!! Just $12.45

#B28

THE OFFICIAL U.S. CUSTOMS SERVICE GUIDE TO IMPORTING INTO THE UNITED STATES. "The indispensable handbook to the millions of business owners and collectors who buy or want to buy overseas." Find out how to enter goods into the U.S.; how to prepare invoices; how duty is assessed; what goods are dutiable; how to get refunds on duty; how to deal with currency conversions; how to deal with import quotas; forms needed for importing, *etc.* 85 info-packed pages. $10.45

"Reading your book HOW TO MAKE A WHOLE LOT MORE THAN $1,000,000 ... Talk about value for money spent! Hope you never stop writing about marketing."
Delford Day, Ft. Thomas, KY

Boy, have I got a hot list broker now! Venture Communications is going gangbusters with my list. If you'd like to rent it and get access to lots of super, mail responsive people, call Bette Anne Keane at (212) 684-4800. Take a good look at what's in this catalog. If you're selling compatible items, you want this list! It's priced very competitively, too!

Collection Techniques For The Small Business

#B46

You've got uncollected and uncollectible invoices sitting in your drawer right now. If you used the techniques in **PAYMENT IN FULL: A GUIDE TO SUCCESSFUL BILL COLLECTING,** some of them wouldn't be there. If you'd use it now, you can still collect on some of them. $27.95 is also a pretty fair price to pay to cut the anger you feel about the deadbeats who're ripping you off.

Developing And Protecting Ideas And Products

#B40

FROM CONCEPT TO MARKET. Gary Lynn's just published book tells you how to protect your idea without submitting a patent, how to license a new idea, market your innovation, start your own company, raise money, build a prototype, write a business plan and price your product. Developing a product is one of the best ways to get really rich there is. Making a small investment in Lynn's extensive research tells you how to develop it right and launch it fast. 243 pages $22.95.

Order Form

Complete 30-Day Money-Back Guarantee!

Photocopy or return this page to: Dr. Jeffrey Lant, Jeffrey Lant Associates
50 Follen St., #507, Cambridge, MA 02138

CLEARLY write down the item number(s) of what you order here. Each number is composed of a letter and a number. Please make sure to give both!

___, ___,

Remember, if you're ordering my Special Reports (#R1 – #R62), you get **any three for $12**. Individual Reports are $5 each.

Total your order here $ ____________. Are you a Massachusetts resident? ☐ Yes ☐ No
If so, add 5% sales tax here $ ___________. Total enclosed $ ___________.

Shipping. If you are ordering books, tapes and Special Reports by Dr. Jeffrey Lant, they are sent the day you order (unless you are using a post office box address that is not guaranteed by a MC/VISA). Other books are sent to you direct from their publishers by fourth class/book rate shipping. Allow four-six weeks. If you want them faster, add $3 per item for first class or UPS shipping. Remember: to ship UPS, I must have a street address!

Canada and overseas. If you want your items shipped to Canada, add $1 for *each* item ordered and $1 to the total for our bank's fees, even if you pay in U.S. dollars. If you want shipment to any other country, you must pay by credit card. I'll charge your account surface or air shipping, as you like. Check ☐ surface ☐ air.

Premiums. If your order totals at least $150, you can select any one of my three 60 minute audio cassettes as my gift to you. The three titles are listed on pages 273 & 274. Write down the one you want here # _____. If your order totals over $225, you get your free audio cassette and any one of my seven "Get Ahead" books (#B1 – #B7). List the item number of the one you want here _____. Remember to get these free premiums, you must order from this catalog by 02/01/92. Also, if your order totals over $25, you get the "First Step Review" IBM compatible software FREE.

Payment & Billing. Unless you are a government agency, college, library or other official public organization (in which case, include your Purchase Order # here _______________), COMPLETE PAYMENT MUST ACCOMPANY YOUR ORDER. I cannot invoice individuals and private businesses. If paying by check, make it payable to Jeffrey Lant Associates, Inc. If you are using a post office box number for shipment, I require a Master Card/VISA number and expiration date to guarantee your check, or else I wait for the check to clear. Sadly, several rip-off artists use post office boxes to defraud reputable merchants like me, so I have to inconvenience good people like you.

If paying by credit card (or using a post office box for shipment):
✓☐ MasterCard ☐ Visa. #_______________________________________
Expiration date___________ Signature_______________________________________

For faster service, place your order by telephone twenty-four hours a day at (617) 547-6372. (Yes, I really do answer my own phone). Before calling make sure your credit card is handy. The order tape doesn't last forever!

Send materials to:

Name _______________________________________

Organization _______________________________________

Street Address _______________________________________

City ___________________________ State ___________ Zip ___________

Telephone (   ) _______________________________________

GET YOURSELF A CHECK FOR UP TO $3,000 — FOR JUST A FEW MINUTES' WORK

Dr. Jeffrey Lant is one of America's top speakers providing dozens of lectures, seminars, workshops and conference programs every year both in the U.S. and abroad.

What's that got to do with you? Simply this...

Spend just a few *minutes* of your time networking Jeffrey into a speaking engagement, and you get 10% of his speaking fee and gross product sales on the day of the program. What does this mean for you? Just for recommending this very marketable guy *you can make up to $3,000*! No sweat. No heavy lifting. Just big bucks.

What do you have to do? Think.

What professional associations do you belong to? What trade groups? What companies are you affiliated with that have sales meetings? Where do your friends and business colleagues work and which organizations do they belong to? Do you know meeting planners? Just who uses speakers that you know — or have access to? Get your prospects and start recommending Jeffrey to them. It's as simple as that.

The people you tell will be grateful to you. Especially when you tell them a little about what Jeffrey talks about...

- developing a marketing plan that minimizes expense and targets the right people for whatever they're selling;
- writing and using marketing documents that get people to buy... instead of trashing them. We're talking about ads, flyers, brochures, cover letters, proposals, reports, and all the other stuff people are (usually unprofitably) creating.
- creating irresistible offers;
- raising money for non-profit organizations;
- getting free publicity to sell products and services.

In short, the kinds of subjects Jeffrey has been successfully writing — and speaking — about for over a dozen years and which have helped literally millions of for- and not-for profit organizations.

You'll find Jeffrey is easy to sell. Why?

- People can see for themselves the quality of his message by reviewing his books and articles. Jeffrey will make available review copies of all his books and the right kinds of articles for each prospect.
- We've got pages and pages of testimonials from satisfied clients.
- Meeting planners get access to a 60-minute video cassette of one of Jeffrey's recent appearances on national t.v... as well as audio cassettes of Jeffrey's programs.

Jeffrey's an established specialist and speaker with all the credentials and essential sales aids which help confirm your recommendation.

Once you've made your recommendation, tell Jeffrey right away. He'll follow up the lead and work with the meeting planner or decision maker. You don't need to do anything else — except wait for Jeffrey to speak. As soon as he's paid, you get your check. Immediately. And it'll be good sized, too — up to $3,000!

Now what? If you want more details on Jeffrey's program topics, biographical details, testimonials, etc., call (617) 547-6372. We have plenty of materials available to help you make the best possible case!

Or just start bringing Jeffrey's name and programs to the attention of the organizations you belong to... people you know in other organizations... anyone who needs speakers. You'll have the satisfaction of knowing you're recommending one of America's most dynamic and practical speakers... and, of course, you'll soon have a fat check as compelling evidence that working smart is better than working hard.

Jeffrey Lant Associates, Inc. ◆ 50 Follen St., Suite 507 ◆ Cambridge, MA 02138

(617) 547-6372

Here's why it's real easy to get Dr. Jeffrey Lant speaking engagements... use these testimonials when you're making a referral and watch your prospect's eyes light up!

"Your book CASH COPY is the best book on writing I've ever read. I am putting to use the many methods you mention in my mail order catalog. I am also telling friends and associates how sensible and reasonable your means of involving the customer are. I am very impressed." Michael Schwartz, Chester, NY

"There seems to be an overabundance of useless 'how-to' books. It is time more people wrote books like CASH COPY which gives its readers information they can put to use to profit. Now!" James Heikka, Phoenix, AZ

"I've read CASH COPY through once (couldn't put it down, actually!) and am more than pleased with it. It will get many readings and will be used to make our marketing efforts 'cash copy'." Edward Lee, Honolulu, HI

"I've really enjoyed HOW TO MAKE A WHOLE LOT MORE THAN $1,000,000 WRITING, COMMISSIONING, PUBLISHING AND SELLING 'HOW-TO' INFORMATION, as I did CASH COPY. It's really amazing what passes for marketing/advertising once one adopts the 'think like a client' Lant viewpoint... What I really wonder is how on earth you get everything done that you apparently do get done. Amazing." Jim Gibson, Atlanta, GA

"After reading CASH COPY which had been recommended by a friend I have found it to be one of the most exhilarating books I have ever read... I find it's an A+ must read business book." B. Eric Rhoads, *The Pulse of Radio*, Palm Beach, FL

"Thanks for writing such excellent how-to guides on marketing and information products. Without your assistance, I wouldn't be nearly this close to achieving my goals." Dr. Michael Anderson, Albuquerque, NM

"We have benefit now! Your 'Cash Copy' seminar provided the focus that our staff needed to gain the competitive edge in our daily selling endeavors. Thank you!" C. Michael Garavalia, Newstand Sales Director, The Conde-Nast Publications, Inc., New York

"You gave me the keys to the Magic Kingdom! LONG LIVE THE KING! 'When did I did that?' you ask. When you wrote CASH COPY." Doris Boggs, Olympia, WA

"I have spoken so highly of you and DEVELOPMENT TODAY to so many people. I first discovered it on campus (University of Montana) at our Mansfield Library, when I was working on a project for the Missoula Children's Theatre... I found your book delightful, informative and a necessity for anyone going into development." Mardi Milligan, Missoula, MT

"I just completed CASH COPY and MONEY MAKING MARKETING. Thank you, thank you... a thousand times thank you. There is so much valuable information in your books. Each one deserves to be read and worked through... I won't even lend them because I am constantly referring to them." Peg Martorella, Pittsburgh, PA

"Your book CASH COPY is thorough, up-to-date and helps those who really want to succeed. CASH COPY went with me everywhere until I finished it. When I buy a book I turn down the corners of important pages — only your book has almost all of its corners turned down." Marie Vevik, Austell, GA

"I find real value in the information you offer! In fact, I recommend your books and tapes to people I meet. Anyone who is open minded to what really works. And believe me, a lot of 'professionals' don't want to know. They want to continue to pump out the same garbage... Jeffrey, you're bold, you're bright, you're honest. You're genuine. Thank you for sharing yourself, your talents. I'll tell a lot of people about you. You deserve prosperity in abundance." Ronald Ball, CalComp, A Lockheed Co., Anaheim, CA

"HOW TO MAKE A WHOLE LOT MORE THAN $1,000,000 WRITING, COMMISSIONING, PUBLISHING AND SELLING 'HOW TO' INFORMATION is simply the best book ever written on how to make a lot of money selling information. I know. I've read all of them." Daniel Hopwood, Paducah, KY

"True story: your CASH COPY in the Asheville Public Library is on and off the shelves — on the shelves, then off, then on. Once I 'captured it'... started reading in the library, had to leave, put the book back. Large error. Because of course when I wanted to drink once again from that well of wisdom the book was gone... Very lean, 'mean' book... no fat." Thomas Streissguth, Asheville, NC

"Your book MONEY MAKING MARKETING is awesome! After getting your book from the library and reading the first 3 pages I knew I had found exactly what I had been looking for for the past two years. Very seldom do I ever write to an author to express my gratitude for the product they have produced, but you deserve such a letter." Dan Dube, Puyallup, WA

"THE UNABASHED SELF-PROMOTER'S GUIDE, CASH COPY, and HOW TO MAKE A WHOLE LOT MORE THAN $1,000,000... have answered every question that came to mind. In fact, the books answered hundreds of intelligent questions that I had not even thought of! The bottom line is this: your books have made me a lot of money. I can honestly say that without them I'd still be sitting in the dark. Instead The Wealthy Barber *has, in less than a year, eclipsed the forty-thousand-copies sold mark. Your books work! I paid you $90 for three books. Your advice earned me tens of thousands. I'd say I owe you."* David Chilton, Kitchener, Ontario

"I thoroughly enjoyed your presentation 'Cash Copy: How To Offer Your Products And Services' at the Best of America HR Conference. It was the most relevant and practical educational session on marketing that I have ever attended." Robert E. Christenson, Home Builders Institute, Washington, DC

"MONEY MAKING MARKETING and CASH COPY are bulging with a wealth of information, thought provoking ideas, tips, and genuine expert advice. In the myriad of business information manuals available on the market today, your two books are without doubt absolute gems. I have read several other titles on some of the subjects covered by your books, and I can truthfully say none of them gave the shear bulk of fully informative, value for money enclosed within the covers of your books." James Smith, Birkenhead, Merseyside, England

"I ran across your book in the library while looking for some information on writing selling copy. CASH COPY has changed my whole way of thinking in regard to selling." W. Douglas Pomroy, Odessa, TX

"Just finished reading CASH COPY. This publication should be Required Reading *for all career realtors."* Charles Flannigan, Pensacola, FL

"I love CASH COPY. It's an encyclopedia of direct mail marketing information. It improved my skills and helped my business." Peter Sickles, Leominster, MA

"I was lucky enough to have been in the audience for your talk on marketing at the American Library Association Conference in Dallas last June. Frankly, it was worth my trip to Texas, and I would like very much for librarians in Ohio to hear you also." Stephen D. Wood, Cleveland Heights-University Heights Public Library, Cleveland Heights, OH; Program Chair, 1990 Ohio Library Assn. Conference

"If I was told that all my books were being taken away, never to be replaced, except for just a very few of my choosing, your books would be my choice. With your books & my abilities, I would recover any loss in no time." Paul Hartunian, Montclair, NJ

"I've read many books on advertising and marketing and most fall short of my expectations. Yours do not!" Phil Oels, El Cajon, CA

"I am studying MONEY MAKING MARKETING, and I find it to be a truly amazing textbook on business success! Simply amazing." William Bowie, Los Angeles, CA

"CASH COPY, to my mind, ranks among the top five seminal volumes on marketing ever penned." Cal Brown, Sharon, MA

"I've been buying your books since 1983 (CONSULTANT'S KIT) and I've learned so much from you through the years... This is the Jewish New Year — a time to inscribe in the Book of Life — a time for renewal. And today your guide arrived. What else could it be but a message from the above?" Alice Beckerman, Los Angeles, CA

"I just completed my first workshop since ordering your six books. I made $2100. Not bad considering for years I have been doing this same program FREE... Thank you for the hard work and insights. My financial planning skills are as good or better than my competition. But so what, if no one knows about it or pays for it. Your books were worth every penny." Dennis Zaderaka, Wheaton, IL

"CASH COPY is the only book that explains how to make and not waste money with promotional material. It will save Big Business billions if they read it. Us small guys will smile all the way to the bank." Lon Hosford, New Milford, NJ

"Jeffrey, your books CASH COPY and MONEY MAKING MARKETING have literally transformed my life... They are my constant references. Your guidance will be a vital part of my future." Michael D. Murray, O.M.D., Glendale, CA

"I'm not in the habit of writing fan letters. Nonetheless, having reviewed only two of the books in your 'Get Ahead' Series, I feel compelled to say that you, Jeffrey Lant, are a certifiable national treasure!" Dr. Don Asmus, Delmar, NY